Main

zed

"This is a well-written and well-organized book that is highly recommended for health care professionals, health educators, and even parents."
—Dr. Charles E. Yesalis, professor of health and human development at Penn State University and coeditor of *Performance Enhancing Substances in Sport and Exercise*

"Drug education ought to be sober but it doesn't have to be dour. The authors [of *Buzzed*] have come up with an informative book about the ways people get high. It is also realistic and interesting to read." —*Dallas Morning News*

"Everyone who is interested in drugs will enjoy reading this. . . . The authors approach the subject with neither bias nor exaggeration. . . . A wonderfully interesting and accurate handbook of drug information."
—Carlton K. Erickson, head of the Addiction Science Research and Education Center, College of Pharmacy, University of Texas at Austin

"There is no talking down or trying to be hip in this guide to recreational drugs. A sound, thorough, authoritative resource that, though aimed primarily at college students, will be a solid asset in every public library."
—*Booklist*

"A well-written book that dispels some of the myths associated with drug abuse. I would recommend it to anyone looking for a readable, factual account of the physiological and behavioral effects of drugs of abuse."
—Dr. Charles Schuster, director of clinical research on substance abuse, Wayne State University School of Medicine, and former director of the National Institute on Drug Abuse

"To those who question if we really need another drug dictionary, the answer is that we definitely need this one!"
—*Library Journal*, starred review

BUZZED

THE STRAIGHT FACTS ABOUT THE MOST USED AND ABUSED DRUGS FROM ALCOHOL TO ECSTASY

FOURTH EDITION

CYNTHIA KUHN, PhD

SCOTT SWARTZWELDER, PhD

WILKIE WILSON, PhD

Duke University and Duke University School of Medicine

with LEIGH HEATHER WILSON

and JEREMY FOSTER

W. W. NORTON & COMPANY | NEW YORK · LONDON

For information about permission to reproduce selections from this book,
write to Permissions, W. W. Norton & Company, Inc.,
500 Fifth Avenue, New York, NY 10110

For information about special discounts for bulk purchases, please contact
W. W. Norton Special Sales at specialsales@wwnorton.com or 800-233-4830

Manufacturing by Courier Westford
Book design by JAM Design
Production manager: Louise Parasmo

Library of Congress Cataloging-in-Publication Data

Kuhn, Cynthia.
Buzzed : the straight facts about the most used and abused drugs from alcohol
to ecstasy / Cynthia Kuhn, Ph.D., Scott Swartzwelder, Ph.D., Wilkie Wilson,
Ph.D., Duke University and Duke University School of Medicine ; with Leigh
Heather Wilson and Jeremy Foster. — Fourth edition.
pages cm
Includes bibliographical references and index.
ISBN 978-0-393-34451-6 (pbk.)
1. Drugs of abuse—Popular works. I. Swartzwelder, Scott II. Wilson, Wilkie
III. Wilson, Leigh Heather. IV. Foster, Jeremy. V. Title.
RM316.K84 2014
615.7'8—dc23

2014011441

W. W. Norton & Company, Inc., 500 Fifth Avenue, New York, NY 10110
www.wwnorton.com
W. W. Norton & Company Ltd., Castle House, 75/76 Wells Street,
London W1T 3QT

1 2 3 4 5 6 7 8 9 0

TO OUR FAMILIES

CONTENTS

PART II

ACKNOWLEDGMENTS

THIS BOOK AROSE from our recognition of how little most adolescents, parents, lawmakers, and even medical advisers know about drugs that we regularly use and abuse. Informal talks with Leigh Heather Wilson and Jeremy Foster (contributors to this book) about their college experiences, and our interactions with a large number of college students in our courses, led to our realization of the need for this book. These students asked hard questions, shared their experience honestly, and provided background research of their own. We thank each of them.

W. W. Norton representative Steve Hoge deserves our thanks for bringing the book to Norton's editors. Our agent, Reid Boates, was superb. He was recommended by Dr. Redford Williams, another Duke author. Thank you, Red. The editorial staff at Norton has seen us through the ups and downs of getting a book out, and we appreciate the good advice and editing of the first edition from Alane Mason and Ashley Barnes. We now thank Anna Mageras for her superb editorial assistance during the preparation of the fourth edition of *Buzzed*.

Two individuals were exceptional in helping us understand the rudimentary principles discussed in the "Legal Issues" chapter. First we thank Mr. Rick Glaser, former first assistant United States attorney of the Northern District of Florida who is now partner, board member, and head of Government Investigation and the White Collar Crime Team for Parker Poe Adams & Bernstein in Charlotte, North Carolina. He clearly and carefully explained some important parts of the federal laws that deal with illicit drugs as well as discussed the general nature of drug prosecutions at the federal level. He was remarkably insightful and helpful. (Mr. Glaser made it clear that his views do not necessarily represent the views of the Department of Justice, the Northern District of Florida, or the Middle District of North Carolina.) The Honorable James E. Hardin Jr., former district attorney for Durham County, North Carolina (now a superior court judge in North Carolina), spoke extensively with us about drug prosecutions at the local and state levels. He was most patient with us nonlawyers and quite helpful in explaining the basic laws regulating search and seizure as well as giving us an understanding of how local law enforcement is dealing with the drug issue.

We also thank Mr. Mark Goldrosen, a defense attorney in San Francisco, for particular insights into recent legal issues.

Despite the fact that we received the best advice we could get, we want to be clear that the words written here are those of the authors, who are not lawyers, and should not be taken as legal advice.

In addition, Cindy thanks her husband, Mark, for patient listening; her children, Elena and Eric, for stories about what young adults are doing and for their helpful advice; Dr. Donald McDonnell, chairman of the Department of Pharmacology and Cancer Biology at Duke, for facilitating her undergraduate course, Drugs and the Brain; and all of her students who ask her questions that she can't always answer and who share information and experiences. Scott thanks Elizabeth Kaufman and his children—Sara, Nicholas, and Rita—for immensely helpful discussions as this project has evolved, and Drs. James Koury, Robert S. Dyer, Anthony L. Riley, and R. D. Myers for helping him learn how to think.

Wilkie thanks his daughter Heather, who, seeing her friends and acquaintances exposed to drugs in all sorts of social situations, was amazingly articulate in describing what she saw and absolutely relentless in pushing him to find some way to inform all of these people about the complexities of the drug issues in a user-friendly way. She became involved in this book as a research assistant, but she deserves enormous additional credit for her advice and counsel. He thanks her for her openness, her dedication to this project, and the grace she showed during some of the hard times. In addition, he thanks his wife, Linda, and his daughter Stephanie for support during some difficult moments when this book was being written. Their love is beyond description. He also thanks Joe for great discussions.

BUZZED

INTRODUCTION

FOR ALL OF our history, we humans have believed that it is possible to reach beyond our simple consciousness. We hunger to expand ourselves into a universe that we feel but cannot touch. Chemicals that alter the way we perceive the world have played a large role in this search. In some instances, people have believed that the chemicals themselves had spiritual powers and mystical properties.

Others use chemicals to reduce a particularly painful state. They use drugs to reduce anxiety or suppress shyness, or they are prescribed drugs to treat serious illnesses like depression and schizophrenia. Some seek the stimulation and power they do not have in their social situations and choose drugs to help them attain this. Some use chemicals as part of their daily life to stimulate or calm themselves as the situation dictates. As science has progressed, the laboratory has replaced nature as a source of chemicals, and the number of chemical choices has grown. There is every reason to believe that this trend will continue almost without bounds. So whether a person is seeking a way to expand his understanding or only trying to make normal life less painful, that person will have many, many choices of chemicals to use.

As scientists, we have devoted years to the study of the effects of drugs on the brain and behavior. We have seen the stunning advances in understanding the actions of the chemicals that have been with us for thousands of years. Yet surprisingly, little of this information is effectively translated for the public. We have become convinced that contemporary efforts to educate people about the effects of alcohol and other drugs are inadequate and misdirected. There is a lot of important information in the scientific literature about addiction and the effects of drugs, but it is not reaching the people who need to know it. The actions of drugs on the brain are complicated and vary tremendously from drug to drug and person to person, making it impossible to make blanket statements like "drugs kill" and have them believed by anyone who has any drug experience.

Imagine two trains headed at high speed in different directions, one being the scientific understanding of drug actions and addictions, the other being the public understanding of drug problems. The gap between scientific information and public information is growing hour by hour. This is the image portrayed in a speech by Dr. Alan Leshner, then director of the National Institute on Drug Abuse. In his words, "There is a unique disconnect between the scientific facts and the public's perception about drug abuse and addiction. If we are going to make any progress, we need to overcome the 'great disconnect.'"

We agree that it is crucial to get these trains headed in the same direction. Each of us must understand what different drugs do to our brains and our consciousness, and what the physical consequences of their use might be. The number of consciousness-altering chemicals is increasing rapidly as medical scientists and pharmaceutical companies take advantage of new discoveries in neuroscience. Every time a new brain circuit or a new neurochemical is discovered, that discovery provides an opportunity to develop drugs that alter brain function in a new way. Some of these prove to be valuable treatments for mental illness, and many of the drugs that are currently abused (e.g., amphetamines, barbiturates, and "roofies") come directly from this same medical research.

Because of the incredible complexity of the brain, most drugs that affect it have actions in addition to those for which they were developed. Often dangerous drugs remain on the prescription market because they offer the only opportunity to treat a medical condition; their potential side effects seem worth the risk if they are used under medical supervision. Yet recreational use may not be worth the risk of the known and unknown effects on health. The fast-acting opiate fentanyl used in the operating room is a great example. This chemical is very safe and effective if there is a medical professional monitoring body functions such as heart rate, blood pressure, and the amount of oxygen getting to the brain. But with just a small error, it can turn dangerous and deadly. So imagine how risky using it could be in some alley or dorm room, where it might be sold as "Apache" or "Jackpot."

It is easy to see how drug information can become subject to distortion. The public can be easily confused and manipulated. For example, some people (especially those in the drug culture) know individuals who have consumed various drugs in various combinations in various settings over long periods of time and do not seem permanently impaired or addicted, or are not involved with the legal system. Yet they may not realize that many drug effects can be subtle enough to do a good deal of harm before the damage is recognized.

Conversely, others routinely carry out drug education by telling the worst horror stories they can recall, and often place any illegal substance in the category of "terribly dangerous." Stories of celebrity deaths from basketball players to musicians are used to illustrate the dangers of drug use. However, most people who use addictive drugs like cocaine and heroin do not die as a result, and the users and their friends certainly know it. Therefore, when horror stories are used as the principal tools in drug education, people soon recognize that such stories do not represent the whole truth. The educator then loses credibility.

Good drug education requires a lot of effort. The scientific and medical literature is often difficult for most people to find and even more difficult to understand. Most interpretations of this literature to the general public are oversimplified, inaccurate, or disseminated by organizations that slant the research to further political and moral agendas.

The marijuana controversy is an excellent example. Some organizations have taken a hard line that this drug is devastating to anyone who uses it. Other organizations view it as harmless and support its legalization for totally unregulated consumption. In our opinion, the truth is somewhere in between. As you will read in the marijuana chapter, marijuana causes memory problems and interacts with the immune system in unknown ways. It has effects many hours after it enters the body, even if the user is unaware of those effects. So it is not harmless. But people do not die from marijuana overdoses (as they do from overdoses of alcohol). Any truthful discussion of marijuana must include a range of topics and a realistic representation of risk, which cannot be accomplished by exchanging slogans.

Drugs should be viewed individually on a continuum of risk. Those we review in this book vary remarkably in their chemical structures; in target systems in the brain; and in their pharmacological, behavioral, and psychological effects. Also, people vary markedly in their reactions to drugs. The rapidly expanding literature on genetic and hereditary predispositions toward addiction is just one example of our growing understanding of individual differences in drug reactivity.

The Internet is also making it difficult to carry out good drug education. An immense amount of easy-to-read information about drugs is accessible there, but much of it is wrong. Anyone can create an Internet site and say whatever he or she pleases; the astute reader must weed out fact from fiction. A naïve reader, on the other hand, may get into serious trouble by following website advice. The drug GHB, for instance, can be deadly at doses not far above those that produce a high. Yet some of the Internet literature would lead us to believe that the drug is not only safe but will treat alcoholism, insomnia, narcolepsy, sexual problems, and depression. One Internet site that we accessed in October 2007 provided directions for making GHB and stated that "GHB is the safest recreational drug ever used by humanity." This information could not be further from the truth, and readers who believe it are at great risk.

The primary goal of this book is to provide an unbiased, readable, and detailed presentation of the scientific facts about the drugs most commonly abused. We expect that this book will have its largest impact on people who are not addicted to drugs but are in a position to use drugs socially. During adolescence and young adulthood, most people—newly independent from parental control—will find themselves in situations in which drugs are available. College dorm rooms are often active, misguided psychopharmacology labs. We do not expect that this book will end drug abuse, but we hope it will prevent some bad experiences and some real tragedies.

We also hope that this book will facilitate a dialogue between scientists and legislators. The use of illegal drugs in the United States is rampant, and the social and legal reactions to that use have placed enormous stress on the resources of this country. The debate about drug laws in the United States is raging and has been driven in part by this usage and the huge increase in the prison population. It is very costly to keep a person in prison, and the number of sentenced prisoners in state and federal institutions has skyrocketed from about 300,000 in 1978 to more than 1.5 million in 2012.[*] About 47 percent of the people in federal prisons are there

[*] Bureau of Justice Statistics (http://www.bjs.gov/index.cfm?ty=pbdetail&iid=4737)

for drugs,[*] and as bad as these numbers are, they are an improvement over those we found as we wrote the previous editions of this book. It appears there is a trend toward reducing prison populations.

The distinction between drugs that are considered legal or illegal in a given society is often based on much more than just scientific information. Traditions, economics, religion, and the popular media all influence the stance that a community takes on drugs. The religious rituals of some Native American communities include the use of hallucinogens, while many of those in Judeo-Christian traditions include the use of alcohol. Other cultures take very hard-line stances against the use of any substance that is considered intoxicating. Even within a given culture, the legality of drugs can change over time. In the United States, the use of alcohol was legal for more than a century, was declared illegal during Prohibition, and is now legal again. Similarly, marijuana was legal until the 1930s, when its use was prohibited. Several recent state initiatives have permitted the use of marijuana for medical purposes and rekindled the debate about its legalization.

Again, in the words of Dr. Leshner, "Science must replace ideology as the foundation for drug abuse and addiction prevention, treatment, and policy strategies." The legislative authorities of developed societies must understand that no matter what legal efforts are taken, their citizens will have access to increasing numbers of chemicals that can cause addiction and impair human function. Effective protection from the kind of societal disruption being experienced in the United States rests in good education that is accessible to everyone and good scientific research that addresses the problems that drugs cause.

We hope that this book will be part of that process. The first twelve chapters are devoted to particular drugs or classes of drugs. Each one starts with a quick-reference summary of the effects and dangers of the drug. Next we present a detailed picture of how the drug works. We describe how the drug gets into and out of the body, its effects on physical and psychological functions, and its long-term effects. We've organized the drugs by class—even though some drug classes, like the entactogens, are much less familiar to most readers than the specific drug names— because drugs in the same class generally have the same mechanisms of action, effects, and risks. However, the table of contents, the chapter contents, and the index make it easy to determine where to go for informa-

---

[*] US Federal Bureau of Prisons (http://www.bop.gov/news/quick.jsp)

tion on a specific drug. In the second part of the book, we've provided general chapters on the brain, how drugs work, addiction, and legal issues. We recommend that any reader using the book for a broad general understanding, rather than as a quick reference, read those chapters first, as they provide an important background for all of the scientific information relating to specific drugs.

We believe that when provided with an unbiased and authoritative source of information about drugs and drug interactions, individuals are empowered to make healthy decisions.

JUST SAY KNOW

(A College Student's Perspective by Leigh Heather Wilson and Jeremy Foster)

This section was written by our college interns for the first edition of Buzzed. *We feel the advice is still as good and relevant as it was then and so we include it in this edition.*

"JUST SAY NO." Well, no thanks. We would like a bit more information before making decisions about drug use. And when you say "Just say no," does that mean you're telling us alcohol is as dangerous as cocaine? Before you start lumping together everything from smoking cigarettes to shooting heroin, could we have a little bit more information? "Just say no" might not always be the right choice. Hasn't research shown that a glass of wine can be healthy? It is only natural that phrases like "Just say no" are not sufficient to satisfy many young people. It is the very basis of our society to value proof, logic, and fact above all. Instead of asking us to respond blindly, convince us!

We have been friends all our lives. Because Heather's dad is a neuropharmacologist, we knew about psychoactive drugs early on. Ever since we can remember, drugs and how they do this or that to the something-or-another region of the brain has been a familiar topic of conversation.

Like many kids, in high school we became bored with the same-old, same-old that radio and MTV offered and wanted to broaden our musical horizons. This sparked an interest in some of the bands popular in the sixties and seventies. Consequently, we developed a fascination with the surrounding culture. It was clear that drugs, of one character or another, were cast in many roles during those times. The deaths of Janis Joplin, Jim Morrison, and Jimi Hendrix were all related to their drug use, and still, by way of their association with these and other musicians, drugs have an air of romance and intrigue.

Around the same time that we became aware of these issues, similar concerns about the nineties' music culture became a trendy topic in the media. The flurry of publicity on the rising use of drugs again among young people, as well as the resurgence of heroin use, in particular, has led many to compare our times to the sixties and seventies. All the hype—not to mention the allure of the positive feelings people say they get from taking drugs—made us quite curious about the subject.

We were both way past believing the slogans and hyperbole on the subject of drugs. Heather began nagging her dad with question after question about drugs in a struggle to understand their effects, and the questions evolved into a series of great conversations with him and some of his colleagues. We were so interested because finally we were getting straight, unbiased information about the actions of drugs in our bodies.

We learned a lot about heroin, which had seemed so attractively mysterious. Its "rush" is commonly described as better than experiencing an orgasm. Its associated dangers, however, included several major risks: addiction, overdose, and contracting HIV from needles. The risk of overdose, we learned, is unpredictable because of individual responses to the drug and varying degrees of purity of the compound sold by dealers. The particular compounds used to cut it can also be dangerous. So it became clear to us that with heroin, as with many other drugs, the safety issues are very complicated and often the danger is not limited to the specific effects of the drug but can include many other peripheral issues. For heroin, some of these issues arise from economic considerations because its high street value and relative scarcity lead dealers to cut it in unpredictable ways.

After all these conversations with Heather's dad and his colleagues, heroin seemed far less alluring and mysterious, and we avoided it. We felt lucky to have learned the truth, and with the new knowledge we felt armed. If someone offered heroin to one of us, we wouldn't be "just saying no," but defending an informed decision to stay away from the drug.

Through learning about heroin we realized that not all the threats have direct causes and that by giving people good information, some of the dangers can be lessened (some people will use drugs regardless). We know that a drug's effects can change in a novel environment, that the risk of overdose increases when the drug purity is not consistent, and that some drugs taken together become lethal. Making people aware of these kinds of issues could decrease some risks of using drugs.

Overall we were struck by the lack of unbiased and complete information available to people like us, and the contrast between the formal education we had received and the scientific facts we had learned.

During high school, we had had experiences with alcohol, many of them positive. It wasn't until Heather's freshman year in college that she had her first really adverse experience with drugs. During Parents' Weekend, she, her roommate, and their parents went to her best friend's room and found her soaked in blood and tears on the floor. Heather's friend had a history of depression, and the combination of this, a bottle of Jack Daniel's Black Label, and too much cold medicine left her ravaged and suicidal. She didn't know that alcohol and antihistamines have a synergistic, depressing effect and that at high levels the combination can even be lethal. They found her in time to save her, but she will always carry the scars where she cut her wrists.

Heather's friend wasn't the only girl left with scars. Everyone involved was affected. She and Heather were part of an unusually close-knit group of five. They had, unknowingly, become a family to each other. By doing almost everything together, they had become a source of strength and love for each other as they adjusted to college life. When Heather's friend went home, she left a hole, a missing link in that safety net. An irresponsible act, taken without knowledge of drugs and their interactions, changed the lives of everyone who found her, all of her friends, and all of her family.

A second experience occurred on the same dormitory hall. Heather and her friends were invited to share some Ecstasy with boys from a nearby school. They were excited, having heard that Ecstasy was a lot of fun. But Heather remembered one of the strongest statements about drug use her dad had ever made. He had said, "Ecstasy permanently alters your brain, Heather. It is a bad drug, and frankly, this is one that I would like to ask you, as a personal favor because I'm your dad and I love you, not to try. There are some kids who have used it and suffered problems with sleep, anxiety, and depression. These poor kids have changed their own brains, and they will never be the same."

Cindy Kuhn had loaned Heather a neuropharmacology textbook the year before; the students used it to read about Ecstasy. With a clear view of what the drug could do to their brains, most of them chose not to try it, though others decided to take the risk.

With these experiences still vivid in our minds, the vast and cavernous difference between what we know from the most current research on drugs and what drug education and prevention programs teach was obvious. We realized that we are all being sold a bill of goods when it comes to recreational drugs. There are dangers involved in using drugs, but the issue is much more complicated than that. Each drug works differently in the brain, and there are very different issues to consider with each drug. Also, some drugs pose risks that are far greater than others. We do an injustice to ourselves when we try to make blanket statements like "Drugs Kill" or "Users Are Losers."

We realized that not everybody has a scientist to talk to and that the world needed a book that would not use scare tactics but would have reliable, in-depth information—a book that would not insult our intelligence. This book is about making the most current research on the pharmacological and psychological effects of drugs available to you in a friendly and useful way. We hope you enjoy reading it, but most of all, we believe that with information that is both clearly presented and unbiased, you will be qualified to make better decisions for yourself about drugs.

TEST YOUR DRUG KNOWLEDGE

1. The effects of smoking pot can last for two days. True or false?

2. Chocolate and marijuana stimulate the same receptors in the brain. How much chocolate would you have to eat to get the same effect as one joint?

3. Which cup of coffee has more caffeine—the one brewed in the office coffeemaker from grocery-bought beans or the expensive cup from the new gourmet coffee bar?

4. Ecstasy was first popularized by California psychotherapists who tried to use it for "empathy training" in marriage counseling. True or false?

5. What popular recreational drug was originally developed as a treatment for asthma?

6. What popular nightclub drug is actually an animal tranquilizer—and the difference between a recreational dosage of it and an overdose is dangerously small?

7. What are the most dangerous drugs and also the ones most often used by children under age fourteen?

8. Which drug prescribed each year to millions of Americans impairs memory?

9. Put these drugs in the order of addictiveness: marijuana, nicotine, heroin.

10. Tonight you are at a club sipping on a soft drink, or still on your first beer, when suddenly you begin to feel very drunk and uncoordinated. What might have happened?

11. What was the drug misinformation promulgated by the movie *Pulp Fiction*?

12. What was the drug effect correctly portrayed by the movie *Trainspotting*?

13. Which drug carries a greater danger of fatal overdose—alcohol or LSD?

14. Right or wrong: alcohol before bed makes you sleep better.

15. Are the herbal remedies sold in health-food stores actually drugs?

16. Why do people inject a drug instead of just taking a pill?

17. What is the most popular illegal drug in America now?

18. If a child or an animal eats a cigarette, will it cause harm?

19. Does marijuana kill brain cells?

20. Does alcohol kill brain cells?

21. Isn't it safe to drink a glass or two of wine with your dinner when you're pregnant?

22. Is caffeine addictive?

23. Are crack babies doomed to mental retardation and behavioral problems?

24. What drug, popular on the club scene and among high school students, causes definitive brain damage in rodents and monkeys?

ANSWERS

1. True. THC, the active ingredient in marijuana, is extremely fat-soluble and can still enter the bloodstream from the fatty tissues and have effects on the brain for up to two days after being smoked. Its by-products can turn up in the blood many months after the last use if the smoker suddenly loses a lot of weight. (See chapter 7.)

2. About twenty-five pounds. (See chapter 2.)

3. The office cup. The African robusta beans found in grocery stores can contain up to twice as much caffeine as the more expensive arabica beans found in specialty coffee shops. Plus you can add as much coffee as you want. (See chapter 2.)

4. True! (See chapter 3.)

5. Amphetamine, which was originally synthesized as a derivative of ephedrine, the active ingredient of the Chinese herbal drug mahuang. (See chapter 12.)

6. Ketamine, otherwise known as Special K (not the cereal!). (See chapter 4.)

7. Chemical solvents such as toluene, benzene, propane, and those found in glue and paint. More than 12 percent of eighth graders have used such inhalants. (See chapter 6.)

8. Valium and other drugs of its class. (See chapter 10.)

9. Nicotine, heroin, marijuana (actually, there is little evidence that marijuana is addictive). (See chapter 7.)

10. Someone probably slipped a sedative into your drink, like a roofie (Rohypnol) or GHB (gamma-hydroxybutyrate), also known as Easy Lay. These drugs can be fatal, so seeking medical attention is wise. (See chapter 10.)

11. The movie shows a heroin overdose being treated by an injection of adrenaline into the heart, which is useless and dangerous. The opiate-blocking drug naloxone reverses heroin overdose after injection by more conventional routes. (See chapter 9.)

12. The main character in the movie is overcome with diarrhea after coming down off heroin. Because heroin causes constipation, once it's eliminated from the body just the opposite effect kicks in. (See chapter 9.)

13. Alcohol. Many deaths each year are caused by alcohol overdose. There is little danger of LSD overdose unless it is combined with or contaminated by other drugs. (See chapter 1.)

14. Wrong. Alcohol might make you sleepy at first, but its by-products can cause sleeplessness, so after a night of drinking you might fall asleep quickly but wake up in the middle of the night feeling agitated. (See chapter 1.)

15. Anything you take with the intention of changing how your body acts is a drug. Any drug that comes from a plant is herbal. This includes nicotine, ephedrine, and cocaine. "Herbal remedies" are completely unreg-

ulated and the amount and purity of what you buy is unknown. (See chapter 5.)

16. For the speed with which the drug gets into the bloodstream and into the brain. The faster it gets to the brain, the better the "rush." This faster delivery also means a greater chance of overdose because the amount of drug can reach fatal levels before the user can do anything about it. (See chapter 13.)

17. Marijuana is used by far more people than any other illegal drug: 77 percent of all illegal drug users use marijuana, and almost 5 percent of the population used marijuana in the last month. (See chapter 7.)

18. Yes. There is enough nicotine in a cigarette to make a small child or animal very sick, or even to kill one. (See chapter 8.)

19. Probably not, but it does interfere with learning and memory. (See chapter 7.)

20. It is unlikely that a single drink kills brain cells, but long-term chronic drinking can cause permanent memory loss and definite brain damage. (See chapter 1.)

21. No. Studies have shown that even very moderate drinking during pregnancy can permanently hinder a child's ability to learn and to concentrate. (See chapter 1.)

22. Not really. People who stop drinking coffee may experience mild withdrawal that includes drowsiness, headaches, and lethargy, but people very rarely engage in the compulsive, repetitive pattern of drinking coffee that typifies use of addictive substances. Addiction is not defined simply by the presence of withdrawal. (See chapter 2.)

23. Not necessarily. In fact, the most common problems that crack babies experience are the same as those experienced by children of women who smoke cigarettes: low birth weight and the associated health risks, and subtle developmental delays in childhood. Cocaine can cause very severe problems, including premature separation of the placenta from the uterus, premature birth, and intrauterine stroke, but these are rare. (See chapter 12.)

24. Ecstasy (MDMA). Studies show dramatic damage to nerves containing the neurotransmitter serotonin that is irreversible at doses approximating those consumed by humans. (See chapter 3.)

Part
I

1

ALCOHOL

Drug Class: Sedative hypnotic

Individual Drugs: beer (3 to 7 percent or less alcohol); wine (8 to 14 percent alcohol); "fortified" wine (17 to 22 percent alcohol); spirits, liquor, whiskey (40 percent or more alcohol)

Common Terms: liquor, whiskey, booze, hooch, wine, beer, ale, porter

The Buzz: When people drink alcohol, they feel pleasure and relaxation during the first half hour or so, often becoming talkative and socially outgoing. But these feelings are usually replaced by sedation (drowsiness) as the alcohol is eliminated from the body, so drinkers may become quiet and withdrawn later. This pattern often motivates them to drink more to keep the initial pleasant buzz going.

Overdose and Other Bad Effects: Under most circumstances, the chances of life-threatening overdose are low. However, people get into trouble when they drink a lot of alcohol very quickly—such as in a drinking game, on a dare, or when they can't taste the alcohol (as in punch or Jell-O shots). Drinking on an empty stomach is particularly risky. If a person becomes unconscious, is impossible to arouse, or seems to have trouble breathing, it is a medical emergency and immediate attention is necessary. Some very drunk people vomit, block their airway, suffocate, and die. Call for emergency medical assistance.

When drunk people pass out, their bodies continue to absorb the alcohol they just drank. The amount of alcohol in their blood can then reach dangerous levels and they can die in their sleep. Keep checking someone who has gone to sleep drunk. Do not leave him alone.

"Binge drinking" is particularly dangerous because it is during binges that most fatal overdoses occur.

Unique Risks for Adolescents: Young people may respond quite differently from adults to alcohol. Although the research is still developing, it looks like alcohol may impair learning more in adolescents but be less potent at making them sleepy. The newest studies indicate that adolescents may be at greater risk than adults for long-lasting effects of alcohol on the brain—even down to the cellular level.

Dangerous Combinations with Other Drugs: It is dangerous to combine alcohol with anything else that makes you sleepy. This includes other sedative drugs, such as opiates (e.g., heroin, morphine, or oxycodone), barbiturates (e.g., phenobarbital), Quaaludes (methaqualone), Valium-like drugs (benzodiazepines), sleep medications like Ambien, and even the antihistamines found in some cold medicines.

All sedative drugs share at least some of alcohol's effects and each increases the other's effects. Drugs can become deadly when combined. Even doses of drugs that do not cause unconsciousness or breathing problems alone can powerfully impair physical activities such as sports, driving a car, and operating machinery when taken together.

Finally, non-narcotic pain relievers such as aspirin, acetaminophen (the pain reliever in Tylenol), and ibuprofen (the pain reliever in Motrin) can each have bad side effects if taken with alcohol. Aspirin and ibuprofen can both be highly irritating to the stomach when taken with alcohol, and under some circumstances the combination of extremely high amounts of acetaminophen with alcohol can damage the liver.

CHAPTER CONTENTS

The use of chemicals to alter thinking and feeling is as old as humanity itself, and alcohol was probably one of the first substances used. Even the earliest historical writings make note of alcohol drinking, and breweries can be traced back some 6,000 years to ancient Egypt and Babylonia. In the Middle Ages, Arab technology introduced distillation—a way to increase the alcohol content in beverages—to Europe. In those times alcohol was believed to remedy practically any disease. In fact, the Gaelic term *whiskey* is best translated as "water of life."

These days, beverage alcohol is clearly the drug of choice for much of Western culture, and we need only to look closely at much of the advertising in this country to see that it is still sold as a magic elixir of sorts. We use alcohol to celebrate successes, to mourn failures and losses, and to celebrate holidays of cultural and religious significance. Implicit in these uses are the hope and promise that alcohol will amplify the good times and help us through the bad ones.

Nowhere is the alcohol advertising more targeted, or the peer pressure to drink more powerful, than on adolescents and young adults—particularly young men. And the advertising works. We know that people's choices about the alcoholic beverages they drink are powerfully influenced by advertising. While young people do most of the drinking in American society, they are also the ones who need their brains to be functioning at their highest levels because of the intellectual demands of education and career preparation.

For most people alcohol is not a terribly dangerous drug—but it is a powerful drug and must be treated accordingly. No one would take a powerful antibiotic or heart medication without the advice of a physician. But alcohol is available to virtually anyone who wants to have it, without a prescription. The vast majority of people in the United States face the decision of whether to use alcohol, and how much to use, during their high school or college years. The responsibility for making these decisions falls on each individual. This chapter will provide the latest information about alcohol and its effects.

TYPES OF "ALCOHOLS"

The alcohol that is used in beverages is called ethanol. It is actually only one of many different types. The alcohol a nurse rubs on the skin as a disinfectant before giving an injection or drawing a blood sample is not the same—it is isopropyl alcohol. The chemical structures of most alcohols make them quite toxic to the human body. Ethanol is the only one that should ever be consumed, but people regularly poison themselves with other alcohols. For example, methanol, produced in home-distilling operations, can cause blindness. A case of methanol poisoning requires immediate medical attention. Therefore, home-distilled liquor, or "moonshine," should always be avoided.

HOW ALCOHOL MOVES THROUGH THE BODY

The amount of alcohol a person consumes at any given time will influence how it moves through the body, but it's important to standardize the amount that we're talking about first, because beer, wine, and spirits contain significantly different concentrations of ethanol. A standard drink is often classified as the amount of alcohol consumed in one twelve-ounce beer, one four-ounce glass of wine, or a mixed drink containing one ounce of hard liquor.

GETTING IN

Ethanol is a relatively small molecule that is easily and quickly absorbed into the body. Once a drink is swallowed, it enters the stomach and small intestine, where a high concentration of small blood vessels gives the alcohol ready access to the blood. About 20 percent of a given dose of alcohol is absorbed through the stomach, and most of the remaining 80 percent is absorbed through the small intestine. Once they enter the bloodstream, the alcohol molecules are carried throughout the body and into direct contact with the cells of virtually all the organs.

Often a person who goes out for a drink in the early evening before dinner reports, "The alcohol went straight to my head." Actually, the alcohol went very rapidly throughout the whole body, and shortly after it was absorbed it became fairly evenly distributed. This process is called equilibration. But because a substantial proportion of the blood that the heart pumps at any given time goes to the brain, and because the fatty material of the brain absorbs alcohol (which dissolves in both fat and water) very well, that is where the effects are first and predominantly felt. In fact, before equilibration, alcohol's concentration in the brain is actually higher than its concentration in the blood. Since it is alcohol's effects on the brain that lead to intoxication, soon after drinking a person may be more impaired than her blood alcohol level would indicate. So, there is some truth in the statement, "That drink went right to my head."

Indeed, the presence or absence of food in the stomach is perhaps the most powerful influence on the absorption of alcohol. When someone drinks on an empty stomach, the blood absorbs the alcohol very rapidly, reaching a peak concentration in about one hour. By contrast, the same amount of alcohol consumed with a meal would not be completely absorbed for nearly two hours. The food dilutes the alcohol and slows the emptying of the stomach into the small intestine, where alcohol is very rapidly absorbed. Peak blood alcohol concentration could be as much as three times greater in someone with an empty stomach than in someone who has just eaten a large meal.

The concentration of alcohol in the beverage consumed also significantly influences its absorption—in general, the higher the concentration, the faster it will be absorbed. So, relatively diluted solutions of alcohol, such as beer, enter the bloodstream more slowly than more highly concentrated solutions, such as mixed drinks or shots. More rapid absorption usually means higher peak blood alcohol concentrations, so a person who drinks shots might have a higher blood alcohol level than a person who drinks the same amount of alcohol in the form of beer or wine. While you can prove this principle in tightly controlled scientific studies using subjects who have completely empty stomachs when they ingest only the dose of alcohol they receive from the researcher, this effect is pretty minimal when people are drinking recreationally, perhaps two to three drinks an hour. Furthermore, people rarely drink under such carefully controlled conditions, and so the safest assumption is that the most important determinant of what your blood alcohol concentration is going to be is the amount of alcohol you consume in an hour and whether you have just eaten—not the type of alcohol you consume.

The rapid absorption of high concentrations of alcohol can suppress the centers of the brain that control breathing and cause a person to pass out or even die. People who get into this kind of extreme medical emergency sometimes do so by accepting a challenge to drink a certain amount of alcohol in a short period of time, by playing drinking games that result in the rapid consumption of multiple drinks, or by taking something like Jell-O shots, which get a lot of highly concentrated alcohol into the body in a short time. Often, young people who cannot legally buy alcohol "drink up" before going out to a mall or to a school dance. Some people do a lot of drinking before leaving for an event where alcohol is not permitted. (College students, most of whom are underage and must therefore conceal their drinking, refer to this as "pregaming.") Given the rapid accumulation of alcohol in the brain, under these circumstances the drinker may be very impaired in terms of her ability to drive or think clearly, though her blood alcohol level would not suggest this degree of impairment.

A person's body type also determines alcohol distribution. A particularly muscular or obese person may seem to be "really holding his booze" because he has more fat and muscle to absorb the alcohol. A heavy person would register a lower alcohol level in the blood than a lean individual after an identical dose. However, the extra weight also slows the elimination of alcohol, so he would retain it longer.

In pregnant women, alcohol is freely distributed to the fetus. In fact, because of the large blood supply to the uterus and developing fetus, some studies actually indicate that the tissues of the fetus may achieve a higher alcohol concentration than those of the mother. Later in this chapter, we will discuss the effects of alcohol on the fetus, and the lasting effects that prenatal exposure has on the child later in life. For now, it is important to recognize that when alcohol is distributed in the body, it does not discriminate between the tissues of the mother and those of the fetus.

GETTING OUT

The roadside Breathalyzer test is actually an excellent way of estimating the amount of alcohol consumed, even though 95 percent of the alcohol a person drinks is metabolized before the body excretes it. Only about 5 percent of the absorbed alcohol is eliminated unchanged, in the urine or through the lungs, but it is enough to result in "alcohol breath"—and the proportion exhaled stays constant enough to give a very accurate estimate of how much alcohol is in the blood.

Most alcohol is metabolized by the liver, where an enzyme called alcohol dehydrogenase, or ADH, breaks ethanol down into acetaldehyde, which in turn is broken down by another enzyme called acetaldehyde dehydrogenase into acetate, which then becomes part of the energy cycle of the cell. The intermediate product, acetaldehyde, is a toxic chemical that can make a person feel sick. Although under normal conditions acetaldehyde is broken down quite rapidly, if it accumulates in the body, intense feelings of nausea and illness result. One early drug therapy for alcoholism was a drug called disulfiram (or Antabuse), which allows the concentration of acetaldehyde to accumulate, making a person feel quite ill after drinking and less likely to drink again. While this strategy appeared promising initially, it has not resulted in consistent positive clinical outcomes with alcohol-dependent patients.

The rate at which alcohol is metabolized and eliminated from the body is critical for understanding how long a person can expect to be affected by drinking. The rate of alcohol metabolism is constant across time. In general, an adult metabolizes the alcohol from one ounce of whiskey (which is about 40 percent alcohol) in about one hour. The liver handles this rate of metabolism efficiently. If the drinker consumes more than this amount, the system becomes saturated and the additional alcohol simply accumulates in the blood and body tissues and waits its turn for metabolism. The results are higher blood alcohol concentrations and more intoxication.

In addition, continued drinking increases the enzymes that metabolize alcohol. The increased level of these enzymes promotes metabolism of some other drugs and medications, harming the drinker in a variety of ways. For example, some medications used to prevent blood clotting and to treat diabetes are metabolized more rapidly in chronic drinkers and are thus less effective. Similarly, these enzymes increase the breakdown of the painkiller acetaminophen (found in Tylenol) into substances that can be toxic to the liver. Finally, metabolic tolerance to alcohol results in similar tolerance to other sedative drugs, such as barbiturates, even if the individual has never taken barbiturates. This is called cross tolerance and may place the drinker at greater risk for the use or abuse of such drugs.

EFFECTS ON THE BRAIN AND BEHAVIOR

Once alcohol has been absorbed and distributed, it has many different effects on the brain and behavior. To a large extent these effects vary with the pattern of drinking. Therefore, we discuss the effects of acute, chronic, and prenatal alcohol exposure separately.

ACUTE EXPOSURE

Effects on Behavior and Physical State

Although the effects that a given dose of alcohol will have on an individual vary considerably, the following table shows the general effects of a range of alcohol doses:

Ethanol Dose (oz/hour)	Blood Ethanol (mg/100ml)	Function Impaired	Physical State
1–4	up to 100	judgment fine motor coordination reaction time	happy talkative boastful

4–12	100–300	motor coordination reflexes	staggering slurred speech nausea, vomiting
12–16	300–400	voluntary responses to stimulation	hypothermia hyperthermia anesthesia
16–24	400–600	sensation movement self-protective reflexes	comatose
24–30	600–900	breathing heart function	dead

Still, there is often a substantial difference between being impaired and appearing impaired. In one study, trained observers were asked to rate whether a person was intoxicated after drinking. At low blood alcohol concentrations (about half the legal limit for intoxication), only about 10 percent of the drinkers appeared intoxicated, and at very high concentrations (greater than twice the legal limit), all of the drinkers appeared intoxicated. However, only 64 percent of people who had blood alcohol concentrations of 100–150 mg/100 ml (well above the legal limit in most states) were judged to be intoxicated. So, in casual social interactions, many people who are significantly impaired—and who would pose a real threat behind the wheel of a car—may not appear impaired even to trained observers.

Alcohol and Brain Cells

You've probably heard some variation of the following statement: "Every time you take a drink of alcohol you kill ten thousand brain cells." Although it is highly unlikely that anyone would drink enough alcohol in a given sitting to kill brain cells directly, as with many such generalizations there is a grain of truth in the warning.

One way that researchers have tried to determine which brain regions control which behaviors in animals is by destroying, or lesioning, a specific brain region and then testing the animal on a particular behavioral task.

Early in the use of this lesioning technique, some researchers found that if they injected a very high concentration of alcohol into the brain (far higher than would be achieved by a drinking person), the cells in that region would die. There is also another grain of truth in the warning about alcohol and brain cells: chronic, repeated drinking damages and sometimes kills the cells in specific brain areas. And it turns out that it might not take a very long history of heavy drinking to do so. We will address this in the "Chronic Exposure" section of this chapter.

There are fundamentally only two types of actions that a chemical can have on nerve cells—excitatory or inhibitory. That is, a drug can either increase or decrease the probability that a given cell will become active and communicate with the other cells to which it is connected. Alcohol generally depresses this type of communication, or synaptic activity, and thus its actions are similar to those of other sedative drugs, like barbiturates (such as phenobarbital) and benzodiazepines (such as Valium). Despite this general suppression of neuronal activity, however, many people report that alcohol activates or stimulates them, particularly soon after drinking, when the concentration of alcohol in the blood is increasing. Although we don't know exactly why alcohol produces feelings of stimulation, there are a couple of possibilities. First, there is the biphasic action of alcohol. This refers to the fact that at low concentrations alcohol actually activates some nerve cells. As the alcohol concentration increases, however, these same cells decrease their firing rates and their activity becomes suppressed. Or it might be that some nerve cells send excitatory signals to the other cells with which they communicate, prompting them to send inhibitory messages, actually suppressing the activity of the next cell in the circuit. So, if alcohol suppresses the activity of one of these "inhibitory" cells, the net effect in the circuit would be one of activation. Whatever the exact mechanism, it appears that there are several ways in which alcohol can have activating as well as suppressing effects on neural circuits.

Effects on Specific Neurotransmitters

GABA and Glutamate

For many years it was generally thought that alcohol treated all nerve cells equally, simply inhibiting their activity by disturbing the structure of the membrane that surrounds each cell. In this sense the effects of alcohol on the brain were thought to be very nonspecific. However, it is now clear that alcohol has specific and powerful effects on the function of at least two particular types of neuronal receptors: GABA receptors and glutamate receptors. GABA and glutamate are chemical neurotransmitters that account for much of the inhibitory and excitatory activity in the brain. When the terminals of one cell release GABA onto GABA receptors on the next cell, that cell becomes less active. When glutamate lands on a glutamate receptor, that cell becomes more active. It is in this way that many circuits in the brain maintain the delicate balance between excitation and inhibition. Small shifts in this balance can change the activity of the circuits and, ultimately, the functioning of the brain.

Alcohol increases the inhibitory activity of GABA receptors and decreases the excitatory activity of glutamate receptors. These are the two primary ways alcohol suppresses brain activity. While the enhancement of GABA activity is probably responsible for many of the general sedating effects of alcohol, the suppression of glutamate activity may have a more specific effect: impairment in the ability to form new memories or think in complex ways while intoxicated. We know that the activity of a particular subtype of glutamate receptor, called the NMDA receptor, is very powerfully inhibited by alcohol—even in very low doses. The NMDA receptor is also known to be critical for the formation of new memory. Alcohol's powerful suppression of activity at the NMDA receptor may therefore account for the memory deficits that people experience after drinking.

Dopamine

The neurotransmitter dopamine is known to underlie the rewarding effects of such highly addictive drugs as cocaine and amphetamine. In fact, dopamine is thought to be the main chemical messenger in the reward centers of the brain, which promote the experience of pleasure. Alcohol drinking increases the release of dopamine in these reward centers, probably through the action of GABA neurons, which connect to the dopamine neurons. Studies in animals show that the increase in dopamine activity occurs only while the concentration of alcohol in the blood is rising—not while it is falling. So, during the first minutes after drinking the pleasure circuits in the brain are activated, but this "dopamine rush" disappears after the alcohol level stops rising. This may motivate the drinker to consume more alcohol to start the pleasure sequence again—"chasing the high." The problem is that although the dopamine rush is over, there is still plenty of alcohol in the body. Continued drinking in pursuit of the pleasure signals could push the blood alcohol concentration up to dangerous levels.

Effects on Memory

One of the most common experiences people report after drinking is a failure to remember accurately what happened "the night before." In more extreme cases, after heavy drinking, people often report that whole chunks of time simply appear to be blank, with no memory at all having been recorded. This type of memory impairment is often called a "blackout." (Less extreme versions of this type of memory loss have been called "brown outs" or "gray outs," in which the person may have only very hazy or incomplete memory for the events that occurred during the period of intoxication. In these instances, and even in blackouts, the drinker may remember more about events when reminded of them.) In the past, blackouts were thought to be relatively rare and were viewed as a strong indicator of alcoholism by many clinicians. However, it turns out that blackouts are far more common than previously thought and don't just occur in people with serious alcohol problems. Researchers are now beginning to look more closely at how and when blackouts occur, and there appear to be some disturbing trends. First of all, blackouts appear to be quite frequent among college students, with as many as 40 percent reporting them. But it's not just the memory loss that's disturbing—it's what happens during the periods for which no new memories are made. In one survey, students reported that after a night of heavy drinking they later learned about sexual activity, fights with friends, and driving, for which they had no memory at all. So it seems that blackouts may well be a serious health risk over and above the direct effects that alcohol has on the brain. Sadly, many people joke about blackouts as an embarrassingly funny result of heavy drinking. But they are no joke. Think about it this way: anything that impairs brain function enough to interrupt memory formation is very dangerous. If it were a blow to the head, exposure to a toxic chemical, or a buildup of pressure in the brain that caused the blackout, it would be taken very seriously. Alcohol-induced blackouts should be taken seriously as well. Short of blackouts, though, it is also clear that alcohol impairs the ability to form new memories even after relatively low doses. Therefore, having a couple of beers while studying for an exam or preparing for a presentation at work is probably not a good strategy. The alcohol may promote relaxation, but it will also compromise learning and memory.

Hangover

One of the best-known symptoms of a hangover is a pounding headache. The cause is not exactly clear, but it is probably related to the effects of alcohol on blood vessels and fluid balances in the body. In any case, it is much easier to prevent the onset of pain than it is to relieve the pain once it has started. Therefore, the sooner a pain reliever is taken, the better. Some people take one before going to bed after a night of drinking. This way the chemicals in the pain reliever can prevent the pain signals in the brain from getting started as the alcohol is eliminated from the body. However, Tylenol (acetaminophen) should not be taken to treat a hangover because it can interact in a very dangerous way with alcohol and its by-products and damage the liver in some people. Aspirin or ibuprofen can be used instead, but both of these drugs can irritate the stomach and small intestine and together with alcohol may cause gastric upset.

The upset stomach and nausea associated with a hangover are harder to deal with. These may be caused by the toxic by-products of alcohol elimination, irritation to the stomach, or both. No medicines treat these effects specifically. Rather, the best strategy is to eat foods that are gentle on the stomach and to drink plenty of fluids. Morning coffee may help to start the day after a night on the town, but its irritating effects on the stomach may make it an unpleasant waking. And because caffeine is a diuretic, it may also contribute to the dehydration that often accompanies alcohol drinking.

CHRONIC EXPOSURE

Everybody wants to know how much drinking is bad for them. Some want to know how much drinking they can get away with before they cause themselves health problems. This question always reminds us of a common response to the old warning that masturbation would cause blindness: some people just wanted to know how much they could do it before suffering blurred vision.

The long-term effects of drinking depend on how much alcohol is consumed. Although there appear to be some health benefits associated with very moderate drinking in adults (this will be discussed later in the chapter), chronic heavy drinking creates very serious problems in a number of body systems, including the brain, liver, and digestive system. Between the extremes of heavy and light drinking lies a "gray area" that is not completely understood. Moreover, this gray area appears to be rather small. That is, while an average of one-half to one drink per day may be healthy for your heart, it is perfectly clear that an average of two drinks per day significantly increases your risk of dying from heart disease or cancer.

The Incredible Shrinking Brain

Brain-imaging techniques create a window into the effects of alcohol on the brain. Using these techniques, researchers have observed shrinkage of brain tissue in people after long-term use of alcohol. But there is also recovery of brain tissue volume in people who stop drinking and remain abstinent, so this "shrinking" effect appears not to be due exclusively to the loss of brain cells. Interestingly, some studies indicate that certain parts of the brain may be more vulnerable to damage by alcohol than others, such as the cortex—the folded, lumpy surface of the brain (it gets its name because of its resemblance to the bark of a tree), which endows us with consciousness and controls most of our mental functions. One region of the cortex that appears to be particularly vulnerable is the frontal lobe. The frontal lobes are unique in that they act like a kind of executive manager for the rest of the brain. They monitor and help to coordinate the actions of the other cortical lobes—much like an executive does in a corporation. The analogy is so apt that the functions of the frontal lobes are often called "executive functions." They endow us with the ability to bring together our mental abilities to solve complex problems, to make and execute plans of action, and to use judgment in service of those plans. Even in people who have never been diagnosed with an alcohol use disorder, chronic drinking can contribute to frontal lobe damage. Another vulnerable region is the mammillary bodies, which are very important for memory. (These small, round structures near the base of the brain got their name from the neuroanatomists who first noticed them and thought that they looked like breasts. Actually, their resemblance to breasts is quite remote, but neuroanatomists do have good imaginations!)

Although many of the studies of brain shrinkage have been done with alcoholics, some of the more recent ones have assessed social drinkers and found similar effects, though less severe. The shrinkage occurs while the person is still using alcohol. If she stops drinking for a prolonged period, her brain will recover somewhat—not because new nerve cells grow, but because support cells, or parts of the remaining nerve cells, grow. Therefore, the regrowth of brain size does not mean that the deficits in mental functioning that many alcoholics experience will be erased simply by abstaining from alcohol.

It is not known if there is a safe level of chronic drinking. Clearly many people who drink do not appear to suffer any damage to their mental functioning. Still, as with acute intoxication, the lack of any obvious impairment does not mean that there is none. Studies using animals instead of humans can look more closely at nerve-cell damage. Such studies have shown that more moderate alcohol exposure can damage and kill brain cells. A number of these studies have shown large areas of nerve-cell loss in a region of the brain called the hippocampus, which is known to be critical for the formation of new memories. This could be one reason why people who drink chronically can end up with relatively poor memory function, though of course this will vary with the person's drinking history.

Another study in animals has shown that in the case of very heavy drinking, brain damage may occur much sooner than previously thought. Using a model in which animals are exposed to a heavy "binge" of alcohol around the clock for four days, it was discovered that cells in some of these same regions started to die off after the first two days of the binge. If this holds true for humans, it will show that even one very heavy episode of binging across a couple of days could damage the brain. These effects were particularly pronounced in adolescent animals, raising some concern that teenage binge drinking may have more serious long-term consequences than we once thought.

Effects on Mental Functioning

Five areas of mental ability are consistently compromised by chronic alcohol abuse: memory formation, abstract thinking, problem solving, attention and concentration, and perception of emotion. As many as 70 percent of people who seek treatment for alcohol-related problems suffer significant impairment of these abilities.

Memory Formation

By memory formation we mean the ability to form new memories, not the ability to recall information that was learned in the past. That is, an individual with a chronic drinking habit might vividly and accurately recall what he learned early in life but not be able to tell what he ate for lunch four hours ago. And the richness and detail of his memories during the past few years of drinking might be significantly less than in those earlier memories. On some tests of mental ability that assess different kinds of brain functions, chronic drinkers often perform just fine on most of the categories but perform poorly on the memory sections. This selective and profound memory deficit may be a result of damage to specific brain areas, such as the hippocampus, the mammillary bodies, or the frontal lobes.

Abstract Thinking

By abstract thinking we mean being able to think in ways that are not directly tied to concrete things. We think abstractly when we interpret the meaning of stories, work on word puzzles, or solve geometry or algebra problems. Chronic drinkers often find these abilities compromised. One way to measure abstract thinking is to show someone a group of objects and ask her to group the objects according to the characteristics they share. Chronic drinkers will consistently group things based on their concrete characteristics (such as size, shape, and color) rather than on the basis of their abstract characteristics (such as what they are used for, or what kinds of things they are). It is as if abstract thoughts do not come to mind as easily for the chronic drinker.

Problem Solving

We all have to solve problems each day. Some are simple ones, like determining whether to do the laundry or the grocery shopping first. Some are more complicated, like setting up a new personal computer or deciding on what inventory to order for the next month's needs in a business. In either case, one of the required abilities is mental flexibility. We need to be able to switch strategies and approaches to problems (particularly the complicated ones) to solve them efficiently. People with a history of chronic drinking often have a lot of difficulty with this. Under testing conditions, it often appears that they get stuck in a particular mode of problem solving and take a lot longer to get to a solution than someone who is better able to switch strategies and try new approaches. This difficulty could relate to the effects of chronic drinking on the "executive functions" of the frontal lobes.

Attention and Concentration

Chronic drinkers also develop difficulty in focusing their attention and maintaining concentration. This appears to be particularly difficult when related to tasks that require visual attention and concentration. Again, the deficits may not appear until the person is challenged. In casual conversation, the sober chronic drinker may be able to concentrate perfectly well, but placed in a more challenging situation (like reading an instruction manual, driving a car, or operating a piece of equipment), she may be quite impaired.

Perception of Emotion

One of the most important elements of our social behavior is the ability to recognize and interpret the emotions of other people. Alcoholics have a deficit in the ability to perceive emotion in people's language. There is a specific brain function that normally gives us the ability to detect attitude and emotion in conversation. It turns out that chronic, heavy drinking markedly reduces this ability. It is important to realize that this deficit is one of perception and does not reflect the alcoholic's own emotional state. It's as if the subtle things like the tone and cadences of the other person's language that convey attitude and emotion are simply not perceived by the alcoholic. This is particularly interesting because we know that chronic heavy drinkers often have difficulty in social relationships. Perhaps this perceptual deficit causes some of these problems.

Do These Deficits Go Away?

Chronic heavy drinkers who quit recover these functions partially during the first month or two after the last drink. However, once this time passes, they have gotten back all that they will recover. It is difficult to identify precisely how much recovery occurs, but clear deficits do appear to persist permanently in these individuals. In one study, people who had quit drinking completely after many years of alcohol abuse were examined for seven years. Even after this time they had significant memory deficits. This persistent pattern of memory deficits in previous alcoholics is common enough to have a specific diagnosis. It is generally called either alcohol amnestic disorder or dementia associated with alcoholism.

What about "Social Drinkers"?

It is important to define exactly what we mean when we say that someone is a social drinker. The most consistent definition, looking across the literature on alcohol use and treatment, would be this: someone who drinks regularly but does not get drunk when he drinks or have any of the clinical signs of addiction to alcohol. People who fit this pattern of drinking generally do not have nearly as severe deficits in mental functioning as those who drink heavily.

Among social drinkers, the pattern of alcohol consumption plays a very important role in determining whether the person will develop deficits in mental functioning. The more alcohol he drinks during each drinking session, the higher the likelihood that mental deficits will develop. Consider two people who each drink five drinks per week, on average. The first person has one drink on each of the five days of the week, and the second person has four drinks on each Saturday night and one in the middle of each week. The second person will be more likely to develop the kinds of deficits in the aforementioned abilities for chronic alcoholics. This is a particularly important point for young people, because heavy drinking on weekends is a typical pattern for many high school and college students as well as for young people in the work world.

It is difficult to say what amount of drinking over time will result in deficits in mental function. There have been many studies addressing this issue in different groups of people, and it's very hard to boil all of these down to a clear and concise statement of risk. However, when all the complexities of the research are taken into consideration, it is reasonable to estimate that people who drink three or more drinks per day on average are at substantial risk of developing permanent deficits in certain cognitive abilities. This is not to say that drinking less is perfectly safe—indeed, we know that there are health risks associated with drinking less—but in terms of causing irreversible cognitive deficits, three drinks per day appears to be something of a threshold.

Tolerance

Development across Several Drinking Sessions

Tolerance means that after continued drinking, consuming an identical amount of alcohol produces a lesser effect—in other words, more alcohol is necessary to produce the original effect. The development of tolerance indicates that alcohol exposure has changed the brain. In some ways it is less sensitive to the alcohol, but in other ways it may remain quite sensitive. The brain effects that produce the high may diminish, while the effects that are toxic to the brain cells themselves may remain the same. Another problem is that as tolerance develops, the drinker may drink more each time to get the high. As we just learned, such a drinking pattern is more likely to produce deficits in mental functioning over time. Also, because the brain is the organ of addiction, the tolerant person who increases her drinking runs a greater risk of addiction. Finally, although the brain may need more alcohol to produce the high, the liver and other internal organs are dealing with more and more alcohol, and they are at risk for permanent damage.

Development within One Drinking Session

Although tolerance to most alcohol effects develops gradually and over several drinking sessions, it has also been observed even within a single drinking session. This is called acute tolerance and means that the intoxication is greatest soon after the beginning of drinking. Acute tolerance does not develop to all the effects of alcohol, but it does develop to the feeling of being high. So, the drinker may drink more to maintain the feeling of being high, while the other intoxicating effects of alcohol (those that interfere with driving, mental function, and judgment) continue to build, placing the drinker at greater and greater risk.

Dependence

It is important to distinguish between alcohol dependence and alcohol abuse. Generally, alcohol abuse refers to patterns of drinking that give rise to health problems, social problems, or both. Alcohol dependence (often called alcoholism) refers to a disease that is characterized by abnormal seeking and consumption of alcohol that leads to a lack of control over drinking. Dependent individuals often appear to crave alcohol. They seem driven to drink even though they know that their drinking is causing problems for them. The signs of physical dependence begin within hours after an individual stops drinking. They include anxiety, tremors (shaking), sleep disturbances, and, in more extreme cases, hallucinations and seizures. Until a chronic drinker actually stops drinking, it is quite difficult to make a definitive assessment of alcohol dependence. But for most practical purposes, this formal diagnosis is unnecessary, because the social and medical problems that most alcoholics experience should be recognizable to health professionals. See the section "How to Spot a Problem Drinker" on page 55 for some general guidelines.

PRENATAL EXPOSURE

The dangers of prenatal alcohol exposure have been noted since the time of Aristotle in ancient Greece. However, it was not until 1968 that formal reports began to emerge. The early studies of fetal alcohol syndrome (FAS) described gross physical deformities and profound mental retardation among children of heavy-drinking alcoholic mothers. Although this was a very important set of findings, at first there was no evidence that women who drank more moderately were placing their children at risk. In fact, for many years, pregnant women were often encouraged to have a glass of wine with dinner or take a drink now and then during pregnancy to help them fall asleep or just to relax.

It took a while for the effects of moderate prenatal drinking to be noticed, because the children have none of the very obvious defects associated with the full-blown fetal alcohol syndrome. However, it is now clear that there is a less severe, but very well documented, pattern of deficits associated with more moderate prenatal drinking—a pattern described as fetal alcohol effects (FAE). School-age children with FAS or FAE are frequently described as hyperactive, distractible, and impulsive, with short attention spans—behaviors similar to those observed in children with attention deficit disorder (ADD). However, the FAS and FAE children differ from ADD children in that they are more intellectually impaired. In recent years the term *fetal alcohol spectrum disorders* (FASD) has emerged as an umbrella term to include the full range of neurological, cognitive, behavioral, and learning disabilities associated with prenatal alcohol exposure.

The impairments of intelligence and behavior in people with FASD appear to persist into adulthood and are probably lifelong, resulting in IQ scores markedly below average, often well into the moderately retarded range. Those with FAS scored worse than those with FAE, but both were significantly below normal, hampered in reading and spelling and most profoundly deficient in mathematical skills. More important, the FAE patients did not perform any better than the FAS patients on academic achievement tests, though their IQs were somewhat higher. What all this means is that even moderate drinking during pregnancy can create permanent intellectual disabilities. Some studies using animal models of FAE even suggest that just one drink per day impairs the function of brain areas related to learning in the adult offspring.

The bottom line is that there is no identified safe level of drinking during pregnancy. The smart decision for a woman is simply not to drink if she is pregnant or thinks that she might be.

RISK FACTORS FOR ALCOHOL ADDICTION

Anyone can become dependent on alcohol. Continued exposure to alcohol changes the brain in ways that produce dependence. Although there are large differences in individuals' risk for dependency and addiction, any person who puts enough alcohol into his brain over a long enough time will become physically dependent on the drug. Putting aside for a moment the risk factors that have been identified for alcohol dependence, the numbers generally show that the chances of a man becoming addicted to alcohol increase markedly if he drinks more than about three to four drinks per day. For women, the number of drinks is about three. Another consistent finding is that people who become addicted to alcohol are often those who report that they drink to relieve their emotional or social difficulties. In other words, if someone drinks to self-medicate—to block out emotional or social problems—he is especially likely to become addicted. But self-medication simply cannot account for all of the alcohol addiction in the world, and the big question remains: Why do some people choose to drink enough to get addicted?

GENETIC FACTORS

Much of the evidence that genetic factors may lead to alcohol dependence has come from studies on twins and children of alcoholics who were adopted at birth and raised by nonalcoholic adoptive parents. Studies like these allow researchers to begin to tease apart the separate influences of nature and nurture in the development of alcohol addiction. At present it seems clear that the basis of alcoholism is partly genetic but that genetic factors alone cannot account for the development of the disease. The real value of the nature versus nurture studies so far is that they have identified certain traits, or markers, that run in families and predispose people to alcohol dependence. Thus, they help to identify individuals who may be at risk for developing alcohol problems. If a person knows that he is at more risk than normal for this disease, then he can make better decisions about drinking.

It is very clear that alcoholism, like diabetes, runs in families. With no family history of alcoholism, the risk of developing alcohol abuse problems is about 10 percent for men and 5 percent for women. However, the risk nearly doubles if there is a family history of alcohol problems. For example, for women who have a first-degree relative (child, sibling, or parent) who is an alcoholic, the chances rise from 5 percent to 10 percent. For men with a first-degree relative who is an alcoholic, the risk goes from 10 percent to 20 percent. So, for both men and women, the risk is doubled. The risk goes to 30 percent for men and 15 percent for women who have both a first-degree relative and a second- (e.g., uncle, aunt, grandparent) or third-degree relative (e.g., cousin, great-grandparent) who is an alcoholic. So, being the child of an alcoholic increases the risk of developing alcohol abuse problems, but boys are at considerably more risk than girls.

It is important to know that these family studies do not conclusively demonstrate a genetic basis for alcoholism. It is likely that factors other than biological ones, such as being raised by an alcoholic parent, also contribute to drinking behavior. A number of studies show that being raised in a family in which alcohol is abused increases a child's chances of becoming alcohol dependent.

A SPECIAL RISK FOR MEN

Although genetic influences significantly affect the risk of alcoholism in both men and women, these influences appear to be particularly powerful in men. A number of studies compare the sons of alcoholic fathers with sons of nonalcoholic fathers. In general, it appears that the sons of alcoholic fathers are less impaired by alcohol than those of nonalcoholic fathers. However, early in the drinking session (when the pleasurable effects of alcohol prevail), the sons of alcoholics appear to be more affected by alcohol than others. This difference suggests that sons of alcoholic fathers may have a more powerful experience of the pleasurable effects of alcohol and a less powerful experience of the impairing effects of alcohol than other men, creating a setup for these men to continue drinking over time and making them more susceptible to addiction.

In addition, a specific type of alcoholism seems to occur mostly in men. This is called Type II alcoholism and is characterized by an onset of drinking problems in adolescence, aggressive behavior, trouble with the law, and the use of other drugs. Type II alcoholism is considered to be very strongly influenced by genetics. Type I alcoholism is more common and less severe than Type II alcoholism, occurs in both men and women, and begins in adulthood. Men with fathers or brothers who show signs of Type II alcoholism should be particularly careful about alcohol use.

HOW TO SPOT A PROBLEM DRINKER

Health-care practitioners use several simple screening tests to assess whether an individual may have an alcohol problem. Before describing them, though, we must make two cautionary notes. First, a diagnosis of alcohol abuse, alcohol dependency, or alcoholism can only truly be made by a health professional trained specifically in addiction. These are very complex medical and psychological states, and no simple screening tool is adequate to make a foolproof assessment. Second, it sometimes does considerably more harm than good to confront a friend or relative with the impression that she may have a drinking problem. Although a concerned person may have the best of intentions and may be acting out of true concern, the other person may simply feel accused and withdraw from the very help being offered. The screening tests we describe in what follows are often used in doctors' offices and clinics as a first indication that there might be a problem.

The most widely used screening test is called the CAGE:

- Have you ever felt the need to **C**ut down on your drinking?
- Have you ever felt **A**nnoyed by someone criticizing your drinking?
- Have you ever felt **G**uilty about your drinking?
- Have you ever felt the need for an **E**ye-opener (a drink at the beginning of the day)?

If the person gives two or more positive responses to these questions, there is a good chance that she has some degree of an alcohol problem. But remember that screening tests are, by their nature, imperfect. For example, it is easy to imagine that a person with a history of heavy drinking might answer yes to all of the questions, even if she hadn't had a drink for years.

Another screening test, which has proven particularly useful with women, is called the TWEAK:

- **T**olerance: How many drinks does it take to make you high?
- **W**orried: Have close friends or relatives worried or complained about your drinking?
- **E**ye-opener: Do you sometimes take a drink in the morning to wake up?
- **A**mnesia (memory loss): Has a friend or family member ever told you things you said or did while you were drinking that you could not remember?
- **(K)**Cut: Do you sometimes feel the need to cut down on your drinking?

This test is scored differently from the CAGE, but a positive score of three or more is considered to indicate that the person likely has a drinking problem.

One final word of caution regarding these screening techniques: they all rely on one critical component (which is not always so reliable)—the person's own responses. There are any number of reasons why a person might not respond fully accurately. Therefore, while these screening tools may be useful as a first-pass indicator of a possible problem, they must not be used in isolation to form impressions about a person.

SPECIAL CONSIDERATIONS FOR WOMEN

DIFFERENT SENSITIVITY

Alcohol does not treat all people equally, and there are some big differences between the effects of alcohol on women and on men. As women have taken a more visible role in our society, they have found more freedom (and perhaps more encouragement) to drink. Consequently, drinking is on the rise among women in general. Surveys indicate that the percentage of women who drink alcohol has increased from 45 to 66 percent over the past forty years and that as many as 5 percent of women are heavy drinkers.

Women's bodies differ from men's bodies in a number of ways that make them react differently to alcohol. For one, women are generally smaller than men, and their bodies have a larger percentage of fat, which causes them to develop higher blood alcohol concentrations than men after drinking similar amounts of alcohol. There is also a chemical called alcohol dehydrogenase (ADH) that breaks down some of the alcohol in the stomach before it gets absorbed into the blood. Women under 40 years of age appear to have less of this in their stomachs, so, compared to men, more of the alcohol they drink gets absorbed into the blood. In fact, after a given dose of alcohol, a woman may achieve a blood alcohol level 25 to 30 percent higher than a man. Women should know that they will likely be considerably more impaired than their male companions if they drink comparable amounts of alcohol.

HEALTH EFFECTS

Women who drink are at significantly greater risk for liver damage than men even if they drink less alcohol or drink for a shorter period of time. This increased risk has been reported for women who drink from one and a half to three drinks of alcohol per day and may be due to the differences in the way a woman's body eliminates alcohol.

The pancreas, too, is more likely to be damaged by alcohol in women. The cells of the pancreas make chemicals that are used for digestion. When alcohol damages the pancreas cells, the digestive chemicals begin to leak out and can actually begin to digest the pancreas itself. Although this happens in both women and men, women tend to develop the disease sooner.

Women are also more likely than men to develop high blood pressure due to drinking alcohol. High blood pressure is one of the major causes of heart attack and stroke. Women who have two to three alcoholic drinks per day have a 40 percent greater risk of developing high blood pressure. The good news is that this additional risk diminishes when the woman stops drinking. Still, for women who drink even moderate amounts of alcohol, the increased risk of high blood pressure is substantial.

The risk of breast cancer is also increased in women who drink. The minimum amount of drinking that it takes to increase breast cancer risk has not been established. However, there is solid evidence that even as few as one to two drinks per day can increase a woman's risk of breast cancer. And it does not take much more drinking to push the risk up considerably higher. For example, one analysis indicated that women who had two to four drinks per day increased their breast cancer risk by 41 percent while another showed that women who drank three or more drinks per day on average suffered a 69 percent higher risk of getting breast cancer.

Finally, women appear to be more sensitive to the effects of chronic alcohol drinking on brain function and seem to be more likely to show deficits in cognitive function.

SOCIAL AND PSYCHOLOGICAL ISSUES

Despite the increased acceptance of drinking by women during the past several decades, a number of studies have shown that women who drink a lot meet with more disapproval of their drinking than do men. In addition, the divorce rate for alcoholic women is higher than for alcoholic men. This suggests that women are less likely to leave relationships with alcoholic men than the reverse.

It is also clear that women who drink heavily are at a much higher risk for domestic violence and sexual assault than other women. One particularly compelling study of more than 3,000 college women found that the more alcohol a woman consumed, the higher her chances were of being sexually victimized. This might occur because a woman impaired by alcohol may have more trouble accurately interpreting a man's behavior as threatening or resisting unwanted sexual advances.

ALCOHOL AND SEX

Anyone who has ever watched a commercial for beer can tell you that your sex life will improve considerably with drinking. The truth of the matter is that most of the effects of alcohol on sexual functioning are bad. Of course, a person may feel more suave and sexy after drinking, and he may more easily convince himself that his sexual prowess is unparalleled. But all too often the mind makes a promise that the body can't keep after a night of heavy drinking. Men, in particular, should consider the meaning of the term "brewer's droop."

As many as 40 to 90 percent of chronic male drinkers (depending on the study) report reduced sex drive. Chronic drinkers show reduced capacity for penile erection, decreased semen production, and lower sperm counts. In fact, in alcoholic men the testes may actually shrink (a fact generally not presented in beer commercials). In extreme cases of chronic heavy alcohol abuse among men, a feminization syndrome can develop, which involves a loss of body hair and the development of breast tissue. Although these effects are most often seen in men who drink heavily over a prolonged period, some sexual and reproductive functions are impaired even by lesser intake. For example, evidence is accumulating that consuming two to three drinks per day may decrease sperm counts.

CHILDREN AND ADOLESCENTS

By far, alcohol is the drug used most often by high school students. Although most seniors cannot buy alcohol legally, 80 percent of them have tried alcohol and about one in five report that they have drunk heavily (more than five drinks in a row) in the past two weeks. This is actually good news, because the number of teens drinking heavily has declined somewhat in recent years. But that's not the end of the story. Recent studies show that among students who engaged in heavy drinking, half had consumed ten or more drinks in one episode and a quarter had consumed fifteen. So, while heavy drinking at the "low" end of the scale (about five drinks in an episode) has declined recently, the rates of extreme heavy drinking have remained high.

The story among college students is not as simple as the media sometimes portray. Reports of "binge drinking" among college students can be misleading. First, the term *binge drinking* is a bad one. Many people think of an alcohol binge as a period of several days during which a person stays drunk nearly all the time. This, of course, is a very dangerous pattern of drinking but is not what is meant by the media when they report on binge drinking among college students. In that context, binge drinking refers to a man having five or more drinks in one sitting or a woman having four or more—clearly enough to put a person at risk for trouble, but hardly a binge in the traditional sense. We prefer to think of the four- or five-drink level as "high-risk drinking"—a more descriptive term. About 40 percent of college students report this level of high-risk drinking in the past two weeks, but there are also a significant number of college students who don't drink at all—about 20 to 25 percent depending upon the college. So it's important for students to know that, while a lot of students drink, not everybody on campus gets drunk every weekend, and a solid number of students don't drink at all. Still, there are often negative consequences for those who do. Nearly 600,000 college students suffer unintentional alcohol-related injuries each year, and more than 1,800 die from those injuries. In addition, 25 percent of college students report negative academic consequences related to their drinking each year, and more than 150,000 develop a health problem related to alcohol use. Clearly, college drinking remains highly prevalent and continues to take a toll on students' lives.

The problems associated with underage drinking are well known, and in recent years research has continued to show that alcohol affects the brain of younger people very differently from the way it affects that of adults. Part of this may be related to brain development. For example, we know that the brain does not finish developing until a person is in his midtwenties and that one of the last regions to mature is the frontal lobe area, which is intimately involved with the ability to plan and make complex judgments. Young brains also have rich resources for acquiring new memories and seem to be "built to learn." It is no accident that people in our society are educated during their early years, when they have more capacity for memory and learning. However, with this greater memory capacity come additional risks associated with the use of alcohol. Studies using animals have shown that when the brain is young, it is more susceptible to some of the dangerous effects of alcohol, especially on learning and memory function. And one study in humans showed that people in their early twenties were more vulnerable to the effects of alcohol on learning than were people just a few years older, in their late twenties. So it appears that children and adolescents who drink are powerfully impairing the brain functions on which they rely so heavily for learning. This is already indicated by very detailed cellular studies on learning-related brain regions. In these studies (which, of course, can only be done using brain tissue from animals), it is clear that alcohol decreases the ability of brain circuits to change in the ways they must for learning to occur, and this effect is much more pronounced in the adolescent brain than in the adult brain.

Although these studies suggest that alcohol has a more powerful effect on learning and learning-related brain functions in adolescents than in adults, there is at least one way in which the adolescent brain appears to be far less sensitive to the effects of alcohol—brain functions that make us sleepy are less activated by alcohol in adolescents, compared to adults. Again, it is only possible to do these studies in animals, but the results are striking. It takes much more alcohol to put an adolescent animal to sleep than it does for an adult. And even at the level of single brain cells, the kinds of brain functions that promote sedation (sleepiness) are activated far less in the brains of adolescent animals than in adults. This could mean that an adolescent may be able to drink far more than an adult before feeling sleepy enough to stop and along the way be impairing her cognitive functions more than an adult would be. It also important to recognize that sleepiness is one of the effects of alcohol that many people find unpleasant, rather than reinforcing. Most people like the initial buzz that they get after their first drink or two, but they find the sedation that follows that third or fourth drink to be aversive, thus providing motivation to stop drinking. But if the sedative effect is less powerful in adolescents or it takes more alcohol to get them sleepy, then they will be less likely than adults to stop drinking as the dose increases.

Some brain-imaging studies suggest that drinking during the teen years might be particularly bad for the hippocampus (the brain region that is critical for learning new information). The data indicated that people in their twenties who had been alcoholics as teens had smaller hippocampal volumes. It's important not to overinterpret this kind of study—it could be that those people had smaller hippocampi to begin with—but the data should at least be seen as another word of caution about teen drinking. Additional strong words of caution come from some recent studies in animals. Normally, new brain cells are being born in the hippocampus on an ongoing basis. Alcohol slows this process down—which may be part of why it is so hard on learning and memory—and this slowing effect appears to be more pronounced in the brains of adolescent animals than in those of adults. The newest studies show that when alcohol is given to animals, the functioning of brain cells can be altered at a very basic level, changing the ways that they process incoming information and how they react to it. And these effects are very long lasting. What's particularly interesting (and disturbing) is that some of these changes in basic cellular functioning occur far more strongly when the alcohol exposure occurs during adolescence, compared to adulthood. In other words, it appears that adolescence is not only a time when single doses of alcohol affect the brain differently but also a time of enhanced vulnerability to the long-term effects of repeated alcohol exposure—even down to the level of individual brain cells. This adds to a strong and growing scientific literature that tells us that adolescents should hold off on drinking.

Another very good reason for teens to hold off on drinking is that there is a very strong relationship between the age at which one starts to drink and the likelihood of developing dependence on alcohol. People who start drinking in their early to midteens are far more likely to develop alcohol dependency, and to experience recurring episodes of dependency, than are people who start drinking at age twenty-one or older. There are certainly a number of reasons for this increased risk, and not all of them are biological, but it is clear from animal studies that adolescents develop tolerance to some of alcohol's effects more rapidly than adults. In humans this could lead to a greater motivation to drink repeatedly. So, although it has always been controversial, our current state laws requiring a person to be twenty-one to drink make good sense from this perspective.

Most parents tend to be clueless when it comes to their children's drinking. For example, while 52 percent of tenth graders report having drunk alcohol in the past year, only 10 percent of parents of tenth graders believe that their child has consumed alcohol in that period. Interestingly, parents report believing that about 60 percent of tenth graders have consumed alcohol within the past year. So parents actually tend to *overestimate* the proportion of kids who drink—they just don't think it's *their* kids who are drinking! There are similar gaps between older teens' reported drinking and parents' beliefs about their drinking. Parents of twelfth graders are starting to see the light, but they still underestimate their kids' drinking significantly. The important message for parents is that alcohol is out there and its use is getting thrust at their children from many angles. Talk to your children about them.

DANGEROUS INTERACTIONS WITH OTHER DRUGS

Sedatives

Clearly the most dangerous drugs to mix with alcohol are other sedatives, or "downers," such as phenobarbital and pentobarbital. The depressing effects of alcohol on brain function combined with the effects of the bar-biturates can cause extreme impairment, unconsciousness, or even death. One of the most famous cases in medical ethics was that of a young woman, Karen Ann Quinlan, who drank alcohol in combination with Quaaludes (methaqualone—a powerful sedative drug) and went into a coma from which she never recovered. This tragic case gained national attention because it raised the issue of whether a person should be removed from life-support machines after it becomes clear that he or she will never recover from a vegetative state.

Although few people take alcohol-sedative combinations severe enough to cause coma or death, the combination of even relatively low doses of alcohol and sedatives can be dangerous, powerfully impairing the ability to think clearly, make good decisions, or drive a car. A person who is nor-mally able to perform these tasks perfectly well at the end of an evening after having had three or four beers over the course of several hours might find that he is totally unable to perform them if even a small dose of seda-tives is added to the mix. The effects of the alcohol may be totally unex-pected in the presence of the other sedative drug.

Antianxiety Medications

Antianxiety medications, such as Valium, Librium, and so forth, fall into the general category called benzodiazepines and are used to treat anxiety, sleep disturbances, and seizures. They are also used to treat alcohol-with-drawal symptoms in detoxification clinics. These drugs are sedating and may cause severe drowsiness in the presence of alcohol, increasing the risk of household and automobile accidents.

Antibiotics

In combination with acute doses of alcohol, some antibiotics can cause nausea, vomiting, headache, or even convulsions (seizures). Among the potentially dangerous ones are Furoxone (furazolidone), Grisactin (gris-eofulvin), Flagyl (metronidazole), and Atabrine (quinacrine).

Anticoagulants (Blood Thinners)

Warfarin (Coumadin) is prescribed to decrease the blood's ability to clot. Alcohol increases the availability of warfarin in the body and increases the risk of dangerous bleeding. But in chronic drinkers, warfarin's action is decreased, lessening these patients' protection from the consequences of blood-clotting disorders.

Antidepressants

Many people who are depressed use alcohol, and many alcoholics are also depressed. So, it is quite common for people to use alcohol with antidepressant drugs. Alcohol increases the sedative effects of the tricyclic antidepressants such as Elavil (amitriptyline). This impairs both mental and physical skills such as those necessary for driving. Chronic drinking appears to increase the action of some tricyclic antidepressants and decrease the action of others. Anyone who is on antidepressants should consult closely with her doctor about how her medication reacts with alcohol.

Antidiabetic Medications

Orinase (tolbutamide) is given orally to help lower blood sugar in diabetic patients. Acute alcohol drinking prolongs the action of this drug, and chronic drinking decreases its availability in the body. Alcohol can also cause nausea and headache when taken with some drugs of this class.

Antihistamines

Antihistamines such as Benadryl (diphenhydramine) are available without a prescription and are used to treat allergic symptoms and sometimes insomnia. They have sedative effects that may be intensified by alcohol, increasing the probability of accidents. In older persons these drugs can cause excessive dizziness and sedation, and their combination with alcohol may be particularly dangerous.

Antipsychotic Medications

Drugs such as Thorazine (chlorpromazine) are used to treat psychotic symptoms such as delusions and hallucinations. Acute alcohol drinking can increase the sedative effects of these drugs, resulting in impaired coordination and potentially fatal suppression of breathing.

Antiseizure Medications

One of the most widely used drugs prescribed to treat epilepsy (seizures) is Dilantin (phenytoin). Acute alcohol drinking increases the availability of Dilantin in the body and increases the probability of side effects. Chronic drinking may decrease the availability of Dilantin, dangerously hampering its effectiveness and increasing the patient's risk of seizures.

Heart Medications

There are many medications used to treat disease of the heart or circulatory system. Acute alcohol drinking can interact with some of these to cause dizziness or fainting upon standing up. These drugs include the angina medicine nitroglycerin and the blood pressure medication Apresoline. In addition, chronic alcohol drinking reduces the effectiveness of the blood pressure medication Inderal (propranolol).

Narcotic Pain Relievers

These drugs (e.g., morphine, Darvon, codeine, Demerol) are prescribed for moderate to severe pain, such as after surgery or dental work. The combination of any of these drugs with alcohol magnifies the sedative effects of both, increasing the risk of death from overdose. This is one of the most common drug combinations to cause accidental overdose deaths.

Nonnarcotic Pain Relievers

Some nonprescription pain relievers such as aspirin, Advil, and Aleve can cause stomach bleeding and prevent the blood from clotting normally. Alcohol can worsen these side effects. In addition, aspirin may increase the availability of alcohol within the body, thereby increasing the intoxicating effect of a given drink. As we stated before, the combination of Tylenol (acetaminophen) and alcohol can result in the formation of chemicals that can cause liver damage. This can occur even when the pain reliever is used in recommended doses and even if it is taken after drinking as a treatment for hangover.

HEALTH BENEFITS OF MODERATE ALCOHOL USE

RELAXATION AND STRESS REDUCTION

It is perfectly clear that heavy drinking, either in one session or across decades, carries with it significant risks to health and safety. However, alcohol is not all bad. Used in an informed and moderate way, alcohol can convey some health benefits. For example, the similarity of its actions to those of antianxiety medications such as Valium makes alcohol a potent antianxiety agent for some people. The feeling of relaxation that accompanies an occasional drink of alcohol can help to reduce stress, and stress reduction is healthy. But remember: people who use alcohol heavily or too regularly as a way of coping with the difficulties in their lives are at considerable risk for becoming addicted. Ultimately, the use of alcohol for relaxation and stress reduction is a personal choice that must be made in as informed a way as possible.

PROTECTION AGAINST HEART DISEASE

There is no doubt that chronic heavy drinking damages the heart. However, recent studies show that light (and perhaps moderate) drinkers have a reduced risk for coronary artery disease—a principal cause of heart attacks. Remember, though, that this research is still developing, and it is not possible to arrive at an exact "prescription" of alcohol use for cardiovascular protection. Still, a growing number of studies suggest that an average of a half to one and a half drinks per day may significantly lower a person's risk for coronary artery disease.

A study from Harvard Medical School further supports these early findings—at least in men. A group of more than 22,000 men who ranged in age from forty to eighty-four were studied over a ten-year period. Compared to men who drank less than one alcoholic beverage per week on average, those who drank two to four alcoholic beverages per week were significantly less likely to die of a heart or circulatory disorder. These light-drinking men also suffered fewer cancers over the ten-year period. However, among men who drank two or more drinks per day, the death rate was 51 percent higher. This means that there is a narrow window for the possible health benefits of alcohol for men. Two drinks per week seem to be good; two drinks per day seem to be bad.

For women, however, these findings present a double-edged sword. Moderate alcohol drinking appears to reduce the risk of cardiovascular disease in women. But studies have also shown that women who drink an average of three to nine drinks per week are significantly more likely to develop breast cancer than women who do not drink. Still, the causes of breast cancer are quite complex and much work remains to determine the exact relationship of alcohol drinking to breast cancer. Women who choose to drink moderately, for whatever reasons, should keep in close touch with the latest information related to breast cancer risks.

DIMINISHED RISK OF DEATH

There have now been several large-scale studies, in both Eastern and Western countries, indicating that light to moderate drinking may diminish the risk of death in middle-aged men. A recent study in China showed that men who drank one to two drinks per day over a six-and-a-half-year period reduced their risk of death by about 20 percent—a finding that is consistent with studies in European countries. The protective effect was not limited to death from heart disease—the drinkers were also less likely to die from cancer or other causes. Further, the particular type of alcoholic beverage consumed was inconsequential: Beer drinkers, wine drinkers, and drinkers of hard liquor shared equally in the benefits, as long as their consumption was not more than an average of two drinks per day. Beyond that level the risk of death was increased by about 30 percent. Alcohol appears to have some similar protective effects in women. But, as just noted, women are also more vulnerable to some of the negative effects of alcohol, so most studies suggest no more than one drink per day for women.

The bottom line seems to be that if you want to get the medicinal effects of alcohol, you have to take it like medicine—a little at a time.

2

CAFFEINE

Drug Class: Stimulant

Individual Drugs: coffee (75–150 mg per 8 oz cup), tea (30–60 mg per 8 oz cup), soft drinks (20–50 mg per 12 oz serving), energy drinks (30–80 mg per 8.4 oz serving), other energy formulations (concentrations vary), over-the-counter pain relievers (30–70 mg), over-the-counter stimulants (100–200 mg), some prescription medications (concentrations vary)

The Buzz: At low to moderate doses, many people report increased alertness and ability to concentrate, and even euphoria. Higher doses can result in nervousness and agitation.

Overdose and Other Bad Effects: Fatal overdose with caffeine is extremely rare, but it is possible. Some symptoms of caffeine poisoning include tremors (involuntary shaking), nausea, vomiting, irregular or rapid heart rate, and confusion. In extreme cases, individuals may become delirious or have seizures (convulsions). In these cases, death may be caused by seizures that result in an inability to breathe. In less severe cases, high doses have been associated with panic attacks.

In small children, toxic effects may be observed with doses of around 35 milligrams per kilogram (about 800 milligrams in a fifty-pound child). This level could be achieved by taking four Vivarin tablets or drinking about seven cups of strong coffee.

Dangerous Combinations with Other Drugs: Caffeine can raise blood pressure, so some physicians caution hypertensive patients, or those who experience irregular heartbeats, to limit their use of caffeine. In addition, it should be used cautiously by people who are taking other drugs that can raise blood pressure. These drugs include antidepressants that are MAO inhibitors, such as Marplan, Nardil, and Parnate, as well as high doses of cold medicines that contain phenylpropanolamine. Because caffeine is a stimulant, it can add to the effects of stronger stimulants such as cocaine, amphetamine, or methamphetamine.

CHAPTER CONTENTS

A BRIEF HISTORY

It is difficult to write a brief history of caffeine because the history of its use in human culture is very old and very detailed. Today, caffeine is found in a variety of sodas, "energy" drinks, pain relievers, and other medications, but historically, coffee, tea, and chocolate were the caffeine-containing products consumed by people. The origins of tea use can be traced back to China in the fourth century, when it was thought to have significant medicinal properties. In the 1500s, medical uses also fueled interest in tea in Europe, but soon its stimulant actions came to be appreciated as well. Some ancient legends suggest that the effects of coffee beans on their early users were so powerful that they were thought to have powers given by divine intervention. These legends also indicate that the stimulant properties of these beans were appreciated and sought after from the very beginning. One often-cited story describes how a goat herder began chewing coffee beans after he observed the stimulating effects of the beans on his herd. Soon he and others began chewing the beans regularly to maintain their stamina and concentration through long, isolated hours of work.

Coffee was first cultivated in Yemen in the sixth century. However, many religious leaders of the time thought poorly of coffee, contending that it gave rise to personal (and political) treachery. On the other hand, users enjoyed its ability to combat fatigue and enhance physical endurance. Among some it gained a reputation for stimulating thought and intellectual conversation.

By the 1600s, trade merchants had introduced coffee to Europe, and "coffeehouses" spread rapidly. One of the hallmarks of these establishments was intellectual conversation. Not all of this conversation was viewed as politically correct, however, and coffeehouses were outlawed in England. That ban was very brief, and the growth of coffeehouses and the use of coffee spread even more rapidly thereafter. In fact, coffeehouses came to be known as places where one could go to learn from notable academic and political figures of the day. The environment created in coffeehouses turned out to be one that gave rise to creative thinking in the entrepreneurial and business realms as well. As an example, the giant insurance firm Lloyd's of London actually began as a coffeehouse in the early 1700s.

Coffee and the United States have a strong relationship. Although tea was the caffeinated drink of choice in the English colonies for quite a while, the British Stamp Act of 1765 and the Trade Revenue Act of 1767 levied high taxes on the importation of tea to the colonies. This, of course, gave rise to the tide of rebellion that was symbolized so powerfully at the Boston Tea Party, ushering in the Revolutionary War. In protest of the tea taxes, coffee became our caffeinated drink of choice. By the 1940s, coffee consumption in the United States reached a high of around twenty pounds per person per year. Though by the early 1990s that level had dropped to ten pounds per person per year, this did not mean that Americans were cutting their caffeine consumption in half. While the consumption of coffee was falling off, the consumption of caffeinated soft drinks was growing rapidly. But coffee made a big comeback. Specialty coffee shops and cafés began to spring up on the West Coast in the 1980s, and they have spread across the nation. Americans are now consuming more varieties of coffee and more types of coffee drinks than ever before. It is estimated that more than 80 percent of American adults drink coffee every day—at an average of about three cups each.

Finally, we cannot leave the history of caffeine without mention of another caffeine-containing delight—chocolate. Chocolate was actually introduced to Europe before either coffee or tea, but it did not become popular as rapidly because it was presented mostly as a thick preparation made from processed and ground cacao kernels. In the 1800s, the Dutch developed a process that removed much of the fat from this crude preparation, and the result was a more refined chocolate powder. The fat that was removed was then combined with sugar and the chocolate powder, and the result was the birth of the chocolate bar in the 1840s. As the technology for producing chocolate became better known in Europe, its use spread rapidly. Dark chocolate contains about twenty milligrams of caffeine per ounce. That means that a four-ounce bar of chocolate would contain approximately eighty milligrams of caffeine—about the same as in a cup of percolator-brewed coffee.

HOW CAFFEINE MOVES THROUGH THE BODY

Caffeine is almost always taken by mouth, and so it is absorbed into the blood primarily through the linings of the stomach, small intestine, and large intestine. It is only slowly absorbed through the stomach, and so most absorption occurs at the next step along the gastrointestinal tract, the small intestine. However, once it reaches the intestines, virtually all of the caffeine that was ingested is absorbed. A given oral dose of caffeine takes full effect within thirty to sixty minutes, depending upon how much food is in the stomach and intestines and how concentrated the caffeine is in the substance that contains it.

Caffeine is evenly distributed throughout the body, metabolized by the liver, and its breakdown products are excreted through the kidneys. The body eliminates it rather slowly, with the half-life of a given dose of caffeine being approximately three hours. Thus, some of the caffeine that one consumes in the morning is still around well into the afternoon. A person who drinks several cups of coffee or caffeinated sodas across a morning or afternoon is adding on to an existing load of caffeine with each subsequent drink and may end up feeling rather jittery by the end of the day.

HOW CAFFEINE WORKS

Caffeine is the best known of a class of compounds called xanthines (pronounced "zan-theenez"). Theophylline, another xanthine found in tea, is prescribed for breathing problems because it relaxes and opens breathing passages. However, there is so little of it in brewed tea that it exerts no significant stimulant effects in that form. In addition to a small amount of caffeine, chocolate contains theobromine, another xanthine, but one with far less potency than caffeine.

All the xanthines, including caffeine, have multiple actions. The major action is to block the action of a neurotransmitter/neuromodulator called adenosine, which is in the brain (more on this in the following). There are also adenosine receptors throughout the body, including those in blood vessels, fat cells, the heart, the kidneys, and many types of smooth muscle. These multiple actions create a confusing picture because the direct effects of caffeine on a system can be enhanced or suppressed by indirect effects on other systems.

EFFECTS ON THE BRAIN

Adenosine receptors, the main site of caffeine action, cause sedation when adenosine binds to them. Adenosine, a by-product of cellular metabolism, leaks out of cells. So, as neurons become more active, they produce more adenosine, and this provides a "brake" on all the neural activity—an ingenious self-regulation by the brain. Caffeine thus produces activation of brain activity by reducing the ability of adenosine to do its job. This is a good example of how a drug can produce an effect (in this case, central nervous system [CNS] stimulation) by inhibiting the action of a neurotransmitter that produces an inhibiting effect (a positive coming from two negatives). At moderate doses of around 200 milligrams (about what you get from one to two cups of strong coffee), electroencephalograph (EEG) studies indicate that the brain is aroused. Higher doses, in the range of 500 milligrams, increase heart rate and breathing. Activation of these centers also causes a constriction, or narrowing, of blood vessels in the brain (though outside the brain caffeine has a direct effect on blood vessels that does just the opposite—dilating, or widening, them).

Caffeine also lowers the amount of blood flow within the brain. It seems strange at first that a drug with such strong stimulant effects in the brain would actually decrease blood flow within the brain. But studies have shown that a dose of 250 milligrams (about what you get from two to three cups of coffee) reduces blood flow by nearly one-fourth in the gray matter of the brain (made up mostly of nerve cells) and by about one-fifth in the white matter through which fibers connect groups of nerve cells into functioning circuits. The fact that caffeine has such powerful stimulant effects despite its decrease of cerebral blood flow underscores how powerful its stimulant effects really are. Further, the effects of a single dose of caffeine on cerebral blood flow were the same in heavy caffeine users and in light users, indicating that the blood flow effect is not one to which people become tolerant.

People may develop a mild tolerance to some of the effects of caffeine, but most tolerant people can achieve an arousing effect by increasing the dose. The tolerance that develops to the brain-arousing effects of caffeine is less severe than the tolerance that develops to some of its effects on other parts of the body (see the following).

Dependence on caffeine can develop as well, as indicated by the occurrence of withdrawal symptoms when caffeine intake is abruptly stopped. Between twelve and twenty-four hours after the last dose of caffeine, users generally experience headaches and fatigue that may persist for several days to a week but that are usually strongest during the first two days after quitting. Nonprescription pain relievers such as acetaminophen (Tylenol) or ibuprofen relieve the headaches, and moderate doses can be taken throughout the withdrawal period—just be careful to avoid taking pain medications that include caffeine (see table, page 88).

Many people have found that they enjoy, and indeed rely on, the psychological effects of caffeine. While this wouldn't meet our definition of addiction, most caffeine users find the effects pleasant enough to continue using this drug. Therefore, those who decide to quit should also be prepared to give up those caffeine-aided feelings of alertness and mild euphoria, which may have become a very regular and important part of each day. A related issue is that people who drink caffeinated beverages often do so at the same or similar times of day. In that way the drinking itself may become a part of important daily rituals. It is important to anticipate that changing those rituals may be difficult as well.

EFFECTS ON OTHER BODY PARTS

THE HEART

Caffeine affects the heart in two ways: it acts on brain centers that regulate the cardiovascular system, and it acts directly on the heart. In people who are not tolerant to caffeine, a high dose (generally above 500 milligrams—about four cups of strong coffee) can increase the heart rate by as much as ten to twenty beats per minute (from a baseline of eighty to ninety). In some, this dosage can result in brief periods of irregular heartbeat. However, in general, the morning cup of coffee does not have much effect on heart function in a healthy person.

There is controversy over the issue of caffeine and the gradual development of heart disease. At present, the scientific literature is inconsistent in its findings on the question of whether continued caffeine use increases the risk of heart disease or heart attack. One very large study of men found no relationship between coffee drinking and heart disease, while others have found an increased risk of heart attacks in coffee drinkers. Moderate caffeine consumption (up to 500 milligrams per day) probably does not place the user at significant risk for heart problems. Above that level, however, the risk of heart attack may increase. This would be particularly true for individuals with other risk factors for heart attack, such as smoking, being overweight, or having a family history of heart disease.

Caffeine is also known to increase blood pressure, but generally this occurs with rather high doses and in people who already have difficulties with blood pressure regulation. For this reason, people with high blood pressure are often advised to avoid caffeine.

Cholesterol

An association between coffee drinking and cholesterol levels has been suspected for some time, yet it remains controversial. It is safe to say that the relationship has not been ruled out, but the picture remains unclear. One solid study has shown that five to six cups of coffee per day can increase LDL cholesterol levels (this is the "bad" type of cholesterol as far as risk of heart disease is concerned) by 10 percent or more. This is not the case, however, if the coffee is prepared using a paper filter. While it is not clear exactly why filtered coffee fails to raise cholesterol levels, it is likely that oils from the coffee beans and other substances that promote fat buildup in the blood are trapped by the paper filter as the water passes over the coffee grounds.

THE KIDNEYS

The well-known bathroom break that follows the morning coffee is probably caused both by a direct effect on the kidneys and by effects in the brain. There are adenosine receptors in the kidneys and caffeine acts on these, causing effects similar to those of diuretics, which increase urine production. Caffeine may also slow the release of an antidiuretic hormone from the brain that normally slows urine production.

THE DIGESTIVE SYSTEM

In coffee drinkers, the acids, oils, and caffeine can all irritate the stomach lining and promote secretion of acid, leading to gastritis (inflammation of the stomach). However, caffeine may not be the major villain, as decaffeinated coffee has effects almost as great as caffeine-containing coffee. Although coffee was once blamed for ulcers, the primary cause of ulcers is now thought to be bacteria (*Helicobacter pylori*). Irritating agents like coffee and aspirin can contribute to the process by damaging the protective mucous lining of the stomach walls, but they probably don't cause ulcers on their own. In some individuals, caffeine in coffee can promote the reflux of stomach acid into the throat, resulting in painful heartburn.

THE RESPIRATORY SYSTEM

Caffeine and similar drugs have two quite separate effects on breathing. The first was already mentioned: they stimulate the rate of breathing. Theophylline is sometimes used in treating premature infants with breathing problems. Xanthines also relax the smooth muscle in the bronchioles that take air into the lungs. This is very helpful in treating asthma, a disease in which breathing difficulties arise because these tubes constrict. Theophylline was used widely in the past to treat asthma and is still sometimes used today. However, concerns about side effects (restlessness, stomach upset) and the development of more effective treatments have diminished its use.

THE REPRODUCTIVE SYSTEM

Although studies in humans have not confirmed a link between caffeine consumption and birth defects, some studies report that babies born to women who used caffeine during pregnancy have lower birth weights. There is also some evidence that caffeine consumption (equivalent to more than one cup of coffee per day) can significantly reduce the chances of a woman becoming pregnant. Finally, there have been contradictory findings about the association between caffeine use and fibrocystic breast disease and eventual development of breast cancer. All of these associations are questionable, and most studies do not support an association with the development of breast cancer.

THE EYES

Caffeine causes the tiny blood vessels in the eyes to constrict (become narrower) and thus decreases the flow of nutrients to the cells within the eyes and the clearing of waste products.

CAFFEINE AND STRESS

Caffeine increases some of the normal stress responses because it increases the amount of adrenaline that is active in the body under stressful circumstances. Thus, it seems that caffeine users who find themselves under stress (or who use caffeine even more during stressful periods to work more effectively) may experience more of the effects that stress can produce. Adrenaline release increases blood pressure during stress, and the caffeine-induced rise adds to this. Thus, caffeine and stress together lead to greater bodily stress responses than either does alone.

CAFFEINE AND PANIC ATTACKS

In some people, caffeine can contribute to the experience of panic attacks, which generally come on suddenly and involve powerful feelings of threat and fear. The experience can be very debilitating for a brief period of time. It seems that caffeine is more likely to bring on panic attacks in people who have had them previously. However, relatively high doses of caffeine (greater than 700 milligrams) have been reported to lead to panic attacks in people who have never experienced them.

ENHANCEMENT OF PHYSICAL PERFORMANCE

Caffeine can slightly enhance physical endurance and delay fatigue associated with vigorous exercise in some people. One way that caffeine might accomplish this is by releasing fats into the blood for use as energy, enabling the body to conserve its other energy stores (in the form of stored sugars), thus allowing the athlete to sustain physical activity for a longer period of time. Caffeine may also help muscle performance during physical exercise, although the way this happens is not clear. What we do know is that caffeine dilates the bronchioles, making it easier for air to pass into the lungs. This would seem to have a beneficial effect on certain types of physical performance. Still, the most thorough studies of well-trained athletes are inconclusive. In some cases there appear to be performance-enhancing effects, and in others there are none. So the jury remains out.

Two words of caution, though, for those who use caffeine for this purpose. Because caffeine causes an increased loss of water through urine production, a person exercising on caffeine may become dehydrated more rapidly during long periods of exercise such as distance running or cycling. This caution is particularly important for hot-weather exercisers. The other concern is the effects of caffeine on heart rate and heart rhythms. Strenuous exercise obviously stresses the heart, so a person with cardiovascular disease could experience problems while using caffeine to promote physical performance.

People who worry about their weight might be interested in the issue of fat metabolism. Products based on the supposed ability of caffeine and theophylline to "burn fat" include a theophylline cream placed on the market several years ago that was supposed to melt fat away. Just rub it on the offending fat pad! Unfortunately, the effectiveness of this treatment hasn't been established (one big problem is probably getting the theophylline through the skin and into the fat cells).

Likewise, there is tremendous interest in whether a combination of caffeine and exercise can help to promote the burning of fat as fuel for weight loss. Fat cells really do have adenosine receptors, and xanthines really can cause a small release of stored fat, so some foods that include caffeine have been sold as fat burners. However, the scholarly research on these products has demonstrated only small weight-loss effects. Coffee and its cousins may prove to be a useful part of weight-loss programs in the future, but at this point nothing "melts" fat except old-fashioned exercise and a healthy diet.

POSITIVE HEALTH EFFECTS

Although we always urge caution when interpreting correlational studies, a recent large study based at the National Cancer Institute collected health data from more than 400,000 individuals in their fifties and sixties starting in 1995 and following them for thirteen years. Across that time, men who drank two or three cups of coffee per day were 10 percent less likely to have died, and women were 13 percent less likely to have died. The study was not designed to answer the question of why coffee drinking was associated with better survival, but the findings are worth knowing about.

Two studies published in 2012 suggest that caffeine may also have benefits for memory function when memory is challenged or in decline. In one study, individuals with "mild cognitive impairment"—a strong predictor of Alzheimer's disease—had their memory function evaluated and caffeine levels measured at the beginning of the study and again several years later. Those who had caffeine levels consistent with drinking about three cups of coffee were significantly less likely to have developed Alzheimer's disease than were those with no caffeine in their systems. This doesn't mean that caffeine prevents Alzheimer's disease. It could be that there was something else about the lifestyles of the people who had caffeine in their systems that helped forestall the onset of full Alzheimer's symptoms. For example, because caffeine in a stimulant it could simply have made the subjects more alert, making them more likely to engage in social or intellectual activities, both of which have been shown to promote cognitive health in older people.

The second recent study was a lab experiment with animals that had their memory function impaired when their brains were deprived of oxygen for a brief time. This condition, called "ischemia," often happens when people suffer a stroke and is known to result in memory and other cognitive deficits. Half of the mice received a dose of caffeine before the oxygen deprivation and the other half did not. Later, the mice that had received the caffeine regained their ability to form new memories 33 percent faster than the ones that had received no caffeine. It was as if the presence of caffeine at the time of the ischemia protected the animals' brains from suffering the full effect of the loss of oxygen. This could have been due to the caffeine disrupting the actions of adenosine in the brain. We wrote about how this action is part of why caffeine creates alertness. But when brain cells are injured or under stress, adenosine can reach dangerously high levels and actually damage the cells. Having the caffeine on board when the animals' brains were stressed may have reduced the potential toxic effect of adenosine. Of course, this does not mean that everybody should walk around buzzed on caffeine all the time *just in case* they suffer a stroke or brain injury. But if it happens to be there, it might be protective.

CAFFEINE AND CALCIUM

Calcium is an important part of nutritional health and is particularly important for the development and maintenance of strong and healthy bones. Caffeine increases the excretion of calcium, and thereby lowers calcium levels in the body. This is not a huge effect, but it is worth keeping in mind—particularly for women. There have also been some studies suggesting that caffeine may reduce the absorption of calcium, and thus limit the beneficial effects of calcium that is consumed in the diet or in supplements. Although there are still some questions about this possible effect, some nutritionists recommend that calcium be taken before consuming caffeine to diminish the possible effects of caffeine on calcium absorption.

TREATMENT OF HEADACHES

Caffeine causes constriction of blood vessels, and this is likely the reason that it can be an effective treatment for migraine headaches, especially if it is taken at the first sign of the headache. In general, it is easier to head off growing pain than to remove pain once it is strong, so a cup of strong coffee at the first sign of a migraine can help stop the problem before it really gets started. Caffeine also increases the effectiveness of medications used to treat migraines, if taken at the first sign of the headache. Caffeine has even been touted as an effective treatment for nonmigraine headaches in some individuals, so it is easy to see why some over-the-counter pain relievers (such as Anacin, Excedrin, and Goody's Powders) contain caffeine. However, its effectiveness in this regard really hasn't been proven.

HOW WE TAKE CAFFEINE

COFFEES

The amount of caffeine in a cup of coffee varies tremendously and depends on several factors.

Types of Coffee Beans

Robusta beans are often grown in Africa and may have as much as twice caffeine as arabica beans, which are grown in South America and the Middle East, among other places. Robusta coffees are generally cheaper and are often used in the mass-produced canned coffees sold in grocery stores, though the package label may not indicate what kind of bean it is. Arabica coffees are considered to be of higher grade and to yield a better-tasting cup. Although generally available, they are predominant at specialty coffee retailers and through the rapidly growing mail-order coffee businesses. Arabicas are also much more often sold in whole-bean form than are robustas. For purposes of comparison, a typical cup of coffee brewed from arabica beans generally has 70 to 100 milligrams of caffeine, whereas the comparable amount of robusta coffee may have closer to 150 milligrams.

Method of Roasting

Dark-roasted coffee beans contain less caffeine and less acid than lighter-roasted ones. Many people think that dark-roasted coffees contain more caffeine because they often have a more powerful taste than the lighter roasts. In fact, the additional roasting associated with the darker product allows more time for caffeine to be broken down in the beans.

Fineness of Grind and Method of Brewing

The method of brewing and the size of the granules of ground coffee interact to have a significant influence on the amount of caffeine per ounce of coffee produced. The finer the grind, the more surface area of ground coffee comes into contact with the brewing water. This creates more opportunity for caffeine to be extracted from the ground beans. As for brewing method, a cup of coffee made using a drip-type coffeemaker generally has about 20 percent more caffeine than a cup made in a percolator. French presses, or "plunger pots," can also extract maximal caffeine levels from ground coffee because the grounds are actually soaked in boiling water for several minutes prior to the plunger being lowered to separate them from the water.

Espresso

Espresso is really a different drink from brewed coffee. It is made by passing water rapidly through relatively tightly packed coffee grounds under high pressure. The result is that the oils and other products in the coffee are more fully extracted than under other coffee brewing conditions, and the taste is considerably richer than that of other coffee brews. A typical "cup" of espresso contains about one and a half to two fluid ounces— much less than a cup of coffee. But espresso contains more caffeine per fluid ounce than coffee does. Thus, the amounts of caffeine in a cup of coffee and a cup of espresso are about the same. While an average cup of coffee brewed from arabica beans contains seventy to one hundred milligrams of caffeine, the average cup of espresso usually contains about sixty to ninety milligrams.

Why do so many people believe that espresso creates more of a "caffeine buzz" than coffee does? Perhaps because of the higher concentration of caffeine in the espresso. When a drug is more concentrated in a certain solution, it tends to be absorbed more rapidly across the membranes of the stomach and small intestine. So, even though a single espresso (*espresso solo*) may have the same or less caffeine than a cup of coffee, its more rapid absorption can result in a more rapid onset of the caffeine effects and a greater feeling of "rush." Of course, a double espresso (or *espresso dóppio*) contains twice as much caffeine.

Other coffee drinks, such as cappuccino, caffè latte, and café mocha, are each generally made by adding a single shot of espresso to other ingredients. So, the caffeine content of these drinks should be roughly equal to that of a single espresso, though less concentrated.

Based on this information, it is obviously impossible to present a simple table describing the amount of caffeine in coffee drinks. Remember that these are broad averages based on a survey of the pharmacological and dietary literatures.

AVERAGE CAFFEINE CONTENT IN COFFEES

Drink	Milligrams
Dripped robusta coffee (8 oz)	150
Dripped arabica coffee (8 oz)	100
Percolated robusta coffee (8 oz)	110
Percolated arabica coffee (8 oz)	75
Instant coffee (8 oz)	65
Decaffeinated coffee (8 oz)	3
Espresso (and espresso-based drinks) made from arabica beans (1.5–2 oz)	90

With the rise in popularity of specialty coffees and coffee drinks, there are lots of products to choose from. The following table shows the caffeine content of a number of these drinks in their usual serving sizes.

CAFFEINE CONTENT IN SPECIALTY COFFEES*

Coffee and Origin	Amount	Dose (mg)
Espresso coffees		
Big Bean Espresso	1 shot	75.8
	2 short shots	140.4
	2 tall shots	165.3

Starbucks Espresso, regular, small	1 shot	58.1
Hampden Café Espresso	2 shots	133.5
Einstein Bros.® Espresso, double	2 shots	185.0
Brewed Specialty Coffees		
Big Bean, regular	16 oz	164.7
Big Bean Boat Builders Blend, regular	16 oz	147.6
Big Bean Organic Peru Andes Gold, regular	16 oz	186.0
Big Bean French Roast, regular	16 oz	179.8
Big Bean Ethiopian Harrar, regular	16 oz	157.1
Big Bean Italian Roast, regular (grown in Brazil)	16 oz	171.8
Big Bean Costa Rican French Roast, regular	16 oz	245.1
Big Bean Kenya AA, regular	16 oz	204.9
Big Bean Sumatra Mandheling, regular (grown in Indonesia)	16 oz	168.5
Hampden Café Guatemala Antigua	16 oz	172.7
Starbucks regular	16 oz	259.3
Royal Farms regular	16 oz	225.7
Dunkin' Donuts regular	16 oz	143.4
Einstein Bros.® regular	16 oz	206.3

*Data taken from the *Journal of Analytical Toxicology* by permission of Preston Publications.

TEAS

Tea leaves are harvested from bushes that are grown mostly in India, Indonesia, and Sri Lanka. Leaves are of differing qualities, depending upon how far out on the stalk of the bush they grow. Generally, the bud leaves, which are closest to the stalk, are considered to be of the highest quality. The leaves are dried and allowed to ferment, which turns them to an orange hue. These are used to make black teas. However, some tea leaves are not fermented in this way and remain green. Green teas are brewed from these and are found in most Chinese and Japanese restaurants in the United States.

In general, a cup of tea will contain less caffeine than a cup of coffee. Although there is more caffeine in a pound of fermented tea than in a pound of coffee, that pound of tea might be used to brew three to four times as many cups as a pound of coffee would. In addition, the amount of tea in a "cup" is often less than the amount of coffee, by tradition. As with coffees, the amount of caffeine in a given cup may vary considerably, depending on several factors. As a general guide, the following are caffeine ranges in teas as found in the food science literature:

Black tea	8 oz	14–61 mg
Green tea	8 oz	24–40 mg
Iced tea	8 oz	5–11 mg

There are well-documented positive effects of both green and black teas on health. Studies have shown that people who drink one or two cups of tea per day are more likely to survive a heart attack than those who do not drink tea. It is not clear why there is this protective effect; nor is it clear if it only applies to heart attack survival or to cardiac health in general. But some scientists think the protection comes from the antioxidants contained in tea leaves. These compounds may contribute to lowered cholesterol levels, for example, and thus help protect the heart. It's important to know that these positive effects have not been observed for herbal teas. It seems that the tea leaves themselves may be the source of the protective chemicals. They may also be the source of naturally stress-reducing chemicals. A recent, well-designed study found that people who drank a beverage that contained the components of black tea daily over a six-week period were more able to manage stress than those who drank a control beverage that was identical to the tea beverage (including the caffeine), except that it lacked the chemicals that are found in the black tea leaves. The researchers even took care to serve the beverages cold to avoid the possible stress-reducing effects of sipping a warm beverage. Importantly, the people who drank the active beverage also had lower levels of the stress hormone cortisol in their blood after stressful events, indicating that the noncaffeine components of black tea leaves can help dampen the body's physical stress reactivity.

SODAS

The consumption of caffeinated sodas in the United States has been on the rise for a number of years. Some people are bothered by the gastric upset that is sometimes associated with the acids in coffees and prefer to drink caffeine-containing soft drinks. In general, the concentration of caffeine per ounce in sodas is considerably lower than in coffees, but the typical serving of soda is twelve ounces, compared to six to eight ounces for coffee. The general range of doses in soft drinks is about twenty to fifty milligrams. The diet drinks contain the same amount of caffeine (though sometimes more) as their nondiet equivalents.

"ENERGY" DRINKS

The term *energy drink* is not exactly accurate. These caffeinated drinks don't actually produce more energy, but they can generate a feeling of alertness, and even a solid buzz, because of their caffeine content. The concentration of caffeine in these products is often twice as high as in regular caffeinated sodas, though the serving sizes are smaller (about eight and a half ounces, compared to twelve ounces for a regular soda), and most come in smaller containers. Most of these drinks contain about 50 to 75 milligrams of caffeine. Interestingly, although these drinks have the reputation of providing a big caffeine blast, they actually contain about the same concentration of caffeine as coffee—maybe even a bit less. A notable exception is "5-hour Energy," which contains about 200 milligrams in just a two-ounce serving. These drinks also often contain any of a number of additional compounds that fall generally into the category of "supplements," like ginkgo biloba, taurine, ginseng, B vitamins, and sugar. We will not address these in this chapter, but some of them are discussed in other chapters, and the energy drinks are also discussed in the chapter on stimulants.

Although energy drinks are relatively new in the US beverage market (Red Bull was introduced into the United States in 1997), their sales grew 60 percent from 2008 to 2012, and in 2012 their total US sales were more than $12 billion (up from $3.5 billion in 2005). They have been marketed aggressively to young people and have obviously been successful. What makes these products so attractive as to have such a big market presence? One element of their popularity may relate to how they are consumed. Unlike caffeinated beverages that are hot and are generally sipped slowly, energy drinks tend to be consumed quickly, thus leading to more rapid absorption of the caffeine (and other chemicals) and a more rapid buzz. It is also likely that some of the many other ingredients in these drinks interact with the caffeine, possibly modulating its effects. This may be true for taurine (found in Red Bull) in particular, though there have been very few studies on the interaction between caffeine and taurine.

Combining energy drinks with alcohol has also become popular. Some people believe that the energy drink enhances the pleasant buzz of the alcohol and diminishes the depressant effects. This is almost certainly incorrect. As we pointed out in the "Alcohol" chapter, combining caffeine with alcohol does not make a person less impaired—it just makes him more awake. Although this may seem appealing to someone who wants to be drunk but not sleepy, there is a danger. If a person feels as if he is alert and unimpaired he might feel that drinking more alcohol is safe when in fact it may not be. In general, it is always wise to be wary of combining drugs, particularly when there have been few studies of their interactions. Still, the idea of combining alcohol and caffeine into one drink led to the creation of several caffeinated alcoholic beverages. Perhaps the best known (or most notorious!) is Four Loko, which was sold in 23.5-ounce cans and contained 12 percent alcohol and a high dose of caffeine—quite a blast! In fact, it rapidly gained the nickname "Blackout in a Can" and became very popular on the college drinking scene. Obviously the use of these drinks had little to do with "energy" and everything to do with rapid and sustained alcohol intoxication. However, after multiple reports of alcohol-related illnesses after its use, Four Loko came under scrutiny by the FDA and was banned on many college campuses. The current product contains no caffeine but retains the alcohol, available in a range of concentrations from 6 to 12 percent.

In addition to energy drinks, per se, there are many "energy formulations" on the market. It can be mind-boggling to sift through all of their claims about how they provide energy and good health, but the bottom line is that they rely mostly on caffeine for their effects. One example is guarana, which is sold in capsule form. One formulation on the market provides 250-milligram capsules, each of which contains about 90 milligrams of caffeine (about as much as a cup of coffee). Guarana comes from the seeds of a South American tree and is often described as an "herbal" energy supplement or a weight loss aid. Although there was a time when it was thought to increase alertness because of something specific to the plant, it is now clear that it's just the caffeine.

Some people also think that it is a good idea to exercise after consuming energy drinks. Although the caffeine might make you feel alert and motivated to exercise, it will also promote dehydration that can decrease physical performance. It's important not to confuse these products with sports drinks like Gatorade, which has no caffeine and is rich in electrolytes that the body needs while exercising and afterward. The following table shows the caffeine content and usual serving size of a number of energy drinks and sodas.

CAFFEINE CONTENT IN ENERGY DRINKS AND SODAS*

Beverage	Serving Size (oz)	Caffeine (mg/serving)
Energy Drinks		
Red Devil®	8.4	41.8
Sobe® Adrenaline Rush	8.3	76.7
Sobe® No Fear	16	141.1
Hair of the Dog®	8.4	none detected
Red Celeste	8.3	75.2
E Maxx™	8.4	73.6
Amp™	8.4	69.6
Red Bull®	8.3	78
KMX™	8.4	33.3
5-hour Energy	2	207
Cran-Energy	8	70
Full Throttle	8	71
Monster	8	80
Rockstar	8	80
Vault	8	47
Carbonated Sodas		
Coca-Cola® Classic	12	29.5
Coca-Cola Zero	12	35
Diet Coke®	12	38.2
Diet Coke® with Lime	12	39.6
Caffeine-Free Diet Coke®	12	none detected

Vanilla Coke®	12	29.5
Pepsi®	12	31.7
Diet Pepsi®	12	27.4
Mountain Dew®	12	45.4
Mountain Dew® Live Wire™	12	48.2
Dr Pepper®	12	36.0
Diet Dr Pepper®	12	33.8
Sierra Mist™	12	none detected
Celeste™ Cola	12	19.4
Sprite®	12	none detected
Seagram's® Ginger Ale	12	none detected
Barq's® Root Beer	12	18.0
Pibb® Xtra	12	34.6
A&W® Root Beer	12	none detected
7–Up®	12	none detected

*Data taken from the *Journal of Analytical Toxicology* by permission of Preston Publications.

OVER-THE-COUNTER DRUGS

There are quite a few medicinal preparations that contain caffeine, some in very high amounts. The following table lists some of these.

CAFFEINE CONTENT IN OVER-THE-COUNTER DRUGS

Brand Name	Milligrams per dose
Cold Remedies	
Coryban-D	30
Dristan	16
Triaminicin	30

Diuretics

Aqua-Ban	100

Pain Relievers

Anacin	32
Excedrin	65
Goody's Powders	33
Midol	32
Vanquish	33

Stimulants

Caffedrine	200
NoDoz	100
NoDoz Maximum Strength	200
Vivarin	200

CHOCOLATE

Chocolate is made from the bean of the *Theobroma cacao* bush, which contains a unique xanthine called theobromine. An average cup of cocoa may contain as much as 200 milligrams of theobromine, but this compound is much less potent than caffeine as a stimulant. However, chocolate also contains caffeine. For example, a one-ounce bar of baker's chocolate contains about 25 milligrams of caffeine, a five-ounce cup of cocoa may contain 15 to 20 milligrams, a cup of chocolate chips contains about 100 milligrams, and one Foosh energy mint contains 100 milligrams. On the other hand, a typical eight-ounce glass of chocolate milk generally contains less than 10 milligrams of caffeine, and one Hershey's Kiss contains only 1 milligram.

One final note about chocolate: caffeine and theobromine may not be the only psychoactive compounds in it. A recent report has indicated that one component of chocolate is very similar to the natural chemical in the brain that interacts with our THC receptors—the receptors to which the psychoactive compound in marijuana binds. Although the concentration of this compound is quite low in chocolate (it was estimated that one would have to eat twenty-five pounds of chocolate to stimulate the receptors as much as a typical dose of marijuana), it is possible that its presence could supplement the natural THC-like compound in the brain enough to produce a subtle effect. These results have led some to speculate that the vague sense of well-being and happiness that some people report in response to chocolate may be related to the interaction of the subtle drug effects associated with low-dose caffeine with those associated with activating the natural THC receptors in the brain.

TOXICITY OF CAFFEINE

Overall, caffeine is fairly safe if a healthy person takes it in moderate amounts. The undesirable side effects that most people experience are gastric upset and nervousness or jitteriness. As people age, they tend to have more problems with sleeplessness and often will limit their caffeine consumption in the afternoon and evening. Pills containing fairly hefty amounts of caffeine, however, can result in severe side effects in people who load up on them to stave off sleep (procrastinating students and sleepy truck drivers, for example). It is also important to note that while caffeine may allow you to keep sleep at bay, sleeping is a very important biological need that you should not ignore for long.

Children who take theophylline for treatment of asthma can also experience toxicity if their blood levels get too high. The major symptoms are severe gastrointestinal upset and vomiting, extreme nervousness, and nervous system excitability, which eventually leads to seizures if blood levels get high enough. Remember, too, that people who have other conditions that impair their cardiovascular system (obesity, hypertension, etc.) are more vulnerable to anything that affects heart function.

3
ECSTASY

Drug Class: Entactogens. All of the drugs mentioned in this chapter are legally considered Schedule I drugs (classified by the Drug Enforcement Administration as having a high potential for abuse and no accepted medical uses).

Individual Drugs: methylenedioxymethamphetamine (MDMA), methylenedioxyamphetamine (MDA), methylenedioxyethylamphetamine (MDE), methylone

Common Terms: Ecstasy, Rolls, Beans, Molly, X, XTC, Adam (MDMA); Eve (MDE); Love (MDA)

The Buzz: MDMA, MDA, and MDE increase heart rate, blood pressure, and body temperature and produce a sense of energy and alertness like that observed after amphetamine use (see "Stimulants" chapter). These drugs also suppress appetite. However, the effects of these drugs on mood are quite different from those caused by amphetamine. Instead of an energizing euphoria, MDMA users experience a warm state of "empathy" and good feelings for all those around them.

Overdose and Other Bad Effects: At high doses of MDMA, users often describe jitteriness and teeth clenching that are unpleasant. MDMA has caused a number of deaths when it was used in conjunction with high levels of physical activity in hot environments (at "rave" dance parties). Death is usually typical of stimulant overdose, with greatly increased body temperature, hypertension, and kidney failure. Long-term damage to serotonin neurons is suggested by human and animal studies. Toxicities of MDA, MDE, and methylone are not well described but likely quite similar.

Dangerous Combinations with Other Drugs: These drugs can be dangerous if taken in conjunction with antidepressants that are monoamine oxidase (MAO) inhibitors. They can cause a dangerous or lethal increase in heart rate and blood pressure.

CHAPTER CONTENTS

A BRIEF HISTORY

MDMA was first made in 1912 by Merck and was patented as an intermediate in a chemical synthesis (not, as often asserted, as an appetite suppressant). It was never used clinically and not tested in humans until the 1950s. The first scientific study was conducted in 1953 by the army, but the results of the study were not published until 1969. A related drug, MDA (methylenedioxyamphetamine) was popular with drug users in the sixties, but MDMA did not return to the scene until after it was synthesized and tested by Sasha Shulgin and Dave Nichols in 1978. A group of psychotherapists decided that the empathic state produced by Ecstasy could be useful in psychotherapy by producing a temporary state of openness that could help patients achieve insight and mutual understanding. The therapeutic benefits of MDMA were not realized, but recreational use spread quickly during the 1980s. This led to concerns that, combined with reports of toxicity, led to its classification by the Drug Enforcement Administration (DEA) as a Schedule I drug (a drug with no valid clinical use). Ecstasy moved quickly into the underground drug scene and was popularized through its use at underground dance parties ("raves") in the United Kingdom. From there, it migrated rapidly to the United States. The Monitoring the Future Study showed that the annual use of MDMA rose from 4.6 percent of high school seniors in 1996 to 11.7 percent of high school seniors in 2001. However, rising concerns about the potential risks of MDMA, active education campaigns, and decreased availability have led to an equally rapid fall in reported Ecstasy use, which was down to 5.7 percent of high school seniors in 2005. Use has hovered at about the same level since then, although the increased popularity of raves has triggered a resurgence of interest in some communities. Some groups continue to advocate for its clinical use. Several clinical trials are ongoing in Europe, and at least two are underway in the United States (for post-traumatic stress disorder and anxiety during end-stage cancer).

IS IT REALLY ECSTASY?

Many other substances have been identified in pills sold as Ecstasy. In fact, a 2006 survey of results from the DanceSafe website that tests Ecstasy pills showed that about 40 percent of the pills submitted to the site were entirely MDMA, a little over half contained at least some MDMA, and about half contained no MDMA at all. This survey probably contains more fake pills than average, because a certain number were submitted to the site because users suspected that they were not MDMA. However, the chances of getting something that is not MDMA are pretty good. Sometimes you get something that is less dangerous than MDMA, such as caffeine or dextromethorphan, but methamphetamine, MDA (methylenedioxyamphetamine), and MDE (methylenedioxyethylamphetamine) are also common contaminants. A partial list of contaminants includes methamphetamine, dextromethorphan, ephedrine, pseudoephedrine, caffeine, MDA, some minor hallucinogens, and ketamine. A related drug, paramethoxyamphetamine (PMA), has also been identified. PMA is a similar stimulant-like drug that causes toxicity at doses closer to recreational doses, but it is not a common contaminant in the United States.

Molly is supposedly a form of MDMA that is completely 100 percent pure MDMA. This is not true. The same website reported analyses of samples that were submitted as Molly, and constituents included methylone (a new "bath salt" with MDMA-like effects); MDA (methylenedioxyamphetamine—a close relative of MDMA); mCPP, TFMPP, or BZP (metachlorophenylpiperazine, trifluoromethylphenylpiperazine, or Benzylpiperazine—piperazine compounds with actions that overlap with but are not identical to MDMA); the anesthetic ketamine; cocaine; methamphetamine; or caffeine. The following discussion, as well as the "Stimulants" and "Hallucinogens" chapters, will dispel the myth that MDMA is safe and that only its contaminants are dangerous.

HOW MDMA MOVES THROUGH THE BODY

MDMA is usually taken orally in the form of pills or capsules, synthesized by bootleg labs that make the pills in many different colors (white, yellow, purple, and beige). MDMA (especially as Molly) is also sold as a white powder that users snort, put in their own capsule to swallow, or dissolve in water and then swallow. The actual composition of pills can vary from a few milligrams up to 200 milligrams. An average dose is 100 milligrams. MDMA is well absorbed from the gastrointestinal tract, and peak levels are reached in about an hour. The effects last for three to six hours.

WHAT MDMA DOES TO THE BRAIN AND BODY

MDMA users provide very consistent reports of the feelings that result from taking it. Almost all users say that it causes a feeling of empathy, openness, and caring. The enhancement of positive emotions has been described as a decrease in defensiveness, fear, the sense of separation from others, aggression, and obsessiveness.

One first-time user reported the effects in this way: "What happens is, the drug takes away all your neuroses. It takes away your fear response. You feel open, clear, loving. I can't imagine anyone being angry under its influence, or feeling selfish, or mean, or even defensive. You have a lot of insights into yourself, real insights that stay with you after the experience is over. It doesn't give you anything that isn't already there. It's not a trip.

You don't lose touch with the world. You could pick up the phone, call your mother, and she'd never know." *

In both animals and humans, MDMA seems to cause a combination of amphetamine- and hallucinogen-like effects. MDMA does not cause overt hallucinations, but many people have reported enhanced perception of sensory stimuli and distorted time perception while under the influence of the drug. It causes an amphetamine-like hyperactivity in people and animals, as well as the classic signs of stimulation of the fight-or-flight response. For instance, heart rate and blood pressure increase, and the smooth muscles of the breathing tubes (bronchioles) dilate. The pupils dilate, and blood flow to the muscles increases.

One way to test the qualities of an unknown drug is to give it to an animal that is trained to recognize a certain class of drugs and see if it recognizes this one. This is called a drug discrimination test. When such tests are done with MDMA, some animals trained to recognize amphetamine also recognize MDMA, while other animals trained to recognize LSD or other hallucinogens also recognize MDMA. This confusion almost never happens with other drugs. Amphetamine-like drugs are almost never confused with hallucinogens. This finding points out the unique behavioral effects of MDMA.

People report that MDMA decreases feelings of aggression, and animal studies confirm this impression. MDMA has contradictory effects on sexual function: while some people report greater sensory pleasure with stimulation, studies in animals and human self-report show a delay or inability to achieve orgasm. MDMA shares this effect with other drugs like SSRIs that raise synaptic serotonin. There is mixed information about whether MDMA is pleasurable and addictive the way cocaine is. Primates will take this drug voluntarily, and the general profile of the way the drug acts on the brain indicates that it has the potential to be addictive. However, the typical pattern of human use is quite different from that of cocaine and amphetamine. While people clearly use it repeatedly, it is used most frequently in a specific environment, like rave dance parties. Although compulsive daily use as seen with cocaine or heroin is not typical with MDMA, some people do experience tolerance to the effects of MDMA and increase the number of pills to compensate. A student in a focus group reported, "The more you do it the less good you feel while on it and the worse you feel coming down."

---

* From Nicholas Saunder Londson, *Ecstasy and the Dance Culture*, 1995 (self-published).

Overall, MDMA creates a very unusual behavioral profile. The positive feelings that people report are most similar to the effects of fluoxetine (Prozac) and fenfluramine (the main component of the withdrawn diet pill Pondimin). This makes sense, as we will see in what follows, because these three drugs share some biochemical actions. Overall, MDMA doesn't fit into any other drug category, and the term *entactogen*, meaning "to touch within," has been coined to describe drugs such as this.

MDA is very closely related to MDMA in chemical structure, and though it shares the amphetamine-like effects, its effects on mood are different. MDA acts more like a typical hallucinogen. MDE effects more closely resemble those of MDMA, but it lacks the unusual empathic qualities of MDMA.

HOW MDMA WORKS IN THE BRAIN

Much of what MDMA does is explained by its ability to increase the levels of the monoamine neurotransmitters dopamine and norepinephrine (see the "Stimulants" chapter) and serotonin (see the "Hallucinogens" chapter) in the synapse. Like amphetamine, MDMA actively "dumps" them into the synapse, and the amount of these neurotransmitters that is released is much larger than is usually seen with cocaine. Unlike amphetamine, MDMA does a very good job of increasing the levels of serotonin. While amphetamine is ten to one hundred times better at releasing dopamine and norepinephrine than serotonin, MDMA is the opposite: it releases serotonin far more effectively than it does dopamine.

Most MDMA effects make sense, given its biochemical profile. The increase in body temperature, the relatively low addiction potential, and the decrease in aggressiveness are typical of drugs that produce a big increase in serotonin levels in the synapse. The serotonin-specific reuptake inhibitors (SSRIs), such as fluoxetine (Prozac), do this in a different way that causes more limited effects. While MDMA actively dumps serotonin into the synapse and produces very large increases this way, Prozac and drugs like it prevent serotonin recapture but do not actively release it. This means that the neuron has to release serotonin first before antidepressants can do anything. MDMA can make much more serotonin available because it doesn't have to wait for the neuron to fire.

We don't know if its effects on serotonin alone are enough to explain the unique effects of MDMA on mood, or whether some undescribed effect is responsible for the sense of empathy and positive feelings. Recent research in humans suggests that serotonin release is necessary for most of its effects on mood, because people who receive serotonin receptor–blocking drugs before MDMA experience much less intense mood changes than people who receive MDMA alone. However, fenfluramine, an amphetamine derivative that has a similar ability to dump serotonin, shares some of these actions (like its ability to decrease aggression) but has not been reported to cause the same emotional changes. The actions of MDMA are still a mystery, because no other drug produces an identical state and because the neurochemical effects we have observed so far don't completely explain all of these effects.

MDMA TOXICITY

MDMA can be unpleasant and even dangerous when used in high doses (two to four times greater than a usual single dose of 80 to 120 milligrams). The bad effects are typical of an overdose of serotonin-releasing drugs. People report jitteriness and teeth clenching as the dose moves up, as well as all the classic signs of overstimulation of the sympathetic nervous system. Hunger is suppressed, and people typically experience dry mouth, muscle cramping, and sometimes nausea. At higher doses, MDMA can cause a large increase in body temperature—one reason for its toxicity: the high temperature may be responsible for the muscle breakdown and kidney failure that have been seen in lethal cases reported from raves. When people dance for long periods of time in close quarters, the physical activity and tendency for dehydration can synergize in an especially dangerous way with the effects of the drug. MDMA has also caused lethal cardiovascular effects in people with underlying heart disease. It has caused heart attacks and strokes in a few people. Unfortunately, it is hard to know what dose is actually toxic based on these reports. People have usually taken Ecstasy at a party, often with other drugs, and later had little recollection of how much drug they took. Like most amphetamine-like drugs, MDMA can cause seizures at extremely high doses. PMA is more toxic at recreational doses, and people taking this drug inadvertently are more likely to experience a dangerous elevation of body temperature and cardiovascular function. However, the common myth that MDMA itself is not toxic is wrong. It is possible to take a lethal dose of MDMA in a typical recreational setting, though overall, the number of deaths caused by recreational MDMA use is small. In 2013, a number of deaths across the country at dance parties have been attributed to MDMA or methylone in Molly. In at least a few cases, no other drugs that could have contributed to death were present. It has become popular to ingest MDMA/Molly as a powder, and case reports of deaths indicate that blood levels of those who die are greater than those that occur after a normal recreational dose, suggesting that inexperienced users are colliding with a dosage form in which it is difficult to control how much you take. The Drug Abuse Warning Network (DAWN) reported 22,298 emergency room visits due to MDMA in 2011 (compared to 505,224 for cocaine).

Some deaths attributed to MDMA actually have resulted from attempts to prevent MDMA toxicities. Many people try to protect against MDMA-induced dehydration and hyperthermia (high body temperature) by drinking lots of water. Some people ingest so much water in a short time, however, that they dilute the concentration of sodium in their blood. This condition, called hyponatremia, can lead to headache, nausea, vomiting, seizures, and, in extreme cases, brain swelling and death. MDMA or hyperthermia-induced changes in the level of antidiuretic hormone can contribute to the situation by concentrating the urine and leaving water in the circulation. However, the biggest reason is simple: people drink much more water than needed to replace lost fluid. This happens to marathon runners, too. In the 2002 Boston Marathon, a study showed that 22 percent of the women runners were hyponatremic by the end of the race. This gender balance is relevant to MDMA because recent research shows that women are also more sensitive to the hyponatremia that MDMA causes. How much is too much? It depends on how much you sweat, and there are no experiments with MDMA users. For marathon runners, slow runners who drank about a liter an hour (thirty-six ounces, or one quart) tended to get in trouble. Fortunately, people can usually recover from hyponatremia if they receive medical care.

MDMA use has been responsible for a number of psychiatric/psychological problems. The most common consequence is the "down" that happens a few days after MDMA use. This is almost always temporary, but the mood changes can be severe enough to measure in the range of mild clinical depression. Some people also feel more irritable or aggressive. This effect can persist in heavy users and may be more severe in women than in men. Some patients have complained of panic attacks after repeated use of MDMA. These usually resolve eventually but have continued for months in a few people. Similarly, hallucinations and amphetamine-like paranoid

psychotic symptoms have occurred in chronic, high-dose users. Again, these symptoms waned when drug use stopped.

Are there long-term effects of MDMA use? Understanding the long-term psychological effects of MDMA is difficult because most heavy MDMA users also use other drugs, including marijuana, alcohol, stimulants, and narcotics that influence their health and brain function. Some studies report that heavy use of MDMA (several hundred times) has been associated with reports of persistent anxiety, involvement in risky behaviors, and other psychological problems, but further research is needed to tease out what role MDMA has in these effects. A number of research reports show that heavy use of MDMA can be associated with impaired memory that is due specifically to the MDMA—not to the use of other drugs. We don't know yet if these changes are reversible: the scientific literature is still a little mixed on this topic, although in at least some studies, ex-Ecstasy users perform better than current users. Furthermore, we also don't know if some of the reported changes (like increases in impulsivity) are simply characteristics that the users had before they ever starting using MDMA.

IS MDMA REALLY NEUROTOXIC?

There is still controversy about whether MDMA causes long-term damage to serotonin neurons, a concern that arose from previous experience with similar amphetamine-like serotonin-releasing drugs. Other drugs that release both dopamine and serotonin (methamphetamine, for example) have been shown in laboratory studies to cause long-lasting changes in either (or both) dopamine or serotonin neurons in the brain. None of the usual contents of the ends of the serotonin neurons that normally release serotonin onto the neuron's receptors (nerve terminals) can be detected. The serotonin itself, the serotonin transporter, and other components of the terminal are decreased markedly. With almost all of these drugs, the amount of damage is dose- and time-related. Small doses produce little or no damage; moderate doses produce marked decreases in serotonin indices but leave the serotonin system still functional; and large doses can eliminate the ability of these neurons to release serotonin for months.

MDMA acts like other drugs in the same class. In experimental studies in rats and primates, MDMA produced temporary loss of serotonin,

which doesn't present any real long-term problem but may be responsible for the midweek blues. It also produces the same kind of long-term changes that the other amphetamine-like drugs produce. With some dose regimens, a limited amount of recovery occurred, while with higher dose regimens, no recovery occurred. One of the controversies about MDMA is whether the loss of these markers really means that the nerve endings are gone or just depleted of their contents. None of the studies conducted so far provide incontrovertible proof that the nerve endings are gone or not. However, there is little question that at the very least, the serotonin itself, the transporter, and the main synthetic enzyme are reduced to very low levels for a long time after repeated, heavy exposure to MDMA. In any case, the serotonin neuron is not capable of functioning normally, and so it may be a moot point if the terminal is there and devoid of contents or actually gone. How much MDMA is necessary to produce significant long-term damage? The dose range that produced permanent damage in experiments with squirrel monkeys was about the equivalent of a 150-pound person taking 350 milligrams spaced over four days. Earlier studies showed that this occurred when the drug was administered by injection in the monkeys, but more recent studies using oral administration, resembling the way that humans take the drug, report similar results. An average human dose of Ecstasy is about 100 milligrams.

Does the same type of damage happen in people who take high doses of MDMA for a long time? An increasing number of studies suggest that the answer is yes. Numerous studies show that levels of major serotonin markers like the serotonin transporter or the main metabolite of serotonin in the nervous system are suppressed in Ecstasy users. None of these studies is perfect and the debate continues, but the evidence is mounting that long-term decreases in serotonin neuron function occur in heavy MDMA users (people who use a hundred times or more over several years). We don't know if these effects reverse if someone stops using MDMA, although some studies indicate that this might be so.

What are the long-term effects of this type of serotonin loss? Are some of the anxiety and learning disorders that we discussed caused by this type of damage? Residual anxiety and irritability/hostility have been reported in a number of heavy Ecstasy users. Because increased levels of serotonin have been associated with improved mood (see the "Hallucinogens" chapter), and its loss with depression in some cases, it is not unreasonable to speculate that mood disorders might be in the future for heavy Ecstasy users.

CAN YOU KEEP YOURSELF SAFE?

Advocates and critics disagree about whether people can protect them-selves from MDMA-induced toxicities by taking measures to keep their body temperature down and keep hydrated. Savvy ravers have adopted several practices designed to try to protect themselves from MDMA's dangers. They drink extra water, try to keep their body temperature down by using "mist rooms" in which people spray each other with water, keep the room temperature low, and sometimes even take SSRIs like fluoxetine (Prozac) in an attempt to protect against neurotoxicity and the amino acid tryptophan when they are coming down to help restore serotonin levels. Do these practices work? Certainly, the organ damage caused by high body temperature can be avoided if you stay in a cold enough envi-ronment. Protecting yourself against neurotoxicity is more controversial. There is animal literature showing that changes in serotonin neurons don't happen if animals are kept cold. However, we don't know yet if these findings extend to people. The same story is true of taking SSRIs like Prozac. This approach has worked in studies on animals but is untested in people. If you take SSRIs before taking MDMA, these drugs keep MDMA from getting into the terminal. This prevents the damage completely but also prevents MDMA's effects. So users take it when they are coming down. Could this be dangerous? Theoretically, if you take an SSRI too early, while lots of serotonin is still floating around, you could trigger the "serotonin syndrome." SSRIs keep the serotonin from being recaptured by the nerve terminal, just like MDMA does. In combination, you can get a dangerous elevation of serotonin that leads to the effects of an MDMA overdose. A mild case could cause nausea, diarrhea, increased muscle tone, and increased blood pressure; a severe case could cause greatly ele-vated body temperature and death. Cases of serotonin syndrome have been reported after MDMA alone, and theoretically the combination could increase the risk.

MDMA raises some challenging ethical questions. Should this drug be used clinically? This question is debated actively by some scientists, and there are credible arguments on both sides of the issue. In favor of its use, MDMA does not cause dangerous effects at doses that would likely be used clinically. Certainly, there are many clinically approved drugs like morphine and amphetamine that are equally dangerous at high doses, so the dangerous side effects are hardly unique. Furthermore, certain cir-cumstances exist, like compassionate use at the end of life, when the potential long-term effects are not an issue. Offsetting these "positives" are many open questions: Are there long-term consequences to low-level use that could be dangerous? Can scientists advocating clinical use show convincingly that MDMA offers unique advantages that outweigh the advantages of other medications? What are the benefit and harm caused by a drug that can apparently treat "personality" rather than disease? Would a completely safe entactogen be a valid clinical drug or a "tonic" for treating the ills of normal life? Can insights and positive feelings aroused during a drug-induced state carry over into normal life? (The same issue has arisen with the incredible popularity of Prozac, as addressed in the book *Listening to Prozac* by Peter D. Kramer.) We can't answer these questions here, but we will raise a cautionary note. Sometimes there is a good reason for bad feelings: they are caused by bad experiences, and they often motivate personal change for the better.

MDMA SUBSTITUTES

Some of the drugs that are in pills that are supposed to be pure MDMA have effects that are very similar or overlap with those of Ecstasy. Methylone is one of the "bath salts" (see the "Stimulants" chapter) because its struc-ture resembles cathinone (its chemical name is 3,4-methylenedioxy-*N*-methylcathinone). However, its neurochemical effects resemble those of MDMA. It preferentially releases serotonin, but also dopamine and norepinephrine, and users find its behavioral effects similar to MDMA. Its toxicity is also similar to MDMA, and multiple overdose deaths caused by methylone have been reported in the scientific literature around the world. The pattern of toxicity is the same, with stimulation of the sympathetic nervous system, high body temperature, and the cascading organ failure associated with serotonin syndrome. Little is known yet about its long-term effects, although some preliminary reports indicate that it does not cause long-term decreases in serotonin like those caused by MDMA. However, there are only a few research reports out, so it is early to conclude much about its long-term effects.

The piperazine drugs (mCPP, TFMPP, BZP) are another group of drugs that have appeared increasingly in pills that are supposed to be MDMA. These aren't exactly MDMA-like, although there is some overlap in what they do. Each is a little different. BZP is like a stimulant: it causes stimulant-like behaviors in rodents and increases the release of dopamine and to a lesser extent serotonin. It also has properties common among addictive drugs in animal tests. TFMPP and mCPP are more serotonin selective and have been used to assess serotonin function in research laboratories for many years. Both release serotonin but have hallucinogen-like behavioral actions that probably reflect a stimulation of serotonin receptors. The combination of BZP and TFMPP most closely resembles the effects of MDMA. TFMPP or mCPP alone resemble hallucinogens more than MDMA and can cause severe anxiety, hallucinations, and sympathetic nervous system stimulation.

4

HALLUCINOGENS

Drug Class: Hallucinogens. Almost all of the drugs mentioned in this chapter are legally considered Schedule I drugs (classified by the Drug Enforcement Administration as having a high potential for abuse and no accepted medical uses). The exceptions are atropine, scopolamine, and ketamine, which have valid medical uses for which the user must have a prescription, and dextromethorphan, which is available without a prescription but requires proof of age for purchase in most states.

Individual Drugs: Serotonin-like group: lysergic acid diethylamide (LSD), psilocybin, mescaline (peyote), dimethyltryptamine (DMT), 4-bromo-2,5-dimethoxyphenethylamine (2C-B), ayahuasca; belladonna alkaloids: Jimsonweed; dissociative anesthetics: phencyclidine (PCP), ketamine; dextromethorphan; Salvia

Common Terms: acid, blotter, California sunshine, microdot, trip, yellow sunshine, and many others (LSD); boomers, magic mushrooms, shrooms (psilocybin); buttons, mesc, mescal, topi, peyote (mescaline); caapi, yage, vegetal (ayahuasca); businessman's special (DMT—dimethyltryptamine); atropine, scopolamine, belladonna, deadly nightshade, Jimsonweed, stink weed, mandrake (belladonna alkaloids); PCP, angel dust, T, PeaCe pill (phencyclidine); Special K, K (ketamine); CCC, robo, red devils, poor man's PCP, DXM, Dex (dextromethorphan); ska, Maria, la Maria, ska Pastora (*Salvia divinorum*)

The Buzz: Hallucinogen experiences vary incredibly. Even the same person can have dramatically different experiences with the same drug on different occasions. The experience is strongly shaped by the user's previous drug experience, her expectations, and the setting in which she takes the drug.

Mild effects produced by low doses can include feelings of detachment from one's surroundings, emotional swings, and an altered sense of space and time. Hallucinations, pseudohallucinations, and illusions can all occur. Hallucinations are sensory experiences that are unreal. Pseudohallucinations are sensory experiences that are unreal but understood to be unreal, and illusions are sensory distortions of normal reality. A hallmark of the hallucinogen experience is a sensation of separation from one's body. Some users experience intense feelings of insight with mystical or religious significance. These effects can last for minutes (with DMT) or for hours (with LSD).

Physical effects vary from drug to drug, but with LSD and similar drugs, users report jitteriness, racing (or slowed) heartbeat, nausea, chills, numbness (especially of the face and lips), and sometimes changes in coordination.

Overdose and Other Bad Effects: Hallucinogens should be divided into two groups: the drugs that produce mainly psychological problems—the LSD-like drugs—and the much more physically dangerous belladonna and PCP-like compounds. The belladonna drugs, such as atropine and scopolamine, can be lethal in the usual amounts that people ingest for intoxication. These drugs can stimulate the heart and increase body temperature dangerously. At the point where a user is experiencing hallucinations from these drugs, he is at or very near the life-threatening level. PCP can also be lethal at high doses, causing seizures, coma, or a psychosis-like state that can last for days.

The most likely negative effect of taking hallucinogens like LSD is a bad trip. The most common of these is a frightening experience that leads to acute anxiety and its accompanying physical effects. Users can accidentally injure or kill themselves because they are not thinking clearly about their environment. They may try to fly, for example, and jump from a high place. Actual psychotic reactions are much more unusual, happening in about 1 to 3 percent of cases, but they can require hospitalization. Another problem can be "flashbacks," or hallucinogen persisting perception disorder, which are visual disturbances or other recalled events of the drug experience that emerge long after the drug is out of the body. Flash-backs are more common in heavy hallucinogen users; some surveys have shown that up to 30 to 60 percent of heavy users experience these in one form or another, while incidence across all users is much lower (probably percentages in the single digits).

Finally, as with any street drug, the drug might not be what the seller says it is. Most of these compounds are manufactured and packaged by illegal and uncontrolled laboratories and distributed in a completely unregulated fashion. The old phrase "let the buyer beware" could not be more appropriate.

Dangerous Combinations with Other Drugs: The dangers of these drugs vary by class. The most dangerous combination is that of PCP-like drugs with alcohol or other sedatives. This combination can kill you. Taking atropine-like drugs with anything that stimulates the cardiovascular sys-tem or raises body temperature (e.g., Ecstasy) can lead to a dangerous dis-turbance of heart rhythms or increased body temperature. Hallucinogens with amphetamine-like actions (e.g., mescaline) can be dangerous when taken in combination with stimulants. Any drug that increases blood pressure as it begins to take effect can be dangerous in people with heart disease if they combine it with other drugs that can raise blood pressure (e.g., nasal decongestants). The physical risks of drug combinations with serotonin-like hallucinogens (e.g., LSD) are much less, although an already unpredictable experience becomes even more unpredictable if combined with marijuana, a common practice.

CHAPTER CONTENTS

HALLUCINOGEN HISTORY

This class of psychoactive drugs boasts a longer history; a greater mystique; and more botanical, chemical, cultural, and historical diversity than almost any other. The use of hallucinogens is evident in plant remains from cultures on every continent. Each student of hallucinogens has his favorite "oldest story." One of ours explains how Siberian hunters discovered the fly agaric mushroom (*Amanita muscaria*). Apparently the hunters noticed the abnormal behavior of reindeer grazing on these mushrooms, and decided to experiment with them. They found that not only did the mushrooms have a profound hallucinatory effect, but they were so potent that the urine of those who had ingested the drug still contained active drug, so the drug could be recycled among tribe members. It has been suggested that the same mushroom provides the drug Soma described in the Rig-Veda, the book of religious writings from India that has been dated to at least 3,500 years ago. Hallucinogens were used in early Greece, and the plant riches of the New World provided a wealth of hallucinogenic agents that were known to the earliest migrants into South America from Eurasia. Archeological evidence suggests that the use of the peyote cactus goes back thousands of years.

Who uses hallucinogens today and why do they use them? Even the most commonly used drug, LSD, is only used by a small percentage of the population. Use has fallen from about 5 percent of high school seniors in 1999 to about 2.2 percent in 2013. There are probably several reasons for these low numbers. First and foremost, the use of this drug produces a powerful experience that is not typically "fun." Second, increased law enforcement pressure has decreased the availability of LSD. The typical LSD user is a white teenage male. We don't really have accurate statistics about the use of other hallucinogens, but the primary age group is the same for most. Finally, Native Americans and others also use hallucinogens for religious purposes.

WHAT IS A HALLUCINOGEN?

Hallucinogens are drugs that change one's thought processes, mood, and perceptions. The word itself is derived from the Latin word *alucinare*, which means "to wander in mind, talk idly, or prate." At high doses, these drugs cause people to perceive an experience as actually happening when, in fact, it is not. At lower dose levels, they cause milder disturbances of perception, thought, and emotion, but not the complete fabrication of unreal events.

Hallucinogens have often been called psychotomimetics or psychedelics. All of these names suggest that these drugs induce or mimic mental illness, but they are wrong to varying degrees. Hallucinogens do not really mimic psychosis or mental illness. Although they can trigger a psychotic experience in a vulnerable person, the drug experience itself is probably quite different. For example, the hallucinations caused by most of these drugs are usually seen, whereas the hallucinations of schizophrenia are usually heard. However, there is some overlap in effects, and recent research with psilocybin has found similarities between hallucinogen effects and some aspects of psychosis, especially feelings of detachment from one's surroundings and feelings of universal understanding. The term *psychedelic* developed in the late 1950s to describe drugs that were "mind-expanding," a vague term that was popular at the time but not very descriptive. A similar term used to describe these drugs is *entheo-genic*, which conveys the idea of finding "the god within." None of these terms is completely adequate. The diversity of terminology to describe these drugs almost certainly results from the tremendous variation in the experiences that people have had with them.

This chapter describes three broad categories of hallucinogens. The most familiar is the LSD- or serotonin-like group. The prototype of this group is lysergic acid diethylamide (LSD). Dealers most often package LSD by plac-ing drops of solution onto a piece of absorbent paper (blotter paper) or a sugar cube, although it can also appear in pill form. Psilocybin mushrooms and peyote cacti are also in this category. Psilocybin mushrooms contain the active compounds psilocin and psilocybin, which roughly resemble LSD in the effects they produce. The peyote cactus contains mescaline. Mushrooms containing psilocybin and cactus buttons containing mesca-line are usually consumed as the dried plant, and look like it. There are many other hallucinogens that resemble LSD in their actions, including dimethyltryptamine (DMT) and bufotenine. There is also a group of amphetamine derivatives—including DOM (2, 5 dimethoxy-4-methyl-phenylisopropylamine), also known as STP; TMA (trimethoxyamphet-amine); and DMA (dimethoxyamphetamine)—that resemble mescaline in their actions. Many variations exist, and new versions seem to rise and fall in popularity. Other members of this alphabet soup you may encounter are 2C-B (4-bromo-2,5-dimethoxyphenethylamine) and its variants. Many of these hallucinogens appear in pill form, and the actual content of the pills often differs from what the dealer has described. An herbal tea called aya-huasca, containing a combination of DMT and harmala alkaloids, has migrated from South America to the United States.

The second major group of hallucinogens we will discuss are the bella-donna alkaloids. These have been used medically for thousands of years, and ritually for even longer. However, their recreational abuse is just now becoming popular. Belladonna alkaloids in the United States are most often obtained either through prescription medication that contains them or from tea prepared from the leaves of the wild-growing Jimsonweed (*Datura stramonium*).

The dissociative anesthetics, or "horse tranquilizers," phencyclidine (PCP) and ketamine are the last category. Ketamine is an anesthetic used primarily in children and in veterinary practices. It appears as a solution for injection (that has been diverted from medical use) or as a powder (made from dried-out solution). People usually inject or ingest the solution and snort the powder. PCP appears in several different forms: pills, a powder for snorting, or "rocks" that can be smoked or, more rarely, dissolved for injection. Sometimes tobacco, marijuana, or parsley leaves are coated with PCP solution. These produce a bizarre, dissociative state that comes the closest to resembling psychosis of all the hallucinations. Finally, there are two hallucinogens that have unique mechanisms of action. Dextromethorphan, the main ingredient in many cough syrups, causes a unique, dissociative state at doses higher than those used for cough suppression. *Salvia divinorum* is a plant hallucinogen that causes an intense, brief, and usually unpleasant hallucinatory experience when users smoke the leaves.

HOW HALLUCINOGENS MOVE THROUGH THE BODY

Ritual use of hallucinogens by indigenous peoples involves many routes of administration, ranging from herbal teas to application to the skin to hallucinogenic snuffs. However, the major hallucinogens used in the developed world are almost always taken by mouth. All of the drugs listed in the previous section can be absorbed easily from the stomach or intestines. PCP is an exception because users also smoke or inject it. Only LSD is potent enough to be effective in tiny doses absorbed on paper. Users most often simply chew and swallow the plant-derived hallucinogens such as cactus buttons or dried mushrooms. Most hallucinogens, and frequently LSD or various drugs that are supposed to be LSD, are ingested in pill form.

The lag time between taking the drug and beginning the drug experience, and the duration of the experience itself, depends upon the drug. A typical LSD experience begins between thirty and sixty minutes after a user takes the drug. LSD is absorbed efficiently from the stomach and intestines and enters the brain fairly quickly. LSD trips last the longest of typical hallucinogens: the drug effects typically last four to six—but occasionally up to twelve—hours for a single dose. The reason for this is simple: the liver degrades LSD slowly, so active drug remains in the body for hours.

Despite many rumors to the contrary, LSD is not stored in the spinal fluid for months, nor does it remain hidden in any organ. It is eliminated just like many other drugs, but more slowly. LSD flashbacks do not occur because hidden drug in the body suddenly reappears. We do not understand the neurobiology underlying flashbacks, but it would be reasonable to speculate that they represent a change in the brain that remains after the drug experience. As we will see later, in the "Brain Basics" chapter, the central nervous system has the capacity to recall all sorts of experiences, and flashbacks may be just that.

Peyote trips can last almost as long as LSD trips. In contrast, psilocybin experiences usually last two to four hours. Dimethyltryptamine (DMT) is the shortest-acting of the commonly used hallucinogens, producing noticeable effects within ten minutes, peaking at about thirty minutes, and ending within an hour. This drug is often described as a "businessman's special" for that reason. The differences from drug to drug are caused by differences in two properties. First, the more fat-soluble a drug is, the more quickly it enters the brain (this explains the rapid onset of DMT action). Second, the more slowly the drug gets degraded, the longer the trip. Again, this varies according to the particular chemical structure of the drug. Some drugs, like LSD and mescaline, produce particularly long-lived effects because they are not quickly metabolized by the liver.

PCP deserves some special notice because of the problems its chemical characteristics often cause. PCP is well absorbed when taken by mouth, and peak blood levels are reached even faster (within fifteen to thirty minutes) if it is smoked. However, it is broken down quite slowly, so the effects last a long time. The main drug experience lasts four to six hours, but significant amounts of the drug are present for twenty-four to forty-eight hours. The body's slow metabolism of PCP, along with some users' tendency to use it repeatedly over a day's time, leads to overdose and very persistent drug effects for days after ingestion.

Myths about how to stop a trip abound; drinking milk is the most unlikely we have heard. There is no simple way to speed up the removal of most hallucinogens from the body. Users must simply wait for the liver and kidneys to do their job. PCP is the only exception. In critical situations, emergency room personnel can use a drug that makes the urine more acidic, speeding up the removal of PCP by the kidneys. Some drug treatments (see the following) can help with the symptoms of acute panic, and a drug is being tested that could block the action of LSD. However, at the moment there is no quick fix like there is for opiate overdose.

So it's important to remember that, once begun, the trip on some of these drugs can last for hours. If the trip is unpleasant, there is not much to do except receive support from unimpaired companions. If someone is going to experiment with any of these drugs, it is crucial that he or she do so in a safe and supportive environment. Doing even the least dangerous of these drugs alone invites trouble.

THE HALLUCINOGENIC EXPERIENCE:
WHAT HALLUCINOGENS DO TO THE BRAIN

It is very difficult to describe what a person experiences under the influence of these drugs because each experience is so individualized. The identity and amount of the drug, how it is taken, the user's expectations, and the user's previous experience all play a role. There are some common effects, however. Often, a trip begins with nausea; a feeling of jitteriness; and mild increases in blood pressure, heart rate, and breathing. Then the user usually feels a slight distortion of sensory perception. Visual effects predominate, with wavering images and distortion of size (things may seem much larger or smaller than they are).

At high doses, users experience illusions, pseudohallucinations, or hallucinations that are highly individual and profoundly influenced by the setting. They can range from simple color patterns to complex scenes, often with the drug taker feeling like he is watching his actions from outside his body. The confusion of senses, or synesthesia, such as seeing sounds and hearing colors, is commonly reported. The sense of time is distorted, so that minutes can seem like hours. At the peak of the drug experience, the user frequently describes a sense of profound understanding or enlightenment. Sometimes there is a sense of oneness with the world, which is rarely maintained after the drug experience is over. Profound euphoria or anxiety can occur. As the drug effect wanes, the user usually feels a sort of otherworldly sense and fatigue.

Although eloquent, fantastic, and entertaining reports abound in the literature, one of the best descriptions of the hallucinogenic experience was written by Dr. Albert Hofmann, the chemist who first synthesized LSD. The report is especially believable because Dr. Hofmann wrote it at a time when the effects of the drug had never before been described, so he could not have been influenced by expectations.

This was in the era when scientific self-experimentation was more common than it is today, so after an accidental experience in the laboratory that alerted him to the profound effect of the drug, he took some of it intentionally and recorded what happened. He reports two experiences in his book *LSD, My Problem Child* that demonstrate the incredible range of experiences that can occur even within the same individual.

Last Friday, April 16, 1943, I was forced to interrupt my work in the laboratory in the middle of the afternoon and proceed home, being affected by a remarkable restlessness, combined with a slight dizziness. At home I lay down and sank into a not unpleasant intoxicated-like condition, characterized by an extremely stimulated imagination. In a dreamlike state, with eyes closed (I found the daylight to be unpleasantly glaring), I perceived an uninterrupted stream of fantastic pictures, extraordinary shapes with intense, kaleidoscopic play of colors. After some two hours this condition faded away. . . .

The dizziness and sensation of fainting became so strong at times that I could no longer hold myself erect, and had to lie down on a sofa. My surroundings had now transformed themselves in more terrifying ways. Everything in the room spun around, and the familiar objects and pieces of furniture assumed grotesque, threatening forms. They were in continuous motion, animated, as if driven by an inner restlessness. The lady next door, whom I scarcely recognized, brought me milk—in the course of the evening I drank more than two liters. She was no longer Mrs. R., but rather a malevolent, insidious witch with a colored mask.

Even worse than these demonic transformations of the outer world, were the alterations that I perceived in myself, in my inner being. Every exertion of my will, every attempt to put an end to the disintegration of the outer world and the dissolution of my ego, seemed to be wasted effort. A demon had invaded me, had taken possession of my body, mind, and soul. I jumped up and screamed, trying to free myself from him, but then sank down again and lay helpless on the sofa. The substance, with which I had wanted to experiment, had vanquished me. It was the demon that scornfully triumphed over my will. I was seized by the dreadful fear of going insane. I was taken to another world, another place, another time. My body seemed to be without sensation, lifeless, strange. Was I dying? Was this the transition? At times I believed myself to be outside my body, and then perceived clearly, as an outside observer, the complete tragedy of my situation.[*]

INDIVIDUAL HALLUCINOGENS

LSD

Lysergic acid diethylamide (LSD) is probably the best known and most commonly used hallucinogen in the United States. It is also the most

---

[*] From Albert Hofmann, *LSD, My Problem Child* (New York: McGraw-Hill, 1980).

potent of commonly used hallucinogens. The effects of LSD depend upon the dose. Typical doses today are between 50 and 150 micrograms (typical doses of the sixties were 100 to 200 micrograms). These levels are enough to produce full-blown hallucinations in nontolerant individuals, although some experienced users take multiple "hits."

Because LSD is so potent and so easily dissolved, it is most often diluted and dissolved in liquid and then absorbed into a piece of blotter paper. No other drug is potent enough to be used in this form. Most of the LSD sold in this format is synthesized in just a few laboratories in northern California, and the product is almost invariably pure LSD. However, enterprising drug dealers sometimes sell other compounds as LSD. LSD is also sold in gelatin squares (window pane) and in tiny pills (microdots).

Although LSD itself was originally synthesized in a laboratory in the 1940s, the hallucinogenic and toxic effects of lysergic acid derivatives (the ergot alkaloids) have been recognized for thousands of years. Certain species of morning glory seeds that provided a drug called ololiuqui (the exact species are not clear but may include *Turbina corymbosa*) or tlitlitzin (*Ipomoea violacea*) in ancient Mexico contain a related chemical, lysergic acid amide. A tea made from the seeds, an alcoholic beverage made by extraction of the seeds with a favorite form of alcohol, and chemically extracted hallucinogens all cause an LSD-like hallucinatory experience. As with most plant hallucinogens, the seeds contain other chemicals, and the combination can cause nausea, vomiting, and other unpleasant side effects. Lysergic acid compounds were recognized in the Middle East several thousand years ago through the poisonings that resulted when a fungus (*Claviceps purpurea*) infected rye that was used to prepare bread. This fungus produced a number of LSD-related ergot alkaloids and amino acids that caused hallucinations and constriction of the blood vessels that could lead to gangrene, loss of limbs, spontaneous abortion, and sometimes death. The disease caused by eating ergot-infected rye became known as St. Anthony's fire, after the patron saint of the order of monks founded to care for the victims of these poisonings and the burning sensation caused by the intense constriction of blood vessels. This plant product was well understood in medieval Europe, and midwives used its ability to cause uterine contractions to accelerate labor.

As the LSD experience begins, many people report unusual sensations, including numbness, muscle weakness, or trembling. A mild fight-or-flight response occurs: heart rate and blood pressure increase a little, and pupils dilate. Nausea is quite common. These changes are rarely large enough to be dangerous, although they can be in individuals with underlying heart disease. Some users report phantom pains. Internet discussions of hallucinogen experiences usually reveal several conversation threads about particular pains. A recent look at these found complaints ranging from chest pain to testicular pain.

PATTERNS OF CLINICAL EFFECTS FOR HALLUCINOGENS OF THE LSD GROUP*

Time	Clinical Effects
0–30 min.	Dizziness, nausea, weakness, twitches, anxiety
30–60 min.	Blurred vision, increased contrasts, visual patterns, feelings of unreality, lack of coordination, tremulous speech
1–4 hr.	Increased visual effects, wavelike motions, impaired distance perception, euphoria, slow passage of time
4–7 hr.	Waning of above effects
7–12 hr.	Returning to normal
Late effects	Headache, fatigue, contemplative state

*Adapted from R. M. Julien, *A Primer of Drug Action*, 11th ed. (New York: Worth, 2008).

Rapid tolerance develops to LSD. Probably this effect, as well as the lingering exhaustion from a drug experience that lasts so long, is the reason why most users take LSD at fairly widely spaced intervals (once a week to once a month). The tolerance diminishes quickly, so that a week's abstinence is usually enough to restore sensitivity to the drug.

PSILOCYBIN MUSHROOMS

Hallucinogenic mushrooms are probably the second most frequently used hallucinogen in the United States. The popular cottage industry that has arisen promoting sales of home-growing kits has increased public awareness of these agents. However, there is probably almost as much misinformation about "shrooms" as there is about LSD.

The shrooms to which most users refer belong to several genera of mushroom (*Psilocybe*, *Panaeolus*, and *Conocybe*). The most commonly used species in the United States are *Psilocybe mexicana* and *Psilocybe cyanescens*. These mushrooms contain two related compounds: psilocin (4-hydroxy-N, N-dimethyltryptamine) and psilocybin (4-phosphoryloxy-N, N-dimethyltryptamine). Although many people think that psilocybin is the active agent, this is probably not the case. Only after the liver has removed the extra chemical group (a phosphate group) can the remainder of the molecule (psilocin) enter the brain. Although there are rumors that phosphorylated serotonin or phosphorylated DMT are alternative hallucinogens that provide a unique new high, these molecules have an additional piece that slows entry into the brain and actually prevents rather than promotes psychoactivity. Psilocybin is distributed both in the dried mushroom form and as a white powder of purified crystalline compound. A typical dose is four to ten milligrams (two to four mushrooms of the genus *Psilocybe cyanescens*).

Use of these mushrooms is ancient. Statues of mushrooms dating from AD 100 to 1400 appear throughout Mexico and Central America, and a group of statues from central Guatemala that are even older (about 500 BC) are widely interpreted as mushroom stalks associated with mushroom worship. Use of *teonanactl*, or "flesh of the gods," persisted in Mexico until the arrival of the Spanish, who attempted to extinguish its use. Ethnobotanists, including R. Gordon Wasson, Richard Schultes, and others, worked in central Mexico in the 1930s to identify almost twenty species of mushrooms belonging to the genera *Psilocybe* (the majority), *Conocybe*, *Panaeolus*, and *Stropharia* that were used for healing and religious purposes.

Psilocybin has come full circle in some ways, from careful ritualistic use by native peoples to college students' recreational shroom use during spring break and at weekend parties to the object of current research and religious interest regarding its ability to cause persevering beneficial psychological effects. This experience is generally viewed as a milder and shorter LSD-like experience. At low doses, psilocybin causes simple feelings of relaxation, physical heaviness or lightness, and some perceptual distortions (especially visual). At higher doses, more physical sensations occur, including lightheadedness; numbness of the tongue, lips, or mouth; shivering or sweating; nausea; and anxiety.

The psychological effects mirror those of LSD. The records of a group of scientists who gave LSD, psilocybin, and PCP to college students during the mid-1960s provide a good description of the effects in contemporary terms. They published the verbatim transcripts of the experiences of three students. The following is an excerpt from a transcript of a female college senior (who previously had never taken hallucinogens) that was recorded during a psilocybin experiment.

About an hour after the drug: "When I close my eyes, then I have all these funny sensations. Funny pictures, they're all in beautiful colors. Greens and reds and browns and they all look like Picasso's pictures. Doors opening up at triangular angles and there are all these colors . . . an unreal world. It must be my subconscious or something. If I open my eyes, now the screen is, the dome gets darker. Looks like something is moving on the outside. Right along the edge. Some writhing. There's a figure—isn't exactly a figure, huge wings like a hawk, head of a hawk, but legs of a man beneath a bed. Now it's gone."

About two hours after the drug: "Ho, ho, I wonder if, I know I can sing as I sang before, but there's some flower vines running up. They start at one point, like at the bulb, and then they go up over an archway or something. And they have flowers on them: the vines are green . . . I have the feeling that someone is sticking their high-heeled shoe into the cotton in my right hand. But I can't feel it, it's not there. When I move my hand, my hands are very wet. And the lower part of my body, body, well, my body's bent. Freud. I think he went too far. Ohh. I'm moving. I look like I'm just moving. I just looked down at my body. I wish I had a mirror. I suppose that wouldn't help my seeing. . . . Now I can see a fire. It looks like a key and there's the crackling again. There's a cage and someone is opening the door of the cage. And there's a spider inside. But I'm not going in. I could stay here forever. It's so pleasant. Move slowly up and down, up and down, back and forth, ripple and wave. I keep my eyes closed now and I see a purple flower." [*]

Trips are not always as benign as this one, and in some cases they can be terribly frightening. The following is a description of a very unpleasant trip experienced by a friend of ours.

"It was late in the evening and I had been hanging out with two friends since the afternoon. We were all pretty tired, but decided to take some mushrooms. I remember as the trip began that every time I closed my eyes huge, vividly colored plants would seem to grow really rapidly in the darkness behind my eyelids. I found this pretty interesting and entertaining. It happened every time I closed my eyes—as though the process and the images were completely beyond my control." Later that night, after a botched attempt to go to a party and a brief spell of unconsciousness, our friend "lay there looking up into the darkness and perceived the darkness to begin to move ever so slightly in a circular motion. It was not a dizzy feeling that happens sometimes to people who are really drunk and think that the room is moving. I had not been drinking heavily at all. In my mind it was the darkness that was moving. I already felt pretty unsettled because of having passed out, and the sense of moving darkness was quite frightening. As I stared into the darkness it began to swirl slightly faster, and I had the feeling that it was moving toward me—bearing down on me. Lightly at first, but the force seemed to increase as the swirling gained speed. Before long I was consciously fighting with that swirling dark force, having to push hard against it with my mind to keep it at bay. The process continued. The swirling got faster, and the darkness now seemed bent on overtaking me. I was overcome with the thought that if I let it get all the way to me I would be dead. So, I mustered all the concentration and focus I could to continue holding it off. I struggled for some time, but very slowly it seemed to wear me down.

"I remember thinking that it was going to win, and I was going to die. I held it off with all the will I could muster, and finally, feeling quite exhausted, gave up with the thought that fighting that force was useless and I should just let it take me. So I did. I relaxed and felt that at least I was facing my death calmly. The swirling malevolence seemed to enter my body in the middle of my belly. Then everything was calm and quiet again. I really thought I was dead. After a brief moment, I remember suddenly feeling that an intense white light was bursting from within me, moving outward. It was as if single, white laser beams were shining out through each and every pore of my skin. Later I remember interpreting the experience in terms of my fear of, and struggle with, my image of my own death. But while it was going on, I was more afraid than I can ever remember having been."

A Cautionary Note on Mushrooms: Psilocybin mushrooms are not the only ones that produce discernible mental effects. However, they are the only mushrooms in wide use in North America. The other well-described hallucinogenic mushrooms can be dangerous. *Amanita muscaria*, which we discussed at the beginning of this chapter, contains a number of compounds that produce hallucinations, including muscimol and ibotenic acid. These compounds can cause a marked intoxication in which speech is slurred, coordination is impaired, and users experience nausea and often vomit. After this phase, a dreamy/sleepy state ensues followed by an intense hallucinogenic experience. However, this mushroom also contains muscarine, which stimulates acetylcholine receptors in the body. This compound mimics stimulation of the parasympathetic nervous system, causing intense salivation, nausea, vomiting, spasm of the bronchioles (breathing tubes), slowed heart rate, and extremely low blood pressure. These last two effects can theoretically lead to shock and death, although muscarinic effects are usually mild. Recreational use of amanita is rare, because the experience is often unpleasant and the mushrooms are not widely available.

Scientists are currently exploring both the basis of the hallucinogenic properties of psilocybin and its therapeutic potential. Studies in Switzerland by Franz Vollenweider have provided a quantifiable rating scale for its behavioral effects, confirmed the role of 5-HT2 receptors in its actions (see the following), and produced brain scans conducted in people who were experiencing drug effects. Studies by Roland Griffiths in the United States have investigated its effects in certain clinical situations like end-of-life care and in the treatment of migraines, and laboratory studies are underway. These studies have established dosage ranges that cause significant effects (twenty to thirty milligrams), and participants report persevering insight as a result of the experience. These studies, among the first in the United States in decades, used careful experimental controls, recruited both hallucinogen users and nonusers, and were reported in the peer-reviewed scientific literature.

OTHER LSD-LIKE HALLUCINOGENS

There are many other molecules with chemical structures that resemble serotonin (tryptamines) or amphetamine (phenethylamines) that scientists or bootleg drug preparers have made. 2C-B is one example, but there are many, and odd variants pop up all the time. Those that have been studied scientifically owe their hallucinogen properties to the same mechanism as LSD. However, each one has the potential to exert additional effects due to interactions with multiple receptor types, and so the effects can be individual and perhaps not what the user expects. A former synthetic chemist, Alexander Shulgin, and his wife published two books that describe the synthesis and use of these drugs, which some use as a guidebook. Those with amphetamine-like structures often have amphetamine-like activities along with their hallucinogenic properties, which can lead to dangerous levels of sympathetic nervous system stimulation and increased heart rate and blood pressure, for example. All such drugs are illegal in the United States (see the "Legal Issues" chapter).

DMT

Dimethyltryptamine (businessman's special) is one of the other serotonin-like hallucinogens that appear on the drug scene in North America. The compound originally derives from the beans of the tree *Anadenanthera peregrina* (sometimes referred to as *Piptadenia peregrina*), which grows in northern and central South America, and related species in southern South America. It has been used by South American tribes as a hallucinogenic snuff called *yopo* or *cohoba*. However, it is most often available today as the pure compound, which users prepare as a tea or smoke by itself or in conjunction with marijuana by first soaking the leaves in a solution of DMT and then drying and smoking them. The drug takes effect very rapidly: the entire experience develops and finishes within an hour. Probably because the onset of action is so fast, DMT causes anxiety attacks much more frequently than LSD, although the basic experience is similar.

Some serotonin-derived compounds, such as 5-methoxy dimethyltryptamine (5-MeO-DMT) or bufotenin, are found in the skins of some toads, including the Colorado River toad. Milking the glands on the back of the toad to obtain the hallucinogens, which are then smoked or ingested, was an old Native American trick that has been repopularized to the extent that the *Wall Street Journal* reported it. The high that is produced is extremely brief and accompanied by much worse side effects than most hallucinogens, including increased blood pressure and heart rate, blurred vision, cramped muscles, and temporary paralysis. These are due mainly to the bufotenin. The same compounds also appear in the seeds of a number of trees that grow in the Caribbean, Central America, and South America (*Piptadenia peregrina*). The powdered seeds provide the basis for hallucinogenic snuffs used by indigenous peoples and have been identified as a component of voodoo powders. DMT, 5-MeO-DMT, and some other variants including 4-Acetoxy-DMT and 5-MeO-DiPT (N,N-diisopropyl-5-methoxy-tryptamine) also show up in pill form. The basic effects of these drugs are similar, although the duration of action varies.

Peyote Cactus (Mescaline)

The peyote cactus has likely been used as a hallucinogen by native tribes in Mexico for thousands of years, and its use by North American tribes is an accepted part of their histories. The species that is typically the source of hallucinogens in the United States is a cactus that grows in northwest Mexico: *Lophophora williamsii*. It produces mescaline, the active hallucinogen, as well as many other compounds. The dried "button" of the cactus is the usual form in which the drug is sold, although it also appears in other dried forms (powders, etc.), as well as in a tea. While it can be smoked, the button is usually swallowed without chewing, and the active agent is absorbed from the stomach and intestine. There are other cacti that produce hallucinogens, including the San Pedro cactus (*Trichocereus pachanoi*), which grows in the Andes Mountains of South America.

Mescaline's chemical structure does not resemble LSD or psilocybin and the other serotonin-like hallucinogens. Instead, the structure looks more like amphetamine. The physical effects also resemble those of amphetamine—dilated pupils, increased heart rate, and increased blood pressure. The mental effects as described by ritual and recreational users, however, are surprisingly similar to LSD. Nausea and vomiting are common, especially soon after ingestion of the cactus buttons. After a user ingests a number of cactus buttons, he often feels an increase in sensitivity to sensory images and sees flashes of color followed by geometric patterns and sometimes images of people and animals. Time and space perception are distorted, as with LSD, and people often feel that they are outside themselves. The effects of ingesting pure mescaline versus the cactus button are similar but not identical, because there are at least thirty other compounds in the cactus.

The ritual use of this cactus by the shamans of native tribes, such as the Huichol in Mexico, persisted into recent times, and North American tribes adopted it in the late nineteenth century. The ritual use by North American tribes was then integrated with a number of Christian practices in the form of the Native American Church. The use of peyote as a part of this church's religious rituals has been protected by the First Amendment and then later by the Religious Freedom Restoration Act (1993). The act states that the government can limit a person's exercise of religious freedom only if "it is in furtherance of a compelling government interest, and is the least restrictive means of furthering that compelling interest." Although the 1993 law was declared unconstitutional by the US Supreme Court in 1997, some states have since enacted protective legislation for religious use to replace the protection no longer provided by federal law.

"Designer" Mescaline-like Drugs

A large number of variations on the structure of mescaline were first "designed" during the original chemical studies of mescaline. The names sound like an alphabet soup: DOM (2, 5 dimethoxy-4-methylphenyliso-propylamine, also known as STP), MDA (methylenedioxyamphetamine), DMA (dimethoxyamphetamine), MDMA (methylenedioxymethamphetamine, or Ecstasy). All of these drugs are less specific than mescaline and produce strong amphetamine-like effects in addition to hallucinations. As a result, all are more toxic than mescaline and appear much more rarely on the street today. Ecstasy provides a unique profile of effects, discussed in the "Ecstasy" chapter.

The spices nutmeg and mace deserve a final note as we discuss the mescaline-like hallucinogens. Someone who takes several teaspoons of nutmeg (if he can figure out how to avoid the overwhelming taste) might experience a very mild hallucinogenic state that includes perceptual distortions, euphoria, and sometimes mild visual hallucinations and feelings of unreality. The active compounds in nutmeg and mace are myristicin and elemicin, compounds with structures somewhat like mescaline. These compounds are very weak hallucinogens, and the dose required to evoke changes in perception causes a number of unpleasant side effects, including vomiting, nausea, and tremors. Furthermore, an aftereffect of sleepiness or a feeling of unreality can persist into the next day.

Ayahuasca

Ayahuasca (caapi, yage, vegetal) is a plant-based hallucinogen that users ingest as a drink containing a combination of plant products. Although formulations vary, the two essential components are the bark of the vine *Banisteriopsis caapi* and the leaves of *Psychotria viridis*. The active ingredients provided by this combination are the beta carbolines harmine and harmaline, and DMT (see previous section). This combination produces a period of intense nausea and vomiting, a period of anxiety or fear, followed by an intense hallucinatory and dissociative experience. The hallucinations are predominantly visual, although users report increased sensitivity to sensory stimuli also. Users frequently experience the dissociation common to other hallucinogens and a profound sense of insight. The experience lasts a number of hours.

Ethnobotanists including Richard Schultes documented use of this drug by indigenous peoples of the Amazon that probably goes back centuries. The Beat writer William Burroughs recorded his experiences with this drug in *The Yage Letters*, and the sixties generation learned about it from *The Teachings of Don Juan* by Carlos Castaneda. Use of ayahuasca has migrated to the United States from South American religious groups like the União do Vegetal (UDV) and Santo Daime that have revitalized the once common use of this drug by native shamans for magico-religious purposes, such as healing and divination. Unlike many hallucinogens, ayahuasca is almost never used recreationally, but more typically as a pharmacologic aid to personal insight and enlightenment.

SALVIA DIVINORUM

Indians of Mexico use a plant called *Salvia divinorum* (a rare member of the mint family) for religious purposes, and it has generated some curiosity in the United States mainly because it is not yet illegal. Indians chew the leaves, but in the United States, people more typically smoke the leaves. Salvia causes an intense and sometimes unpleasant hallucinatory experience that lasts about an hour. Users report a unique experience that resembles neither LSD nor other hallucinogens. This drug is more likely than other hallucinogens to produce an unpleasant experience due to its novel mechanism of action, and so repeated use is somewhat unusual. The active agent is probably a compound called Salvinorin A, the second most potent hallucinogen known after LSD. A smoked dose of as little as 200 to 500 micrograms produces hallucinations.

BELLADONNA ALKALOIDS

Belladonna alkaloids are a group of plant-based compounds that affect the central nervous system. They are produced by the plant *Datura stramonium*, or Jimsonweed, and other closely related plants of the nightshade family. The name "Jimsonweed" comes from records of a famous poisoning that left the settlers of the Virginia colony of Jamestown deathly ill. Someone unfamiliar with the edible plants of the New World included the leaves of this plant in a salad, resulting in severe intoxication in the diners. The plant became known as Jamestown weed, which later was corrupted to Jimsonweed. Teas prepared from any part of the plant, or the chewed seeds alone, produce a bizarre dream state at extremely high doses. Most users do not remember the experience because the drug causes amnesia. Ingesting doses large enough to produce this mental state causes dangerous effects on heart rate, breathing, and body temperature.

The active agents in Jimsonweed are the belladonna alkaloids atropine and scopolamine. Atropine is responsible for many of the effects outside the brain. At low doses, this compound or similar drugs are used to treat asthma and some stomach problems, and also to diagnose eye problems. However, at higher doses atropine can be lethal. The dramatic effects on thought and perception are caused by the scopolamine. Scopolamine, unlike atropine, enters the brain easily and is responsible for all of the behavioral effects of this plant.

The belladonna alkaloids mimic the complete shutdown of the parasympathetic nervous system—the mouth becomes dry, the pupils dilate, the heart speeds up, the bronchioles (breathing passages in the lungs) dilate, and digestion slows. These drugs also affect regions of the brain involved in the control of body temperature, which can rise to dangerous levels. Finally, they block one receptor for the neurotransmitter acetylcholine that is important for memory, so users often don't remember the experience. These compounds and related ones also exist in other plants, including the deadly nightshade (*Atropa belladonna*) and the mandrake root (*Mandragora officinarum*). Used properly, they are important and effective medicines. They have also been used for divining and other religious purposes by many cultures. However, recent recreational use, mainly by teenagers who don't understand the drug's effects, has resulted in an increasing number of hospitalizations and occasional deaths. The mandrake root is showing up in herbal remedies and has caused accidental poisonings in this form.

Belladonna alkaloids have very different actions from the serotonin-related hallucinogens. They induce a bizarre delirium that users remember only as strange dreams. These dreams often include the sensation of flying.

These compounds have been used throughout history, as often for poisoning as for hallucinations. The term *belladonna*, or "beautiful woman," comes from their use during the Middle Ages to dilate the pupils of the eyes for the enhancement of beauty. These drugs also were supposedly used by practitioners of female-deity worship in Europe and Eurasia during the rise of Christianity, when those using these drugs were depicted as "witches" by the early Church. These compounds were used in medicine at the time, and it is possible that famous stories of witches flying on broomsticks may derive from vaginal application of these drugs to treat gynecological disorders. Recent news that criminals in Colombia drug tourists with "burundunga," a plant-based drink containing scopolamine that causes a dissociative state that the victims do not remember, proves that the historic uses of these plants are still with us.

PHENCYCLIDINE (PCP) AND KETAMINE (SPECIAL K): HALLUCINOGENIC ANESTHETICS

Phencyclidine (PCP, angel dust, etc.) has a bad reputation—and deserves it. Both PCP and ketamine were initially marketed as general anesthetics under the names Sernyl and Ketalar. However, so many patients experienced hallucinations and delirium as they were waking up that doctors stopped using it in humans unless they received a Valium-like drug to minimize the hallucinations. Currently, ketamine is used mainly as a veterinary anesthetic. Use in humans is limited to situations in which it is essential to avoid depression of heart function with an anesthetic, or in children. PCP is sold in many different forms: as rocks that are smoked like crack, as PCP-impregnated marijuana joints, as white powder, or as pills. It is taken orally, snorted, or injected intravenously. The main effects of a single dose last four to six hours, although the effects can linger for up to two days. Ketamine is usually obtained by diversion from medical use. It is typically injected, or dried powder prepared from the solution is snorted.

PCP and ketamine are among the most complicated drugs we discuss in this book, because they have so many different effects on brain activity. PCP can produce a state similar to getting drunk, taking amphetamine, and taking a hallucinogen simultaneously. It is most frequently taken for the amphetamine-like euphoria and stimulation it produces. Many of PCP's bad side effects also resemble those of amphetamine, such as increased blood pressure and body temperature. However, at the same time, it causes a "drunken" state characterized by poor coordination, slurred speech, and drowsiness. People under the influence of PCP are also less sensitive to pain. Finally, at higher doses it causes a dissociative state in which people seem very out of touch with their environment. Observers frequently report that a PCP-intoxicated person has a blank stare and seems very detached from what is going on around her.

Not surprisingly, PCP-intoxicated people frequently find themselves in trouble with the law. Their driving skills are poor, their judgment worse, they are not attending to their environment, and they are insensitive to pain. This condition indeed can resemble the "drug-crazed," sometimes violent state that many misinformed people attribute to any drug of abuse. In the case of PCP, the stereotype has some truth. Few drugs cause a person to be more difficult to treat in an emergency room situation because she is so out of touch, belligerent, and agitated. At high doses, muscle rigidity and general anesthesia occur. Extremely high doses can result in coma, seizures, respiratory depression, dangerously high body temperature, and extremely high blood pressure.

Ketamine doesn't have quite the bad reputation that PCP has, perhaps because its stimulatory effects are less pronounced. People who take low doses of ketamine achieve a drunken state—they are a little spacey and uncoordinated, but more sociable. At higher doses, the intoxicated, dissociated feeling and loss of coordination get more intense. People describe "going down into a K-hole" to describe the feeling of being cut off from reality. They describe out-of-body and near-death experiences. This dissociated state is probably pretty similar to the one induced by PCP. Both of these drugs can cause amnesia, and so users often don't remember the drug experience well.

DEXTROMETHORPHAN

Dextromethorphan is the main constituent of many over-the-counter cough remedies. At appropriate doses (a teaspoon or two), this drug decreases coughing and doesn't do much else. However, it is a cousin of the hallucinogenic anesthetics PCP and ketamine, and some resourceful drug users—usually teenagers—have discovered that if they take excessive doses (equivalent to drinking an entire bottle of cough syrup—about 300 milligrams—or taking anywhere from ten to sixty DXM-containing pills), they can experience a dissociative state that is dose-related. While the lower end of the abused range (10 pills) leads to a mild state, very high numbers of pills (60 pills) can lead to an intense dissociated, hallucinatory state, and there are case reports of psychotic behavior in people taking extremely high doses. Recent research shows that it indeed acts much like ketamine. Dextromethorphan also shows up in the guise of fake Ecstasy pills—it is a common substitute for MDMA. Toxic doses cause confusion, disorientation, elevated body temperature, high blood pressure, and vomiting or nausea. Some users develop patterns of repeated chronic use, although there is not much in the scientific literature about dextromethorphan tolerance, dependence, or addiction. Although it can cause toxicities, the lethal dose is still considerably above (roughly double or more) the highest doses the recreational users typically employ. However, the other constituents in cough syrups can add to the toxicities. Cough syrups with decongestants in them can raise blood pressure markedly, and the combination of DXM and the antihistamine (chlorpheniramine maleate) in some preparations can cause a serotonin syndrome–like toxicity in rare cases. Ingestion of high doses (thirty to sixty pills) of formulations with acetaminophen can deliver enough of this analgesic drug to damage the liver. While DXM is not illegal, most states have laws that prevent sales to anyone under the age of 18.

HOW HALLUCINOGENS WORK

Neuroscientists know less about hallucinogens than most other psychoactive drugs. In part, this is because hallucinations can be studied most accurately in humans. No one would volunteer for the careful brain-lesion studies that can determine where critical drug effects reside, but imaging studies in living humans have proven useful. In addition, we do have a lot of information about the neurotransmitter systems involved from studies in animals. Because there are so many hallucinogenic drugs, it will come as no surprise that there are several different neurochemical routes to hallucinatory states and that each drug produces a somewhat distinct state caused by a distinct mechanism of action.

LSD, PSILOCIN, MESCALINE, AND DMT

The suspicion that drugs like LSD have something to do with the neurotransmitter serotonin (5-HT) has been prevalent since scientists first described the similarity of the chemical structures of LSD and psilocin to serotonin in the 1940s. It has been a long and tortuous road from this initial suspicion to a molecular understanding of what these drugs do. Serotonin is an important neurotransmitter that helps regulate sleep, modulate eating behavior, maintain a normal body temperature and hormonal state, and perhaps limit vulnerability to seizures. Drugs that enhance all of the actions of serotonin are useful for treating depression and suppressing overeating. How, then, can drugs that affect serotonin produce such bizarre effects on perception without disrupting many of these other actions of serotonin?

Part of the difficulty in understanding hallucinogens came from using LSD as a test hallucinogen. All of the early test systems involved organs other than the brain. For example, serotonin can make the heart of a clam beat faster, so these hearts were an early favorite test system. Scientists would hang the clam heart from a wire attached to a pen that would move if the heart muscle contracted. When serotonin was dripped on the heart, it contracted. LSD prevented the effects of serotonin on clam hearts and other test systems, and for years it was thought that hallucinogens acted by preventing the actions of serotonin. When more sophisticated tests of serotonin action in the brain became available, they seemed to support this idea. Scientists measuring the rate at which serotonin neurons were firing showed that LSD inhibited their firing. However, this didn't make a lot of sense, because shutting down the serotonin neurons so dramatically should have affected all of the other processes that rely on serotonin, but LSD did not produce such effects. Furthermore, mescaline did not have the same effect as LSD in these types of experiments, but because the structure of mescaline, unlike the other drugs, did not resemble serotonin, scientists were willing to assume that mescaline was working in some different way.

The answer to the question of what hallucinogens have to do with serotonin had to wait for scientists to discover that the neurotransmitter serotonin acts on a number of different receptors. At least thirteen types of serotonin receptors are now recognized, and we know that some seem to have very specific effects on behavior. Only one of these (as we already described) can trigger hallucinations. The thirteen receptors can be grouped into big classes (1–7), which themselves are subdivided. Virtually all serotonin-like hallucinogens are agonists (they stimulate) at two subtypes of the 5-HT2 receptors (5-HT2a and 5-HT2c). Researchers think that the hallucinogenic activity results from the stimulation of 5-HT2a. So far, every experimental drug tested that stimulates the serotonin-2a receptors causes hallucinations. We don't know how this happens, but we are pretty sure that stimulating these receptors can do it. Most of these receptors are in the cerebral cortex, where we think hallucinogens have their major action.

One mystery that remains about serotonin drugs is why the antidepressant drugs that increase the amount of serotonin in the synapse (see the "Brain Basics" chapter) do not usually cause hallucinations. These drugs increase serotonin everywhere in the brain, including sites that have 5-HT2a receptors, but although a rare patient taking one of these drugs experiences hallucinations, when the 5-HT2a receptors are stimulated in balance with all of the other serotonin systems, there are generally no hallucinogenic effects.

BELLADONNA ALKALOIDS

The belladonna alkaloids work by a completely different mechanism, which explains the different state that they cause. They act by preventing the actions of the neurotransmitter acetylcholine at one of its receptors. Acetylcholine is the neurotransmitter that nerves use to stimulate muscle and allow movement, and it is also the neurotransmitter mimicked by nicotine. It has two types of receptors: one is stimulated by nicotine, and the other (called the muscarinic receptor, because researchers discovered that it was stimulated by the compound muscarine from the *Amanita muscaria* mushroom) slows the heart and probably helps to form memories. We'll describe this in more detail in the chapter on nicotine.

PCP, KETAMINE, AND DEXTROMETHORPHAN

All three drugs block the actions of the neurotransmitter glutamate at one of its receptors, although PCP and ketamine are much better at it than dextromethorphan. This blockade can, on its own, produce most of the effects of these drugs, including feeling disconnected from your body or environment after either recreational use or medical use in anesthesia. This feeling has made it impossible to use these drugs to treat stroke, a medical use for which there was great hope when the ability of these drugs to limit stroke-induced brain damage was discovered. However, in clinical trials of these drugs, patients hallucinated. As you can imagine, it was terrifying for patients to wake up in the hospital, seriously ill, afraid that the stroke rather than the treatment was causing hallucinations.

PCP and to a lesser extent ketamine act like amphetamine to release the neurotransmitter dopamine. This accounts for the locomotor activation that PCP-intoxicated people can experience. Scientists once thought that these drugs directly affected dopamine neurons, but now they think PCP effects are the result of glutamate receptor blockade. In any case, this causes some good feelings and is why both drugs are somewhat addicting.

These drugs also decrease sensations of pain to a varying extent. NMDA receptor blockade likely plays a major role in the effect, but it also may reflect some activity on a group of receptors called "sigma" receptors that when activated cause a spectrum of effects including hallucinations and a loss of pain sensations. These receptors were once classified as opiate receptors, but they are not anymore. We do not know what they do in regulating normal brain function. Interest in this system has risen in recent years because researchers found that drugs that specifically stimulated this receptor system produced hallucinations without affecting the other opiate systems. Dextromethorphan is also a very weak stimulant of this receptor, which might contribute to its effects.

The most useful drugs are those that are most selective. PCP, ketamine, and dextromethorphan suffer from being the opposite—they block the action of the major neurotransmitter in the brain that excites other neurons, and so they affect many important brain functions.

SALVIA

Salvia has its own unique mechanism of action. Research on Salvinorin A, the likely psychoactive agent in the plant, has shown that it acts most like an agonist for the kappa opioid receptor—the receptor that causes dysphoria rather than euphoria (see the chapter on opiates). This explains the general lack of euphoria and repeated use of this drug. It does open a new area of research into the role of these receptors in hallucinations, as none was suspected before characterization of Salvia biochemistry.

ENLIGHTENMENT OR ENTERTAINMENT?

The use of hallucinogens by many indigenous peoples is tightly controlled by their cultures, which restrict such drugs to ritual use for purposes of healing, enlightenment, or prophecy. In many cases, only particular individuals in a society are permitted to use the drugs at all.

Has the use of hallucinogens evolved from this spiritual purpose to recreational use/abuse in contemporary society? If you talk to college student users, the reasons they give for using these drugs vary tremendously. Some clearly and simply aim for a novel and exciting experience. However, interviews with regular and heavy users reveal a substantial percentage who use the drug for the sense of enlightenment they feel they gain by separating from themselves.

The difference between the novelty seekers and those seeking enlightenment may simply be in how they frame the experience. For example, many users report a sense of "dissolving boundaries" while under the influence: A user might be sitting on the ground and feel that the boundary between the ground and his body no longer exists. This feeling could lead to the very exciting (or unsettling) feeling of being sucked into the earth, or it could lead to a calming sense of "oneness" with Mother Earth.

Dr. Timothy Leary (1920–1996) provides an example of varying perspectives on LSD. He started out as a professor at Harvard, pursuing a traditional academic study of the potential therapeutic utility of hallucinogens. The stories his subjects told him convinced him that LSD had tremendous spiritual value, and he became famous (and lost his job at Harvard) for his advocacy of the free use of LSD. Today he is better known for coining the phrase "turn on, tune in, drop out" during the 1960s than he is for his academic research.

Unfortunately for LSD advocates, their attitudes conflict directly with the illegal status of these drugs. Both sides can argue this issue persuasively, but the fact is that the majority of Americans prefer that use of such drugs be tightly restricted, as native societies seem to have decided as well. One person's enlightenment can be another person's hell.

DANGERS AND MYTHS

RESEARCH ON HALLUCINOGENS

One myth we want to dispel is that there is no credible scientific research conducted on hallucinogens. Research on hallucinogens (including LSD) can be legally conducted in the United States and Europe. Admittedly, the research history of hallucinogens is colorful and not always credible, ranging from military experiments on unsuspecting subjects to the blithe self-experimentation of Dr. Timothy Leary in the sixties. However, in recent years, research by credible biomedical researchers has expanded, focusing on a variety of topics ranging from what hallucinogen experiences can tell us about psychosis to the specific mechanisms by which these drugs act to cause persevering effects on religious insight.

IDENTIFICATION

Users can never really be sure which hallucinogen they are taking. Blotter-paper-like preparations are most likely to be actual LSD because other hallucinogens are not potent enough for an effective dose to be delivered in this way. However, a pill/capsule/powder could be anything, or any combination of things. Laboratory analyses of blood from people admitted to emergency rooms for LSD toxicity indicate that in some urban settings, only about 50 percent of the drug samples that were thought to be LSD by their possessors actually were LSD. Finally, any drug that has been synthesized in an underground laboratory can contain various by-products that arise from poor chemical synthesis.

Hallucinogenic mushrooms represent another identification problem. It takes an educated and practiced eye to identify any mushrooms in the field, and this is always a dangerous proposition. Many mushroom species, including the aforementioned *Amanita muscaria*, contain psychoactive compounds that are extremely dangerous or lethal. Other species (*Amanita phalloides*, for example) contain toxins that produce fatal damage to the liver and kidneys. While simple "home" tests are much touted ("if the stem turns blue, it is psilocybin"), none of these are foolproof. A number of mail-order operations exist that claim to send out psilocybin-containing mushrooms, but the identity of the spores for "grow your own" operations can be very difficult to establish.

PHYSICAL AND PSYCHOLOGICAL PROBLEMS

LSD, psilocybin, and mescaline do not generally cause dangerous physical reactions; and blood pressure, body temperature, and other vital signs remain reasonably stable unless there are acute anxiety reactions. A user is in little danger of seizures or coma. Furthermore, there is little evidence that these drugs activate the pleasure centers, and addiction and physical dependence do not occur. In this sense, they are remarkably safe. However, the psychological consequences for some users can be extreme. The bad trip, in which the drug user feels acute anxiety and perhaps fears that he will not be able to return, is the most common. Fortunately, this reaction ends as the drug is eliminated from the body. Acute anxiety can usually be treated with a dose of a benzodiazepine (a Valium-like drug—see the "Sedatives" chapter). "Talking down" can be helpful, but it is not always practical. While antipsychotic medications like Thorazine (chlorpromazine) were once popular, they are not always effective on bad trips and, in fact, can make things worse. Now that we understand that many hallucinogens act on serotonin-2 receptors, it's possible that an antagonist (blocking) treatment will become available that would terminate the trip immediately. Research studies show that a 5-HT2 antagonist called ketanserin effectively blocks most psychoactive effects of psilocybin. Such drugs exist but have not yet been investigated or approved for this purpose in the United States. Similarly, the narcotic antagonist naloxone should stop a Salvia trip, but this hasn't been tested yet.

What about the myth that taking LSD will make you crazy? Hallucinogens can worsen the symptoms of people who are already psychotic, but we don't know if they can cause psychosis. They certainly don't very often. However, a number of studies have shown that hallucinogen users are disproportionately represented among psychiatric inpatients, and that one to five people out of one thousand who take hallucinogens experience an acute psychotic reaction.

There is a "chicken and egg" problem in understanding this statistic. Most people who are hospitalized for a psychotic reaction to hallucinogens have never before been seen by a psychiatrist. So, it is impossible to know whether they were completely healthy before the drug experience.

We do know that a small number of people have very serious reactions to LSD and similar drugs, including prolonged psychotic states. Also, people with a family history of, or other predisposition toward, mental illness should be particularly careful. Sometimes a hallucinogenic experience can bring out symptoms in such individuals.

FLASHBACKS

The issue of flashbacks, or posthallucinogen perception disorder (PHPD), is clearer. Flashbacks are the reemergence of some aspect of the hallucinogenic experience in the absence of the drug. They are most commonly reported in frequent LSD users, although isolated case reports exist about flashbacks in individuals after use of other serotonin-like hallucinogens. The most common form includes altered visual images, wavering, altered borders to visual images, or trails of light. While flashbacks can occur after a single use of the drug, they may become increasingly common as the number of hallucinogenic experiences increases. Use of other drugs, like marijuana and alcohol, and even extreme fatigue, can trigger this phenomenon. The overall incidence is hard to judge because use of other drugs or psychiatric conditions must be ruled out. By our best guess, incidence for the common user is low.

People's reactions to flashbacks vary widely. Some users experience anxiety and depression while others view flashbacks as an acceptable side effect of an otherwise positive experience. In many cases, flashbacks diminish with abstinence, although symptoms that persist for years have been reported.

Persistent symptoms might actually reflect long-term changes in how the brain processes sensory images. Studies of vision of habitual LSD users (when they are not under the influence of the drug) show that their brains may continue to respond to visual stimuli after the stimuli are removed. This response suggests that repeated LSD usage may cause some neuroplastic changes that persist. In the "Brain Basics" chapter, we discuss the brain's capacity to remember all sorts of experiences, including repeated drug applications.

CHROMOSOMAL DAMAGE

We have one final myth to discuss: the idea that LSD will break chromosomes. This concern, based on scanty research, was raised during the

1960s. While women who used LSD during pregnancy have given birth to children with birth defects, this rate is not higher than that of the general population. Furthermore, most of these women also used other drugs during pregnancy. Most animal research has not shown remarkable effects of LSD on the developing fetus. Some concern about the effects of LSD goes back historically to the widespread use of related ergot alkaloids to induce abortion. However, LSD itself does not have this effect. Nevertheless, women who are pregnant, or who might be, should avoid drugs in general.

DEATH

Conventional LSD-like hallucinogens are fairly unlikely to produce serious physical effects. However, some newer and fortunately rare designer hallucinogens have blurred the lines between stimulants and hallucinogens. For example, one of these—25I-NBOMe, 4-Iodo-2,5-dimethoxy-N-(2-methoxybenzyl) phenethylamine—has been reported to cause deaths. This drug and some like it sometimes are marketed as bath salts, and sometimes as LSD. The particular problem with this drug is its extraordinary potency: like LSD, it has big effects at very small doses. This drug and several close relatives may represent serious risks to human users, but almost nothing is known about them.

The belladonna alkaloids represent a particular danger. These drugs prevent the action of one of the major neurotransmitters in the body (acetylcholine) at many of its synapses. At doses that cause hallucinations, they increase heart rate and body temperature to dangerous levels: death can result. It is important to understand that there is not a dose that produces significant behavioral effects that is not toxic: the behavioral effects, like delirium, are signs of overdose. These effects are easily treated by medical personnel if they know what the intoxicating drug is. Therefore, it is extremely important to seek medical attention.

PCP also can cause dangerous side effects or death from overdose (two to five times a single recreational dose). As the user increases the dose, general anesthesia can result (remember, this was the reason the drug was invented). However, a number of dangerous effects occur after high doses, any one of which can be lethal. Body temperature can rise to 108 degrees Fahrenheit, blood pressure can rise so much that a stroke occurs, breathing can cease, or a prolonged period of seizure activity can result. PCP can also cause a prolonged state resembling paranoid schizophrenia. This most often happens in people who use PCP for a long time; however, an abnormal psychiatric state that persists for days can result from a single use. The acute delirium caused by PCP or ketamine can be alleviated with benzodiazepine drugs, such as Valium.

INTERACTIONS WITH OTHER DRUGS

Many people who experiment with hallucinogens combine them with other drugs. For example, it is not uncommon for people to take LSD or mushrooms and smoke marijuana at the same time. The effect of these combinations is highly individual and depends on the previous drug experience of the user, the doses, and the particular drugs involved. For example, smoking marijuana often triggers PHPD (flash-backs) in heavy LSD users. Many of these combinations produce bizarre, anxiety-provoking—but not dangerous—states.

The most troublesome reactions are those that are caused by the user taking something without knowing it. PCP is a frequent culprit in this regard. Marijuana can be adulterated with PCP without the user's knowledge and can induce a terrifying or dangerous state in the unsuspecting users.

What about interactions with prescription drugs? Not surprisingly, other drugs that influence serotonin systems have been involved in reported interactions. There are multiple reports of serotonin-specific reuptake inhibitors (SSRIs) like Prozac (fluoxetine) triggering flashbacks in heavy LSD users. The opposite interaction also can happen: some patients who are taking SSRIs to treat depression report that they do not experience the effects of LSD. A more dangerous interaction could theoretically happen if people combine SSRIs and ayahuasca. The MAO inhibitor in the ayahuasca can synergize with the increase in serotonin caused by the SSRI, leading to the dangerous "serotonin syndrome" that we discuss in the "Ecstasy" chapter.

5

HERBAL DRUGS

Drug Class: Herbal drugs. The drugs mentioned in this chapter are not scheduled by the Drug Enforcement Administration. However, there are legal restrictions on some. Ephedrine requires a prescription.

Individual Drugs (just a few examples): Herbal X-tacy, beta phenylethylamine (PEA), dimethylamylamine (DMAA), synephrine, smart drugs, ginseng, melatonin

The Buzz: Most of these drugs are either members of other classes we have discussed or don't have a buzz because they are ineffective or because they are used to improve brain function—not to intoxicate.

Overdose and Other Bad Effects: The biggest danger of these drugs is that many are untested and unregulated. For some, there is some research support for effectiveness and safety, or evidence of traditional use by other cultures for centuries. For most, claims of efficacy are based on sometimes-skimpy research that may or may not include credible clinical studies. Even for effective medicines, the actual contents of herbal preparations are unknown. Furthermore, the user cannot rely on the instructions to be a reliable guide for effective or safe use. In the worst cases, instructions suggest use of dangerous amounts of the drug. In the best cases, the doses are estimations based on sparse research.

Dangerous Combinations with Other Drugs: Ephedrine and similar stimulants can be dangerous when taken in combination with mono-amine oxidase inhibitors, which are used to treat depression. The combination of these two drugs can lead to fatal increases in blood pressure or heart rate. The combination of ephedrine-like stimulants with caffeine is much more likely to lead to symptoms of cardiovascular activation, jitteriness, anxiety, and arousal than either drug alone.

CHAPTER CONTENTS

WHAT IS AN HERBAL DRUG?

Herbal drugs are simply drugs from plant matter. Many of the drugs discussed in this book fall under that large umbrella. Many of the most common intoxicants are ultimately derived from plant products. Nicotine comes from tobacco plants, and many forms of alcohol are prepared by the fermentation of yeast in the presence of grain products. Most of the hallucinogens, ranging from psilocybin mushrooms to belladonna alkaloids, could be described as herbal drugs, along with many natural stimulants, including caffeine, ephedrine, and cocaine. There are also herbal sedatives—hypnotics such as kava—that act very much like alcohol.

Herbal drugs are touted as safe and effective because they are "natural," or a "normal constituent of the body." This drug classification is an effective marketing device: the current market in herbal drugs in this country amounts to millions of dollars. Because most of these preparations are sold as nutritional supplements rather than as drugs, they are not subject to FDA requirements. Therefore, neither their safety nor their effectiveness has been established in controlled scientific studies. This doesn't mean that none of the drugs are effective; some certainly are. Furthermore, we should never discount the placebo effect: the promise of a remedy can have a powerful healing effect. And remember—herbal drugs are still drugs, because if they are effective, they change how your body works. That means when you visit the doctor, you should be sure to tell her about any supplements you are using. As you will see in this chapter, they can interfere with the effects of medications you may be prescribed.

This chapter will discuss a subset of these drugs that are widely used to change mental status—either to optimize function or treat mental illness. This subject could be the topic of an entire book, so we have focused on the most common ingredients in the many supplements that are out there. It is important to bear in mind that these drugs are most often components of complex mixtures, and it is very difficult to know how much (or whether) a particular component contributes to the desired effect. A quick survey of energy supplements available online showed ingredient numbers ranging from three to more than fifty!

HERBAL DRUGS ARE NOT REGULATED
LIKE REGULAR DRUGS

Herbal drugs are not regulated the way normal prescription and nonprescription medications are controlled in the United States. In 1994, Congress passed the Dietary Supplement Health and Education Act, or DSHEA. This law says that the FDA will not regulate any natural product (which they define as any product intended for ingestion as a supplement to the diet, including vitamins and minerals; herbs, botanicals, and other plant-derived substances; amino acids and concentrates; metabolites;

constituents; and extracts of any of these substances). Therefore, such drugs can be marketed without proof that they are safe or effective. The FDA can only remove them from the market if they can prove they are dangerous—a strict requirement, and one that shifts the burden of proof from those marketing the drug to the FDA. Not all herbal drugs are ineffective or dangerous, but the buyer should consider several issues. First, what is the source of claims for effectiveness? Some herbal drugs have been tested by credible, well-controlled scientific studies. Others have been used by other cultures for centuries in a carefully documented way. Unfortunately, there is little evidence to back up claims about many other drugs. Furthermore, there is a growing interest in Eastern medicine that can sometimes lead to uncritical acceptance of herbal healing techniques. While many effective medicines derive from herbal sources, many ineffective ones do as well.

The second consideration is the safety and reliability of formulation. A frightening example happened in the early 1990s in the marketing of the amino acid tryptophan. Tryptophan, a normal constituent of the body, is used by some as a so-called smart drug to improve mental functioning and facilitate sleep. It is a component of many foods and has no known hazards when taken as a nutritional supplement. However, a still unknown contaminant in a tryptophan preparation from one particular supplier caused a serious and fatal disease—eosinophilia-myalgia syndrome. In addition, with almost daily revelations about contaminated food products from both foreign and domestic sources, caution with "herbal" preparations is warranted. A recent survey of melatonin products showed that the melatonin content of some preparations was half or double the amount listed on the label. Finally, an increasing number of "herbal" compounds actually contain a synthetic drug that is far more efficacious—common problems in this regard are diet aids that contain the drug sibutramine, and "herbal" sexual enhancers that contain sildenafil (Viagra). Such substitutions can lead to greater-than-expected results.

Most people who use herbal drugs must rely upon self-experimentation to establish effective doses that lack side effects. Unlike in Europe, where the use of herbal drugs and homemade formulations is broader and pharmacists are more informed, there are few professionals in the United States who are qualified to give knowledgeable advice about herbal drugs, so users must depend upon an informal (and often uninformed) network of advocates—usually those marketing the compounds.

In 1998, Congress established a new division of the National Institutes of Health (the National Center for Complementary and Alternative Medicine) to study alternative and complementary medicines, including herbal drugs, and research is extremely active right now. We know more about the safety and effectiveness of these drugs all the time.

EPHEDRINE AND ITS SUBSTITUTES

Ephedrine is a molecule found in many plants that was sold widely as a sports supplement to enhance workouts, cause weight loss, and best of all, melt fat. It also was sold as an herbal (and safer) substitute for Ecstasy (methylenedioxymethamphetamine, MDMA). Ephedrine has been banned since 2004 (a ban upheld in 2007), although it sometimes crops up on the Internet in some forms including herbal teas, in Chinese herbal remedies, and in a chemically synthetic form as an asthma treatment. Ephedrine is an effective medicine for treating asthma and has been used medically as such in appropriate doses for thousands of years because it acts as a mild stimulant to the sympathetic nerve endings to dilate bronchioles, increase heart rate and blood pressure, and raise blood glucose. However, this drug does not enter the brain well and at best causes a jitteriness that most people find discomfiting even when used in appropriate amounts for the treatment of asthma. At higher doses, ephedrine causes an arousal and anxiety state that most people find unpleasant, although some report positive feelings with the arousal. Relative to other stimulants, these effects are mild.

These characteristics explain why ephedrine, especially at excessive doses, can be mistaken for MDMA and is popular for improving athletic performance. Ephedrine increases heart rate and blood pressure and can give the feeling of greater physical activation, which can be mistaken for improving athletic performance. If high enough doses are taken, these effects are associated with some increase in arousal and anxiety, so the users can "feel" a drug effect. But in fact, ephedrine does nothing to improve muscle development.

There may be some truth to claims that ephedrine can help contribute to weight loss due mainly to its effects on the body to facilitate fat breakdown and increase energy production, but the effects are minor. Ephedrine and ephedrine/caffeine preparations have been tested on obese humans and have been found to have a modest benefit (one well-controlled study reported a five-pound weight loss in two months, and a total of ten pounds of weight lost in five months).

The FDA banned ephedrine because of many (thousands) reports of adverse events including milder side effects like tremors, headache, insomnia, nausea, vomiting, fatigue, and dizziness as well as a number of deaths in young, healthy people who experienced heart attacks or strokes (especially when using this drug while exercising).

Numerous substitutes for ephedrine have entered the marketplace. Some of these are relatives of ephedrine (p-synephrine), and some are plant products whose active ingredients aren't known or listed (Hoodia, Cha de Bugre). Three common ingredients are beta phenylethylamine (PEA), p-synephrine (the active ingredient in bitter orange), and dimethylamylamine.

Beta phenylethylamine is a drug that works very much like ephedrine and so has very similar effects: it raises blood pressure and heart rate due to the release of norepinephrine. In addition to its ability to mimic sympathetic stimulation, it also stimulates "trace amine receptor 1," a minor receptor that exists throughout the body through which it constricts arteries and probably has other actions. Unlike ephedrine, PEA enters the brain, and at high doses it causes the release of dopamine and norepinephrine and causes stimulant-like behavioral effects. Normally, these effects are limited by the rapid metabolism of PEA by monoamine oxidase in the liver and in the brain. Little is known about how high PEA levels get when humans ingest pharmacologic amounts as supplements: there has been almost no investigation of this.

PEA has another unique characteristic: it is a natural constituent of the brain (albeit a minor one), and over the years scientists have measured levels in the urine and blood of patients with a variety of disorders including ADHD, schizophrenia, depression, and Parkinson's disease in the hopes of understanding whether there is a link there. These research findings are mixed between speculations that it is beneficial (lifting depression after exercise) or harmful (contributing to the acceleration of dopamine neuron death after monoamine oxidase therapy). So is PEA a natural therapy or dangerous sympathomimetic? We don't know. It is certainly physiologically and behaviorally active, based on a few studies. However, the same caveat exists for this supplement as for many others: you are not guaranteed to get the dose that is advertised, and sometimes not even the molecule that is advertised.

p-Synephrine is a simpler story. This is a *very* close relative of the nasal decongestant m-synephrine, better known as phenylephrine. It was used as a drug in the 1920s but has not been marketed for many years. However, its source as a dietary supplement is usually from immature (green) Seville oranges. It is used primarily for weight loss and as a component of sports supplements. It has been used in traditional Chinese medicines for digestive problems. Its main well-characterized effect from the old animal studies of the sympathetic nervous system is to raise blood pressure, probably by stimulating the alpha-adrenergic receptor for norepinephrine, and perhaps through the weak inhibition of norepinephrine uptake. This effect has been observed in humans in some but not all studies. Its effectiveness as a weight-loss agent is in the eye of the beholder: reviewers who acknowledged their association with its marketing have taken a more positive view of the "modest" weight loss and benign side-effect profile than reviewers without a conflict of interest. Most studies of both its effectiveness as a weight-loss agent and its cardiovascular effects have been conducted on supplement mixtures containing caffeine, so it is hard to know the efficacy of the p-synephrine mixtures that are widely marketed. It would be logical to assume that the benefit-risk profile is similar to ephedrine.

DMAA is marketed as a constituent of rose geranium, although formulations may have geranium extract or synthetic DMAA. It is currently under investigation by the FDA, which has contested its existence as a natural product in geranium and, hence, questioned the freedom to market it under the protection of natural-product legislation. The purified molecule was used as a nasal decongestant for decades, ending in the 1970s. Like p-synephrine, its main action is as an alpha-adrenergic agonist that constricts blood vessels and raises blood pressure. There is little scientific evidence that it lowers weight or improves muscle mass. Furthermore, the first few reports are starting to trickle in of healthy young people experiencing strokes when using DMAA/caffeine combinations during heavy workouts—exactly the scenario that resulted in ephedrine casualties.

Finally, these drugs are often sold in complicated mixtures containing caffeine. Combinations of ephedrine and similar stimulants with caffeine are much more likely to lead to effects on the heart and circulation, jitteriness, anxiety, and arousal than either drug does alone. Furthermore, the potential for overdosing is high given the free availability of both drugs. The effects of ephedrine and PEA can be exaggerated, leading to dangerous increases in blood pressure in patients taking monoamine oxidase inhibitors for the treatment of depression (Marplan, Nardil, Parnate).

These are just three examples of the continual challenge users face in evaluating the effectiveness and safety of herbal drugs, especially those used as sports supplements when people are working out. Manufacturers are not required to prove efficacy or safety. If all that happens is that you waste your money on an ineffective product (which might have placebo value for you), then it isn't a big problem. But with drugs that simulate the effects of norepinephrine on the heart and blood vessels like many of these sports supplements, the outcomes of taking excessive amounts can be catastrophic.

ST. JOHN'S WORT

St. John's wort may be the most widely used herbal preparation currently on the market. It is an extract prepared from a plant of the same name (*Hypericum perforatum*) that achieved recognition as an antidepressant following reports from Europe of clinical trials showing that it improved mild depression. Many people take St. John's wort to stave off depression or just to improve their state of mind. Most research shows that St. John's wort may have some effectiveness but not as much as pharmaceutical antidepressants, especially in cases of severe depression.

So why not take a little St. John's wort? By itself, it isn't particularly dangerous. However, it has proved to have many negative interactions with other drugs, including some important medications. St. John's wort can stimulate the production of enzymes in the liver that break down other drugs. This allows the liver to break down some drugs so fast that a normal dose doesn't work. Birth control pills are affected in this way, and there are cases in which women taking St. John's wort have become pregnant because their birth control pills were being degraded too quickly. Even more serious consequences have occurred. There are more than ten case reports of transplant patients who experienced tissue rejection when levels of their immunosuppressant medication fell drastically after they started taking St. John's wort.

Finally, St. John's wort can interact dangerously with one class of antidepressant, the serotonin-specific reuptake inhibitors (SSRIs). Taking both St. John's wort and SSRIs can lead to "serotonin syndrome" because serotonin is inactivated more slowly than usual, resulting in higher-than-normal levels of serotonin in the synapses. At its mildest, people just feel flushed and jittery; at its worst, it leads to an increase in body temperature, heart rate, and blood pressure, and can be fatal.

MELATONIN

Melatonin is widely sold in capsule or tablet form in health-food stores as a treatment for jet lag and other sleep disorders, as well as a cure-all that can prevent aging and such diseases as cancer. It could be called the prototype herbal drug. Melatonin is the molecule released by the pineal gland, so it is a normal part of the human body. It has been the object of scientific study, and some of the claims of substantial effects have been borne out in these studies. In fact, one of the most recently marketed sleep aids (ramelteon, Rozerem) is a melatonin mimic, and several more are in development. On the negative side, however, scientists have not established a clear-cut safe and effective dose, the safety of long-term use has never been established, and the content of preparations marketed as melatonin is unregulated and varies widely.

WHAT IS MELATONIN?

Melatonin is a neurotransmitter that is structurally related to serotonin. It is produced mainly by the pineal gland (a tiny gland that sits on top of the brain), by the retina, in the GI tract, and by some immune cells. Melatonin is released only at night. Visual signals travel from the eye to an area in the brain that sets the circadian rhythm, and then to the nerves that travel to the pineal gland and cause it to release melatonin into the bloodstream, where it has some of its actions. Melatonin is very fat soluble and easily enters the brain (whether from a pill or your own natural melatonin) and acts on receptors at certain places in the brain. Melatonin mainly acts on two receptors (MT1 and MT2) and also has actions mediated by nuclear hormone receptors and the direct interaction with cellular constituents.

MELATONIN AND SLEEP

The very marked day-night rhythm in melatonin release is one reason why melatonin is associated with sleep. Normally, when darkness falls, the nerves that stimulate melatonin release become active, which then acts on its receptors to trigger sleep.

A growing number of research studies show that if melatonin is taken at a time earlier than normal bedtime (such as in the early evening or late afternoon), it can help people fall asleep faster. Scientists have studied

melatonin for jet lag, night-shift workers, some insomniacs—even astro-
nauts in the space shuttle! Melatonin can help with jet lag if people take it
at the time that they would go to bed in their destination. Results are
more mixed in other situations.

MELATONIN AND FERTILITY

Does melatonin actually create day-night rhythms in other aspects of
body function? It may contribute to the fall in body temperature that
occurs at night. In species other than humans, melatonin may be very
important in allowing animals to breed at appropriate times of the year.
The shorter days and longer nights of winter cause an increasing release
of melatonin. For some species, like sheep, which breed during the short
days of winter, this increasing release of melatonin improves fertility,
while it decreases fertility in animals like hamsters, which breed in the
summer, when days are long. Melatonin has a much less certain role in
human reproduction. Humans are not "seasonal breeders": they maintain fertility throughout the year. This fits nicely with the fact that the
nightly rises in melatonin are not as great in humans as they are in other
animals. Can human reproduction be affected by causing a larger night-
time rise in melatonin? Some scientific studies suggest that melatonin
can decrease fertility in humans, although there is little research in this
area. Melatonin (in doses that exceed usual doses by tenfold) has even
been tested as a contraceptive, but given the possible side effects on
sleep, it has some real disadvantages in comparison to more completely
tested medications.

MELATONIN AND AGING

Melatonin has a measurable antioxidant action in model systems,
although we are less certain that it has this action in humans who take
supplemental melatonin. Much of aging-related tissue damage and disease may result from by-products of oxygen metabolism (oxygen radicals)
that damage tissue. Certain compounds, such as vitamin E, are known to
"scavenge" and eliminate these products before they interact with proteins and DNA and thus produce tissue damage. The melatonin molecule
can act directly as a radical scavenger, and giving melatonin to experimental animals can prevent the DNA damage caused by compounds

known to produce such oxygen radicals. However, this research is in its early stages, and effectiveness in lower primates or humans has not been tested. Again, taking a psychoactive compound that might suppress fertility for years to delay aging seems like a strategy that offers more risks than rewards.

MELATONIN AND OTHER HEALTH BENEFITS

Melatonin is also claimed to improve immune function, lower blood pressure, prevent bone loss due to aging, influence GI motility, and even reverse the graying of hair! While there are isolated studies to support these claims, research in these areas is not abundant.

IS MELATONIN SAFE?

Melatonin may be effective in some situations, but is it safe? In animal studies designed to test toxicity, it proved to be pretty safe. However, we don't really know what an effective dose is for a person. Doses in scientific studies range from 0.1 to 5 milligrams, but in most health-food stores, melatonin is sold in amounts ranging from 1 to 5 milligrams. Further, users can purchase and consume unlimited quantities. Excessive doses might affect reproduction or other aspects of body function. Finally, we do not know conclusively the long-term effects of this drug. It isn't even known whether melatonin is effective if given for a long period of time. Most sleep medications lose their effectiveness with time, and it wouldn't be surprising if melatonin did as well. If so, a dangerous situation could develop if a person started increasing his dose to compensate for the loss of effect.

GINSENG

The ginseng root has been used in Chinese medicine for thousands of years for a variety of ailments ranging from fatigue and stress to high blood pressure and even cancer. Traditionally it is used as a daily tonic. It is available here in the United States in a wide variety of forms, from teas to the root (which is chewed). Ginseng comes from several members of the plant family Araliaceae. American, Korean, and Japanese ginseng are members of the genus *Panax*, and Siberian ginseng is a member of the genus *Eleutherococcus*. It is being used widely in the United States for reasons that include improving athletic performance, decreasing anxiety, and as a tonic to increase resistance to stress.

Does ginseng have real biologic activity? If you listen to testimonials by happy users, then the answer is yes. The most biologically active ingredients in ginseng (the ginsenosides) have some activities in the brain. In some studies, extracts of ginseng improved the ability of rats to learn a maze. Studies showing effects on human memory are mixed and suffer from small subject numbers and mixed results. Part of the confusion arises from different approaches to testing ginseng and many other nutritional supplements: while some studies try to show effects of a single dose in a highly controlled laboratory setting, others have used population studies in people who are self-medicating with supplements. The latter studies may be the best test of the efficacy of available supplement preparation. Unfortunately, these have been less successful than the more controlled tests with well-defined doses. One problem that arises in understanding the results of such studies is that people who choose to self-medicate with herbal drugs may be, in general, more health conscious than those who don't, and may do a lot of other things that improve their health and maintain good brain function. Ginseng has a variety of effects in experimental cell systems including effects on cell growth and immune function. Its ability to lower blood glucose in animal models of diabetes has attracted some notice, and studies are underway in humans.

The recommended dose on preparations sold in a local health-food store come in the same range as doses used in the experimental studies (about 700 milligrams for a normal adult male). However, the exact content of these formulations is unknown, so potency can vary widely. In addition, the effectiveness of a single dose is not clear. Some studies fail to show significant effects except with repeated dosing. Fortunately, no dangerous side effects of single, high doses are known. The safety of repeated doses is unknown. Some case reports of uterine bleeding in postmenopausal women indicate that ginseng has effects resembling those of estrogen. As with many ancient herbal cures, there is active research ongoing to test the safety and efficacy of ginseng in treating disease. This is another drug that might have potential, but we just don't have enough information yet to judge.

GINKGO

An extract of the leaves of the ginkgo biloba tree is a popular herbal cure that is supposed to improve circulation in small blood vessels in the brain, and so improve memory and alertness. Like ginseng, it has many advocates. Unfortunately, it has even less in the way of research to back up the claims of satisfied users. Numerous studies of memory in healthy adults offer conflicting results—some show benefits, while others do not. Investigations of its benefits in treating diseases of memory are sparser. One study in Alzheimer's patients suggests that ginkgo provided some help, and studies are underway of the effects on dementia and normal aging. However, other studies do not support its effectiveness. One potential problem with ginkgo is that it can slow blood clotting, which can lead to dangerous hemorrhages if it is used in combination with prescribed anticoagulant medication. It is often marketed in combination with ginseng for similar conditions, such as stress. Its effectiveness as a stress cure remains to be proved.

HERBAL "SMART DRUGS"

The so-called smart drugs may win the contest for ingenious marketing of marginally effective agents. Their popularity has been fueled in part by the general enthusiasm for cleansing and lack of intoxication in a drug-weary culture. The recent explosion of "energy" drinks shows little sign of abating. Although taking a drug to improve mental quickness instead of getting bombed certainly seems innocent, nowhere is superstition more rampant than in the marketing claims for drugs that improve memory and general mental acuity. There is truly a desperate need for such drugs in medicine to retard the memory loss caused by Alzheimer's disease and some other forms of dementia. However, despite years of effort, only a few marginally effective drugs have been developed (this is discussed in the "Nicotine" chapter).

The herbal smart drugs are often a concoction of various amino acids and similar compounds. The most common supplements in energy drinks and herbal "smart" supplements are the sulfur-containing amino acid taurine, carnitine, and precursors to neurotransmitters including tyrosine, phenylalanine, and choline. Should you take "smart" nutrients? First, if you are eating a normal American diet with the typical excess of protein, there is more than enough of most of these micronutrients in your diet to maintain optimal levels in your blood and brain. Second, these compounds act over hours to days. They don't produce the advertised immediate "energy boost." Finally, even if enough amino acid is provided to boost the production of a neurotransmitter, it doesn't automatically mean the neuron is releasing more to have greater effect. A newly made neurotransmitter is simply stored, awaiting the arrival of a nerve impulse to release it. So simply making more adds to the store that is ready for release. Adding more is effective only if stores are truly depleted. This generally happens only after life-threatening stresses (not a bad day at work).

Let's look at a couple of examples. Phenylalanine is reputed to have marvelous pleasurable qualities as the precursor to dopamine. There is some truth to this claim. Tyrosine and phenylalanine are both amino acids that are required for the synthesis of proteins. Tyrosine is the basic building block for the neurotransmitters dopamine and norepinephrine, and it is logical to think that increasing tyrosine might improve mood. However, the average American eats enough protein to provide adequate levels of these amino acids. Taking a pharmacologic (big) dose of tyrosine may be able to boost catecholamine production for a short time, but the benefits are transient, and scientists are just starting to study the behavioral outcomes (if any) of supplementing tyrosine.

There may be more truth to the claims that taking large doses of other neurotransmitter precursors can influence the production of the neurotransmitter. Choline supplements can indeed enhance the production of the neurotransmitter acetylcholine, which is important for many aspects of brain function, including memory. The death of acetylcholine neurons may contribute to the disabling memory loss of Alzheimer's disease, and supplementing acetylcholine production can produce slight and temporary improvement in the memory of Alzheimer's patients. The choline precursor citicoline actually may improve memory a bit in both healthy people and those who have experienced brain injury and Alzheimer's disease, but whether the effect is large enough to overcome the disease process remains to be seen. Similarly, the tryptophan in high-protein foods like milk can enhance the production of serotonin in the brain. Because increases in serotonin are speculated to enhance sleep, there may be some truth to the old wives' tale that warm milk enhances sleep. Another claim that might have some credibility is that ingesting extra tryptophan could help to prevent the loss of serotonin that occurs when a person takes Ecstasy. There is a rapid loss of serotonin in this case, which perhaps can be lessened by providing an extra precursor. Unfortunately, this does not diminish the dangerous side effects of MDMA at all.

Taurine and carnitine are the most common additions to energy drinks. Taurine is a sulfur-containing amino acid and is very abundant in the body, including in the brain, and it seems important for maintaining many body functions including blood pressure and metabolism. It may function as an inhibitory neuromodulator, especially in situations like ischemia or stroke where it may counteract the release of excitatory neurotransmitters. Studies in animals seemed to indicate it was a panacea—it lowered blood pressure, improved glucose tolerance in diabetes, possesses valuable antioxidant properties, and best of all, burns fat. Unfortunately, human studies are fewer, but they offer some opposing concerns—it may raise blood pressure in women, does not burn fat, and lowers glucose unless rats also eat fructose (or presumably people drink soft drinks). Clearly, more work is needed to understand the benefits and risks of taurine supplementation. Similarly, carnitine is also an important normal constituent of the body that is necessary for the production of energy by mitochondria, and a lack of carnitine caused by a genetic deficiency can have extremely adverse effects on brain function. There are some published studies of carnitine supplements in various neural disorders including Alzheimer's disease and Parkinson's disease with mixed results at best. Does this mean that giving dietary supplements to healthy young adults improves memory? Again, we have no evidence, and many compounds that show marginal effects in impaired populations have even less action in healthy adults. So will these "energy" drinks give you a better edge mentally in studying for exams? Perhaps, but the reason may be the 100 to 280 milligrams of caffeine that they contain! Many other "nutraceuticals" including SAMe (S-adenosylmethionine) and various vitamins often appear in supplements and benefit people who are deficient—not normal, well-nourished adults.

Nevertheless, hope springs eternal that we will find the natural product to optimize mental function or stave off the effects of aging. The findings that resveratrol, a molecule present in red wine, prolongs life and improves functioning in aging mice led to another wave of hope until we learned that the amounts required equal the resveratrol in 750 to 1,500 bottles of wine a day!

HAZARDS OF HERBAL DRUGS

Most of the herbal preparations that people use are innocuous, and some are effective, especially in people with deficiencies in the molecule that is in the supplement. Additionally, there is some benefit in taking a milder, endogenous version of a prescribed drug that may have intense side effects. However, some have real dangers. Of the group mentioned here, stimulants related to ephedrine pose the greatest risk, because people can easily take enough to cause high blood pressure, stroke, or heart attack. Often, the marketers of the herbal preparations recommend taking excessive doses. Such supplements are clearly dangerous for someone already experiencing high blood pressure or any kind of cardiovascular problem.

Some of the nutritional supplements can be quite dangerous for people with certain medical conditions, or those taking certain drugs. Taking anything that increases the production of monoamine neurotransmitters (e.g., phenylalanine or tyrosine) is dangerous for someone who is taking a certain type of drug to treat depression (the monoamine oxidase inhibitor class, such as Nardil or Eldepryl). These drugs prevent the breakdown of monoamine neurotransmitters, and dangerous high blood pressure can result if they are taken in combination with nutritional supplements that increase the production of these same neurotransmitters. Furthermore, taking phenylalanine can be dangerous for a person who suffers from phenylketonuria, a disease that prevents the normal metabolism of phenylalanine, which can build up in the blood to dangerous levels. The long-term effects in otherwise healthy people of taking high doses of many herbal drugs are not known. The current enthusiasm for herbal remedies will provide the data that we need but, unfortunately, at the likely expense of unwary users of these products. Our advice is to keep your eyes on the scientific research about nutritional supplements and brain function, because science is catching up fast.

6

INHALANTS

Drug Class: Mixed

Individual Drugs: nitrites (butyl or amyl); anesthetics (nitrous oxide—Whippets; gaseous anesthesia agents used for surgery—halothane, ether); solvents, paints, sprays, and fuels (toluene, gasoline, glues, canned spray paint, etc.)

Common Terms: bolt, bullets, climax, locker room, rush, poppers, snappers, aimes

The Buzz: The chemicals in this category have very little in common in chemical structure, pharmacology, or toxic effects, except that they are all taken by inhalation.

The nitrites relax the smooth muscle tissue that regulates the size and shape of blood vessels, the bladder, the anus, and other tissues. The relaxed blood vessels produce a drop in blood pressure, an increased heart rate, and a sense of warmth and mild euphoria. Visual distortions can also occur.

Nitrous oxide is by far the mildest of the anesthetics; it produces mild euphoria, reduction of pain, and reduction of inhibitions, followed by drowsiness as the concentrations increase. Other anesthetics produce the same effects but cause major sedation at modest levels.

Solvents produce effects similar to those of alcohol, with stimulation, loss of inhibitions, and mild euphoria, followed by depression. Distortions of perception and hallucinations may occur.

Overdose and Other Bad Effects: The risk of a lethal overdose with inhaled nitrites is small. Because they dilate blood vessels, nitrites cause a reduction in blood pressure. This can produce heart palpitations (rapid, hard heartbeats), loss of consciousness upon moving from lying down to standing up, and headaches. No one who has heart or blood vessel disease should use these compounds without the supervision of a physician. Long-term use of nitrites can produce negative effects that are described later. And when they are ingested, nitrites can cause major medical problems, including death.

The overdose risk for anesthetics ranges from relatively low (nitrous oxide) to very high (modern surgical anesthesia agents). For nitrous oxide, the major risk is not breathing enough oxygen while breathing the gas. For the others, the risk is disruption of heart function and the suppression of respiration, followed by death. Anyone who has inhaled enough anesthetic to become unconscious is in danger and should receive medical attention immediately.

Serious solvent intoxication is like that of alcohol, with muscular incoordination, headache, abdominal pain, nausea, and vomiting. Many of these agents are flammable, so serious burns can occur. The risk of a lethal overdose with solvents is significant. Death usually occurs because the heart rhythm is disrupted (cardiac arrhythmia) or because there is a lack of oxygen. Accidents and suicide are also significant risks. A significant percentage of people who die from inhalants are first-time users.

Dangerous Combinations with Other Drugs: As with alcohol and sedatives, it is dangerous to combine inhalants with anything else that makes a person sleepy. This includes alcohol and other sedative drugs, such as opiates (e.g., heroin, morphine, or Demerol), barbiturates (e.g., phenobarbital), Quaaludes (methaqualone), Valium-like drugs (benzodiazepines), and cold medicines, including antihistamines.

Drugs can become deadly when taken together. Even dose combinations that do not cause unconsciousness or breathing problems can powerfully impair physical activities such as playing sports, driving a car, and operating machinery.

CHAPTER CONTENTS

Of all the chemicals and drugs described in this book, it is disturbing that those used by the youngest people are the most toxic. Because of their easy access to glues, gasoline, solvents, paints, and sprays, many children begin to use drugs by inhaling these common chemicals. They get a buzz, but along with that buzz comes toxic effects that would horrify any chemical safety expert. As this is written, about 10 percent of 8th to 12th grade students report using inhalants at least once in their life.[*]

While inhaling substances for highs has been with us since the Greeks, it has only been since the late 1700s, when nitrous oxide was first synthesized, that people used a chemical regularly for this purpose. This "laughing gas" was prominent in England and was even offered at London theaters for recreational purposes.

As science and industry progressed, a number of volatile compounds, such as gasoline, became readily accessible to the public, and serious inhalant abuse and toxicity became prominent in the 1920s. Beginning in the 1950s, glue sniffing was recognized as a problem, and as more and more chemicals have been marketed, the menu for abuse has grown.

Because of the diversity of the chemicals in this group, we have divided this chapter into three parts—the nitrites, the anesthetics, and the solvents. The anesthetics and some of the nitrites are made for human con-

---

[*] Monitoring The Future Study (http://www.monitoringthefuture.org/pubs/monographs/mtf-overview2012.pdf)

sumption, and at least we understand the effects these have on body function. The solvents, including gasoline, sprays, glues, paints, and cleaning fluids, were never intended for human use. We consider these among the most toxic substances used for drug recreation, and we believe that they should never be used by anyone under any circumstances.

NITRITES

WHAT THEY ARE AND HOW THEY WORK

These chemicals are yellow, volatile, and flammable liquids that have a fruity odor. The nitrites are part of a large class of drugs (including amyl nitrite, butyl nitrite, isobutyl nitrite, and the nitrates like nitroglycerin) that relax the smooth muscles that control the diameter of blood vessels and the iris of the eye, keep the anus closed, and keep us from dribbling urine. When these muscles relax, the blood vessels enlarge and blood pressure falls, more light is let into the eye, and the bowels are let loose.

The medical uses of these compounds have a long and successful history, beginning with the synthesis of nitroglycerin in 1846. That's right—nitroglycerin, the explosive that we all know about, is also a very important drug. Chemists first noticed that just a bit of it on the tongue produced a severe headache (they did not know that this was because it dilated blood vessels); within a year it was medically used by placing it under the tongue to relieve heart pain caused by blocked blood vessels. Like all of these compounds, nitroglycerin relaxes blood vessels, and today it is very commonly used to relieve the pain that patients with heart disease feel when one of the vessels supplying blood to their heart has a spasm (angina pectoris). Remember the scene in movies when an old person grabs his heart, falls to the floor, and struggles to get his medicine out of his pocket? Then the bad guy takes the medicine away and the victim dies? Almost certainly, it was nitroglycerin that he needed.

The nitrites, like the amyl nitrite "poppers" that some people use for recreation, have the same basic effects as nitroglycerin. They were first synthesized and used medically in 1857, but soon physicians found them to be short lasting and unreliable, so nitroglycerin under the tongue has remained the medicine of choice. Amyl nitrite is now used clinically only when the very rapid absorption through inhalation is necessary for some cardiac medical procedures.

The side effects of nitrates and nitrites are common and consistent, and they are related to the dilation of blood vessels. When physicians pre-scribe these drugs, they tell their patients to expect headache, flushing of the skin, dizziness, weakness, and perhaps loss of consciousness if body position is changed rapidly.

As with almost all drugs, there is a lot we don't know about how they work. In this case, we really don't know exactly why the nitrites have the mental effects that make them attractive for some people to use. Users report a physical sensation of warmth, a giddy feeling, and a pounding heart. The psychological sensations are the removal of inhibitions, skin sensitivity, and a sense of exhilaration and acceleration before sexual orgasm. There is a rather common visual disturbance consisting of a bright yellow spot with purple radiations.* These effects may arise from the dilation of some blood vessels in the brain. Finally, some people use these drugs not for the mental effects but for their muscle-relaxing prop-erties to permit anal intercourse.

TOXICITY

Only amyl nitrite is specifically manufactured and packaged for legiti-mate medical use in humans. Unless a product is approved by the FDA, it should be considered an industrial chemical not manufactured for human consumption, because even if it is supposed to be pure, it may contain contaminants that are harmful.

Compared to many drugs, amyl nitrite has less toxicity as long as it is inhaled as intended. Of course, there is always the possibility that the dila-tion of the blood vessels will cause someone with blood circulation prob-lems to have a bad experience. As with all drugs, check with your physician before taking it.

However, there is a major toxicity problem with nitrites if they are swallowed rather than inhaled. When they are ingested, nitrites can cause major medical problems by interfering with the ability of the blood to transport oxygen. Blood carries oxygen to the tissues by way of the red blood cells, which contain hemoglobin to bind the oxygen and then release it to the cells of the body. If the hemoglobin cannot bind oxygen, then a person will die rapidly because the tissues will be suffocated. This

---

* This description of nitrite effects is taken from a paper titled "The Psychosexual Aspects of the Volatile Nitrites" by Thomas P. Lowry, MD, which appeared in the *Journal of Psychoactive Drugs*, vol. 14 (1–2), pp. 77–79.

is the way that cyanide (as used in Nazi gas chambers) works, although nitrites, when ingested, interact a little differently with hemoglobin than cyanide does.

This danger from nitrites is illustrated by an unfortunate incident that occurred in New Jersey in 1992. On October 20 of that year, forty children in an elementary school visited the school nurse because their lips and hands were turning blue, they were vomiting, and they had headaches after lunch. They had a hemoglobin disorder produced by nitrite poisoning. This was not caused by drug abuse but by something much more surprising. The boiler in their school was used to heat the water, and somehow the boiler fluid, which contained a lot of nitrites, was mixed with the hot water used for preparing their soup. Fortunately, the kids received medical care and recovered completely.

TOLERANCE AND WITHDRAWAL

Frequent and repeated use of nitrites and nitrates can produce tolerance and symptoms upon withdrawal. Workers in the explosives industry are a case in point. When a worker first goes on the job and is exposed to nitroglycerin in his environment, he might experience headaches, weakness, and dizziness. After a few days, these symptoms disappear as tolerance develops. However, when he stops working on the weekend, he might suffer headaches and other symptoms due to withdrawal. A few workers have been found to have cardiac and circulatory problems upon withdrawal, and these were treated by giving them nitroglycerin. Since the advent of the nitroglycerin patch for continuous administration of the drug to heart patients, many people have been continuously exposed to nitroglycerin and have developed tolerance to it. The medical profession has become quite concerned because tolerance reduces the effectiveness of the compound, and withdrawal can produce cardiac problems.

NITROUS OXIDE AND OTHER GAS ANESTHETICS

WHAT THEY ARE AND HOW THEY WORK

One of the most important drug experiences anyone can have is that of proper anesthesia in the operating room. Most surgery could not be carried out without proper anesthesia, because it serves three important functions: pain relief, muscular relaxation, and loss of consciousness. All of the gas anesthetics produce the loss of consciousness, and some of them produce the muscle relaxation and pain relief. The reason for pain relief is obvious: No one would want to be cut and probed without pain suppression. Because most general anesthetics produce only loss of consciousness and not pain relief, a pain suppressor is added by an anesthesiologist. Muscular relaxation is required so that involuntary muscle contractions will not get in the way of the surgeon's work. Finally, the loss of consciousness provides the patient relief from the anxiety and boredom of the operating room and perhaps some very welcome amnesia for the whole experience. It is probably this characteristic of gas anesthetics that leads to their abuse.

Surgery wasn't always so easy. Until 1847 it was carried out without the help of anesthetic agents. Before then, there might have been a little help from alcohol or opium, but mostly the patient was held down by an array of strong men while the surgeon worked in spite of the patient's screams. But in 1847 things changed at the Massachusetts General Hospital when ether was first used. Ether had been synthesized recently, and dentists had begun to notice that it had anesthetic properties. A dentist named Morton claimed that he could produce surgical anesthesia with this miracle compound and that he would demonstrate it at Mass General. With the observation gallery full and the men arrayed to hold down the patient as usual, the dentist appeared with the anesthesia machine he had invented to administer the ether. For the first time a patient underwent major surgery while asleep but with his heart and respiration safely intact. Within a month the word had spread and ether became a powerful part of medicine and surgery.[*]

Ether was a great general anesthetic because it fulfilled the requirements for anesthesia, but it was flammable and could cause operating room fires. Modern nonflammable anesthetic agents, like halothane, are both effective and potent, and anesthesia is achieved by breathing air containing just a small percentage of these gases. This makes them great for the operating room and bad for drug abusers, because it is so easy to overdose with them. As higher levels of anesthesia are achieved, three significant systems are impaired: respiration, blood pressure, and heart contractions.

Breathing is produced by the firing of a group of nerve cells deep in the

[*] This description is taken from chapter 13, "The History and Principles of Anesthesiology," in *Goodman and Gilman's The Pharmacological Basis of Therapeutics*, 11th ed., edited by Joel G. Hardman and Lee E. Limbird (New York: McGraw-Hill, 2006).

brain. They are a little resistant to anesthetics, but at high levels their activity is suppressed, and respiration is depressed. Also, the smooth muscle cells that keep blood vessels at a set diameter relax, and this causes a drop in blood pressure. Finally, anesthetics can have a direct effect on the ability of the heart to contract, so it becomes weaker and prone to disruptions of its rhythm. Halothane is particularly tricky because the difference between the concentration that is effective and the one that causes problems is small.

Lots of chemicals and gases can be anesthetic agents, ranging from inert gases like xenon to the most modern compounds. Scientists still do not know exactly how anesthetics work. We know that they suppress the firing of nerve cells, and some can relax various muscles. At this point the best evidence is that, in part, they suppress consciousness by increasing the action of the neurotransmitter GABA (see the "Brain Basics" chapter for an explanation of GABA), which inhibits excitable activity in neural networks.

When an anesthetic gas is inhaled, the sequence of responses is fairly uniform for many of the agents. There can be a brief period of excitation or stimulation, like after the first drink of alcohol. This is followed by pain relief, dizziness, weakness, and general depression of functions. At higher levels, reflexes such as eye blinking, swallowing, and vomiting can be lost. Finally, heart function and respiration are lost and the person dies. Some agents (such as enflurane) have more excitatory effects at overdose, and at high levels these effects can cause epileptic seizures. Other agents produce little in the way of stimulation and only depress the nervous system.

The window of concentration between anesthesia and death is very narrow for these drugs. In medical settings the gases are carefully mixed with oxygen and survival body functions are monitored continuously. The anesthesiologist is fully capable of maintaining breathing for the patient or administering cardiac stimulants if necessary. Even with this level of care, problems can occur. Without careful surveillance, a person is at enormous risk of either dying or sustaining permanent brain damage.

NITROUS OXIDE

Nitrous oxide was first synthesized in the late 1700s as a colorless and almost odorless gas, and its anesthetic and pain-relieving properties were appreciated almost immediately. For quite a while it remained out of the mainstream of medicine, being used mostly for recreation and entertainment at carnivals. The first medical usage of this gas came in the mid-1800s when dentists found it to be an excellent way to suppress pain.

One cannot easily achieve deep surgical anesthesia with nitrous oxide alone, unless it is applied in an environment where the atmospheric pressure is raised. Now it is used medically only to augment other anesthetics and sedatives, or for minor procedures that do not require the loss of consciousness. When nitrous oxide is inhaled in sufficient quantity, there is a euphoric feeling that comes along with the pain relief. The term laughing gas arises from the giddy state that it produces. By comparison to any of the other drugs that people inhale for recreation, nitrous oxide is safer, because it has little effect on critical body functions including respiration; brain blood flow; and liver, kidney, and gastrointestinal tract processes.

The pharmacological mechanisms of nitrous oxide have not been completely determined. Certainly it acts like a general anesthetic and under high pressure can cause loss of consciousness, so, as we suspect with other anesthetics, it may increase GABA inhibition of nerve cells. Part of its effect may also be through the brain's built-in opiate system—the same receptors that morphine and heroin activate. One of the best bits of data that support this is that the specific opiate antagonist naloxone blocks the pain-relieving properties of this gas in animal experiments. In fact, nitrous oxide has been used to treat opiate and alcohol withdrawal symptoms.

The latest research studies suggest that nitrous oxide may also act on a neuronal receptor for the neurotransmitter glutamate, the N-methyl-D-aspartate (NMDA) receptor. This is the same site at which ethanol and ketamine act to produce their dissociative effects—that feeling of being out of your body.

NITROUS OXIDE TOXICITY AND TOLERANCE

As we described, in clinical settings nitrous oxide is rather free of toxic effects. However, for recreational users, there are four dangers: not getting enough oxygen, getting hurt if the gas-delivery device works improperly, experiencing a vitamin B12–related problem that might occur with repeated use, and suffering possible brain toxicity if nitrous oxide is used in combination with other drugs that are NMDA antagonists.

First, remember that nitrous oxide is an anesthetic gas that can cause unconsciousness, or at least make you so disoriented that you lose good judgment. Major problems occur when the user arranges some sort of mask or bag to deliver pure gas and then becomes unconscious and breathes only nitrous oxide: the person is asphyxiated by lack of oxygen.

Second, there is the physical damage to tissues exposed to any gas that is expanding. Anyone who has ever held her hand in front of an air or gas jet knows that expanding gas is cooling. That's the principle underlying air-conditioning units. Some users try to inhale the gas right out of the tank with no regulation of the flow rate, actually injuring their mouths, tracheas, and lungs from the cooling gas. Also, there is the direct physical risk of overexpanding (blowing up) the lungs as the gas flows at a high volume and pressure.

Third, there is an odd complication of prolonged nitrous oxide use that is similar to a vitamin B12 deficiency. A B12-dependent enzyme is inactivated by nitrous oxide, and that leads to the destruction of nerve fibers (a neuropathy) and thus neurological problems. These can include weakness, tingling sensations, or loss of feeling. There are several case reports in the medical literature of nitrous oxide causing severe nerve damage. Some dentists who regularly administer this gas have been found to experience this type of neuropathy.

Fourth, animal studies now suggest that NMDA-receptor blockers like nitrous oxide can be neurotoxic in certain brain areas. The combination of ketamine and nitrous oxide suggests that using these drugs together might be particularly problematic. In animals, they are synergistic, producing much more damage together than would be expected from the simple combination of the two drugs. This should serve as a strong caution to recreational users of nitrous oxide not to combine that use with any other NMDA antagonist like ketamine or ethanol.

Tolerance to nitrous oxide can develop, and the euphoric properties diminish with repeated usage. However, in the recreational setting, where it is used only occasionally, tolerance is unlikely.

SOLVENTS

If there were ever a drug category to "just say no" to, this is it. This category of chemicals is literally a wastebasket of anything that anyone can get in vapor form and then inhale. It consists of all sorts of industrial chemicals, such as toluene, benzene, methanol, chloroform, Freon and other coolants, paints, glues, and gases. **We take the position that these compounds are so toxic to both the first-time user and the long-term**

user that they should never be used under any circumstances. However, we all know that people do inhale these chemicals, and so in the paragraphs that follow, we will describe a few of the more common agents and talk about their toxicity.

WHAT THEY ARE AND HOW THEY WORK

These compounds have only two characteristics in common (other than their toxicity). First, they form gases that can be inhaled. Second, they produce more or less the same feelings that alcohol and anesthetics do.

Solvent abusers usually inhale these chemicals through crude methods, generally called "huffing." They soak rags with the chemicals and breathe through the rags, or put the chemicals in a can or cup and breathe the fumes. As with inhalational anesthetics, once the user begins to inhale, the blood levels peak in a few minutes and most of the agents are absorbed by body fat. As blood levels rise, there is dizziness, disorientation, perhaps an initial period of stimulation followed by depression, and a sense of being light-headed. Some users describe changes in their perception of objects or time and/or have delusions or hallucinations involving any of the senses. Muscular incoordination occurs as levels increase, along with ringing in the ears (tinnitus), double vision, abdominal pain, and flushing of the skin. These are followed by the standard symptoms associated with chemical depression of the central nervous system: vomiting, loss of reflexes, cardiac and circulation problems, suppression of respiration, and (possibly) death.

The most dangerous effect of inhalant use is "sudden sniffing death," which occurs during the abuse of coolants and propellants (like Freon), and fuel gases (like butane and propane), which probably induce abnormal heart rhythms. Death may occur because the chemicals depress the excitability of the heart cells that set the beating pattern, while at the same time increasing the sensitivity of these and other heart cells to the stimulant epinephrine (adrenaline).

We do not know exactly how these compounds produce their mental effects. However, based on the physical effects, we can assume that they work in the same manner as anesthetics.

TOXICITY

There is such a large number of diverse compounds that it is impossible to list all of the toxic effects of every one of them. Also, long-term inhalant users almost always use other drugs, so it is difficult to sort out which toxic effect belongs to which drug or which combination of drugs. But there is one common thread that runs through all of these compounds. Many users are injured not from direct toxic effects of these agents but from trauma related to their use. Disorientation and loss of muscular coordination make accidents more likely, and because many of these chemicals are flammable, serious burns occur. In one well-respected study, 26 percent of deaths associated with inhalant use were from accidents.

Also, people commit suicide under the influence of inhalants. In the same research study, 28 percent of the deaths associated with inhalant use were from suicide. Did the inhalants cause depression and suicide, or did the suicide-prone individuals use inhalants to relieve their pain? Both are probably true, as is the case with so many other drugs.

First-time users can and do die. In a British study of 1,000 deaths from inhalant use, about one-fifth of the deaths were to first-time users. The deaths were from a variety of causes, but each was associated with inhalant use. This is a remarkable statistic, and it should make anyone wary of ever trying these chemicals.

If a person lives long enough to be classified as a chronic inhalant user, what are the long-term effects? Many research studies have been published on this subject, but almost all of them involve case studies of people that were referred with specific medical problems. There are no broad studies covering large numbers of inhalant users without reported medical problems. So we don't know from a statistical perspective what the long-term toxic risk is. However, the medical studies of individuals who do report problems are sobering. One neurological study of abusers referred for medical treatment showed that thirteen out of twenty people (65 percent) studied had central nervous system damage as revealed by clinical examination and neurological imaging. Another study showed damage in 55 percent of a different group of people.

One of the best-studied chemicals is toluene. It is a common industrial solvent and a component of glues. In one study of chronic abusers, eleven out of twenty-four patients had damage to the part of the brain called the cerebellum. This area of the brain is well known for controlling fine, delicate muscle movements, and new studies suggest that it might also play a part in learning. Whether cerebellar impairment clears when the abuse stops has not been determined. Some studies suggest that the cells in this area die. Other brain areas, including the visual and other nerve pathways, are affected as well, but we caution that complete and controlled human studies are impossible to do.

Tests of intellectual function show that abusers have problems with memory, attention, and concentration. Like the physical studies, these studies also considered small numbers of patients who were ill, so we have to be careful in the interpretation of these results. However, there is no question that some people get very sick and suffer substantial central nervous system damage from the chronic use of inhalants.

Other body functions also suffer. The combined list of compounds and the body functions they impair is huge, and it gets larger every day as research shows new effects of these chemicals. It is enough to say that long-term usage of inhalants can damage the heart, lungs, kidneys, liver, blood, and many other areas, in addition to the nervous system. These chemicals are truly not for human consumption.

7

MARIJUANA

Drug Class: No specific class, but legally considered a Schedule I narcotic (classified by the Drug Enforcement Administration as having a high potential for abuse and no accepted medical uses). State laws vary.

Individual Drugs: low-grade marijuana (average 1 to 3 percent delta-9-tetrahydrocannabinol [THC]); high-grade marijuana—sinsemilla (average 10 percent THC, up to about 20 percent); hashish (7 to 20 percent THC); hash oil (up to 70 percent THC)

Common Terms: marijuana, reefer, pot, herb, ganja, grass, old man, Blanche, weed, sinsemilla, bhang, dagga, smoke (dried plant material); hash, tar (hashish); hash oil, oil, charas (extracted plant resin)

The Buzz: People's experiences with marijuana vary widely and depend upon the potency of the drug taken. In general, smoking marijuana first relaxes a person and elevates his mood. These effects are usually felt within a few minutes and followed about a half hour later by drowsiness and sedation. Some people experience this as stimulation followed by a relaxed feeling of tranquility. Users may shift between hilarity and contemplative silence, but these swings often reflect the user's situation.

When hashish or high-grade marijuana is eaten, the effects take much longer to be felt (up to one to two hours) and may produce a more hallucinogenic-type response.

The effects of marijuana on mental functions, including learning and memory, can last far beyond the feeling of being high. Because it takes so long for the body to eliminate THC and its by-products (some of which also affect brain function), a person's cognitive functions can be affected for a day or more after a single dose.

Overdose and Other Bad Effects: Lethal overdose is virtually impossible. Occasionally people report feeling anxious or fearful soon after smoking or after a particularly heavy dose. Relaxed and reassuring conversation with the user is often the best treatment for such an episode.

Although no one has ever died from an overdose of marijuana, it does impair judgment and the kinds of complex coordination needed to drive a car. Automobile accidents and dangerous mistakes are the largest risks of marijuana intoxication. However, people with heart disease or high blood pressure may be at risk because marijuana use increases the heart rate and places a greater workload on the heart. Marijuana can also endanger unintended users. There have been reports of small children unknowingly eating large amounts of cannabis in cookies and going into a coma.

Although the research is still emerging, there is evidence that the repeated use of marijuana during adolescence may result in long-term effects on some brain systems such as those controlling certain aspects of vision. In addition, recent studies have indicated that adolescents may be at greater risk than adults for THC-induced impairment of learning and memory and that prolonged use during adolescence may increase the risk of psychological difficulties later in life (more on these emerging studies later). Finally, there is a troubling association between the incidence of schizophrenia and early onset cannabinoid use. We don't yet understand if this is a causal relationship or merely a correlation.

Dangerous Combinations with Other Drugs: There has been very little work on this topic, but possible dangers include interactions with heart or blood pressure medications or with drugs that suppress the function of the immune system. In addition, one study shows that the combination of marijuana with cocaine can lead to very dangerous effects on the heart.

CHAPTER CONTENTS

A BRIEF HISTORY

All of the marijuana preparations people use for their psychoactive properties derive from the cannabis plant. The first written accounts of cannabis cultivation appear in Chinese records from as far back as 28 BC, though the plant was likely cultivated for thousands of years before that. The Chinese writings indicate that the plant was grown for fiber, but they also recognize its intoxicating and medicinal properties. In fact, THC (and also nicotine and cocaine) have been identified in the internal organs of an Egyptian mummy from approximately 950 BC. By around AD 1000, use of the cannabis plant as an intoxicant had spread to the eastern Mediterranean region, and European explorers to this area returned with fascinating stories of the effects of hashish.

Cannabis had been introduced to eastern Europe much earlier (around 700 BC), but not until Napoleon ventured to Egypt in the early nineteenth century did European culture fully acquaint itself with hashish. By the 1840s, recreational use of cannabis products (as well as a number of other drugs) had grown to be quite chic among the artists and intellectuals of France, many of whom used the drug in their search for new ways to enhance creativity and to view the world.

Although the original European explorers brought cannabis seeds to the New World to produce hemp for rope and cloth, it was not until the early twentieth century that marijuana began to impact United States society directly.

THE CANNABIS PLANT AND ITS PRODUCTS

Cannabis is a highly versatile plant. Hemp, a strong fiber in the stem, has been used to make rope, cloth, and paper. When dried, the leaves and flowers are used as marijuana for their psychoactive and medicinal effects. The roots of the plant have also been used to make medicines, and the ancient Chinese used the seeds as a food. Cannabis seeds are still used for oil and animal feed.

The two most prevalent species of cannabis are *Cannabis sativa* and *Cannabis indica*. In years past, people cultivated *C. sativa* to make hemp. Under natural conditions, it will grow as high as a lanky fifteen to twenty feet, and it still grows wild as a weed across the southern United States.

C. indica has been cultivated throughout the world mostly for the psychoactive properties of its resins. These plants generally grow to no more than a few feet in height and develop a thicker, bushier appearance than *C. sativa.*

The cannabis plant contains more than four hundred chemicals, and several of them are psychoactive. By far the most psychoactive of these is delta-9-tetrahydrocannabinol (THC), found in the plant's resin. The resin is most concentrated in the flowers. In an unfertilized plant, it provides a sticky coating that protects the flowers from excessive heat from the sun and enhances contact by grains of pollen. The vegetative leaves contain a small amount of resin, as do the stalks, but the concentrations in these parts of the plant are so low as to have little intoxicating effect.

Today, much cultivation of "drug" strain marijuana plants has occurred, but the amount of THC present in the flowers of individual plants varies considerably. In addition to the genetic makeup of the plant, the growing conditions, timing of harvest, drying environment, and storage environment can all significantly influence the potency of the final product. As the plant matures, the balance of various chemicals in the resin changes, as does the amount of resin secreted at the flowering tops of the plant. Early in maturation, cannabidiolic acid (CBDA) predominates and is converted to cannabidiol (CBD), which is converted to THC as the plant reaches its floral peak. The extent to which CBD is converted to THC largely determines the "drug quality" of the individual plant. When the plant matures into the late floral and senescent stages, THC is converted to cannabinol (CBN). A plant that is harvested at the peak floral stage has a high ratio of THC to CBD and CBN, and the psychoactive effect is often described as a "clear," or "clean," high, with relatively little sedative effect. However, some cultivators allow the plants to mature past this peak to produce marijuana with a heavier, more sedative effect. The difference between the feelings associated with peak- versus late-harvested marijuana has been described as the difference between being "high" and being "stoned."

Burning marijuana for smoking produces hundreds of additional compounds. So when someone smokes a single joint, hundreds upon hundreds of chemical compounds enter the body. We know that many of these compounds act on various organs and systems in the body, but we don't know what effects most of them have, either acutely or after prolonged use. Many scientific studies have, therefore, restricted their attention to THC, allowing us to evaluate at least some of the effects of cannabinoids on the brain and behavior.

DRUG PREPARATIONS: FROM "HEADACHE POT" TO "HOSPITAL POT"

The products made from marijuana plants for psychoactive effects vary markedly in their THC content and therefore in their psychoactive potency.

Low-grade marijuana is made from all the leaves of both sexes of the plant. These vegetative leaves contain very little THC compared to the pistillate flowers of the female plant or to the smaller leaves adjacent to them. The THC content of such a preparation may be only 1 percent or lower. Smokers sometimes call this "headache pot" because smoking it can produce more of a headache than a high.

Medium-grade marijuana is made from the dried flowering tops of female cannabis plants raised with and fertilized by male plants. Fertilization limits the psychoactive potency of the resulting marijuana because the female flowers secrete THC-containing resin only until fertilization. After that time the flower no longer needs the protective resin, and it begins to produce a seed.

High-grade marijuana is made from the flowering tops, or "cola," of female plants raised in isolation from male plants. The resulting marijuana is called *sinsemilla*, which means "without seeds." As the female flowers mature without fertilization, they continually secrete resin to coat the delicate flowers and small leaves surrounding them; the flowers grow in thick clusters, heavy with resin. When these "buds" are harvested and dried, they contain an average of around 7 to 8 percent THC. Some samples of sinsemilla test as high as 20 percent.

Such powerful marijuana has been called "hospital pot" because occasionally an unsuspecting smoker, expecting the usual gentle high of medium-grade marijuana, gets frightened by the sudden and powerful high of sinsemilla, panics, and winds up in the emergency room. Actually, the best treatment for such a scare is a calm and reassuring "talk down" by a friend. The feeling of panic often arises from an unexpected sense of loss of control, and the individual needs only to be reassured that he is safe and that nothing will threaten him.

Some cultivators in the United States, using well-controlled indoor growing conditions, produce marijuana with THC concentrations as high as 24 percent, but the THC content of most marijuana in the United States is in the range of 10 percent. In recent years United States marijuana has been touted as being ten times more potent now than it was in the 1960s and 1970s. This claim isn't exactly true. Since the 1970s the THC content of marijuana seized by US law-enforcement officials has been measured by the Potency Monitoring Project in Mississippi—a government-funded project. In the early 1970s they generally reported that samples of seized marijuana contained low concentrations of THC—in the range of 0.4 to 1 percent—but those samples often came from low-potency, high-volume Mexican "kilobricks," which probably contained considerably less THC than most of the marijuana that was actually being smoked in those days. Also, it was not until the late 1970s that the higher-potency cannabis products available to smokers, such as buds and sinsemilla, were included in the samples analyzed by the Potency Monitoring Project. Thus, estimates of THC content in the 1970s probably underestimated the average THC content of the marijuana smoked during that period. When independent laboratories analyzed marijuana samples during the 1970s, THC contents were often considerably higher than those reported by the Potency Monitoring Project—in the 2 to 5 percent range—though lower than most marijuana samples today. After 1980 the seized marijuana tested by the Potency Monitoring Project included more representative samples of what was available on the street, and between 1981 and 2000 the THC content hovered between 2 and 5 percent—consistent with the average range of independently tested samples during the 1970s. Still, marijuana cultivators have gotten better at their business, and it is reasonable to assert that THC concentrations in recreationally used marijuana have increased significantly. They may continue to increase as well. The recent changes in both medical marijuana and recreational marijuana laws in some states will probably help to fuel further refinements in both genetic plant selection as well as growing techniques. Although there are alternatives to smoking marijuana, such as eating it or vaporizing it, most marijuana is still smoked, and for most people the less smoke they need to take in, the better. The higher the concentration of cannabinoids in marijuana, the less needs to be smoked, so our bet is that cultivators will be motivated to continue looking for ways to increase the cannabinoid content in marijuana.

Hashish is produced when the resin of the cannabis plant is separated from the plant material. The purest form of hashish is virtually 100 percent resin. In India this pure material is called *charas*. Most hashish, however, is not pure resin and contains varying amounts of plant material as well. It often appears as a dark-colored gummy ball that is rather hard, but not brittle. The average THC content of hashish is around 8 percent but can vary quite a bit—up to 20 percent. Hashish is often smoked in a pipe or rolled into a cigarette along with tobacco or lower-grade marijuana. A more traditional means of smoking hashish is to ignite a small piece and let it burn under a glass or cup. The user then tilts back the glass and inhales the smoke from underneath.

Hash oil is the most potent of the preparations made from the cannabis plant. After the plant is boiled in alcohol, the solids are filtered out, and when the water evaporates, what's left is hash oil. Hash oil is generally a thick, waxy substance that is very high in THC content—ranging from 20 to 70 percent. It can be scraped onto the inner rim of a pipe bowl for smoking or used to lace tobacco or marijuana cigarettes.

HOW THC MOVES THROUGH THE BODY

When marijuana is smoked, the rich blood supply of the lungs rapidly absorbs the THC. This applies to marijuana that is "vaporized" as well. Even though it is not burned, the THC that is mobilized from the plant material in the vaporizer is absorbed through the lungs. Because blood from the lungs goes directly from the heart to the brain, the high, as well as the effects on heart rate and blood vessels, occurs within minutes. Much of the THC is actually gone from the brain within a few hours after smoking. However, THC also accumulates in significant concentrations in other organs, such as the liver, kidneys, spleen, and testes. THC readily crosses from the blood of a pregnant woman into the placenta and reaches the developing fetus.

How the smoker smokes makes a difference in how much of the THC from the marijuana actually gets to the body. A cigarette allows for approximately 10 to 20 percent of the THC in the marijuana to be transferred. A pipe is somewhat more efficient, allowing about 40 to 50 percent to transfer, and a water pipe (or bong) is quite efficient. Because the water pipe traps the smoke until it is inhaled, theoretically the only THC lost is what the smoker exhales. Vaporizers allow a very efficient transfer of THC because, in addition to taking advantage of the rich blood supply in the lungs, vaporized pot does not create smoke that can be irritating to the lungs and cause a person to limit his inhalation or to cough out a "hit" that is too big. This can be a problem as well, particularly when a smoker first switches to a vapor system. Smokers are used to the feeling of smoke in their lungs and often use that feeling as a gauge by which they estimate their intake. The vapor does not irritate the lungs, so that gauge is missing and some new vapor users take in far more THC than they intend until they figure out a new way to estimate their intake.

Although much of the high wears off relatively soon after smoking, THC remains in the body much longer. About half of the THC is still in the blood twenty hours after smoking. And once the blood carrying the THC passes through the liver, some of the THC is converted into other compounds that may remain there for several days. Some of these metabolites have psychoactive effects as well, so that although the initial high may disappear within an hour or two, some of the effects of marijuana on mental and physical functions may last for days.

Not only may THC and its metabolites stay in the blood for days but they also stay in the fatty deposits of the body much longer because they are very lipid-soluble—they easily get absorbed into and stored in fat. THC stored in fatty deposits is released from these tissues slowly over a rather long period of time before finally being eliminated. What all this means is that about 30 percent of ingested THC (and its metabolites) may remain in the body a full week after smoking and may continue to affect mental and physical functions subtly. In fact, the remnants from a single large dose of THC may be detectable up to three weeks later.

All of these rules also apply when marijuana is eaten instead of smoked, except that less THC gets to the brain and it takes a lot longer for it to get there. When marijuana (or any drug) is taken into the stomach, the blood that absorbs it goes to the liver before flowing to the rest of the body (including the brain). This means two things: First, the liver breaks down some of the THC before it ever has a chance to affect the brain. Second, the remaining THC reaches the brain more slowly because of its indirect route through the bloodstream. However, because the body absorbs THC more slowly when marijuana is eaten, the peak levels of the drug last longer (though they are lower than they would be if the same amount were smoked).

Whether the user eats or smokes marijuana and the accompanying differences in the way THC is distributed and metabolized appear to have a substantial impact on the kind of experience he has. Rather than experiencing a sudden change from being straight to being high, the marijuana eater experiences a slow and gradual shift that lasts longer. Many experienced users report that what happens after eating marijuana is more reminiscent of a mild mushroom or LSD trip; it's not simply "getting high." Because high levels of THC can cause hallucinogen-like experiences, people who have eaten marijuana and reported such feelings may actually have achieved higher levels of THC than many smokers—despite the fact that some of it is metabolized by the liver before it gets to the brain—because they ate a larger amount than they would likely have smoked.

EFFECTS ON THE BRAIN

THE BRAIN RECEPTOR FOR THC

Perhaps the most striking finding from research on cannabinoids has been the discovery of a cannabinoid receptor in the brain. In recent years there has been a striking increase in studies of the brain's natural cannabinoid receptors and the chemicals that our brains make to interact with them (the "endocannabinoids"). There is a lot of interest in how these receptors work and what they do. The research is new, but it seems that they play a role in a number of important functions such as learning, control of anxiety, and maybe responsiveness to other drugs, like alcohol. This is not the first time that researchers had located a specific brain receptor for a plant material. The opiate receptor, which was discovered years ago, is involved in the modulation of pain and possibly of stress in a broader sense as well. But while it makes sense that our brains have evolved a chemical system for dealing with pain, it's less clear why it would evolve a receptor for THC and what the implications of this study are for human beings.

Because the brain provides its own cannabinoid receptors, it must also provide its own compound to activate those receptors. Anandamide (the name comes from *ananda*, the Sanskrit word for *bliss*) is one compound, found naturally in the brain, that binds with cannabinoid receptors. Another is called 2-AG. It also activates THC receptors in the brain and is present there in amounts 170 times greater than anandamide. There are likely several other such naturally occurring compounds, because several different subtypes of cannabinoid receptors have been discovered.

THE HIPPOCAMPUS

Although we must leave it to the anthropologists and ethnobotanists to figure out why we have cannabinoid receptors, we do know where they are in the brain, and that might help us to understand the effects of marijuana. The hippocampus is critically involved in the formation of new memories (as we discussed in the "Alcohol" chapter) and has a very high concentration of cannabinoid receptors. Not surprisingly, the inhibition of memory formation by marijuana is its most well-established negative effect on mental function.

In animal studies, when rats are given THC, they show significant deficits in memory formation—not the ability to recall previously learned information, but the ability to store new memories. In fact, an animal treated with THC performs a memory task as poorly as an animal with a damaged hippocampus. Normally the cells in the hippocampus become active and communicate with one another while an animal learns such a task. However, the hippocampal cells in the animals under the influence of THC did not activate in normal ways. These experiments make a compelling case that the memory deficits associated with acute marijuana use are due to the THC suppressing the activity of hippocampal cells and hindering the acquisition of new memory. After the animals' bodies eliminated the THC, their memory and hippocampal function returned to normal. The compound 2-AG, which exists naturally in the brain and stimulates THC receptors, also decreases the ability of the hippocampus to carry out some of its memory-related functions.

But the story is more complicated. Very recent animal studies have shown that several of the effects of THC are quite different in adolescents compared to adults. For instance, with respect to learning and memory, THC disrupts the learning ability in adolescent animals far more potently than it does in adult animals. At this point we're not sure if this is due to a more powerful effect on the memory-related actions of the hippocampus, but some very early findings suggest that might be the case. In addition, THC produces fewer unpleasant side effects like anxiety and aversiveness in adolescents than in adults. Consider that whether users continue to use a drug often depends on whether the pleasure outweighs the pain. So, if the negative effects of THC are felt less by adolescents, they might simply find it more pleasant to use THC than adults do, thus increasing adolescents' risk for more frequent use and the negative consequences that can follow, just as with alcohol.

Whether talking about effects in adults or adolescents, these studies raise an important question about the effects of repeated marijuana use. Does marijuana kill brain cells? At present the weight of the scientific evidence suggests that at the doses, and for the periods of time, that most people use marijuana, the answer is no. A number of studies in rats have investigated the effects of THC on various areas of the brain, including the hippocampus, by giving the rats very large doses of THC for very long periods. While some of these studies suggest that some damage can occur, the way the experiments were done raises questions about the relevance of the results. The studies that show these effects on hippocampal cells generally exposed animals to high concentrations of THC nearly every day for several months (a substantial percentage of the life span of a rat). In many animal studies of this kind, the doses given are hundreds of times higher than a human user would take at any given time. When researchers gave lower doses, far less severe effects were observed in the hippocampus, even when the drug was given for more than twice as long. And even the low doses in many of these animal studies were much higher, were administered much more frequently, and were administered for longer periods of time than most marijuana smokers would ever self-administer the drug. One study did use realistic concentrations of THC to see if they would decrease the chances of young hippocampal cells from rats surviving in culture (i.e., growing on their own in an artificial medium outside the body). Indeed, the presence of THC did appear to decrease the chances of those brain cells surviving. Another study also showed that THC-like drugs decreased the ability of cultured hippocampal cells for making connections with other cells in the culture. While these studies should raise some flags about marijuana use, it's very important to take these results with a grain of salt because the circumstances under which the effects were observed were so unusual.

Generally, science of this sort progresses first by finding significant results in rats or mice and then by attempting to see if the effects show up in nonhuman primates, such as rhesus monkeys, whose brains (and behavior) are more similar to those of humans. Some experiments have used rhesus monkeys to assess the effects of daily exposure to a reasonable amount of marijuana smoke for one year. At the end of the study, the animals' brains were examined, and no evidence was found of permanent gross changes in neurons or of neuronal death. Chronic exposure to THC could conceivably cause long-lasting changes in the organization of the brain, or in the chemistry of neurons, but that would be hard to detect. If the prolonged THC exposure occurred while the brain was maturing (childhood or adolescence), then the changes might be quite important. At this point no biological data support this. However, as we will see later, some human studies show that prolonged marijuana use can have long-lasting effects even after people quit using the drug, and subtle brain changes may underlie these effects.

So what do we make of the animal research? It's not perfect and cannot give us final answers, but there are good reasons to take the results seriously. This is particularly true for studies of the hippocampus, because that structure in the rat is remarkably similar to that in the human, both in how it looks and in what it does (i.e., promote memory). Although profound damage to the hippocampus, as observed in those studies, is unlikely to occur in any but the heaviest of marijuana users, less severe effects could occur with more moderate use. The user might risk subtly damaging hippocampal circuits without causing obvious memory deficits. Her circuits might just be less sharp than they otherwise would have been. We don't know for sure.

OTHER BRAIN REGIONS

Two other areas of the brain particularly rich in cannabinoid receptors are the cerebellum and the basal ganglia. These regions help to coordinate and fine-tune our movements, and marijuana is known to disrupt these functions as well. Cannabinoid receptors, however, are not found in the brain stem, which is critical for breathing. That may be why it's virtually impossible to take a fatal overdose of marijuana.

EFFECTS ON OTHER BODY PARTS

THE IMMUNE SYSTEM

THC receptors are located in many different places outside the brain and affect body functions in a range of ways. One of these is the immune system—the complex of structures, cells, and chemicals that fight infection and disease. In fact, two different main types of cannabinoid receptors have been identified: one that is highly concentrated in the brain, and one that is highly concentrated in certain immune-system cells.

Some animal studies indicate that THC can reduce immunity to infections, but the doses used in these studies were far greater than any human user would take. Unfortunately, at present, there are not enough reliable studies of the effects of THC on human immune function to make a convincing case either way. Still, a lot of basic research is being conducted that suggests that THC may compromise the function of immune cells. We will simply have to wait to see if these early studies prove to be relevant to the human marijuana user.

THE HEART

Smoking marijuana increases the heart rate. Laboratory studies have shown that this increase measures in the general range of twenty to thirty beats per minute. Relatively frequent smokers do develop some degree of tolerance to this effect, but even tolerant individuals experience substantial increases in heart rate after smoking. There have been a number of good studies showing that marijuana also increases heart rate and lowers the heart's pumping efficiency during exercise—essentially increasing the workload on the heart. Clearly these effects on the function of the heart could pose a risk for some individuals, particularly those with heart disease or high blood pressure, or those who take medications that alter heart rhythms. Still, there is no clear evidence that marijuana smoking leads directly to heart disease or produces heart attacks.

THE LUNGS

Two separate and important questions bear on this topic: Does chronic marijuana smoking impair the functioning of the lungs? Does chronic marijuana smoking promote lung cancer?

The answer to the first question is yes. Some studies of chronic, heavy marijuana smokers show that their lungs do not produce as much airflow as the lungs of nonsmokers. In addition, solid studies have found both an abnormal clinical appearance and an abnormal organization of cells in the airways of heavy marijuana smokers relative to nonsmokers and to those who smoked tobacco alone.

Although there have been rumors that marijuana smoke is ten or even one hundred times more toxic to the lungs than tobacco smoke is, the truth is that marijuana smoke and tobacco smoke are rather similar. Many of the toxic compounds, such as tar, carbon monoxide, and cyanide, are found in comparable levels in both types of smoke. One known carcinogen, benzopyrene, is found in both but occurs in greater concentration in marijuana smoke, while tobacco-specific nitrosamines appear only in tobacco. So far, no definitive evidence links marijuana smoking with lung cancer, but eventually such a link will probably be established. One study measured DNA damage (thought to be a precursor to the development of cancer) in lung cells from marijuana smokers, tobacco smokers, and nonsmokers. The study found a trend toward DNA damage in cells from marijuana smokers regardless of whether they also smoked tobacco. This finding suggests that marijuana smoking alone might predispose a person to developing lung cancer. Finally, a recent study of lung cancer patients suggests that people who smoke both tobacco and marijuana regularly may run a greater risk of developing lung cancer, and at an earlier age, than smokers of tobacco alone.

But how much marijuana smoke will prove to represent a risk? Very few marijuana smokers inhale even a significant fraction of the amount of smoke a typical cigarette smoker does in a given day. On the other hand, marijuana is smoked differently from tobacco. The amount of marijuana smoke inhaled per puff is two-thirds larger than a typical puff of a tobacco cigarette. Marijuana smoke is also inhaled more deeply into the lungs and is held in the lungs four times as long. So, the toxins in the marijuana smoke get greater access to the lungs and may do that much more damage than cigarette smoke. One study showed that a marker for carbon monoxide in the blood measured five times higher after smoking a marijuana cigarette than it did after smoking a tobacco cigarette of comparable size. The amount of tar inhaled from the marijuana cigarettes was three times higher and, of that amount, one-third more was retained in the respiratory systems of the subjects who smoked marijuana than in those who smoked tobacco.

Finally, one study indicates that chronic marijuana smokers who smoke three to four joints per day suffer from chronic bronchitis as often as cigarette smokers who smoke a pack or more per day. People in these two groups also showed comparable changes in the structure of their lung cells. These changes do not indicate the presence of lung cancer, but many investigators believe that such changes may foreshadow later development of lung cancer.

THE REPRODUCTIVE SYSTEM

Although marijuana does not make people sterile, as some rumors have asserted, long-term use of marijuana does have some effects on reproductive function. Through its effects on the brain, marijuana suppresses the production of hormones that help to regulate the reproductive system. In men this translates to decreased sperm counts and, occasionally, erectile dysfunction (impotence) from high doses over a long period of time. A woman who uses marijuana regularly over a long period of time may experience irregular menstrual cycles. Though these effects almost never cause complete infertility, they could decrease the probability of conception.

Another hormonal effect of marijuana in men may result in the development of breast tissue (the scientific term for this is gynecomastia), an effect that is generally not enjoyed by men. This is caused by marijuana's ability to increase secretion of the hormone prolactin.

SUBJECTIVE EFFECTS: THE "INTERNAL" EXPERIENCE

As a drug, marijuana defies characterization. It does not fit neatly into any of the general categories into which most other psychoactive drugs can be placed. However, it shares characteristics with many of them. So, rather than try to squeeze the effects into a simple category, we will first describe the range of effects and then try to unify the information in a practical way.

Many, perhaps most, people don't even get high the first few times they use marijuana. This unusual lack of effect may be due to the need to learn the techniques of smoking, such as inhaling the proper amount and holding the smoke in the lungs. It also appears that the user has to learn how to appreciate or perceive the high that the drug provides. This is in marked contrast to most drugs, whose effects lose power with repeated use (tolerance).

People's subjective experiences of THC vary widely. Most people report that the high is intellectually interesting, emotionally pleasing, or both. The "interesting" aspect of the high may relate to what many people call an improvement in sense perception. Some people say that they hear subtleties in speech or music that they wouldn't have recognized without the drug. To some, visual images may seem more intense or more meaningful. Likewise, feelings often seem more intense to the user, or differ from what she'd feel without the drug. Generally, the user interprets these changes in cognition and feeling as positive, but the interpretation also depends on the situation in which they occur. A sense of emotional well-being and intellectual stimulation could switch to something less pleasant in other surroundings.

It's difficult to assess the accuracy of reports of enhanced perception, cognition, or emotional insight because the high does not generally translate well into straight language. Many people who report having tried to write down the subtleties of their thoughts and feelings while on marijuana find afterward that the words they wrote just don't convey the experience. Even if, while they were high, they thought they had captured the moment, the resulting account seems to miss the substance of the experience.

Still, what does this translation problem mean? Are the feelings and thoughts that one has while high not as profound as they seem in the moment? Are they just what one would have thought or felt otherwise, but given a false importance by the drug? Perhaps the drug produces a relaxed and open state in which normal feelings and thoughts can be experienced more fully; but the effect can't be due to relaxation alone because drugs like Valium clearly do not impact perception, thinking, and emotion the way marijuana does. The difference could relate to the effects of THC on memory and the perception of time.

A number of early research reports indicated that marijuana altered the user's perception of time, seeming to slow it down. Users sometimes refer to being on "pot time," when rather brief events seem to stretch on and on; that might be due to wandering concentration or disjointed memory. Perhaps because THC makes it harder to remember one's ideas and feelings, only the most salient or important parts stick in the memory, changing the user's interpretation of the experience. The memory deficiencies that marijuana causes could also contribute to the sense of wonder that many users report. If memory is not being formed as normal, and the usual time-line that one experiences is thereby distorted, things that might otherwise fall from one's attention may remain interesting. A musical phrase, an idea, or a painting might captivate one's attention for far longer than usual if memory is compromised. Is this a bad thing? On one hand it seems reasonable that if one's brain isn't functioning normally, then the resulting perceptions are inaccurate and thus may lack true value. On the other hand, it could be argued that such a cognitive "compromise" may afford one an opportunity to appreciate aspects of an experience that would otherwise be passed over.

TOLERANCE, DEPENDENCE, AND WITHDRAWAL

Although users do develop a tolerance to marijuana, this development is not as simple or as clear-cut as it is in the case of some other drugs. Frequent smokers generally report less of a feeling of being high than infrequent users after smoking a marijuana cigarette or taking oral THC. Interestingly, frequent users also report feeling high after smoking an inactive placebo cigarette (though less so than after a real one). These findings indicate that tolerance to the subjective effects of marijuana does develop and that there is a significant learning effect associated with chronic marijuana use. Perhaps frequent smokers associate the feeling of being high with the various environmental stimuli that surround the act of smoking, so that smoking a joint (even an inactive one) and expecting to get high leads them to feel high despite the lack of drug.

Dependence can be measured in a variety of ways, but in general it seems that even heavy marijuana users do not become dependent in all of the ways that users of some other drugs do. For example, one way to assess dependence is to determine if the individual craves the drug so much that it comes to control much of her behavior. The dependent person will have difficulty in controlling her use of the drug and will sacrifice much to get it. The number of people who have this level of difficulty with marijuana is relatively small, and there does not appear to be a significant degree of craving associated with marijuana. Some individuals have reportedly experienced psychological dependence, but these cases are hard to assess because each is unique and there have been no truly well-controlled studies.

Withdrawal occurs when, after chronic use, a drug is abruptly withdrawn and the user suffers a kind of rebound of unpleasant, often dangerous, effects. The classic symptoms are the agitation and illness associated with opiate withdrawal and the anxiety, and sometimes tremors and seizures, associated with alcohol withdrawal. Even after the most intense exposure, the effects associated with marijuana withdrawal are mild. For example, in one study people consumed ten- or thirty-milligram doses of THC by mouth every three to four hours around the clock for up to twenty-one days. These are very large doses (even taken orally), given continuously over a long time, and do not model the intake of any but the most extreme users of marijuana. When they stopped, the subjects most frequently showed irritability and restlessness. Less prominent symptoms were insomnia, sweating, and mild nausea. When THC was re-administered to these subjects, the symptoms went away, indicating that they had been the result of the THC withdrawal. Another study of people who had smoked several times daily for about fourteen years indicated that they experienced a number of clinically significant symptoms when they quit smoking for a period of three days. These symptoms included irritability, decreased appetite, and difficulty sleeping—the kinds of problems expected after withdrawal from heavy marijuana use. This study is important because it documents that there are clinically significant symptoms that accompany the abrupt cessation of marijuana use. There's a lot more to addiction than withdrawal symptoms, but it will always be tempting for a person to use a drug again if quitting results in uncomfortable withdrawal effects.

One area of the brain that is involved in the rewarding (and possibly addicting) effects of some drugs is the nucleus accumbens, which contains cells that use the neurotransmitter dopamine (please see the "Addiction" chapter). Until recently there was no evidence that THC had any effect on dopamine activity in this region, leading many people to believe that marijuana carried no risk of addiction at all. Although the jury is still out on whether marijuana is addictive, there are some studies in animals that indicate it can increase dopamine levels in the nucleus accumbens. Remember that when it comes to science, it is never wise to bank on the results of just a few studies, but those reports at least raise the possibility that THC has some effect on the brain's reward systems. If so, then marijuana may join the long list of other things that stimulate these circuits, including nicotine, food, heroin, sex, and alcohol. We expect that scientific research will eventually show that anything pleasurable (even a good biscuit) will evoke dopamine, and if the pleasurable experience is repeated enough, then withdrawal from it will produce discomfort. (Who wants to give up tasty food?) But the key here is a matter of degree. Maybe food, sex, and marijuana release some dopamine in the reward circuit, but cocaine is so much more effective that it is therefore much more addicting. As we continue to emphasize, good information is critical to making healthy decisions, and just because someone concludes that marijuana may stimulate the reward circuit, we should not infer that this drug is the pharmacological equivalent of other drugs like cocaine or heroin.

EFFECTS ON MEMORY AND OTHER
MENTAL FUNCTIONS

ACUTE EFFECTS

Although researchers cannot stick electrodes into the brains of human subjects to see exactly how marijuana affects memory, some have conducted revealing studies on the memory effects of acute marijuana intoxication. In general these studies show what the animal studies predicted they would. While people are high, they are significantly less able to store new information than when they aren't. In fact, the single most common and reproducible cognitive effect of marijuana is this interference with memory processing. It is important to emphasize that, as with alcohol exposure, the deficit is not in the ability to recall old, well-learned memories, but rather in the ability to form new ones.

For example, after smoking one joint, people in their twenties were significantly impaired in their ability to recall the details of a story that they both read and listened to while high. However, if they learned the story the day before they smoked the joint, then the subjects could recall the story with no trouble. So, it's probably the case that marijuana compromises the ability to learn new information but not the ability to recall previously learned information.

"RESIDUAL" AND CHRONIC EFFECTS

Because THC remains in the body (and thus the brain) for so long, it is important to know how long memory (and other cognitive functions) may be affected. Researchers have undertaken a considerable number of studies, but most of them are flawed because they fail to control for influences such as smoking experience or intelligence. Even so, when all the findings are boiled down, marijuana appears to have residual effects on cognitive functions (including memory) for up to forty-eight hours. It is therefore probably not wise to take a challenging test or to fly an airplane within a day or two after smoking marijuana. Furthermore, a person who smokes marijuana every few days is probably never completely free of its effects on thinking and problem solving, living consistently in a somewhat compromised cognitive state.

In one well-controlled study, investigators recruited college students in two distinct groups: "heavy" users (those who had used marijuana nearly every day during the month before the study and had THC in their blood when they came to the laboratory) and "light" users (those who had used marijuana on average only once in the thirty days before coming to the laboratory and had no THC in their blood when they arrived). The students spent the night under supervision and were given a battery of mental tests the next morning. The intent was to assess the cognitive function of the heavy users, but a number of interesting differences (and similarities) appeared between the backgrounds of the heavy- and light-using groups. The heavy users tended to come from more affluent families with higher incomes. There were no differences between heavy and light users in psychiatric history: neither group had more psychological problems than the other. However, when their present emotional state was assessed, the heavy users were happier (remember, though, that they still had THC in their systems).

The mental tests revealed two important findings. First, the heavy users showed much less mental flexibility in problem solving than did the light users. They often made the same mistake over and over again on one test, indicating that they tended to become locked in to a particular problem-solving strategy and had a hard time generating new ones even when the current one no longer worked for them. The heavy users also showed impaired memory function, but this problem did not appear on all of the memory tests that they took. They were as good as light users at remembering a short story that was read to them. However, male heavy users (but not female heavy users) did not perform as well as light users at recalling figures that they were shown and then asked to draw from memory. The heavy users also had significantly more trouble learning lists of words over time.

So, what we know from this study is that about one day after their last dose, people who smoke daily are significantly impaired on some measures of memory for words and pictures, and make more errors than would be expected on a problem-solving test that requires mental flexibility. But because none of the light users had THC in their systems when they came to the lab, we do not know the effects of marijuana one day after use in people who use the drug less than daily. The other thing we don't know is how long the residual impairment of heavy users lasts, or if there is any permanent impairment that is due to brain damage rather than residual THC in their brains.

This study did try to address the second question. The investigators looked a bit more closely at the light users and found that although they had all used marijuana very little during the month before the study, some had used it more than others across their lifetimes (and some quite heavily earlier in their lives). When the light users were divided up into subgroups based on their life histories of marijuana use, there was no relationship between the scores they got on the mental tests and how much marijuana they had used in the past. With no THC in their systems at the time of testing, it did not matter how much these subjects had smoked in the past—there were no apparent permanent effects. But once the light users were subdivided, the number of subjects in each subgroup became rather small. So, from a purely statistical point of view, the lack of effects should be interpreted cautiously until more studies are done with larger numbers of subjects.

Another project studied people who had smoked almost daily (about two joints per occasion) for either an average of ten or twenty-four years, and compared their mental performance to a group of nonusers. Some learning deficits were found among the longer-term users, but there were some problems with the study. First, the users were all individuals who were seeking treatment for drug problems, and many of them had chronically used other drugs in addition to marijuana. Even more troubling, the average time between when the subjects had last smoked and when they were tested was only seventeen hours. Clearly, the outcomes reflected residual effects of recently smoked marijuana, so it's impossible to attribute the observed effects to a permanent effect of chronic marijuana use.

A better study looked closely at the cognitive function of two distinct groups of users and comparable control groups of nonusers. The people in the first group were in their midforties and had been smoking heavily (about five joints per day) for an average of thirty-four years. The people in the second group were younger (average twenty-eight years old) and had been smoking about four joints per day for eight years. The performance of these groups was compared to age-matched control subjects who were not marijuana users. The older group of chronic users performed worse than the other groups on tests of verbal learning and memory as well as on a test of divided attention. There are several important points about this study. First, it indicates that after many years of very heavy marijuana use, there are some cognitive deficits that appear to be permanent. But the people who had been smoking heavily for eight years showed no deficits. There is another way in which the two user groups were different—the age at which they started using marijuana. The older group had started using at about twelve years of age while the younger user group had started at about twenty years of age. Starting so young may have had something to do with the deficits that they experienced as adults.

Does this finding suggest that repeated exposures to THC during adolescence may result in damage or deficits that would not occur with the same levels of exposure in adulthood? For now the best answer is that we don't know, but there are some studies that are worth thinking about. One study of visual function suggested that smoking marijuana at an early age may change the way the visual system develops. Regular smokers and nonsmokers were asked to perform a task that forced them to visually scan what they were shown and identify important features of what was presented. This type of visual scanning ability is known to develop quite rapidly between the ages of twelve and fifteen. The investigators found that visual scanning performance was impaired in some of the smokers, and the factor that predicted deficits was the age at which the person had started smoking. Deficits were associated with smoking initiated before age sixteen; those who started after age sixteen showed no deficits. This study is not without its difficulties, though. Again, there is a chance that the smokers may have had acute effects—the average time between their last joint and testing was about thirty hours. Still, the results suggest that those who start smoking marijuana in their early teens may be at greater risk for long-term impairment than are those who start later.

In recent years some reports have emerged suggesting that early marijuana use may increase a person's chances of developing psychological disorders later. The kinds of disorders indicated are serious—delusions and other symptoms characteristic of schizophrenia—so we take this possibility seriously. These studies raise the question of whether exposure to THC during adolescent brain development changes the trajectory of that development in ways that compromise later mental health. The statistical risk of developing these disorders is quite modest, and the vast majority of marijuana users do not develop psychotic disorders, so scientists speculate that for a subpopulation of people who are predisposed to psychosis, perhaps based on genetic characteristics, repeated marijuana smoking in adolescence conveys a relatively high risk of developing a psychological disorder later. Specifically, in people who have abnormal expression of a gene that gives rise to the brain enzyme catechol-O-methyltransferase (COMT—an enzyme that breaks down the neurotransmitters dopamine and norepinephrine), the association between adolescent marijuana use and later psychotic symptoms appears to be higher than in the general population. The relationship between early marijuana use and later psychotic symptoms depends on multiple factors, including the amount of marijuana used, the age at which the use is initiated, and a person's genetic vulnerability. It's complicated. But psychosis is serious and can be life-threatening, so teens need to understand this risk.

Another thing that teens need to understand is that they are probably more vulnerable than adults to experiencing long-term declines in cognitive function after a history of heavy marijuana use. A recent study assessed IQ and other more specific measures of cognitive function in a group of 1,037 thirteen-year-olds. Then they followed the subjects while they went through adolescence and early adulthood. During those years, they kept track of their marijuana use by interviewing the subjects at ages eighteen, twenty-one, twenty-six, thirty-two, and thirty-eight. At age thirty-eight, they also retested their IQ and cognitive functioning. The subjects who had been diagnosed with cannabis dependence across those years showed significant declines in IQ and on a broad range of other cognitive functions, like the ability to think abstractly and process information quickly. Because people who become cannabis dependent often wind up with less education, it was important that the study control for this difference. But even when the education level was controlled in the statistical analysis, those subjects with histories of cannabis dependence did significantly worse than those without. There were also two additional factors that predicted the amount of cognitive decline in marijuana users—the persistence of their use and the age at which they began using. The more times a subject had been diagnosed as dependent on cannabis between the ages of thirteen and thirty-eight, the greater his or her amount of cognitive decline. This makes sense, of course, but what was really striking was that significant cognitive decline was only observed in subjects who had started using marijuana weekly (or received a cannabis dependence diagnosis) before the age of eighteen. Among those who started using in adulthood, there were not significant declines in cognitive function. This finding is important and is consistent with the results of other studies that have shown deficits in higher order cognitive functions and verbal IQ among chronic cannabis users who started in adolescence but not among those who started in adulthood. And the difference was noticeable. When people who knew the participants well were asked, they reported having observed cognitive problems among the participants who had shown cognitive decline on the formal tests. Finally, and importantly, quitting cannabis use did not fully restore neuropsychological functioning among the subjects who had started using cannabis during adolescence, suggesting that regular marijuana use during adolescence may actually cause long-term damage to the brain.

We went into detail about this recent study because we think it was well done and the results are important. But it's also important to recognize that the study was done in one region, and that although there was a large number of subjects overall, some of the groups of cannabis dependent users had only forty to eighty subjects each. This is still a good number, but it's not huge, so some caution is warranted when trying to generalize the results. Another factor to consider is that the subjects who showed cognitive declines were pretty heavy users—having received at least one diagnosis of cannabis dependence and/or engaged in weekly use before the age of eighteen. So these results may not apply to those who engage in occasional, recreational use of marijuana. Regardless, teens and their parents should take this study very seriously. In our view, it represents one of the good reasons why young people should think very carefully before using marijuana.

These and other recent studies that underscore the risks of marijuana use in adolescence occur at a time when teens' perceptions of the harmfulness of marijuana use have been declining. Over the past several years, the Monitoring the Future survey of adolescent drug use and attitudes has shown increasing marijuana use by teens, which is probably associated with their decreasing perception of its harmfulness. This could be related to the increasing public conversation about medical uses for marijuana and the legalization efforts for recreational use in some states. (See the chapter on legal issues for more discussion of the recent changes in marijuana laws.)

It will take time for science to fill in the gaps in this research; meanwhile, it is our view that these findings should be taken as a strong caution about adolescents using marijuana.

DOES MARIJUANA PROMOTE AGGRESSION?

In a word, no. In the late 1920s and 1930s, as US society was beginning to recognize marijuana use, articles appeared in some newspapers associating marijuana with crime. Some government agencies of the time promoted the idea that marijuana use led to aggressive behavior. Even the editors of *Scientific American* wrote in 1936 that when marijuana was combined with other intoxicants, it made the smoker vicious and prone to kill. (It is interesting, given the political climate of the time, that the editors of *Scientific American* chose to attribute the viciousness to the effects of marijuana and not to any of the other "intoxicants," which included alcohol.) This image of marijuana effects is very inconsistent with the 1960s image of a dreamy-eyed, smiling young woman at Woodstock offering a joint to the camera. Though there lingers some debate about the effects of marijuana on aggressive behavior, a clever laboratory study shows clearly that, if anything, marijuana decreases aggressive behavior in people when they are provoked. The study is worth explaining.

Researchers brought young men into the laboratory and showed them two buttons on a table. They were told that by pressing button A, they would accumulate points that would result in a reward. They were also told that pressing button B would remove points from another subject in a different room who would be engaged in the same task (there was actually no other subject). As the men worked at pressing their buttons, every so often they would see that they were losing points. This was attributed to the actions of the other (fictitious) subject. The experimenters could arrange to have more or less points removed to create the impression that the other subject was being mildly or highly aggressive to the actual subject. Not surprisingly, as the fictional subjects became more aggressive, the real subjects began to press button B to retaliate. Then the subjects smoked either a marijuana cigarette or a placebo cigarette that tasted like marijuana but had no THC and continued the button exercise. After smoking the marijuana cigarettes, the subjects showed a clear decrease in aggressive response to the highly provoking actions of the "other subject." Although this was obviously not a study of aggression on the street, it does have the scientific advantage of well-controlled treatments and well-defined measurements. Moreover, it is consistent with the vast majority of anecdotal reports about marijuana effects, which claim that it makes people more peaceful.

EFFECTS ON MOTOR PERFORMANCE AND DRIVING

Some people believe that marijuana does not impair the ability to drive. The truth is that it does. The decrease in attention and concentration that marijuana produces makes operating any kind of heavy machinery very dangerous. A marijuana smoker's reflexes may be in good enough shape to control a car, but they may not be of much use if she stops paying close attention to the road. Similarly, the marijuana-induced changes in perception and sense of time may be entertaining on the couch in the living room but could be deadly on the highway. Laboratory studies using driving simulators have shown that marijuana significantly impairs both the ability to concentrate and the ability to make corrections. This appears to be true on the real road as well. One study showed that young people who reported driving frequently while on marijuana were twice as likely to be involved in accidents as their nonsmoking peers. The best bet is never to drive while using any drug (legal, illegal, or prescription) known to impair motor or cognitive skills.

ARE THERE MEDICAL USES?

This is a hot-button issue. When medical professionals discuss the possible medical uses of marijuana, their emotions seem to escalate, and when passions run high, otherwise fair and reasonable thinkers can sometimes interpret data and draw conclusions in ways that they normally would not. In trying to make sense of the debate, we want to present simply what the scientific and clinical literature tells us about the potential usefulness of marijuana as a medicine: in general, there are indeed valid medical uses for cannabis products.

Prior to 1900, cannabis products were used frequently as appetite stimulants, muscle relaxants, and analgesics (pain relievers). In the early twentieth century, though cannabis was still used, its prevalence began to decline as competitive drugs became available. Finally, in 1937, the Marijuana Tax Act effectively stopped all legal medical use. Marijuana is currently categorized in Schedule I under the Controlled Substances Act, passed in 1970. This schedule lists drugs that have a high potential for abuse, lack an accepted medical use, and are unsafe for use even under medical supervision. In 1972 the National Organization for the Reform of Marijuana Laws (NORML) began a campaign to have marijuana moved to Schedule II so that it could be legally prescribed. NORML asked the Bureau of Narcotics and Dangerous Drugs (now called the Drug Enforcement Administration—DEA) to begin the process of rescheduling the cannabis products. It took more than a decade, but the required public hearings were initiated in 1986. After two years of hearings, the administrative law judge for the DEA, Francis L. Young, wrote that marijuana was "one of the safest therapeutically active substances known to man" and that marijuana fulfilled the legal requirement of currently acceptable medical use. However, his order that marijuana be moved to Schedule II was overruled by the DEA.

As the debate progressed, the demand for marijuana for medical uses grew, and the Food and Drug Administration (FDA) was persuaded to issue a handful of approvals for patients under a special permission called an Individual Treatment Investigational New Drug Application (sometimes called a Compassionate Use IND). By the late 1980s the number of requests for Compassionate Use INDs increased markedly as AIDS patients and their physicians asked for permission to use marijuana to enhance appetite to combat the physical wasting associated with AIDS. However, in 1991 the program was halted because it was at odds with the (first) Bush administration's anti–drug abuse policies. Many AIDS patients were left in the position of having to break the law to use marijuana to fight their physical wasting. In 1997 a group of physicians and researchers in San Francisco, who were trying to initiate controlled studies of the clinical effectiveness of marijuana for this purpose, estimated that there were two thousand AIDS patients in San Francisco alone who were using marijuana in this way. In 1999 the Institute of Medicine of the National Academy of Sciences conducted a study that concluded that marijuana had both potential therapeutic value and potential harmful effects. The harmful effects that were of particular concern were related to smoked marijuana. Thus, marijuana was cast in the same light as many drugs that are under investigation for human medical use. The study recommended that more research be conducted on the effects of marijuana and on the development of nonsmoking delivery systems. This call for more research on medical marijuana usage was echoed by the American Medical Association in 2001.

Two of the chief concerns about smoked marijuana as a medical treatment are the risk to lung function and the presence of carcinogens. Although cancer patients might use marijuana only once every few weeks, AIDS or glaucoma (see the following) patients would use it much more frequently. The proponents of medical usage argue that water pipes would address the concern about the smoke's effect on the lungs to some degree and that nonsmoking systems for delivering marijuana vapors may bypass the concerns about carcinogens that are mobilized by combustion altogether. For example, it might also be possible to extract the therapeutic compounds from marijuana into a fluid suspension delivered with an inhaler. Another concern relates to possible toxic effects to the immune system, particularly in AIDS patients who are already immunocompromised. Although this subject is currently debated in the medical literature, one large-scale study of HIV-infected men found no evidence that marijuana accelerated the process of immune-system failure.

NAUSEA

One of the more unpleasant side effects of cancer chemotherapy (treatment with drugs to kill the cancer cells) is that the medicines make many people feel quite nauseated. THC clearly helps to control this side effect. In fact, THC has been available since 1985 in capsule form for use by cancer patients under the brand name Marinol (dronabinol), categorized by the DEA under Schedule II. Marinol has been shown to help control nausea and also to help patients gain weight. However, some physicians and patients argue that, compared to marijuana (which they use illegally for the same purpose), Marinol's dosage and duration of effect (because it is taken orally rather than smoked) are harder to control and that it is simply not as effective. This might be so because cannabidiol, a component of natural marijuana that is not present in Marinol, has antianxiety effects that patients find helpful in addition to THC's purely antinausea effects. Proponents argue that until a synthetic THC preparation can be made that truly reproduces the effects of the various cannabinoid compounds in marijuana, marijuana cigarettes should be made available for medical use. A 1990 survey showed that 44 percent of oncologists (cancer specialists) had suggested the use of marijuana to some of their patients to help relieve the side effects of their chemotherapy.

GLAUCOMA

Research in the 1970s found that marijuana significantly reduced the pressure of the fluid within the eye that is too high and potentially damaging in glaucoma patients. At present, however, neither marijuana nor Marinol is used as a treatment. Scientists are studying whether THC-like compounds might be effective treatments if kept exclusively in the eye to treat intraocular pressure; in this way, patients would not become stoned.

Mexican brown heroin and Southeast Asian heroin.

Mexican black tar heroin.

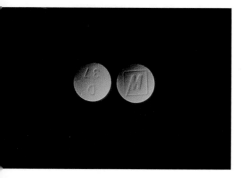

Demerol (meperidine).

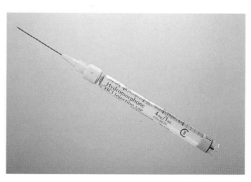

Hydromorphone.

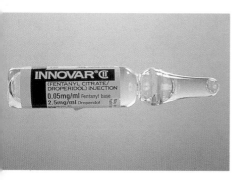

Innovar (fentanyl).

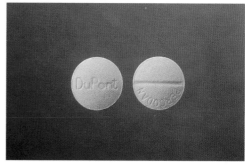

Percodan (oxycodone).

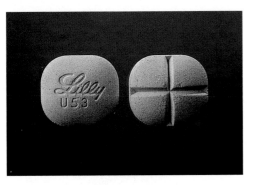

Methadone.

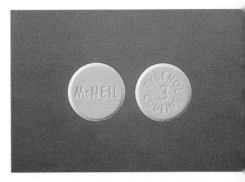

Tylenol with Codeine No. 3 (codeine).

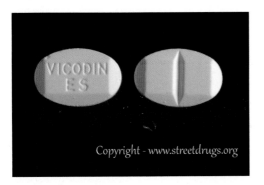

Vicodin (hydrocodone).

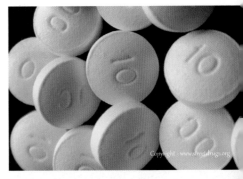

Oxycodone.

OxyContin (oxycodone).

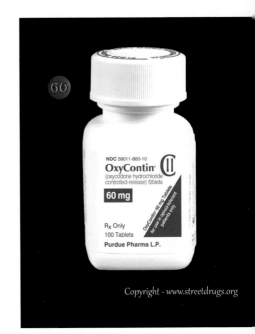

PCP is most commonly sold as a powder (left) or liquid (center), and applied to a leafy material such as oregano (right), which is then smoked.

Collage of LSD blotter paper.

Tryptamines.

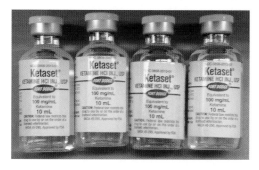

Ketamine, also known as Special K.

Marijuana rolled into cigarettes for smoking.

Marijuana abusers prefer the *colas*, or buds of the plant, because of their higher THC content. Leaves are discarded or used as filler.

Hollowed-out cigars packed with marijuana, called blunts.

Amber, viscous hash oil.

Black, resinous sticks of hashish.

Baby pot plant.

Spice (synthetic cannabis).

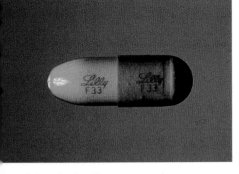

mytal (amobarbital).

Nembutal (pentobarbital).

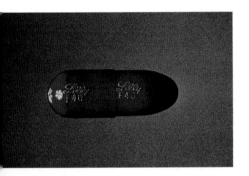

econal (secobarbital).

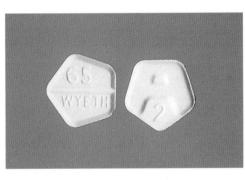

Ativan (lorazepam).

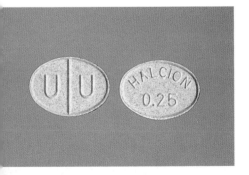

Halcion (triazolam).

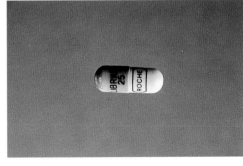

Librium (chlordiazepoxide).

Valium (diazepam).

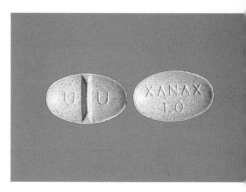

Xanax (alprazolam).

Sniffing an inhalant-soaked rag from a bag is a form of huffing.

GHB is a generally odorless, colorless liquid or white powder.

Rohypnol (flunitrazepam). "Roofies," as they are known on the street, are sold inexpensively in Mexico. They are smuggled into the United States, where they have recently become a problem among American teens. The problem is rapidly spreading from the American Southwest to other parts of the United States.

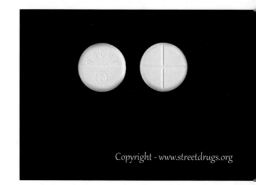

Testosterone.

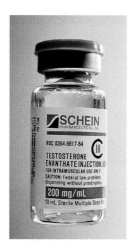

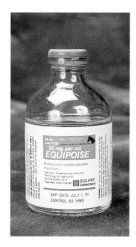

Counterfeiters duplicate packaging for black-market sales.

owdered cocaine.

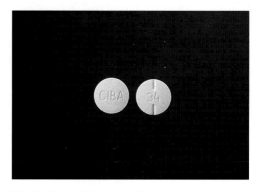

Ritalin (methylphenidate).

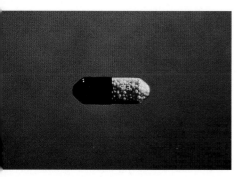

exedrine (dextroamphetamine).

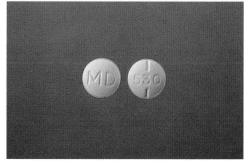

Methylphenidate.

Crack cocaine.

Bath salts.

Ice, so named because of its appearance, is a smokable form of methamphetamine.

Methcathinone, or cat.

SEIZURE DISORDERS

There have been some recent high-profile cases of children with intractable seizures (those that cannot be treated with conventional anticonvulsant medications) being successfully treated with cannabis. The case of Charlotte Figi gained international attention in 2013. She began having seizures at about one month of age and by the time she was five years old, she was having three hundred seizures per week, her cognitive function had declined, and her parents were told there was essentially nothing that could be done. Desperate, her parents tried cannabis, and it essentially put a stop to the seizures. It turned out that the particular strain of cannabis they used had little appeal to recreational users because it didn't create much of a high. It was low in THC but rich in CBD—which is not known to be psychoactive. Studies had shown that both THC and CBD have anticonvulsant properties in animal models, but they control seizures through different mechanisms. Much more research will be needed to fully explore the potential for marijuana as an antiseizure medication. It might only work in the most severe cases, or maybe only in children. But it could be that truly "medicinal" strains could be developed that would minimize the high (for those who don't want it) and maximize the clinical effects.

SPASTICITY

Spasticity is a disabling movement disorder, associated with multiple sclerosis. The drugs that are typically used to treat it—including anticonvulsants and benzodiazepines—are helpful but limited in their effectiveness. Recently, clinicians in Spain and the United Kingdom have begun using a cannabinoid drug, called Sativex, as an "add on" medication in adult patients for whom the usual treatments are not adequate. Like the strain of marijuana that was effective against seizures in the aforementioned children, Sativex has a balance of THC and CBD that diminishes the psychoactive effects of the THC. Studies are underway to evaluate its possible benefits and risks, and early reports indicate that it has long-term clinical benefit for that group of patients in the absence of any serious side effects. It will take time for those studies to be completed, but so far it appears that this type of cannabinoid mixture is safe and effective for this specific group of patients.

Marijuana is by no means the only drug that is effective in treating the aforementioned conditions, but there certainly is a strong argument for the value of marijuana as medicine. Multiple sclerosis and other disorders that produce spasticity with impaired muscle control (marijuana works as a muscle relaxant), seizures, chronic pain, and migraine headaches have also been reported to respond positively to marijuana. The proponents of marijuana as medicine point out that it is hard to beat in terms of safety. As we described, it is next to impossible to overdose on marijuana, and its relative lack of addictive properties makes it safer on that score than many medicines currently used as muscle relaxants or for pain management. On the other hand, to relieve pain, sufferers would have to use enough marijuana to become stoned, which would greatly impact their ability to work or go to school. Many currently accepted pain-relieving medicines don't have such a strong effect on mental function.

LEGISLATIVE ACTIONS FOR MEDICAL USE

In November 1996, Arizona and California passed propositions related to the medical use of marijuana. In California, the Compassionate Use Act of 1996 (Proposition 215) passed by a margin of 12 percent—56 percent to 44 percent. Essentially, the proposition stated that patients or defined caregivers who possess or grow marijuana for medical treatment as recommended by a physician were exempt from laws that otherwise prohibit the possession or cultivation of marijuana. It also stated that physicians who recommend the use of marijuana should not be punished in any way for doing so. The language of this proposition indicated that marijuana need only be "recommended" by a physician and did not specify the conditions for which it may be recommended. The proposition went on to state that persons using marijuana for medical purposes could still be held liable if they engaged in conduct that endangered others or if they diverted marijuana for nonmedical purposes. Still, it is clear from a reading of the proposition that nearly twenty years ago, California voters endorsed a very loose interpretation of which uses might be considered "medical."

In Arizona, the Drug Medicalization, Prevention, and Control Act of 1996 (Proposition 200) passed by a vote of 65 percent to 35 percent. This proposition offered a similar bottom line as far as it concerns the medical use of marijuana, but it went considerably further in that it enabled physicians to recommend the use of other drugs currently grouped with marijuana under Schedule I of the DEA classification. Schedule I drugs include LSD, heroin, and other notorious drugs of abuse. Many people believe that marijuana should not be listed on Schedule I in the first place, arguing that it is not addictive and is far less powerful than most of the drugs on the list. Aside from that debate, however, the Arizona proposition raised serious concerns about other Schedule I drugs potentially being used as medicine.

Within two months of the passage of these two propositions, the US Congress conducted hearings on the issue, and the Clinton administration crafted a response. The DEA (a federal agency) has always issued licenses to physicians that allow them to prescribe controlled substances that are approved for medical use, so that without this DEA license, a physician would be limited in terms of what drugs she could prescribe. To discourage physicians in California and Arizona from recommending marijuana for medical use, the federal government has stated that it may investigate physicians who recommend marijuana and potentially withdraw their DEA licenses. Several physicians, health organizations, and patients sued the government in response.   Since 1996, twenty states and the District of Columbia have either passed medical marijuana initiatives or have passed legislation that is favorable toward the medical use of marijuana, and Washington and Colorado have enacted laws that legalize the possession of small amounts for recreational use. All of these initiatives have generated some degree of conflict with federal laws that strictly forbid marijuana use or possession for medical or personal use. The result has been an ongoing series of legal challenges and responses between state and local interests on one hand and federal authorities on the other. The ultimate outcome of these challenges remains to be seen, but they raise very powerful questions about patients' rights, states' rights, and the role of science in determining medical policy and law. In a marked shift from the past policies of past administrations, President Obama has asked the Justice Department to refrain from enforcing the marijuana laws in certain circumstances for states that permit its possession.

Some people and agencies believe that medical marijuana propositions are thinly veiled maneuvers toward legalizing drugs. The concern is that once a drug (or a group of drugs) is approved for medical use, the next step could be legalization for nonmedical uses. Whether or not this is a legitimate concern, the potential usefulness of marijuana as medicine and the aforementioned initiatives have added considerable fuel to another even more emotional debate: the outright legalization of marijuana.

THE QUESTION OF LEGALIZATION

The subject of the legal status of marijuana (and all drugs of abuse, for that matter) still evokes strong emotional responses in some people. But in recent years, the tone of the debate has shifted away from emotional and moralistic arguments and more toward a discussion that looks closely at the issues from a broad perspective, which includes pharmacological, social, and economic viewpoints. The legal status of any drug depends heavily on the culture in which that drug is evaluated and the prevailing social conventions relative to that drug. For example, in the United States today (at least at the federal level), we choose to have marijuana categorized as a Schedule I narcotic and to keep it illegal, while we allow the sale and advertisement of known addictive drugs such as nicotine and alcohol. Other societies have chosen to prohibit alcohol consumption vigorously while placing little or no sanction on the use of cannabis products. We should recognize the two principal factors that change attitudes and laws about drugs: culture and time.

ATTITUDES AND LAWS IN THE UNITED STATES

What had been a fascination with marijuana in the nineteenth century among artists and intellectuals was quickly overshadowed in this country by fears about an association between marijuana and crime, particularly violent and sexual crime. Although we now know that there is no such relationship, by the mid-1920s the popular media had seized on this idea, and concern began to grow. Although then, as now, there were no scientific data to support the conclusion that the use of marijuana led to violent behavior, by the mid-1930s all the states of the union had laws regulating the use of marijuana. As we mentioned, even magazines devoted to interpreting the science of the day got on the bandwagon. Both *Popular Science Monthly* and *Scientific American* published articles in 1936 portraying marijuana as a "menace" to American society, particularly to the young.

A major player in elevating marijuana to the status of "national menace" was Harry Anslinger, who served as commissioner of narcotics in the 1930s. Mr. Anslinger began something of a crusade against marijuana, skillfully using congressional testimony, the medical establishment, and the popular media to warn of the dangers of marijuana to American society. He was successful, and in 1937 congressional hearings were held to address the association between marijuana and crime. By this time it was

clear that Congress was ready to limit the use and possession of marijuana, and it passed the Marijuana Tax Act of 1937, which did not outlaw
marijuana but created a tax structure around the cultivation, distribution,
sale, and purchase of cannabis products, which made it virtually impossible to have anything to do with the drug without breaking some part of
the tax law.

Interestingly, almost immediately after the passage of the Marijuana
Tax Act, the pendulum began to swing the other way. In the early 1940s,
studies were published that indicated that marijuana was relatively harmless and that any relationship to criminal behavior was likely due to marijuana's association with the use of alcohol, which proved to be the prime
cause of aggression. Other studies during that time began to show that
although acute marijuana use impaired cognitive function, it did not
change the personality of the user, and that it affected thinking and feelings more than behavior. By the late 1960s, when the Marijuana Tax Act
was ruled unconstitutional by the US Supreme Court, Mr. Anslinger's
assertions about the relationship between marijuana and violent crime
were discredited. Still, marijuana was illegal, and this label alone implied
"dangerous" for most people. What has developed since that time has
been an interesting tension between a legal status that implies danger and
a scientific literature that consistently suggests that marijuana (used in
the ways it is generally used) is a relatively safe drug for adult users.

Little scientific work was done with marijuana through the 1950s and
1960s, though its use increased. The media during the 1960s increasingly
focused on "hard" drugs such as LSD (which was legal until 1966, and
placed on Schedule I in 1967), while marijuana became a symbol of youth-
ful rejection of "the establishment." The acceleration in marijuana use
began in the late 1960s and by the spring of 1970, the National Institute of
Mental Health estimated that as many as 20 million individuals had used
marijuana at least once. In December 1970, the Gallup organization estimated that 42 percent of college students had smoked marijuana. Perhaps
the social association between marijuana and hallucinogens during the
1960s can account for its continued inclusion with LSD and heroin under
the category of Schedule I narcotics, despite the profound differences in
the potency of its effects on (and risks to) individuals. The use of the drug
decreased in the 1980s as social and political conservatism grew but rose
again in the 1990s as the perceived risks of using it again dropped. Currently, marijuana use appears to have leveled off, with slight declines
among some age groups, including middle and high school students.

THE CONSEQUENCES OF ILLEGALITY

Because people continue to use marijuana and cannot buy it at the corner store with their coffee, cigarettes, and beer, criminal distribution networks have evolved to meet the demand. Growing out of the competition within these networks comes the violent crime so common to our daily news reports. At the same time, users, by definition, become criminals. We spend a considerable amount of money each year to apprehend, prosecute, and imprison people on marijuana charges. These costly laws apparently did not hinder the marked increase in marijuana use, particularly among young people, during the 1990s, nor do they deter the 30 percent or so of US high school students who have used marijuana during the past year. Clearly, as a society we are not ready to endorse the use of marijuana by selling it in the corner drugstore, but both conservative and liberal sectors are increasingly calling for a dramatic rethinking of marijuana laws and policies.

Aside from the criminal issue, many people feel they have been lied to by the government agencies responsible for educating and interpreting science to the lay public. In the 1960s, as more and more young people tried marijuana and discovered that it did not turn them into insane, violent killers, they began to resent and distrust the authorities who had presented those images. Authority began to lose its credibility relative to drugs. Forty years later, that credibility has not been regained, in part because the scientific truth about marijuana (and other drugs) is often lost among political and moral agendas.

VOICES FOR DECRIMINALIZATION

In 1970, a commission that was formed to take a closer look at marijuana laws recommended that the private possession of small amounts of marijuana for personal use no longer be considered an offense, but that selling marijuana or driving under its influence still be punishable. The same year that that report was released, the American Medical Association and the American Bar Association suggested the reduction or elimination of criminal penalties for the possession of very small amounts of marijuana. Soon thereafter, individual states began taking steps to decriminalize marijuana for personal use, and in 1977, President and Mrs. Jimmy Carter called for the decriminalization of the possession of small amounts of marijuana. The general view of many who supported decriminalization in the 1970s was that the laws against marijuana were more harmful than the drug itself.

THE SWINGING PENDULUM

The "Reagan Eighties," however, brought a new get-tough attitude to the issue of illegal drug usage. The trends toward decriminalization were abruptly reversed and replaced by the War on Drugs. States began to reinstitute tougher policies and penalties. During the 1980s the number of people aged eighteen to twenty-five who reported using marijuana steadily decreased while alcohol usage increased and the use of powder, and then crack, cocaine began to skyrocket. Crack became a major scourge of the urban underclass and for both pharmacological and social reasons has been a major contributor to violent urban crime.

Still, in the early 1990s marijuana use significantly increased, particularly among young people. In just the two years between 1992 and 1994, the use of marijuana by adolescents twelve to seventeen years of age nearly doubled. Perhaps this was just the pendulum swinging back from the more conservative and reactionary 1980s. Or maybe a new generation of users was exploring drugs. Cocaine was the drug of the 1980s, a decade that more than a few financial writers refer to as the "Go-go Eighties." Cocaine is clearly a "go-go" drug, whereas marijuana has a considerably more mellowing and contemplative effect, perhaps reflecting a change in the spirit of the times.

WHAT WILL HAPPEN NEXT?

As a society we have much bigger drug problems to deal with than marijuana. A rational and convincing chorus of voices across the political spectrum, including medical and scientific professionals, political pundits, and members of the business community, are urging a restructuring of our legal response to recreational drugs. Some call for total legalization of all drugs, some for less radical changes, but it's clear that something needs to change. The legal debate over marijuana is still complicated. On one hand, there are now clear medical uses for the drug, and it obviously does less social and medical harm than our legal drug of choice, alcohol. One report indicates that marijuana is the largest cash crop in the United States, larger than those for corn and wheat combined, and the revenues from its controlled cultivation, sale, and taxation could be significant, turning the loss of resources for prohibition and prosecution into gains in the legal economy and national and state coffers. Legalization would eliminate the need for a criminal production and distribution network, along with its violent and antisocial consequences.

On the other hand, marijuana is not harmless, as some of its proponents would claim. Just because it is not as harmful as other drugs that are now legal does not mean it should go unregulated. It has relatively long-lasting effects after even a single dose, may carry significant risks for adolescent users, and the jury is out on whether it produces brain damage or increases the risk of lung cancer after heavy and prolonged use. Finally, despite its benign profile relative to other drugs, marijuana is currently illegal, and that label alone is a difficult obstacle to overcome in the public (and political) mind.

So, the debate remains open and passionate, but our guess is that all drug laws are going to change significantly in the not-too-distant future and that marijuana laws will be a part of that change. The reform of marijuana laws may lead the way because, while there aren't many good reasons to legalize a number of other recreational drugs, there are some good reasons to change marijuana laws.

"SYNTHETIC" MARIJUANA

Before closing this chapter, we need to address the rising use of a group of drug mixtures that are often referred to broadly as "synthetic" marijuana. These mixtures have many names, including Spice, K2, fake weed, Yucatan Fire, Skunk, Moon Rocks, Black Mamba, Mr. Smiley, Incense, and Blaze. They contain any number of different psychoactive compounds, including cannabinoids, though they do not contain marijuana, per se—thus, the term *synthetic*. Indeed, part of the problem with these drugs is that it is impossible to know what is in the mixture. Users are essentially playing a game of "drug grab bag" when they take it. Although the packaging of these drugs often states that the contents are "natural," and they do contain dried plant material, the truth is that their active ingredients are synthetic cannabinoid compounds. Another problem is that the cannabinoids these drug mixtures contain generally bind with the brain's natural cannabinoid receptors either more powerfully or in different ways than THC or the other natural cannabinoids, and this can lead to far more powerful effects. As we discussed with respect to the newly emerging medical uses of marijuana, our understanding of the cannabinoid receptors in our bodies is just beginning to be understood. There are still a lot of unknowns. So when you start messing around with those receptors with new and very powerful compounds, bad things can happen and the user can be in for a wild and very dangerous ride.

Users of these drugs report experiences that are similar to those produced by marijuana, such as relaxation and changes in perception, but they also often report very nasty effects like paranoia, hallucinations, extreme anxiety, agitation, and confusion. Vomiting, rapid heart rate, increased blood pressure, and decreased blood supply to the heart are also observed. There have been multiple reports in the media of users ending up in hospital emergency departments with such extreme symptoms, and some have attributed death to the use of synthetic marijuana. It is very hard to know, however, what actually caused the symptoms in those patients, because many of the compounds that are found in the drugs are so new and so unusual and new ones emerge so rapidly on the market that the usual hospital toxicity screens do not even look for them. So, many times it's not until the patient is stabilized, or a friend comes forward with information, that anyone even knows what the person took. This can lead to an emergency department guessing game that is in nobody's best interest. The bottom line on these drugs is that it's probably best to steer clear.

8

NICOTINE

Drug Class: No specific class—prescription and nonprescription medication for smoking cessation. Legal for use in any form by adults.

Individual Drugs: tobacco, nicotine chewing gum, nicotine skin patch, chewing tobacco, snuff, cigarettes, cigars, pipe tobacco, e-cigarettes

The Buzz: Nicotine is a specific kind of stimulant that increases attention, concentration, and (possibly) memory. Many people also report that nicotine has a calming or antianxiety effect as well.

Overdose and Other Bad Effects: Dangerous overdose from nicotine is quite rare, but it is possible. A serious overdose would cause tremors (shaking) and convulsions that could paralyze muscles needed for breathing, and kill a person. Less serious nicotine poisoning results in dizziness, weakness, and nausea, which disappear as the drug is eliminated. Many people experience such side effects when they first smoke or when they use nicotine gum for the first time in a smoking-cessation program (the gum delivers quite a bit more nicotine than a cigarette).

As with many drugs, nicotine reaches the fetus in a pregnant woman and can cause permanent damage. If the mother smokes, then many of the bad effects specific to smoking also impact the fetus.

Dangerous Combinations with Other Drugs: Nicotine powerfully stimulates the heart and circulation. It can cause problems in combination with other drugs that increase heart rate or blood pressure or that reduce the oxygen-carrying capacity of the blood. Nicotine and cocaine taken together put far more stress on the heart than either drug alone does. This combination increases the risk of sudden death from heart attack.

CHAPTER CONTENTS

A BRIEF HISTORY

Like many drugs that are used recreationally today, nicotine has a history of being used as medicine. In the 1500s tobacco was used to treat a number of ailments, from headaches to colds. So revered was tobacco for its medicinal properties during that time that it became known as a holy plant. In 1828 French chemists isolated the active ingredient in tobacco and called it nicotine, after Jean Nicot, the French diplomat who brought tobacco from Portugal to France. Although tobacco continued to enjoy rave reviews from some quarters for its supposed medical properties, others were beginning to voice the concern that it might be bad for people's health. By the 1890s nicotine was no longer a compound prescribed as medicine in the United States.

All this was before smoking tobacco became at all popular in the United States. In the mid-1800s the vast majority of tobacco factories produced chewing tobacco rather than tobacco for smoking. It was not until the early 1900s that smoking began to replace chewing, at first in the form of cigars, which provided a transitional opportunity to both chew (the cigar is often left in the mouth, allowing nicotine to be absorbed orally) and smoke at the same time.

Cigarettes did, however, catch on, and per capita sales of cigarettes to adults in the United States reached a peak in the early 1960s when about 40 percent of US adults were smokers. Since then smoking has decreased to about 19 percent of the adult US population. This decline is likely due to compelling research showing that smoking causes cancer and other health problems; the use of these research findings in truthful and believable public educational campaigns about smoking; and the ban on TV advertising for cigarettes.

But there are some other factors that are associated with smoking. We now know that there is a clear relationship between educational level and smoking—the more educated the person, the less likely she is to smoke. The percentage of college graduates who smoke cigarettes is less than half the percentage of smokers among people who have not attended college, and in general men (22 percent) are slightly more likely than women (17 percent) to smoke. According to recent statistics, daily smoking increases steadily with age, from 2 percent among eighth graders to over 9 percent among twelfth graders. But smoking increases markedly after that as well. Data from the US Centers for Disease Control indicate that people twenty-five to forty-four years of age are the most likely to be smokers (25.6 percent). It is a sad irony that smoking is higher among adults living below the poverty level (29 percent) than among those who do not live in poverty (16 percent), because the cost of cigarettes has gotten quite high—averaging $6 per pack across the United States.

Why do people still smoke, and why is smoking initiated so often by young people? We don't know, but it could be a combination of effective non-TV advertising and the sense among many young people that they are not vulnerable to the health effects of cigarettes. They may have a parent or other relative who has suffered those ill effects but believe that those are "old people." This is a tough point to argue with because the negative health effects are relatively far off for the young smoker. But the young person will get older, and the time will come when health decisions made in high school may have a powerful impact on quality of life. Nicotine is clearly an addictive drug, and it appears that people who start smoking as adolescents put themselves at very high risk for addiction. In fact, almost all addicted smokers started as adolescents. In studies involving rats, nicotine caused adults to decrease their activity level but did not have the same effect on adolescents. Because rats are quite sensitive to their internal state and tend to become less active when they experience something that is threatening or potentially dangerous, it appears that the adolescents experienced less of the aversive effects of the drug than did the adults. Consistent with this interpretation are the findings of an important study that showed that adolescent rats will self-administer far more nicotine than adults when given the opportunity. Perhaps the adolescents like the reinforcing effects of nicotine more, they experience fewer negative side effects, or both. The bottom line for humans is that by the time a young smoker begins to think about the future or feel some of the ill effects of smoking, his addiction is probably in place. Quitting is then a problem—not impossible, but a problem.

HOW NICOTINE MOVES THROUGH THE BODY

GETTING IN

The speed and efficiency with which nicotine enters the blood and is transferred to the brain depends very much on how it is administered. When a person smokes tobacco, or inhales nicotine using an e-cigarette, the nicotine is absorbed very rapidly into the blood through the lungs and passes within seconds to the brain. The amount of nicotine in a typical cigarette is enough to kill a child or make an adult very sick, but because not all of it gets into the blood through the lungs—most of it is lost in exhaled or uninhaled smoke—a cigarette does not threaten an overdose.

If a person takes nicotine by mouth in the form of snuff (smokeless tobacco), the absorption of nicotine may be more complete than it is with smoking, but the dose is delivered over a much longer period of time. For example, the typical dose of nicotine from a cigarette is about one milligram. However, a plug of snuff maintained in the mouth continuously for thirty minutes delivers a dose in the three- to five-milligram range. The mucous membranes of the mouth are a good site for absorption because a lot of blood flows nearby, but the process is still much slower there than it is in the lungs. So, while snuff delivers a larger total dose over time than a cigarette does, they both result in about the same peak concentration of nicotine in the blood.

Nicotine gum delivers less nicotine than snuff. Even if it is chewed for thirty minutes continuously, nicotine gum generally delivers only about 1.5 milligrams of nicotine. As this is being written, tobacco companies are continuing to develop and test-market tobacco-free oral nicotine delivery devices. One, called "Verve," is a spit-free, oral "disk" that the user either chews or holds in her mouth for ten to fifteen minutes. It contains nicotine and mint flavoring, but no tobacco. As smoking has diminished across several decades in the United States, tobacco companies have done research that indicates that about 30 percent of adult smokers are interested in smokeless products, but many of them are not comfortable with chewing tobacco or snuff, so the companies are designing more creative tobacco-free nicotine products that can deliver nicotine orally. Regardless of the specific oral delivery system, if the nicotine is getting absorbed from inside the mouth, its route into the body will be the same.

Cigars present an interesting case in nicotine absorption, because generally the smoker doesn't inhale. Although some of the smoke still makes it to the lungs, most of it comes into contact with membranes in the mouth and upper airways, across which nicotine can be absorbed. How much nicotine gets absorbed through the direct contact of the cigar tobacco with the mouth depends largely on the style of smoking. Those folks who stick a cigar in their mouth and leave it there until the end looks like the end of a dipstick from an old lawn mower engine will absorb much more nicotine through the mouth than those who hold the cigar in their hand and puff intermittently.

GETTING AROUND

Once nicotine is absorbed, how is it distributed? Again, this depends on how it is taken. Smoking a cigarette results in a peak concentration in the lungs, blood, and brain within about ten minutes. But these concentrations decline rapidly as nicotine is redistributed to other body tissues. Twenty minutes after smoking, the nicotine concentration in the blood and brain is down to half of what it had been just ten minutes earlier. With snuff the distribution is slower, but the peak nicotine concentrations are quite similar to those obtained after smoking a cigarette.

GETTING OUT

Studies on animals that have very closely followed the concentrations of nicotine in the brain have shown very high levels five minutes after administration, declining to near nothing thirty minutes later. Nicotine's rapid absorption from the lungs, coupled with this pattern of distribution to the brain, allows the smoker a lot of control over the peaks and valleys of nicotine exposure. In this sense, cigarettes offer a very effective drug-delivery system.

These characteristics also set up the smoker for addiction in two ways. First, nicotine's rapid route to the brain provides a quick and potent hit. Second, the rapid redistribution out of the brain means that the brain areas that control the behaviors associated with smoking are ready for more nicotine soon after the smoker finishes the last cigarette. After nicotine is absorbed and distributed throughout the body, the liver breaks most of it down into two inactive metabolites: cotinine and nicotine-N-oxide. The kidneys eliminate these metabolites through the urine. Cotinine is the marker used in urine screens for nicotine because it stays in the body for several days.

IS NICOTINE ADDICTIVE?

Yes. Any honest and thorough appraisal of the scientific and medical literature on nicotine must conclude that this is a drug that causes physical dependence and addiction. At least three related lines of evidence lead to this conclusion.

REINFORCEMENT

In the language of psychology, a reinforcer is something that motivates an individual to work toward getting more. Nicotine is known to promote the release of the neurotransmitter dopamine in brain regions that mediate reinforcement (see the "Addiction" and "Stimulants" chapters). It is not surprising, then, that laboratory animals will work for nicotine. When rats have the opportunity to press a bar to self-administer small doses of nicotine, they will do so. And, as we noted, adolescent animals will do this much more than adults.

Humans, too, will work for nicotine once they have been smoking for a

while. In fact, all smokers do, given that they spend their money on cigarettes. The willingness to work for them was typified in an old advertisement for cigarettes that centered on the phrase "I'd walk a mile for a Camel."

TOLERANCE

Studies have demonstrated the rapid development of tolerance to the
effects of nicotine. When people begin to smoke, they experience a range
of rather unpleasant effects, such as dizziness or nausea, but these disappear over days or weeks as the smoker continues to smoke. Tolerance to
other effects of nicotine develops even more rapidly. For example, when a
group of smokers was given two equal doses of nicotine sixty minutes
apart, they experienced more pronounced elevations of their heart rates
and reported greater subjective effects from the first dose compared to
the second.

WITHDRAWAL

On reporting for his first morning of smoking-cessation treatment after a
required day of abstinence, one of my patients summed up his feelings by
saying, "I want to hurt something." As I scanned the room for sharp
objects, I realized that he was in nicotine withdrawal. Although not all
smokers are so extreme (or honest) in their feelings soon after quitting,
most report powerful cravings and irritability during the first two to three
weeks after their last cigarette. These are clearly symptoms of withdrawal.

As with tolerance, withdrawal from nicotine has both short- and long-
term aspects. For example, most smokers report that their first cigarette
of the day is the one that makes them feel best. This effect can be seen as
the termination of a miniwithdrawal after the overnight abstinence.

SUBJECTIVE EFFECTS

Although nicotine, particularly as administered by smoking, is clearly
addictive, it also clearly differs from many other addictive substances. It
lacks the obvious mind-altering effects of alcohol, stimulants, or opiates.
People don't use nicotine because it provides a rush or a high. Rather,
most users report that it calms them and reduces anxiety. But even these
effects are more complicated than they may seem.

Because the vast majority of nicotine users obtain it by smoking, we should consider smoking as a particular kind of drug delivery. Many people derive considerable comfort and calming from small personal habits or rituals—such as tapping a foot or humming to themselves—and many such habits become associated with nicotine delivery during smoking. Lighting up, holding the cigarette, moving it to and from the mouth and puffing—any or all of these small rituals could calm the smoker in and of themselves and become associated with the pharmacological effects of nicotine. The use of e-cigarettes—which deliver nicotine but contain no tobacco—involves many of the same habits associated with smoking and delivers nicotine to the lungs like cigarettes do. So the experience is very much like actual smoking—without the smoke. Adding these habits to nicotine delivery makes it hard to determine what role the nicotine alone plays in the reported calming effect. Another consideration is that the people who report the antianxiety and calming effects of smoking are most often people who have been smoking for a while. Thus, it is hard to know whether the calming is a primary effect of nicotine or simply the reduction of an addicted person's craving.

Another commonly reported effect of smoking is the suppression of appetite. Again, it is not clear if this effect is principally due to the nicotine or the smoking, but animal studies show that nicotine can reduce eating when it is given in the absence of smoke. In humans, smoking one cigarette has been shown to diminish hunger contractions in the stomach. It is also possible that the appetite is suppressed in part because smoking reduces the function of the taste buds in the mouth. Other possibilities include the effects of smoking on energy metabolism and blood-sugar levels. The fact is that we do not know exactly why smoking suppresses appetite, but it seems clear that for some people it does. Of course, there is another side to this coin: when a smoker quits smoking, his appetite often increases and he gains weight. This could be due to the effects of the physical withdrawal of nicotine from the system or to the need to replace the oral habits associated with the act of smoking.

EFFECTS ON THE BRAIN AND MENTAL FUNCTION

Before the 1980s, it was not at all clear how nicotine affected the brain. We now know that nicotine stimulates a specific subtype of receptor for the neurotransmitter acetylcholine—the nicotinic acetylcholine receptor.

These receptors are distributed rather widely on nerve cells throughout the brain, so nicotine has effects on a wide variety of brain structures. In general, it excites nerve cells and increases cell-to-cell signaling. Several studies have shown that nicotine increases the activity in brain regions that are associated with memory and other mental functions, as well as in some structures involved with physical movement.

When acetylcholine receptors in the brain are blocked, animals (and people) have a difficult time remembering new information. Conversely, some reports show that stimulating these receptors improves memory somewhat. Because nicotine promotes the release of acetylcholine and also activates its own subtype of acetylcholine receptors, some investigators predicted that nicotine might enhance memory function. This appears to be generally true in studies with animals, and a number of studies have been undertaken to determine whether nicotine can help patients with memory deficits, like those with early Alzheimer's disease. In such studies researchers generally administer nicotine either by injecting it or by using a patch that allows it to be absorbed slowly through the skin. Although it's still uncertain whether nicotine may be of use to Alzheimer's patients, some convincing studies show that nicotine does improve some mental functions for at least a brief time after its use. In a study that used the nicotine patch, patients with mild to moderate Alzheimer's disease showed increased attention while exposed to nicotine.

This does not mean, however, that a person should smoke cigarettes or chew nicotine gum while studying or during an exam or other activity that demands concentration or memory. The carbon monoxide in the cigarette, combined with the lack of oxygen exchange in the lungs due to the smoke, would likely lead to other side effects, such as dizziness, which could easily overpower any potential attention- or memory-enhancing effects of the nicotine. In addition, chewing nicotine gum often delivers enough nicotine to make even experienced smokers feel nauseated the first time or two.

Another potential medical use for nicotine is in the treatment of adult attention deficit/hyperactivity disorder (ADHD). Although work on this problem is not extensive, one study indicates that nicotine patch treatments reduce ADHD symptoms in both smokers and nonsmokers. When nicotine patches were used for four weeks, the capacity for attention in both children and adults with ADHD was improved.

Nicotine may also prove helpful in people with schizophrenia—not as a treatment for the psychotic symptoms but rather as an aid for cognitive function. Schizophrenics often suffer learning and other cognitive deficits that are likely due to impaired nicotinic receptors in the hippocampus. The thinking is that if nicotine is given, it will make up, in part, for that deficit in the function of the hippocampus and thus improve cognitive function in the patient. Although this research is still in the early stage, there is some compelling evidence that nicotine may indeed diminish some cognitive deficits in adult schizophrenics.

Although these studies appear promising and may lead to more effective treatments for these disorders, it is critical to remember three things. First, the studies we mentioned have not yet led to any approved medical uses for nicotine beyond its approval for use in smoking cessation. Second, several of the studies have involved injections of nicotine, which, of course, should never be undertaken without medical supervision. Third, those results should never be interpreted as a reason to smoke. The health costs of smoking far outweigh any potential health benefits of nicotine.

SMOKING AND EMOTIONAL FUNCTION

Depression is a common problem among adolescents. As many as 15 to 20 percent of adolescents may become depressed at some time during this period. Smoking has generally been regarded as a consequence of depression in young people, but it may be that smoking leads to depression in some. It turns out that adolescents who are smokers are twice as likely as nonsmoking adolescents to suffer an episode of major depression and that teens with long-term depression are more likely to be smokers than teens without depression. Recent studies also show that depression at the age of fourteen predicted smoking progression as teens age from fourteen to eighteen. This suggests that increased smoking during the teen years could represent a form of self-medication for depression. Although these findings do not tell us why a teen smoker is more likely to become depressed or vice versa, they may provide valuable warning signals. A young person who has problems with depression may be at higher risk than normal for smoking, and it may be wise for such people to take special care to avoid situations in which smoking is prevalent. Likewise, a teen who smokes may be more susceptible to depression and should watch for early signs of it so that antidepressant treatment can be started, if necessary.

EFFECTS ON THE HEART

It is well known that smoking causes lung cancer and other chronic lung diseases. What is less well known is that smoking also contributes to diseases of the heart and vascular system, which actually kill more people in the United States annually than any cancer. Nicotine affects the heart in several ways. The heart is a big muscle, and like all muscles it needs a rich supply of oxygen to do its work pumping blood throughout the rest of the body. When nicotine is in the system, it results in the release of adrenaline, which increases heart rate and blood pressure. The heart then needs more oxygen to increase its workload, but its oxygen supply doesn't increase, so it must do extra work with no extra help.

What's worse, the carbon monoxide in smoke also decreases the ability of the blood to carry oxygen, making the situation even more stressful for the heart. Repeatedly stressing the heart in these ways leads to damage and compromises its function. Cigarette smoke is also directly toxic to the inner lining of the blood vessels. Something in the smoke makes them hard and inflexible, adding to the cardiovascular problems. It is estimated that as many as 30 percent of the deaths attributed to heart and vascular disease relate to smoking.

All of these negative effects on heart and circulatory functions may have another, less dangerous but unwanted effect. Smokers develop thinner skin. A 1997 study of identical twins in which one twin smoked and one did not showed that the smokers had skin that was thinner than that of their twin siblings. Investigators think that this may be why some smokers tend to have more wrinkles and look older than they are. One possible explanation for this effect on the skin is that smoking can decrease the blood supply to the topmost layer of the skin and thus damage it.

SECONDHAND, THIRDHAND, AND SIDESTREAM SMOKE

There are two sources of smoke from cigarette smokers: the smoke they exhale (secondhand) and the smoke rising off the lit cigarette, cigar, or pipe itself (sidestream). It is worth knowing that sidestream smoke has a higher concentration of carcinogens than either secondhand smoke or the smoke that a smoker takes into his lungs through a cigarette filter. Whatever the source, smoke can cause disease. The Environmental Protection Agency, after considerable study of this issue, determined that secondhand smoke is indeed a carcinogen in and of itself and is responsible for a significant number of lung cancer deaths each year in the United States. Of course, the amount of exposure to secondary smoke is a critical factor in the risk of developing lung disease (as is the smoker's own amount of exposure), and a few parties in smoky rooms will probably not kill anyone. However, people who spend a lot of time in smoky places, like bars, or who live with smokers are clearly placing themselves at some risk for lung disease.

The effects of secondhand smoke on the development of heart disease are even more alarming. A ten-year study published in 1997 showed that regular exposure to secondhand smoke can double a person's risk of heart disease. This study of more than thirty thousand women suggests that as many as fifty thousand people may die each year in the United States as a result of heart attacks related to secondhand-smoke exposure.

In enclosed areas where smoking occurs, the residue of the nicotine on surfaces can react with normal chemicals present in the air to create carcinogens that are found in tobacco. This toxic feature is referred to as "thirdhand" smoke, though obviously it is not smoke per se. The actual health risks of such residues are not clear. But it is a matter of current study and some public health researchers are concerned that toddlers and young children may be at greater risk of exposure because they are more likely than adults to touch and explore surfaces and put their hands in their mouths or eat without washing their hands first.

PRENATAL AND POSTNATAL EFFECTS

As with most psychoactive drugs, nicotine passes to the fetus in the blood of the pregnant woman who smokes (or otherwise uses nicotine). Babies born to smoking moms have been shown to have levels of cotinine in their urine that are nearly as high as those of active smokers. As time passes after birth and their nicotine levels fall, these babies show symptoms of nicotine deprivation. The pregnant smoker also passes along cyanide and carbon monoxide to her baby, both of which are very bad for the developing fetus. Remember that carbon monoxide reduces the ability of blood to carry oxygen and thereby depletes body tissues of oxygen. Also, nicotine constricts blood vessels bringing blood to the fetus, further limiting oxygen supply. In the fetus, this oxygen depletion is thought to account for the fact that babies born to smoking mothers are smaller, lighter, and have smaller head circumferences than babies born to nonsmoking mothers. In addition, as with alcohol, smoking during pregnancy likely has lasting (perhaps permanent) effects on the brain and mental function of the child after birth. Some studies have linked maternal smoking with difficulties in verbal and mathematical abilities and hyperactivity during childhood. There's also a greater likelihood of nicotine addiction in adulthood for people whose mothers smoked during their pregnancy. Interestingly, maternal smoking did not change the likelihood of people trying cigarettes, but it did significantly increase the chances of them becoming addicted if they did initiate cigarette use. This finding may suggest that while experimenting with smoking may be driven largely by social forces, the liability to addiction may be tied more closely to specific biological characteristics.

Once a baby is born, an immense amount of brain development is still going on. Exposure of babies and small children to secondary smoke should also be avoided. For example, some studies have suggested that there is an increased risk of sudden infant death syndrome (SIDS) in babies of smoking mothers and that this could be due to smoke in the environment. It is also possible that this could be due to damage that the baby suffered before birth due to the mother's smoking or to the combination of prenatal and postnatal exposure.

Studies also indicate that the children of fathers who smoke are more likely to develop childhood cancers than the children of nonsmoking dads. Based on the Oxford Survey of Childhood Cancers, the study of some three thousand parents showed that fathers who smoked twenty or more cigarettes per day had a 42 percent increased risk of having a child with cancer and that those who smoked ten to twenty cigarettes per day increased the risk by 31 percent. The risk was increased by 3 percent for fathers who smoked fewer than ten cigarettes per day. These results suggest that smoking may damage sperm in ways that could lead to cancer-causing alterations of the DNA.

The message is very clear—babies are best raised in a smoke-free environment.

HEALTH RISKS OF SMOKELESS TOBACCO

We should also stress that the chewing of tobacco and snuff represent significant health risks in their own right. In addition to the nicotine they deliver, their prolonged use can increase the likelihood of cancers of the mouth and esophagus. Many users develop thickening lesions in the mouth that may develop into cancer of those tissues. Smokeless tobacco also causes gum disease, which can result in inflamed and receding gums and can expose the teeth to disease. In addition, because smokeless tobacco products generally contain very high amounts of sugar, they also promote the development of dental cavities. In short, smokeless tobacco is not a safe substitute for smoking.

It is also not a good "performance enhancing" drug for athletes, though a staggering number use it that way. Many young people believe that the nicotine in smokeless tobacco products increases their physical reaction times and the power of their movements in various sports like baseball, track and field, and football. This is actually not true. There is no evidence of significant gains in reaction time, and there are studies that indicate that nicotine actually decreases the speed and force of leg movements during reaction-time studies. Its negative effects on heart function also argue against the use of nicotine during athletic activities.

QUITTING

Not so many years ago, the prevailing wisdom was that the ability to quit smoking was a matter of simple willpower. This attitude implied that smoking was not really an addiction, that no special techniques were required for quitting, and that anyone who could not quit simply lacked the internal fortitude to do so. We now know that none of this is true. Nicotine is an addictive drug, and quitting is a complicated change of behavior that is not easy.

Many former smokers report having quit on their own, but there are also plenty of treatments available to help. Unfortunately, there is no one treatment that works for everyone. Probably because the behavioral habits of smoking are tied up with the physiological addiction to nicotine, many people require a number of different treatment strategies to address the whole problem. On the behavioral side, these can include educational counseling, group or individual smoking-cessation training, hypnosis, or stress-management training. On the medical side, they can include the use of nicotine chewing gum or nicotine skin patches. Also, a medication called Zyban, which is also used as an antidepressant under the name Wellbutrin, is sometimes used as one component of smoking-cessation programs, and a number of other drugs are being actively studied or are in initial clinical trials. Some of those trials contain some interesting twists that might be of great value. It turns out that starting nicotine replacement therapy (the patch, specifically) a couple of weeks before one's "quit date" can increase the likelihood of successfully quitting. Initial studies sponsored by the National Institute on Drug Abuse have demonstrated this, and ongoing studies are looking for the optimal time at which therapy should begin relative to the quit date. Other studies are exploring the value of taking a flexible view of which medications to use, and when, in the quitting process. Some people have more success than others with different treatments, and current studies are looking for the best ways to "rescue" smoking-cessation patients who are not having success with one approach by replacing it with another at just the right time in the quitting process. Although these studies are still being conducted, they show promise for helping clinicians to refine their treatments to give patients their own personal best chance for success.

As smoking-cessation treatments become more sophisticated and the options for treatment multiply, it becomes more and more valuable to seek professional consultation about quitting. The best first step to quitting is to get a referral from a physician, psychologist, or pharmacist to an established smoking-cessation program. Sometimes these are run in hospitals or clinics, but they may also be operated as part of a community mental health clinic or by a private practitioner. In any case, the people in charge of the program should be trained professionals prepared to discuss the various options in detail.

The bad news is that although most of these programs can help people quit for a brief time, many people return to smoking within six months. It appears that programs that use multiple approaches (such as nicotine replacement and/or other drug therapies, behavior training, and hypnosis) have a somewhat better record of keeping people off cigarettes longer than single-method programs do. Still, many people in multiple-approach programs return to smoking within a year. Why is this the case? We're not sure, but it probably has to do with how much behavioral habit the act of smoking involves, and how many places, people, and things out in the real world the smoker has associated with the act of smoking over the years. The very uncomfortable cravings for nicotine diminish rapidly within days of quitting, and nicotine gum or skin patches can help during this time. The first few days are clearly the worst, but most people report that by about two weeks the cravings are mostly gone. What remain are all the cues that used to be associated with smoking—the morning cup of coffee, the evening beer, the talk with a friend on a break at work (the list can go on and on).

These are powerful stimuli that can exert considerable control over behavior. Many people will report that they felt well on their way to really kicking the habit when an old friend with whom they used to smoke came back for a visit, or that they went back to a bar where they used to smoke and drink and have fun, and before they knew it, the cigarette was back in their hand. A smoking-cessation program must anticipate these situations and provide strategies for dealing with them. It's a valuable help to schedule follow-up sessions to talk such things over, learn strategies, and get support. This can be particularly helpful because it has been shown that stressful conditions can lead to relapse as well.

Before leaving the topic of the behavioral and environmental cues that perpetuate smoking and challenge those who try to quit, it's important to discuss e-cigarettes, which were initially developed as an aid for people trying to quit smoking. As we mentioned, these are devices that deliver nicotine to the lungs without burning tobacco. In fact, they contain no tobacco at all. They look like cigarettes, right down to the red LED that turns on and looks like a glowing cigarette ember when the user draws air into it (although at least one brand comes in a slick-looking black color with a blue LED). A sensor turns the device on when a drop in internal pressure is created by the user taking a drag. Powered by a rechargeable battery, an atomizer converts liquid nicotine (mixed with other chemicals and flavorings) into a warm mist, allowing it to be drawn into the lungs. The user then exhales a mist that looks a lot like smoke but is odorless. Clearly, e-cigarettes allow the smoker to engage in most of the behavioral aspects of smoking and may thereby turn out to be a very good quitting aid, though their usefulness has yet to be thoroughly studied. But even if they did not help anyone quit and just resulted in smokers switching over to e-cigarettes, they would still have some value as a "harm reduction" option for smokers. Essentially they amount to a nicotine delivery system that mimics the actions associated with smoking without delivering any known cancer-causing agents to the user. However, e-cigarettes should not be viewed as risk-free. After all, users may remain addicted to nicotine, even though they eliminate their exposure to carcinogens. Furthermore, the cardiovascular stimulation that contributes to the cardiovascular disease risk of smoking is still present. It's analogous to switching heroin addicts to methadone—the user may remain addicted, but to a less dangerous compound. There are also concerns about people starting nicotine addiction through e-cigarette use: e-cigarettes could serve as a "gateway" to smoking for those who have never smoked or as a path back to smoking for those who have quit. Once a person becomes addicted to nicotine, it might be easy to slip from e-cigarette use into (or back into) smoking. If that were the case, then e-cigarettes would clearly be causing great harm. We will know more as research studies address this issue. Meanwhile, e-cigarettes are gaining popularity rapidly in the United States among both adults and teens.

One final point on quitting: if at first you don't succeed, try again. Every person is different and every addiction is different. If trying on your own did not work, a treatment program might. If one treatment program did not work, a different one might. Enough types of help are available that there is a good chance one will work for any motivated person who wants to quit smoking.

9
OPIATES

Drug Class: Opiate analgesics. All of the drugs mentioned in this chapter are scheduled by the Drug Enforcement Administration, but they vary from Schedule 1 (heroin) to Schedule IV (propoxyphene) based on their likelihood of abuse and medical use.

Individual Drugs: Opium, heroin, morphine, codeine, hydromorphone (Dilaudid), oxycodone (Percodan, OxyContin), meperidine (Demerol), diphenoxylate (Lomotil), hydrocodone (Vicodin), fentanyl (Sublimaze), propoxyphene (Darvon)

Common Terms: Chinese molasses, dreams, gong, O, skee, toys, zero (opium); Big H, dreck, horse, mojo, smack, white lady, brown (heroin); speedballs (heroin and cocaine); Oxys, OCs, Hillbilly heroin (oxycodone)

The Buzz: People who inject opiates experience a rush of pleasure and then sink into a dreamy, pleasant state in which they have little sensitivity to pain. Their breathing slows, and their skin may flush. Pinpoint pupils are another hallmark of opiate effects. Opiates taken by ways other than injection have the same effect, except that a pleasant drowsiness replaces the rush. Nausea and vomiting can accompany these effects, as well as constipation. An injected heroin/cocaine combination (speedball) causes intense euphoria, the dreaminess of heroin, and the stimulation of cocaine. People who take opiates by mouth experience the same effects, but the pleasure has a slower onset and is less intense.

Overdose and Other Bad Effects: Opiate overdose can be lethal whether users inject it or take pills. This is not a cumulative effect of years of misuse—it can happen the first time. Breathing slows to the point that it ceases. Fortunately, the opiate antagonist naloxone (Narcan) can almost immediately reverse the dangerous effects of opiates if the user gets medical help quickly. Opiate overdoses are most common with injectable forms of drug but can occur with any dosage form if enough is taken. Medical attention is critical.

Dangerous Combinations with Other Drugs: Opiates are especially dangerous when used in combination with other drugs that suppress breathing. These include alcohol, barbiturates (e.g., phenobarbital), Quaaludes (methaqualone), and Valium-like drugs (benzodiazepines).

CHAPTER CONTENTS

WHERE OPIATES CAME FROM

No less a cultural icon than Dorothy of *The Wizard of Oz* has experienced the effects of opiates (remember the field of poppies?). As we saw in *The Wizard of Oz*, you pretty much have to lack a brain to resist the effects of opiates. For those with a more classical bent, morphine derives its name from Morpheus, the Greek god of dreams, who was often depicted with a handful of opium poppies. Use of opiates began in prehistoric times, probably with teas prepared from opium poppies. The oldest historical references to the medicinal use of opiates arise from the Sumerian and Assyrian/Babylonian cultures (about five thousand years ago). Opium pipes recovered from archeological sites in Asia, Egypt, and Europe document the smoking of opium between 1000 and 300 BC. Arab traders introduced opiates to China between AD 600 and AD 900. Paralleling developments in Europe, medical use gradually evolved into recreational use, and the number of opium addicts grew. The importation of opium into China became a major source of trade for England and helped start a war between China and England when China banned its importation in the early nineteenth century.

Use (and abuse) of opiates in Europe was common during the Middle Ages. One agent of its popularity was Paracelsus, who coined the term *laudanum*—meaning "to be praised"—for an opiate preparation. Later, many poets (Samuel Taylor Coleridge and Elizabeth Barrett Browning, among others) used and abused opium. Coleridge reported an opium experience in his famous "Kubla Khan."

Opium has been used widely in the United States throughout its history. It was popular long before the wave of Chinese immigration introduced opium smoking to this country. Opium was a major ingredient in many of the patent medicines available before the FDA was started, and the average housewife was a major consumer in nineteenth-century America. As in the story of cocaine, the rising availability of increasingly potent preparations led to greater recognition of the drug's toxicity and addictive qualities.

In 1805 morphine, the major active ingredient in the opium poppy, was purified; in 1853 Alexander Wood invented the hypodermic syringe. The first major wave of addiction to injectable narcotics followed the wide use of injected morphine during the American Civil War. The final improvement came courtesy of the Bayer Company in 1898, when the company's scientists discovered that adding an extra chemical group onto morphine made it more soluble in fat, so that it would enter the brain faster. This improvement produced heroin, once a trade name for the narcotic produced by Bayer.

Today, opiate drugs are a mainstay of the medical treatment of pain. There just aren't substitutes for their effectiveness at reducing pain. However, all opiate drugs are addictive. Some doctors so fear addiction in their patients that they withhold needed treatments. This was the reason for the introduction of national programs that rightly promoted the use of adequate medication to treat pain. Unfortunately, this opened the door for a small number of unscrupulous doctors to run "pill mills" that prescribe these drugs to patients with very little verification of their medical need for such medication. Unfortunately, opiate drugs are also the form of drug more abused than any other except alcohol and marijuana. The majority (90 percent) of opiate abusers use pills that have been diverted from medical use, although heroin use remains a significant problem as well.

WHAT OPIATES ARE

Opiate drugs are any drugs, natural or synthetic, that produce the characteristic opiate effects: the combination of a dreamy, euphoric state; lessened sensation of pain; slowed breathing; constipation; and pinpoint pupils. Sometimes scientists use the more generic term *opioids*, which includes drugs resembling the substances in the opium poppy as well as endogenous opioids that serve as neurotransmitters in the brain.

Opium refers to a preparation of the opium poppy (*Papaver somniferum*). It is obtained in a very low-tech, labor-intensive manner throughout the world. Opium farmers cut the developing seedpod of the opium poppy and collect the gummy fluid that oozes out of the cut over the next few days. The sap is refined in several ways. It may be dried into a ball and used directly (gum opium) or dried and pounded into a powder (opium powder). Raw opium appears as a brown tarry substance. Opium can also be made into an alcohol-water extract called tincture of opium. This is the famous laudanum of your great-great-grandmother's era, or the paregoric of that age.

Morphine, which is one of the mainstays for pain management, is a major constituent of the seedpod. It is a potent opiate and is used in injectable or pill form to relieve pain after surgery and for extreme pain, such as in advanced cancer. Codeine is a much less potent opiate that is used mainly in pill form for milder pain. Many people have encountered it as an acetaminophen-codeine preparation that is used commonly for dental pain or in prescription cough medicine. To compensate for the lower potency of codeine, some drug abusers simply drink an entire four-ounce bottle, which does contain an intoxicating amount. These cough syrups used to be available over the counter until recreational use became too popular. Now most states require a prescription for codeine-containing cough syrups.

Heroin is a chemically modified form of morphine that is created from partially purified morphine, usually in "refineries" close to sites of opium production. It is broken up into small amounts and usually appears on the street in bags of loose powder containing about one hundred milligrams. The actual color can range from white to brown to black depending upon the source and quality of the preparation technique. Highly purified heroin hydrochloride is a white powder that is prized for its purity, while Mexican "black tar" heroin at the other end of the spectrum is recognized by its black appearance. The user either snorts the powder directly or dissolves it in saline and injects it. The actual composition of the powder depends upon the supplier and can range from 10 to 70 percent heroin (in combination) with various contaminants, including talc, quinine, and baking powder, making up the balance.

Opium poppies grown in Southeast Asia (Burma and Thailand), Afghanistan, South America (Colombia), and Mexico provide the starting material for illegal heroin that enters the United States. Southeast Asian poppies mostly provide heroin for Europe, although some makes its way to the United States. Heroin production from Afghanistan still represents the majority of worldwide production (tenfold more than the next highest supplier, which is Mexico), but heroin in the United States mainly comes from South America (East Coast) or from Mexico (West Coast) (US Department of Justice National Drug Intelligence Center, Threat Assessment 2011).

The purity of heroin varies widely. In the most recent report from the DEA (from 2011), the average purity in the United States was 30 percent, with ranges from 5 percent to 66 percent, depending upon the location. If heroin is just morphine that has been slightly changed chemically, what advantage does it have? In fact, once heroin enters the brain, it is converted back to morphine. However, the improved fat solubility does serve a useful purpose—it gets heroin into the brain faster. Many physicians are lobbying for its use in terminal cancer patients, as this difference means faster pain relief. The government is weighing the balance between this medical benefit and heroin's long and unpopular legal history.

Scientists have made many derivatives of morphine. The original hope was to find a drug that would eliminate pain but not cause tolerance or addiction. That mission has been unsuccessful—all of the effective opiate analgesic drugs are also addictive. However, the attempt has led to many man-made opiates with desirable characteristics for particular clinical uses. There are at least five important opiate analgesics that are either direct products of the seedpod of the opium poppy or minor modifications of it. These chemically modified drugs are widely used in medicine, and prescription opiate abuse is a major health concern today. Ten times more people abuse prescription opiates than abuse heroin, and rates have increased dramatically in the last ten years, as have overdose deaths from these drugs. Therefore, we will spend some time describing them in detail.

Some of the most widely used and abused prescription narcotics are modifications of morphine. These are hydromorphone, oxycodone, and hydrocodone. Hydromorphone (Dilaudid), a very strong opiate, is an effective analgesic that is widely abused. Oxycodone is synthesized from a nonanalgesic in opium (thebaine) and ranks between morphine and codeine in its effectiveness against pain. Its use has spread dramatically in the United States in the last few years, due in part to its appropriate use to treat pain. It is also marketed in combination with aspirin under the prescription name Percodan. Hydrocodone (Vicodin) is a moderately strong opiate that is also widely abused.

Meperidine (Demerol) is used like morphine for intense postsurgical pain, but it works well even with oral use. Meperidine has a definite downside: it can cause seizures at high doses—a feature that has led to decreased use by physicians in recent years. Methadone is a long-lasting opiate that is taken as a pill. Its unique time course makes it particularly useful for replacement therapy for treating opiate addiction as well as chronic pain. The gradual and mild onset of action staves off withdrawal signs but doesn't provide a "high." Its use for these purposes is controversial in some circles: although tolerance and physical dependence clearly develop, it provides safe and effective treatment without the same liability for abuse. One important characteristic of methadone is its very long half-life—it remains in the body for hours. This is a helpful characteristic in suppressing opiate withdrawal and in treating chronic pain. However, it also represents a danger to people who do not follow instructions about its use. Overdose deaths from methadone have increased 800 percent in the last five to ten years. Most of these deaths have occurred in people who were using it for pain relief, not abusing it. Fentanyl (Sublimaze) and its relatives are very fat-soluble, very fast-acting analgesics that anesthesiologists use when they put patients to sleep. Fentanyl is also used in patches that release the drug slowly through the skin to provide more long-lasting pain relief. Its most unusual formulation is a lollipop designed to deliver the drug to young children before surgery. Many addicts use fentanyl in its injectable form, and it is a common cause of overdose. Fentanyl's high comes on fast and is intense, brief, and just a step away from fatal suppression of breathing. Finally, there is propoxyphene (Darvon). This drug is such a poor opiate that most physicians won't use it, because clinical studies find it to be no more effective than a placebo. However, some people swear by it, although it's really little stronger than aspirin.

All the opiate drugs bind to the same molecule in the brain, but they do so with varying degrees of success. What follows is a list of drugs that bind very well, bind okay, and bind poorly. The clinical use of these drugs is determined in large part by this quality. Obviously, a drug like codeine won't do much good with the pain caused by major abdominal surgery, and hydromorphone would be overdoing it for a simple headache. Therefore, the form in which each of these is prepared and administered is tailored to its typical use.

OPIATE DRUGS

High Efficacy	Medium Efficacy	Low Efficacy
morphine	hydrocodone	codeine
hydromorphone	oxycodone	propoxyphene
meperidine		
fentanyl		

HOW PEOPLE TAKE OPIATES

Most opiate drugs enter the bloodstream easily from many different routes because they dissolve in fatty substances and so can cross into cells. Heroin and fentanyl represent one extreme—they are so fat-soluble that they can be absorbed across the mucosal lining of the nose. Most other opiates are not quite that fat-soluble and cannot be absorbed well after snorting. However, some opiates including the natural ingredients of the opium poppy form a vapor if heated and can be absorbed into the body if they are smoked—that is the basis of the use of the "opium pipe" as the traditional device of ancient as well as more recent history. Almost all opiates can be absorbed from the stomach, although injection is a much more efficient route for some, like morphine, that are more poorly absorbed from the stomach than others.

Intravenous injection is the route that delivers opiates into the bloodstream the fastest. Because intravenous injection is more difficult and more dangerous than other routes, many users do not start this way. Instead, they start by skin-popping—injecting drugs subcutaneously (just beneath the skin). Heroin powder is dissolved and injected. Morphine, fentanyl, and meperidine almost always appear as legally prepared injection forms that have been diverted from medical use. Snorting heroin has become a common route for new drug users. In part, users are avoiding the stigma—and risk of infectious diseases including hepatitis and AIDS—that come with injecting a drug. In part, they may believe mistakenly that they cannot become addicted if they don't inject drugs. Prescription opiates like codeine, hydromorphone (Dilaudid), oxycodone (Percodan, OxyContin), meperidine (Demerol), and, of course, methadone (Dolophine) are available as pills. Sometimes drug users resort to grinding up pills of codeine, hydrocodone, or methadone and injecting the suspension when they cannot get opiates any other way. This is an extremely risky business because the other pill components do not dissolve in saline. Injecting particles into a blood vessel can irritate the blood vessel, thus setting off a chain of reactions that lead to vascular inflammation and permanent damage. In addition, a pill particle can lodge in a small vessel and block off the blood supply to an area of the body.

HOW OPIATES MOVE THROUGH THE BODY

The rate at which opiates enter the brain depends mainly on how the user takes them. The fastest way to get high is to inject the drug directly into the bloodstream. The second fastest is to smoke it. When opiates are smoked or injected, peak levels in the brain occur within minutes. Fentanyl is the most fat-soluble and achieves maximum brain concentrations in seconds. Heroin is a little slower; it takes a couple of minutes. Morphine is slower still, but not by much (five minutes). The faster the buzz, the greater the danger of death by overdose, because drug levels in the brain can rise so quickly. Snorting heroin causes slower absorption because the drug must travel through the mucous membranes of the nose to the blood vessels beneath.

After taking a pill, the high is much slower because the drug must be absorbed from the small intestine into the bloodstream, then pass through the liver, which can metabolize much of a dose, before it ever gets into the circulation. This process takes about thirty minutes, so there's no rush after oral administration. This lack of a "rush" is why methadone is so useful in treating addicts, and as a pain medication. Sometimes users figure out how to circumvent opiate preparations that are designed to have a slow onset—the formulation of OxyContin provides a now-notorious example. OxyContin is a delayed-release form of oxycodone that is designed to release drug gradually, providing pain relief over hours. However, users discovered that crushing the pills causes a quick release of drug and gives a "high" that the manufacturer did not intend. Following its introduction in 1996, OxyContin rapidly gained a reputation as the hot "new" drug of abuse. It has since been reformulated to make abuse more difficult.

The duration of action depends upon how quickly the drug-metabolizing enzymes in the liver degrade the particular drug. Most of the drugs mentioned last for four to six hours. The exact time can vary from two hours (morphine) to up to six or so (propoxyphene), but all opiates are pretty similar. There are two important exceptions. Methadone lasts for twelve to twenty-four hours, so it can be given as a single daily dose. Fentanyl goes to the other extreme: the effects are over within an hour.

OPIATE EFFECTS ON THE BRAIN AND THE REST OF THE BODY

Morphine hits the backs of the legs first, then the back of the neck, a spreading wave of relaxation slackening the muscle away from the bones so that you seem to float without outlines, like lying in warm salt water. As this relaxing wave spread through my tissues, I experienced a strong feeling of fear. I had the feeling that some horrible image was just beyond the field of vision, moving, as I turned my head so that I never quite saw it. I felt nauseous. A series of pictures passed, like watching a movie: a huge neon-lighted cocktail bar that got larger and larger until streets, traffic and street repairs were included in it; a waitress carrying a skull on a tray; stars in the clear sky. The physical impact of the fear of death; the shutting off of breath; the stopping of blood. I dozed off and woke up with a start of fear. Next morning I vomited and felt sick until noon.

The character in William Burroughs's novel *Junkie* describes his first experience with morphine fairly accurately. The only thing missing from this description is the rush that comes with intravenous injection that most users compare to orgasm.

All opiates cause a pleasant, drowsy state in which all cares are forgotten (nodding off), and there is a decreased sensation of pain (analgesia). The feelings are the most intense after injection, which brings the rush. After the orgasmic feeling, sexual feelings usually diminish, and people experience decreased sexual desire and performance. This happens because opiates affect the release of many hormones and neurotransmitters, including those involved in the regulation of sexual behavior. People under the influence of opiates will often say that they just don't worry about their troubles anymore: they are in a special, safe place where cares are forgotten. The allure is understandable, and at the beginning it is impossible to understand the misery of addiction and withdrawal.

While the opiate user is in a dreamy, pleasant state, breathing slows, pupils are constricted, and he typically experiences nausea and perhaps even vomits. Although the effects on breathing can be quite dangerous, the other physiologic effects are fairly benign. For example, opiates do not produce big changes in blood pressure in healthy individuals. Most of the effects of narcotic drugs are caused by effects of the drugs on specific opiate receptors in the parts of the brain involved with the control of breathing and other involuntary functions. For example, opiate users vomit because morphine stimulates a center in the brain (the chemoreceptor trigger zone) whose job it is to cause vomiting in response to the ingestion of a toxic substance. So, in the movie *Pulp Fiction* the injection of adrenaline into the heart to reverse opiate overdose was not accurate. The effects on breathing that were causing the woman to OD were happening in the brain, and injecting a drug directly into the heart to get it started again was good theater, but bad pharmacology. Injecting an opiate receptor–

blocking drug (naloxone, or Narcan) into the bloodstream instead would have effectively treated the OD. The movie *Trainspotting* does a much better job of depicting the reversal of opiate effects with naloxone. The protagonist is dumped at the doors of a hospital emergency room, taken into a room, and given naloxone. In a matter of seconds he leaps up from the gurney.

One very important effect of opiates on the body has made life easier for generations of foreign travelers. Opiates increase the tension in certain muscles in the gastrointestinal tract so that the normal propulsive movements that move food along cannot operate effectively—hence their well-known ability to cause constipation. This can be a good thing if you are in Mexico and have traveler's diarrhea. Diphenoxylate (Lomotil) takes advantage of a neat chemical trick to stop diarrhea without affecting the brain. The typical opiate molecule is slightly changed so that it is not fat-soluble enough to enter the brain. This gives you a very safe, very effective medicine that can treat mild diarrhea without the risk of addiction. Through a similar action, opiates constrict the muscles of the urinary bladder and can cause difficulties in urination.

There is active research ongoing to use a similar strategy to develop drugs that bind to one special population of mu receptors that are not behind the blood-brain barrier but still involved in suppressing pain. This could be the holy grail of narcotics research—a nonaddictive narcotic drug.

HOW OPIATES WORK IN THE BRAIN

The efforts of the opium poppy to make opium alkaloids may reflect ingenious plant evolution to match the biology of their predators/pollinators. The poppy plant figured out how to make a compound that acted in their brains. The poppy is not alone—many plants make compounds that are psychoactive. The marijuana plant, numerous species of hallucinogenic mushrooms, and the coca shrub, to name a few, also influence the behavior and physiology of animals that ingest them. Furthermore, the production of opioids is not limited to plants—certain frogs produce opioid-like compounds in their skin, perhaps for the same reason(s).

Opiates act on specific receptor molecules for the endorphin/enkephalin class of neurotransmitters in the brain. These endogenous opioids are chemical neurotransmitters that control movement, moods, and physiology. They help to control many bodily activities, including digestion, regulation of body temperature, and breathing. They also help to process pain sensations, and they activate reward circuits (see the "Addiction" chapter), which is why stimulating them makes you high. All of these behaviors arise when neurons in different parts of the brain release endorphins or enkephalins. Normally, each neuron is doing its job, firing away only if it is called upon; activation of all the endogenous opioid neurons virtually never happens. Taking heroin is like every endogenous opioid neuron in the brain firing all at once.

Which of the many endogenous opioid neurons in the brain are responsible for the opiate high? The first is a small group of neurons in the hypothalamus of the brain. The neurons that use the main endorphin neurotransmitter beta-endorphin all start here and they spread out throughout the brain. These neurons become active during extremely intense stress, perhaps for the purpose of calming us down. The theorists speculate that in the body's most extreme time of stress, when it is on the verge of death, a sense of calm relaxation is helpful. The beta-endorphin neurons fire like crazy and induce an opioid-like pleasant state. Injecting beta-endorphin in the brain creates many aspects of this state, including slowed breathing, analgesia, and drowsiness.

The enkephalins are a different story. Many different kinds of neurons use enkephalins to communicate with other neurons. They appear in parts of the brain involved in processing painful sensations, controlling breathing, and other actions influenced by the opiates. They are also found in the gastrointestinal tract, where they regulate digestive function. Most important, they are found in several places involved in the reward system and may be important there. However, they probably do not function as a cohesive unit like endorphin neurons.

Endorphins and enkephalins are different members of a closely related "family" of neurotransmitters. Dynorphins, the third member of the family, share some actions, like analgesia, but actually cause unpleasant rather than pleasant feelings. These three neurotransmitters share receptors. This is perhaps a resourceful evolutionary trick played by the brain to get the most "bang for the buck" out of neurotransmitters and their receptors. By combining different opioid peptides with their receptors, a large number of possible combinations can produce a great diversity of effects.

The main opiate receptor (named with the Greek letter *mu*) provides the major effects of opiates: analgesia, euphoria, respiratory depression—

almost everything opiates do. The second major receptor (delta) cooperates with mu in some places to help produce these same effects. The third receptor (kappa) is the weird one. The drugs that are specific for this receptor produce analgesia, but they do not produce a high. This should be the perfect nonaddicting analgesic drug. There is only one problem: stimulating this receptor alone causes the opposite of euphoria, or dysphoria. Unfortunately, all of the clinically useful drugs we have now are specific for the mu receptor, and they are all addictive—the addicting properties of opiates cannot be distinguished from their painkilling properties.

NATURAL HIGH: OUR OWN ENDORPHINS

Are the joys of nature (music, sex, meditation, whatever) as great as drugs? There may be a crumb of truth in this. The brain does produce its own opiates—the enkephalins and endorphins. If we inject these into animals, they cause the same effects as morphine or heroin. The big question is, are they released in circumstances in which we feel great? Can we learn to release them ourselves? The latter question is a premise of the science fiction book *Earth*, by David Brin, which depicts a future world where drug abuse no longer exists: the new social outcasts are the brain addicts who have learned to release their own opioids.

Naturally released endorphins do affect behavior. One enterprising scientist showed that the release of endorphins went up in animals undergoing experimental acupuncture, lending credence to this ancient Chinese healing technique. How can we tell if we are releasing endorphins? First, we could give a drug like naloxone (Narcan) and see if the endorphin high stopped. This approach has actually been tested on people listening to their favorite music, who found that they didn't enjoy the music as much if they were treated with an opiate antagonist (and pleasure is in the ear of the beholder—it has to be music the listener likes, whether it is Beethoven or Florence and the Machine). However, playing the music instead of listening to it may be even more effective. A recent study that used increased pain threshold as a surrogate for endorphin activity in the brain showed that playing music or drumming elevated the pain threshold of the musician. How about runner's high? Do endorphins kick in at the end of a marathon? A recent experiment suggests that may happen. Scientists showed that endogenous opioids were released in the brains of people who had just completed a two-hour endurance run.

Overall, endogenous opioids play an important role in suppressing pain and in promoting reward. Recent studies showed that animals with no beta-endorphins will not take care of their babies, implicating endorphins as a critical element in nurturing behavior as well. These neurotransmitters are crucial to an important and related group of behaviors essential to human survival. Dynorphins also have an important role to play, telling us that stressful experiences make us feel bad, hopefully teaching us to avoid such experiences in the future.

ADDICTION, TOLERANCE, AND DEPENDENCE

While the buzz from opiates might sound alluring, it comes at a cost. Opiate drugs stimulate all opioid systems simultaneously, so there are many unwanted effects that accompany the desirable ones. One of these is the cycles of withdrawal that opiate users experience. People who take opiates for a while (weeks) can develop significant dependence and addiction and undergo withdrawal when they stop. Most opiate addicts use heroin or other opiates several times a day. With this pattern of use, tolerance develops to many of the actions of opiates, but it develops to different effects at different rates. In experimental studies, tolerance develops quickly to the ability of opiates to suppress pain. However, patients experiencing intense, chronic pain like that associated with terminal cancer can actually show little tolerance to the analgesic effects of opiates. Tolerance also develops fairly well to the suppression of breathing (this is why opiate users can tolerate higher and higher doses). However, the constipation remains, and the pinpoint pupils are slow to change. The latter is fortunate because it provides a useful sign of OD in a comatose patient and can help identify even a long-time user. While tolerance develops to opiate-induced euphoria, the drug keeps providing enough pleasure that users still get high.

Part of the tolerance results from chemical changes in how cells respond to opiates. The normal chain of events initiated by opiates adapts to the continuous presence of the drug. The adaptation becomes so thorough that cells function normally even though the drug is present. Another part of tolerance is purely a conditioned response. Pharmacologists have learned from animal studies that if you give animals a dose of heroin every day in the same room, they tolerate higher and higher doses. However, if you move them to a strange environment, the dose that they usually tolerated kills them: we think that conditioned responses permit their bodies to anticipate and counter the effects of the drug. This conditioning effect probably does apply to humans. Frequently, very experienced opiate users who OD do so because they took the drug in an unfamiliar environment.

Opiate withdrawal is miserable but not life-threatening (unlike alcohol withdrawal). Again, in *Junkie*, William Burroughs provides a good description:

> The last of the codeine was running out. My nose and eyes began to run, sweat soaked through my clothes. Hot and cold flashes hit me as though a furnace door was swinging open and shut. I lay down on the bunk, too weak to move. My legs ached and twitched so that any position was intolerable, and I moved from one side to the other, sloshing about in my sweaty clothes. . . . Almost worse than the sickness is the depression that goes with it. One afternoon I closed my eyes and saw New York in ruins. Huge centipedes and scorpions crawled in and out of empty bars and cafeterias and drugstores on Forty-second Street. Weeds were growing up through cracks and holes in the pavement. There was no one in sight. After five days I began to feel a little better.

The earliest signs of withdrawal are watery eyes, a runny nose, yawning, and sweating. When people have been using opiates heavily, they experience mild withdrawal as soon as their most recent dose wears off. As withdrawal continues, the user feels restless and irritable and loses his appetite. Overall, it feels like the flu. As withdrawal peaks, the user suffers diarrhea, shivering, sweating, general malaise, abdominal cramps, muscle pains, and, generally, an increased sensitivity to pain. Yawning and difficulty sleeping gradually become more intense over the next few days. The worst of the physical symptoms abates after a few days.

If flu symptoms were all that happened when addicts stopped using, treating heroin addiction would be easy. Unfortunately, there is another symptom that is more intangible but much longer lasting. There is a dysphoria (the just-feeling-lousy feeling), which may be the reverse of opiate-induced euphoria. They experience a craving for the drug that can be so strong that it becomes the only thing they can think about. The craving for a fix can last for months, long after the physical symptoms have abated. This is the symptom that usually triggers relapse.

Most of these withdrawal signs are the opposite of acute drug effects.

For example, opiates cause constipation, and diarrhea occurs when people go through withdrawal. The body of the addict adapts to maintain a level of intestinal tract movement despite the presence of the opiate that is con-stipating. Remove the opiate, and the underlying processes that were counteracting it to keep things normal suddenly find themselves unhin-dered. The character in the movie *Trainspotting* experienced this effect, which necessitated his mad dash for the bathroom in one scene. This rep-resents the sort of yin-yang response the body has to any disruption. (If you shiver and feel cold when you are withdrawing from opiates, what do opiates usually do to body temperature?)

Many addiction researchers think that once people are established addicts, the desire to avoid withdrawal maintains addiction more than the pleasurable effects of the drug. Obviously, when people first get addicted, they haven't been taking the drug long enough to go through intense with-drawal if they stop. However, after several months or years, the withdrawal is stronger and may contribute more to an addict's continued drug taking. If you know taking the drug will solve the problem, it seems an easy solu-tion, doesn't it? In the end, it is a combination of changes in the brain that create the overwhelming compulsion to keep using narcotics (or any other highly addictive drug). Researchers think that the craving for a drug may result from chemical changes in two parts of the brain that unfortunately combine their efforts: the parts of the brain that seek reward are chemically changed to respond strongly to drug cues, and the parts of the brain that create anxiety and bad feelings start firing as soon as the drug wears off.

PATTERNS OF USE: ARE YOU A JUNKIE?

Many people use opiates occasionally for the high. They take a pill, drink cough syrup, or inject heroin or fentanyl, for example. Some people develop a habitual pattern of daily use that accelerates over a period of time and then stabilizes at a certain level. These people take opiates every few hours. After the first week or two, they are tolerant to many of the effects of the drug; every time the drug wears off, withdrawal signs begin and the cycle of use starts again.

What pattern of use defines an addict? Can a person be addicted after the first dose? The answer for opiates isn't very different from the answers for all of the other drugs we discuss. It is not determined by whether a user injects drugs, or uses them only on weekends, or has never shared a needle, or has ever blacked out. The answer is that he's addicted when he has lost control of use: when he must continue to pursue whatever pattern of use he has set. For some, this loss of control might come from taking oxycodone pills or smoking heroin; for others, injecting or snorting heroin; and for still others, even drinking codeine-containing cough syrup.

Is a person an addict if he goes through withdrawal? Or, conversely, if he doesn't go through withdrawal, is he not a junkie? This is a common rule that many people use. As we have said, an opiate user will go through withdrawal if he has been taking the drug regularly enough that his body has adapted to it. This is a clear indication of tolerance. Usually, such adaptation means he is in a regular use pattern, but a user can be addicted before he has taken the drug long enough to show strong withdrawal signs. Conversely, a pattern of use might be compulsive but low, and the withdrawal might be so mild it isn't noticeable. Withdrawal happens also in patients who take opioids as prescribed for pain if they take the drug for a period of days or weeks. This doesn't mean they are addicts—just that their bodies have adapted to the opioids.

The National Institute on Drug Abuse has accumulated statistics about "addiction careers," or the typical drug-use pattern of people who are addicted to opiates. Usually, use begins with occasional experimentation and then gradually accelerates over a period of months to continuous administration at intervals of four to six hours. The surprising part about opiate addiction careers is that they often end. Many opiate users follow this pattern for about ten to fifteen years and then quit, often without prolonged treatment. The reasons are not entirely clear but probably include a host of social and physical factors.

OPIATE OVERDOSE AND TOXICITY

SHORT-TERM EFFECTS

The other downside to taking opiates is that there are many physical effects of stimulating all opiate receptors in the body simultaneously. Death by overdose is a major possibility. The most dangerous thing about the opiate drugs by far—and the usual cause of death—is the suppression of breathing, which can be fatal within minutes after an injection. It's not the result of cumulative toxicity but can happen with a single dose. Usually at this point the patient has become sedated and sleepy and has pinpoint pupils. The most common reason for overdose with opiates is that the user has received a dose that is much higher than expected. The composition of street heroin varies widely, and the user never really knows what he or she is getting. In some inner cities it can be as high as 70 percent pure or as low as 10 percent. Tolerance sometimes is not enough to compensate for such a difference in dose. Seizures can develop with extremely high doses, especially in infants and children who have OD'd by ingesting a drug intended for an adult. Seizures are much rarer in ordinary adult users but obviously can be dangerous. Using narcotics in combination with other depressants like alcohol raises the risk of death. A rash of deaths in Texas from 2005 to 2007 resulted from a black-market combination of black tar heroin and crushed-up cold medication that contained the antihistamine diphenhydramine. This combination of narcotic and antihistamine has long been a favorite of addicts because the antihistamine augments the narcotic high. For the uninitiated teenagers who were taking the drug, the combination proved to be lethal.

The other side effects of opiates are uncomfortable but not dangerous: nausea and vomiting, constipation, and difficulty urinating. Sometimes opiates cause a flushing of the skin and itching. This happens because morphine probably releases histamine, one of the molecules that mediates allergic reactions in the skin.

If opiate addicts were in perfect health, these would be little to worry about. Unfortunately, this is often not the case. Addicts are frequently undernourished, generally in ill health, often addicted to alcohol or other drugs, and if they inject drugs, infected with HIV or hepatitis. For example, in most people the effects of opiates on blood pressure are minor. However, these effects can be worse in people who already have problems with their cardiovascular system. Similarly, the constriction of the bile ducts can cause them to spasm, which is extremely painful in users with bile duct problems.

The existence of contaminants in illegally prepared injectable forms of heroin represents another major hazard. Depending upon the source (which is almost never known), heroin can be contaminated with quinine or other inactive ingredients, including talc. Some apparent heroin overdoses are actually problems caused by these contaminants.

LONG-TERM EFFECTS

What are the long-term effects, and which of them are dangerous? The answer might surprise you. One of our teachers, a wise and ancient British pharmacologist named Frederick Bernheim, was fond of getting up in front of the medical school class and saying that if you didn't mind being impotent and constipated, opiate addiction really wasn't too bad. He probably wouldn't be so blithe about it today, but there is some truth to this assertion.

The long-term consequences for your major body systems of taking opiates every day are, as our teacher implied, somewhat benign. Yes, addicted men can become impotent, and sexual and reproductive function can be impaired in men and women addicts. Women often stop having menstrual cycles, and in men sperm production falls. The people who use opiates over the long term are also chronically constipated, as he described. Users typically lose weight because they spend so much time chasing down the drug, they don't eat well. Otherwise, the opiates themselves are not damaging to organ systems, in marked contrast to regularly ingested alcohol. The death of Jerry Garcia of the rock group the Grateful Dead is a case in point: he was a longtime opiate addict, but he died from complications of his diabetes, not from the heroin. Even more dramatic was the quite amazing long life of William Burroughs, from whose books we have quoted extensively. He died at the age of eighty-three of natural causes, despite living much of his life addicted to opiates.

None of this sounds too bad. However, there are other major considerations. First of all, with any pattern of compulsive drug use, the user tends to ignore anything but obtaining the drug. Therefore, he tends to neglect his health, usually eats poorly, and suffers all of the other complications of not taking care of oneself. Furthermore, addicts often engage in risky behaviors associated with obtaining and using the drug. Many women addicts engage in unprotected sex to obtain money for their drug habit, and thereby increase their risk of contracting sexually transmitted diseases. Many people who inject drugs share the needles, which greatly increases their risk of contracting HIV and hepatitis. In New York City, a substantial percentage of all heroin addicts who inject heroin are infected with hepatitis and HIV. In fact, the recent popularity of snorting heroin is motivated in large part by the desire to avoid needles. These people don't avoid addiction, but they do avoid a potentially lethal side effect from needle-transmitted disease. In the context of HIV and other sexually transmitted diseases, the potential effects of opiates on the immune system present a real concern. Opiates do seem to suppress immune function, and most immune cells are loaded with opiate receptors: numerous recent studies have shown changes in immune-cell function if they are exposed to opiates. There are some other toxicities associated with long-term opiate use. As mentioned earlier, injecting particles or using unsterilized needles can cause an inflammation of the veins, which in turn can cause serious damage to the blood vessels.

New research has shown that the brains of regular opiate users don't work normally. First, many narcotics addicts have trouble with complex decision making—they tend to make poor choices and have some trouble learning new information. We are not sure yet whether this is a cause or a result of the drug taking, but the fact that these problems are worse in people who have used drugs for a long time makes it likely that it is related to the drug. Stimulant abusers have the same troubles, suggesting that changes in the brain reward system that are activated by both types of drugs may be the reason.

Second, although opiates themselves are not particularly toxic to neurons (unlike alcohol), the repeated suppression of breathing that is caused by continuous opiate use can produce changes in the brain associated with hypoxia (low blood oxygen). Long-term addicts simply don't breathe enough to maintain normal levels of blood oxygen. While this problem is not unique to opiates, it is a potential side effect that could have long-term consequences, including impaired cognitive function.

TREATMENT FOR OVERDOSE AND ADDICTION

In case of overdose, the opiate antagonist naloxone (Narcan) almost immediately reverses the life-threatening suppression of breathing. Treating opiate addiction is another matter. As with other addictions, there is no easy solution. People have tried many of the strategies used for alcoholics. A number of groups, such as Narcotics Anonymous, emphasize abstention, attendance at meetings, and so forth.

In addition, two drugs have proved to be very effective in treating narcotic addiction. Methadone is a long-acting opiate that can be given on an outpatient basis to patients in treatment programs. The idea of this strategy is to allow the addict to avoid withdrawal and the constant need to procure the drug. The other advantages of methadone are that the drug is given orally, without the risks of IV administration, and that the dose is controlled and can gradually be worked down. Although some complain that this method just substitutes one addiction for another without addressing the social and psychological reasons for the addiction, patients' lifestyles do improve. The bottom line is that methadone works—it helps users abstain and get back to productive lives and decreases mortality compared to users receiving non-drug-based therapy. Recently, buprenorphine, another opiate drug, has been approved for the treatment of opiate addiction in the form of a pill that you place under the tongue, or an implant placed under the skin to provide the drug constantly. It is somewhat different from methadone. It also stimulates opiate receptors and provides a "substitution" strategy. But when an addict takes buprenorphine, it keeps effective agonists like heroin from getting to the receptors. So it has just enough activity to stave off withdrawal. The addict doesn't get high on buprenorphine and can't get high on heroin. Some formulations of buprenorphine are combined with naloxone, so if users inject it rather than taking it as a pill, he or she cannot get high and likely will experience withdrawal symptoms. The goal of this formulation is to decrease potential abuse. The reason for this formulation is that buprenorphine, unlike methadone, can be prescribed by a doctor. Methadone can only be used in conjunction with a clinic visit: this is a real turnoff to long-term clients who complain that the only time they are around the old drug-taking environment is when they are forced to visit the clinic to receive their medication.

Pellets containing long-term-release preparations of the opioid antagonist naltrexone are also available. Like buprenorphine, they are implanted under the skin and provide the drug continuously. In this case, they keep the user from getting high as long as they last—and that's the problem. The pellets wear out, and the user simply goes back to getting high. The success of this strategy is less than those using methadone or buprenorphine. Another strategy that received some (undeserved) attention was the idea of putting a patient to sleep with a general anesthetic for the first eighteen to twenty-four hours of withdrawal along with an opioid antagonist to help speed the normalization of opioid receptor function. Again, this was based on valid pharmacology—the opioid antagonist would help remove any remaining opioid from sites where it was active. However, it is extremely dangerous to put someone under anesthesia for so long. Furthermore, these programs typically offered little follow-up, and people were just as likely to start using opiates again after this program as if they had not been treated. Most reputable physicians have rejected these treatments. Finally, scientists are studying ibogaine, a chemical contained in an African shrub, after some sensationalistic reports in the addiction underworld that one ibogaine experience led them to give up opioids forever. Ibogaine is a hallucinogen, and although research is progressing, it seems unlikely that it will pan out to be a mainstream treatment for opioid addiction. While there are numerous clinics around the world, the National Institute on Drug Abuse decided that it has too many side effects to commit resources to studying its potential, and so there is little about it in the scientific literature.

10

SEDATIVES

Drug Class: Sedative, hypnotic, anxiolytic. All of the drugs mentioned in this chapter are legally considered Schedule II–IV drugs (classified by the Drug Enforcement Administration as having some potential for abuse as well as accepted medical uses), except for GHB, which is Schedule I as a recreational drug and Schedule III as a prescription drug (Xyrem).

General Sedatives: Barbiturates (phenobarbital, pentobarbital [Nembutal], secobarbital [Seconal], amobarbital [Amytal]), chloral hydrate (Notec, Somnos, Felsules), glutethimide (Doriden), others (Equanil, Miltown, Noludar, Placidyl, Valmid, methaqualone [Quaaludes])

Benzodiazepines: Flunitrazepam (Rohypnol), diazepam (Valium), chlordiazepoxide (Librium), Ativan, Dalmane, Xanax, Serax, Tranxene, Verstran, Versed, Halcion, Paxipam, Restoril (there are hundreds more)

Drugs Designed Specifically to Induce Sleep: Zolpidem (Ambien), eszopiclone (Lunesta), and ramelteon (Rozerem)

GHB: Gamma-hydroxybutyrate (Xyrem)

The Buzz: All of the sedatives produce about the same psychological effects. First there is a sense of relaxation and a reduction of anxiety—a general "mellow" feeling. At higher doses, this is followed by lightheadedness, vertigo, drowsiness, slurred speech, and muscle incoordination. Learning is impaired, and memory for events that occurred while under the influence of these chemicals, especially the benzodiazepines, may be impaired. The duration of action can vary from a couple of hours to more than a day, so it is important to be alert to the possibility of prolonged impairment. Unexpected side effects such as anxiety, nightmares, hostility, and rage (the opposite of the calming effects the drug is expected to have) occasionally occur. All of these drugs impair the ability to drive, and in general, their effects are increased by alcohol. A person who has had a sedative and a drink of alcohol should never drive.

Overdose and Other Bad Effects: With benzodiazepines the risk of fatal overdose is small if they are taken alone. High doses simply cause prolonged sleep and perhaps memory impairment for the period they are active. However, if they are combined with any other sedating drug, fatal suppression of respiration can result. If a person has taken a benzodiazepine and is difficult to arouse, it is best to assume that some other drug may be present and to seek medical attention immediately.

Almost any of the sedatives except the benzodiazepines will cause death by suppression of breathing and heart failure if taken in sufficient quantity. The progression of symptoms is as follows: drowsiness and muscular incoordination with slurring of speech; deep sleep from which the person cannot be aroused; loss of reflexes such as blinking, gagging, and withdrawal from a painful stimulus; suppressed breathing; and death. If a person has taken a sedative and cannot be aroused, seek medical attention immediately.

Dangerous Combinations with Other Drugs: As with alcohol, opiates, and inhalants, it is dangerous to combine any sedative, including benzodiazepines, with anything else that makes a person sleepy. This includes alcohol and other drugs that have sedating properties, such as opiates (e.g., heroin, morphine, or Demerol), general anesthetics (nitrous oxide, halothane), or solvents. Some cold medicines include antihistamines, and sedatives consumed in combination with them can produce depression of heart rate and breathing.

Even drug combinations that do not cause unconsciousness or breathing problems can powerfully impair physical activities such as playing sports, driving a car, and operating machinery.

There are reports that GHB ("Easy Lay") and flunitrazepam (Rohypnol, or "roofies") have been added to drinks to cause sedation leading to rape or sexual assault. If a person begins to feel weak, dizzy, lightheaded, or mentally confused after a drink that should not produce such feelings, consider getting that person medical help.

For all of recorded history, people have sought ways to reduce their anxiety and make themselves peaceful and calm: through meditation, religious practice, psychotherapy, and all kinds of chemicals. Historically, the chemical of choice has been alcohol, and for many it still is. But as biology and medicine have progressed in this century, there has been a growing understanding of how we can manipulate our consciousness with very specific drugs to induce unconsciousness for surgery, to induce sleep, or to reduce anxiety.

The modern pharmacology of sedation began in the mid-1800s with the synthesis of chloral hydrate, a sedative that is still used today. It was followed by barbital, the first of the barbiturates, in 1903. The barbiturates turned out to be a wonderful group of compounds, because small

modifications to the chemical structure of the basic compound produced a variety of sedatives with different properties. For example,
phenobarbital had antiseizure properties at doses that did not make
patients too sleepy. Some barbiturates were extremely short-acting,
while others produced anesthesia sufficient for surgery. More than
2,500 barbiturates were synthesized, and at least 50 reached the commercial market. Not only was this an important milestone for patients
and physicians but it also demonstrated to scientists that slight changes
in a basic molecule could create drugs with very different effects.

As important as the early sedatives were, they had a deadly side
effect. At high doses they depress the brain functions that support life,
particularly breathing. This was a major risk, and thus they could not
be safely prescribed to anxious and depressed individuals who might
use them to commit suicide. This changed in 1957 with the synthesis of
the first benzodiazepine-like compound (chlordiazepoxide, or Librium).
It quickly became clear that this was a remarkable group of drugs. They
could specifically reduce anxiety without making a person too drowsy
and, best of all, they did not excessively suppress respiration. They were
much safer. Even though at that time no one knew how these drugs worked,
they clearly worked very well, and a huge number of different variations of
these compounds were synthesized (more than three thousand).

GENERAL SEDATIVES

WHAT THEY ARE AND HOW THEY WORK

Almost all of the general sedatives that are used for recreational purposes
are compounds that have been manufactured for medical use and are
diverted from legitimate sources. These drugs are obtained by illegal prescriptions, by theft, or by importing them from countries where they can
be bought without a prescription. Thus, they almost always appear as
pills, packaged liquids, or preparations ready for injection. There is nothing distinctive about their appearance; however, the potency of drugs in
this group can vary considerably.

Our best understanding of the general sedatives comes from studies of
the barbiturates. The barbiturates and other drugs act by increasing the
inhibitory function of the neurotransmitter GABA at its binding site on
the nerve cells (see the "Brain Basics" chapter for a discussion of GABA).
So, if a signal comes along that releases a bit of GABA onto a cell or net-

work of cells, then in the presence of the barbiturates that same packet of GABA can be much more effective. They do this by increasing the time that the channels in the cell membrane are open. If they are open longer, then more inhibiting ions flow, and the cell is inhibited from firing action potentials for a longer time. If there is enough GABA and enough barbiturate, then the cells cannot fire at all, and the network shuts down.

With a sedative, shutting down is exactly what we want to have happen, but only in certain areas. What we don't want is for those areas responsible for life to shut down, and there is the secret to good pharmacology— finding a drug that will do exactly what you want and not what it must not do. The barbiturates and other general sedatives are terrific if you know just how to use them, and they can be deadly if you don't.

For instance, the barbiturate phenobarbital is a great barbiturate for mild sedation and perhaps an antiseizure medicine. A clinically appropriate dose of phenobarbital will make you feel a little drowsy and maybe a bit less anxious. More of it will make you sleep, but it takes quite a bit to stop critical life functions such as respiration, and it is not good for surgery. Now assume that a person has experience with phenobarbital and knows how many pills he can take, but cannot get it, so he takes pentobarbital instead. Pentobarbital tends to have a much greater effect on GABA inhibition and is great for surgery, but it does not spare the nerve networks that control respiration. The same dose of pentobarbital that would be appropriate for phenobarbital can fatally suppress breathing. Our experimenter is in real danger of having a lethal overdose.

The message from this is that all of these sedatives are alike in their mechanism of action, but they can be very different in their potency, and maybe even in their specific potency on critical life-support networks. Anytime you take a sedative, know exactly what you are taking and the appropriate dose for that drug.

TOXICITY

The barbiturates, being manufactured for human consumption, do not contain known toxic agents, and in general their toxicity is not great if they are used at clinically appropriate doses. We have already talked about what can happen at high doses—death by respiratory depression. At normal doses, the major concern is that they can have sedative effects that outlast their sleep-inducing properties so that, for example, driving, flying an airplane, or performing other activities requiring muscle coordination can be impaired for up to a day after a single dose. Also, as with any drug that sedates, there is the possibility that excitation rather than sedation will develop. No one knows why this happens, but it seems that some people react as though some part of their nervous system is actually stimulated.

If barbiturates are used for a long period of time, the liver systems that metabolize them become enhanced. This may cause some tolerance to develop, but it also causes other drugs to be metabolized more effectively, including steroids, ethanol, and vitamins K and D. So, when taking barbiturates with other prescribed drugs, there may be a problem with getting an adequate concentration of those other drugs, and a physician might need to increase the dosage.

Chloral hydrate is a liquid that can irritate mucous membranes in the mouth and stomach and may cause vomiting. It can also cause disorienting feelings, such as lightheadedness, vertigo, muscle incoordination, and even nightmares. There are also reports that chronic users can experience sudden death, perhaps due to overdose or to liver damage. (When the liver becomes damaged, its ability to metabolize and detoxify a compound is impaired, and what may be a normal drug dose becomes toxic.)

In general, all of these drugs are safe if taken under the guidance of a physician and not mixed with other sedating compounds. People who experiment with any of them should be aware that the safety window between the effective dose and the lethal dose may be rather small.

A recent example of the danger of using anesthetic sedatives outside of the hospital is the death of Michael Jackson. It appears that Mr. Jackson had great difficulty sleeping and thus hired a physician to sedate him with propofol, a general anesthetic used for both major and minor operative procedures. Propofol is generally a very safe drug, but allegedly in this case it was administered outside of a medical setting without proper equipment for anesthesia and recovery. In addition, there are claims that Mr. Jackson might have also been under the influence of other sedative drugs.

TOLERANCE AND WITHDRAWAL

Tolerance will develop to all sedatives if they are used in sufficient doses for a period of weeks or more. There is a real risk with sudden withdrawal, because the central nervous system adapts to the drugs by turning down the inhibitory systems that these drugs enhance. It's like if the brakes have been on in a car and the driver has been compensating by pressing the accelerator more, and then suddenly the brakes are off and the driver cannot let up on the gas. The car goes faster and faster and then out of control. That's what happens to the brain. The GABA system stops being enhanced and is in a weakened condition, so the brain, out of control, becomes overexcited and can have electrical discharges that produce epileptic seizures.

Then there is the problem of psychological dependence or, simply, learning to live in a sedated state. Some people who are chronically anxious or agitated may get some relief from these drugs, but upon withdrawal, they are miserable because they have not cured their problems but only suppressed them.

BENZODIAZEPINES

WHAT THEY ARE AND HOW THEY WORK

The benzodiazepines are remarkable because they are one of the closest drugs we have to a "magic bullet" for anxiety. Used in the proper way, benzodiazepines can provide significant relief from anxiety without disrupting normal functions. Most important, they are quite safe from the risk of overdose if they are used alone and not in combination with any other sedating drug, including alcohol. While there are a few known deaths from benzodiazepines, in the vast majority of these cases the person had used them with something else.

The mechanism of action of these drugs is just about the same as that of the general sedatives—the enhancement of GABA inhibitory systems. So, the question arises of why they don't suppress respiration and cause death. It's because they work through a special benzodiazepine-binding site on the GABA receptor molecule (the place where GABA interacts with the nerve cell), and the nerve cells that control respiration and other important functions do not have many benzodiazepine sites on their GABA receptors. They are almost the perfect drug, because the receptors are on cells that participate in thinking and worrying but not on those that keep us alive. It is no wonder that these are among the most prescribed drugs on earth.

PROBLEMS WITH BENZODIAZEPINES

So, is it a perfect class of drugs? No. First, benzodiazepines often cause drowsiness and muscle incoordination, at least during the first few days of use. So operating machinery such as cars and airplanes and saws is a really bad idea. Also, they cause problems with learning, and some of them can cause amnesia. Finally, significant tolerance develops and increasing doses are required, along with a long withdrawal period when use is stopped.

Because they enhance inhibition in the central nervous system, benzodiazepines can impair the process of neuroplasticity that we talk about in the "Brain Basics" chapter. That is, they can prevent the brain from recording and adapting to new information by preventing it from changing its wiring pattern. See the discussion on pages 303–6 about how long-term potentiation of synapses may underlie learning. Benzodiazepines suppress this process. The general sedatives do this, too, but few people take them chronically, while a lot of people take benzodiazepines for prolonged periods. Because general learning is a problem, it is unrealistic for someone who needs to learn new information to expect to do so to her full potential if using these drugs. Once people stop taking benzodiazepines, however, this effect on learning disappears and they return to normal function.

The really dark side of not learning is amnesia—not remembering something important. Benzodiazepines can cause amnesia, and this is part of the major controversy about their abuse in social situations. There are reports of benzodiazepines being put into the drinks of women who are then raped but have amnesia for the whole event. This may have become more prominent because of the availability of flunitrazepam (the brand name is Rohypnol, commonly called roofies), which is an especially potent benzodiazepine. A very small amount (two milligrams) will easily disappear in a drink but be quite effective. This is the worst kind of drug abuse because it is inflicted on someone who does not choose it.

Flunitrazepam is widely distributed in the underground market, and the government has banned importation of it. As far as we can determine, it does exactly what the far more common benzodiazepine Valium does and nothing more. However, it takes only about two milligrams of flunitrazepam to do what ten milligrams of Valium will do; it more easily disappears into a drink; and if mixed with a lot of alcohol, it could lead to a serious overdose.

As for other problems with benzodiazepines, they are about the same as those for the general sedatives—lightheadedness, vertigo, poor muscle coordination, nightmares, and so forth.

DRUGS DESIGNED SPECIFICALLY TO INDUCE SLEEP

Problems with sleeping are a huge issue in our society, and the pharmaceutical companies are responding with new drugs that may be less problematic than the general benzodiazepines. Three of these drugs are zolpidem (Ambien), eszopiclone (Lunesta), and ramelteon (Rozerem).

AMBIEN

Ambien (zolpidem) is an interesting drug because, although it is chemically unrelated to the benzodiazepines, it acts on a benzodiazepine receptor that induces sleep. It does not, however, seem to reduce anxiety, so it is thought to be less rewarding and thus less prone to cause dependence than normal benzodiazepines like Valium. It also has a very short lifetime in the body—its effects are diminished within a few hours—which some scientists argue is what prevents the development of tolerance problems.

Zolpidem received FDA approval in 1993 and now has been on the market long enough for any problems to emerge. In general, it appears to be a reasonably safe drug if, as with all prescription drugs, it is taken as prescribed by a doctor—that is, it should be taken just before sleep, and then the user should actually get in bed and go to sleep. If the user stays awake, zolpidem's hypnotic properties will impair driving or other activities requiring coordinated functions. And like other agents that act at the benzodiazepine receptor, it can produce amnesia for any activities that occur during the time it is effective.

It should not be taken with any other sedating drug, such as alcohol, and its use should be limited to a short period of time—seven to ten days. Epidemiological studies indicate that the abuse potential of this drug is, in fact, lower than that for benzodiazepines, but caution should be used in prescribing it for individuals who have a history of sedative abuse or dependence.

As with all drugs, however, surprises do occur. There are an increasing number of reports of individuals who take zolpidem and then partially wake up enough to engage in fairly complex activities for which they later have no memory. These include sleep driving, sleep eating, sleep shopping, sleep e-mailing, sleep sex, and even criminal activity carried out in a twilight state. We do not know why this happens, but we speculate that for some reason, the sleep-maintaining effects of the drug diminish faster than the effects of the drug on other brain areas. This leaves the user in a twilight state in which some behaviors are possible but high-level cognitive functions are still impaired. One person told us of repeated episodes of sleep shopping from Internet sites. Another reported sending inappropriate e-mails to a friend of the opposite sex. We have consulted on criminal cases that involved driving offenses, the display and firing of a gun, and even murder—all committed while the person was under the influence of zolpidem, and in every case, the person had amnesia for the events.

As we are writing this edition, there has been a 2013 report from the Drug Abuse Warning Network[*] concerning adverse effects of zolpidem. The report states that in the United States, "the number of zolpidem-related emergency department visits involving adverse reactions increases nearly 220 percent from 6,111 visits in 2005 to 19,487 visits in 2010." The report goes on to state that "patients typically use zolpidem to benefit from temporary sedative effects that aid them in attaining restful sleep. Adverse reactions have occurred, including daytime drowsiness, dizziness, hallucinations, behavioral changes (e.g., bizarre behavior and agitation), and complex behaviors such as sleepwalking and 'sleep driving' (i.e., driving while not fully awake)." It is very likely that many more people experience unexpected effects with zolpidem than the number that actually go to the emergency department of hospitals, so our advice is to be cautious in the use of this drug, especially in combination with other drugs.

LUNESTA

Lunesta came to the market in 2005 and is similar to Ambien. It is not a benzodiazepine but acts at benzodiazepine receptors to induce sleep. Like Ambien, it is reported to have lower abuse potential than benzodiazepines, but the same cautions apply. There is not enough market experience with this drug to comment further about unexpected problems.

ROZEREM

Rozerem is an entirely different sleep-inducing agent that works through melatonin receptors. It is discussed in the chapter on herbal drugs.

[*] http://www.samhsa.gov/data/2k13/DAWN079/sr079-Zolpidem.htm

GHB

GHB emerged on the scene of popular culture when *Time* magazine made it a hot topic. On September 30, 1996, *Time* reported the death of a seventeen-year-old Texas girl. An outstanding athlete and a highly responsible student, she went to a dance club, had a couple of soft drinks, then went home complaining of a headache and nausea. Twenty-four hours later she was dead from an overdose of GHB. There was no other toxic agent in her body and no evidence that she knew she took the drug. The speculation is that GHB was slipped into her drinks.

GHB is now a common drug of abuse for teenagers and young adults. The Internet is full of descriptions (many very inaccurate) about the effects of the drug, and there are even instructions for making it in home laboratories. GHB can be lethal, it is easy to manufacture, and it is difficult to detect in a drink—a perilous and dicey combination.

WHAT IT IS AND HOW IT WORKS

GHB—gamma-hydroxybutyrate—is most often available as an odorless and colorless liquid, occasionally with a salty taste. It is used as a general anesthetic in Europe, and it has been sold in health-food stores for bodybuilding, but that is now illegal in most areas, having been banned by the US Food and Drug Administration for over-the-counter sales in 1990. Now most of the illicit market is found in nightclubs and at all-night dance parties ("raves"). GHB is available by prescription (Xyrem) for treating the sleep disorder narcolepsy (a disease in which the patient falls asleep repeatedly during the day).

Originally this drug was thought to work by binding to the GABA receptor on nerve cells and activating that receptor. It does that, but GHB may itself be a neurotransmitter in the brain. It meets many of the requirements that neurobiologists have established for a transmitter. It is synthesized in the brain, it has specific receptor sites and specific receptor locations, and its effects can be blocked by specific receptor antagonists. Thus, it may have a very specific role in the brain, although we don't know what that is.[*] Even so, there is nothing very remarkable about this, and it

---

[*] The latest results from our laboratories suggest that GHB may suppress the function of the NMDA subtype of the glutamate receptor, as does ethanol. This may explain the ethanol-like buzz that some users report.

should not make much difference to anyone but neuroscientists, except for one unusual fact: it easily crosses from the blood to the brain.

Under normal circumstances, the brain is remarkably insulated from the rest of the body by the blood-brain barrier. To get into the brain, substances must dissolve easily in fat to move through tissues. Most neurotransmitters will not cross the blood-brain barrier, and so no matter how much of them is ingested, they never reach the brain. This is a very important property of the body because neurotransmitters are present in much of what we eat, and if we had meals that included a huge amount of a particular neurotransmitter, we would die of either overexcitation or too much inhibition.

So, what does it mean that GHB can cross from the blood to the brain? It means that whatever role GHB plays in normal brain function will be modified by added GHB moving into the brain. Instead of having a normal circuit that is wired and functioning in an orderly manner, the circuit could become disordered as the GHB receptors get randomly activated as the drug courses through the brain. This is a bit different from other sedatives that simply increase the activity of a receptor, more or less preserving the orderliness of the network.

Whatever the neuropharmacology of GHB turns out to be, it is clearly a potent drug. In general, it can be thought of as a major sedative on the basis of its effects. It produces relaxation, mild euphoria, then headache, perhaps nausea, drowsiness, loss of consciousness, seizures, and coma or even death. Given its amnesiac properties, it probably produces subtle effects on learning and memory at doses that don't produce loss of consciousness.

Is GHB addictive? When GHB is used clinically as a treatment for narcolepsy, it is not. However, when it is used recreationally, at doses that are higher than recommended and at frequent intervals, a profound dependence syndrome can develop, as we discuss in what follows.

TOXICITY

As illustrated by the *Time* article, GHB can be quite toxic. We then did not know much about toxicity from long-term effects of its use, but the short-term effects were clear. Overdose can occur easily. The overdose signs are similar to those for other sedatives, with drowsiness, nausea, vomiting, headache, loss of consciousness, loss of reflexes, and suppression of breathing, leading up to death. Epileptic seizures may also occur. Please be aware that routine toxic screens in the emergency room are often not set up to detect GHB. Therefore, if anyone shows signs of these problems, it is critical to get medical help and tell the medical personnel that GHB may be present.

Often GHB is taken with ethanol, and this violates the cardinal rule of not combining sedatives. A very recent pharmacological study in humans indicates that toxic effects of the two drugs are additive, lowering blood pressure and decreasing blood oxygen.

TOLERANCE AND WITHDRAWAL

Perhaps the worst problem with GHB is the development of tolerance and withdrawal. When the first edition of this book was written, we knew nothing about the effects of long-term use of GHB, but now we know a lot, and the news is very bad.

Here's how the problem typically develops, according to a psychiatrist who regularly treats GHB-dependent patients. A person will discover that GHB produces a high somewhat like alcohol, and with higher doses, sedation. That person uses the drug recreationally, at social events, for the euphoria. Then one night the person has trouble falling asleep and turns to GHB as a sedative. After many uses, the person reaches the point that he is using the drug every few hours, twenty-four hours a day, seven days a week. Typically a person in this state can sleep no more than two to four hours before he awakes and needs more of the drug.

The GHB withdrawal process can be devastatingly difficult for a highly tolerant and dependent person. Within hours of stopping GHB, he experiences insomnia, anxiety, and perhaps psychosis. The physical symptoms are somewhat like those associated with profound ethanol withdrawal— tremors, agitation, high heart rate, and high blood pressure. Often the person cannot withdraw without medical help, and usually this means admission to a hospital where physicians skilled in addiction medicine can administer high doses of benzodiazepines or other sedatives to allow the person to slowly come out of withdrawal.

OTHER SOURCES OF GHB

GHB is synthesized in the brain through several metabolic pathways, and this has provided a way for people to get a GHB-like high without having to purchase the now-illegal substance itself. The solvents GBL (gamma-butyrolactone) and 1,4 BD (1,4 butanediol) are metabolized in the brain to GHB; when ingested, they both produce the same effects as GHB itself.

There's a real problem with 1,4 BD—the metabolism of 1,4 BD to GHB is inhibited by ethanol. So if a person drinks alcohol and takes 1,4 BD, then the conversion to GHB is delayed until the ethanol is eliminated, and the user can have an unexpectedly delayed GHB effect.

A CAUTIONARY NOTE

Because GHB is growing in popularity, easy to manufacture, readily found in nightclubs, and hard to detect in a drink, it is important to be alert to the possibility that someone may add it to a drink. If a person begins to feel weak, dizzy, lightheaded, or mentally confused after a drink that should not produce such feelings, consider getting that person medical help. At this point, there is no FDA-approved antagonist for GHB. Good medical support early on can prevent most of the problems that ingesting GHB will cause.

11

STEROIDS

Drug Class: Anabolic steroids. All of the drugs mentioned in this chapter are legally considered Schedule III drugs (classified by the Drug Enforcement Administration as having some potential for abuse but having accepted medical uses).

Individual Drugs: testosterone, methyltestosterone, boldenone (Equipoise), methandrostenolone (Dianabol), stanozol (Winstrol), nandrolone (Durabolin, Dex-Durabolin), trenbolone (Finajet), ethylestrenol (Maxibolin), fluoxymesterone (Halotestin), oxandrolone (Anavar), oxymetholone (Anadrol), androstenedione, dehydroepiandrostenedione (DHEA)

Common Terms: steroids, roids, juice

The Buzz: Steroids do not cause a buzz immediately when they are taken because they don't take action for hours. After a typical "stacking" regimen lasting several weeks, some users report feelings of euphoria, great energy, and increased combativeness/competitiveness. Such users complain of depression when they stop using anabolic steroids.

Overdose and Other Bad Effects: Anabolic steroids do not cause death by acute overdose in the same way that opiates or other psychoactive drugs do. However, they cause many changes in body function that can cause serious injury or death. Serious heart damage and even death from heart attacks or stroke have occurred in people using high-dose anabolic steroids for a prolonged period of time.

WHAT ARE ANABOLIC STEROIDS?

Testosterone and drugs that act like testosterone in the body are called anabolic steroids. The term *steroid* refers to their chemical structure, and the term *anabolic* refers to their ability to promote muscle growth. Testosterone production during adolescence and after is responsible for both sexual maturation and the growth in height and muscle mass that men experience at this time. Physicians prescribe anabolic steroids to men who have inadequate testosterone production. Male and female athletes, both professional and amateur, use anabolic steroids illegally for their ability to increase muscle mass. Most of the steroids used illegally by athletes have been diverted from appropriate medical or veterinary use, or have been prepared by bootleg labs and packaged in a way that resembles the real product. They appear as pills (white, yellow, or pink) or as injectable solutions. There are also topical testosterone preparations including creams, gels, and skin patches that release small amounts of hormone that are absorbed through the skin.

There are other natural steroid hormones, but they are not anabolic steroids. Estrogen and progesterone are the steroids that are present in females, and cortisol is the steroid that is normally released by the adrenal gland under conditions of stress. Cortisol is a catabolic hormone that breaks down muscle. Normally, the only anabolic steroid present in the body is testosterone. Obviously, men have much more than women, but women produce a small amount of testosterone as well. **The steroids that people take to treat asthma are not anabolic steroids; instead, they are**

variations on cortisol. So asthma sufferers who take steroids for their asthma should not worry that they are using a dangerous drug.

In a normal man, testosterone is present from the time of fetal life. During fetal development, it is responsible for the development of the male genitalia, and it contributes to the differentiation of brain functions that are different in men and women like reproduction and sexual behavior. During puberty, testosterone production increases dramatically, causing the rapid growth in height, the thickening and coarsening of body hair, the lowering of the voice, genital development, acne, and the muscle growth that happens at that stage of life. It influences the production of fat-carrying proteins in the blood and lowers levels of the "good" lipid-carrying protein that can protect against heart disease. Testosterone also contributes to the increase in libido that occurs at this age. Once puberty is over, testosterone levels tend to be fairly constant through adult life.

Physicians use testosterone to treat men whose bodies don't produce enough due to disease or surgical removal of the testes. They tend to be anemic, a serious condition that is easily reversed with hormone treatment. It is also used for its anabolic properties to facilitate tissue regrowth in burn patients and in AIDS patients who have severe weight loss. Recently, some doctors are using testosterone to restore libido and energy in men with "low T," although this may be as much an advertising gimmick as a clinical condition.

The Cold War introduced anabolic steroids into international athletic competition. The Communist countries of Eastern Europe started using anabolic steroids to improve performance in both their men and women athletes in the fifties and sixties, and the improvement in performance was not lost on the rest of the world. Some of the athletes (for example, women swimmers from then East Germany) have since claimed that they were given these substances without their knowledge, although they recognized that they were receiving a very active drug because of the dramatic changes they noticed in their bodies. Other countries caught on, and by the mid-1960s, this use was common. By the early 1970s almost three-quarters of the athletes involved in middle- or short-distance running or in field events admitted to using steroids, and most of the weight lifters also used steroids. The use of anabolic steroids in Olympic competition was banned in 1976. Different amateur and professional sports associations have gradually adopted similar prohibitions. For example, major league baseball in the United States did not ban steroids until 1991 and did not initiate a testing program in the major leagues until 2003. As a result of rigorous testing, the percentage of amateur and professional athletes who use steroids has declined markedly. Unfortunately, the use of anabolic steroids has left the mainstream and entered the underground world. Testing has become increasingly successful but has also resulted in a "shell game" in which athletes either use products that are not yet recognized by testers or learn how to stop use long enough before a tournament to avoid detection. The controversy surrounding the designer steroid tetrahydrogestrinone (THG) synthesized by BALCO (Bay Area Laboratory Cooperative) is a recent example. This molecule is a testosterone derivative that had never been used before and so was not banned. When a coach turned in a syringe filled with this unknown steroid, the hunt was on by the testing laboratory of Dr. Don Caitlin at UCLA. He identified the molecule in 2003, and since then, urine from a number of elite athletes has tested positive for THG, and a number of track and field records have been thrown into question. Growing concerns about the rapid spread of anabolic steroid use led Congress to place them under the Controlled Substances Act in 1991. This ban is gradually having some effect, and the number of high school students admitting to anabolic steroid use has gradually declined since 2000 to a current level of about 1 to 2 percent.

HOW ARE ANABOLIC STEROIDS USED AND ARE THEY EFFECTIVE?

Normally, testosterone is released constantly by the testes, and when doctors try to treat male patients who have inadequate testosterone, they try to provide steady, low levels. This is not how steroid users typically use them. One way that sophisticated users take anabolic steroids is by using creams or skin patches to temporarily boost levels of the natural hormone testosterone to levels in the top of the normal range: this can evade some testing approaches. Testers figured out how to thwart this strategy by testing the ratio of testosterone to a minor metabolite, epitestosterone, which is present at no more than a 4:1 ratio normally. When the ratio is very high (over 6:1), it almost always indicates testosterone use. Then sophisticated athletes started using T:E combinations. Testers most recently base assessment on the ratio of C13:C12 in testosterone precursor and metabolites in urine: testosterone from synthetic sources has a different ratio than that produced by the body. Both tests caught Floyd Landis cheating in the 2006 Tour de France. Another way that athletes cause a temporary boost in the body's production of testosterone is by using natural hormones that stimulate the pituitary (gonadotropin-releasing hormone, GnRH) or testes (luteinizing hormone, LH, or human chorionic gonadotropin, HCG) to make more testosterone.

Usually, athletes use anabolic steroids in a "stacking" regimen: a cycle that lasts four to eighteen weeks, starting with low doses of several steroids, gradually increasing the dose every few weeks, then taking some weeks off. The amounts they take are huge in comparison to normal regimens used by doctors. A normal replacement regimen would be about seventy-five to one hundred milligrams of testosterone a week, while a comparable regimen of self-administered testosterone can be from ten to a hundred times the normal medical dose. Some of the anabolic agents used in this way are listed at the start of the chapter, but the list is always changing and expanding.

The huge doses that users often take may explain the difference between public perception and scientific results. For many years, the scientific establishment denied that anabolic steroids could cause any real improvement in athletic performance. This conviction was based on results of controlled scientific studies done on men who were not particularly fit and who already had optimal levels of testosterone. They put them all on an exercise regimen and gave some men testosterone and others a placebo. All of the men usually improved in performance because of the exercise regimen. Because the male body makes about the optimal amount of testosterone, adding a little usually has little impact.

The situation for bodybuilders and others who use anabolic steroids is quite different—they are maximally fit to start, just looking for that slight edge, and taking huge amounts does improve performance enough for that winning edge. Although testosterone normally works only on its own receptor to build muscle, when such huge amounts are taken, scientists have speculated that it "spills over" onto the catabolic steroid receptor and prevents the effects of cortisol. So instead of just muscle building, huge amounts of anabolic steroids might prevent muscle breakdown, too. Finally, it is possible that just the sense of energy that anabolic steroids can give, or even the psychological boost of taking a performance-enhancing drug, can have a real impact on performance in sports. In a highly competitive environment of optimally trained athletes, the appearance of advantage may be all that is necessary.

Anabolic steroids definitely improve muscle deposition in women, even in normal amounts; in the amounts taken by athletes, the improvement in muscle deposition can be dramatic. Because muscle deposition promoted by testosterone tends to be greater in the upper body, this provides the greatest effects (and therefore the greatest likelihood of abuse) for sports like swimming that rely on upper-body strength.

STEROIDS AND THE NATIONAL PASTIME

Even the national pastime, baseball, has been influenced by steroid use. The current focus on steroid use in baseball started in 1998, when Mark McGwire admitted that during the year that he broke the home run record, he used the legal dietary supplement androstenedione (andro) to enhance his performance. (Because andro is a normal body constituent, supplement manufacturers can sell it legally. See the chapter on herbal drugs.) This admission sparked a marketing blitz and created a cottage industry that is still thriving today. The most recent version of the controversy surrounds the use of testosterone and other banned anabolic agents like human growth hormone by baseball players, including New York Yankees star Alex Rodriguez, who were clients of the Biogenesis of America clinic.

Does andro really work? Androstenedione is a normal precursor to steroid hormones that are produced in the human body. If you take a dietary supplement containing andro, a small percentage is converted in the body to testosterone. That much has been proven scientifically. Here is the catch: it takes a lot to increase testosterone enough to improve muscle mass. Remember that slight changes in testosterone in the physiologic range won't do it—it takes levels a hundredfold higher at least. Since McGwire's admission, several good research studies have shown that andro supplements indeed cause a temporary small increase in blood testosterone, but this doesn't translate into strength or muscle mass. However, much larger doses can increase muscle mass and strength. (Mark McGwire has since admitted, however, that he also took other, more active anabolic agents.)

This research hasn't stopped supplement manufacturers from touting their products. As you consider their advertising claims, consider this: more androstenedione is converted to estrogen than to testosterone. Therefore, the breast development that is a side effect of taking testosterone is probably more of a likelihood than getting stronger if you take andro.

There are a number of products containing andro on the market, including androstenediol, DHEA (dehydroepiandrosterone), and norandrostenedione. They all have a common goal: to serve as a steroid hormone precursor to increase the production of testosterone or other androgenic hormones that normally exist in the body in trace amounts. And they all share a common problem: it is difficult (but not impossible) to achieve anabolic levels of the hormones by taking the supplements.

WHAT ARE THE HAZARDS OF ANABOLIC STEROID USE?

There is no question that anabolic steroid use can cause bad health consequences. However, extravagant claims on both sides of this argument have flown back and forth in the media. What is the scientific evidence? In women the evidence is clear-cut. Women usually make only a tiny amount of testosterone, so the very high levels that result from taking anabolic steroids lead to the emergence of masculine characteristics: extra muscle deposits, a deeper voice, thicker and coarser body hair, male pattern baldness, and an enlarged clitoris. The anatomical changes caused by steroid use (deeper voice and enlarged clitoris) are irreversible. Also, women experience changes in the profile of blood proteins that promote heart disease and lose the normal protective effects of their gender on the heart and blood vessels. Similarly, in adolescent males, use of anabolic steroids can cause a premature end to puberty, including a stop to the rapid growth stimulated in part by testosterone during this phase of life. Some of the effects in adolescent boys, like those in women, are irreversible. Normally, the rise in testosterone during puberty stimulates skeletal growth and finally stops it by causing the growing ends of the bone to "close over" and stop lengthening. After this closing over has happened, no further increase in height is possible. Use of anabolic steroids can speed up this process, leading ultimately to a shorter height than expected.

In adult men, the doses that many athletes use suppress libido and halt sperm production. A growing number of case reports indicate that damage to the heart occurs in some users. It is also clear that levels of fat-carrying proteins in the blood of both men and women users change to a pattern that promotes heart disease, although this pattern reverses when steroid use is stopped. The combination of hypertrophy (increased growth) of the heart, increased tendency of the platelets to clot, and increased levels of lipids in the blood likely contributes to the increased risk of heart attack in men who use anabolic steroids to improve athletic performance. There are isolated cases of liver disease and liver cancer that have been attributed to the use of particular steroids. On rare occasions, certain anabolic steroids cause the appearance of blood-filled cysts in the liver that can rupture and cause dangerous internal bleeding. Finally, testosterone can actually cause some feminizing effects in men. Breast development is the most common. This happens because a little bit of the testosterone in the body is converted to the female hormone estradiol. This condition commonly develops in weight lifters who use anabolic steroids. Most importantly, death (from any cause) is more common in men who use anabolic agents than in men of comparable age and health who do not.

What about "roid rage"? Do anabolic steroids really make people incredibly aggressive and prone to uncontrollable outbursts of rage and violence? This is the most controversial effect of these drugs. There is no question that anabolic steroids can affect behavior. They have been used successfully to treat depression in experimental studies, and there have even been a number of cases of anabolic steroid-induced manic episodes. Furthermore, as we note in the following, stopping use can cause depression.

However, evidence for the specific effects of testosterone on aggression is hard to find in controlled studies in humans. There have been small, much-publicized studies showing that testosterone levels were high in a subset of criminals who were known to have committed particularly violent crimes. There are many studies in rats and some in monkeys that show that high levels of steroids can affect aggressive behavior in specific tests. The behavior they describe is not the sort of irrational destructiveness that is so popular in the lay press. Instead, animals often simply compete better or fight more quickly when provoked. To extrapolate from these studies to explain the behavior of individual men requires a leap. For the moment, we are left with reports of users who describe their own absolutely uncharacteristic impulsive aggressive behavior while under the influence of anabolic steroids. Learning from the wrong conclusions scientists drew from their first inadequate experiments with muscle deposition, we should take these reports seriously because there simply aren't controlled laboratory studies of the behavioral effects of the tremendous dosage regimens that some athletes use.

ARE ANABOLIC STEROIDS ADDICTIVE?

Anabolic steroids certainly meet the first criterion of addiction—that users take them in the absence of medical need and despite the knowledge of negative health consequences. This was the basis for their being placed under the Controlled Substances Act. But are they addictive? Users do feel differently when they take steroids, and the feelings are mostly positive. They also experience a withdrawal syndrome when they stop. Some users report fatigue, depression, loss of appetite, insomnia, and headaches as the effects of the drugs wane. However, users don't report a rush of euphoria when they take steroids; there are no recognizable effects of taking an injection. Furthermore, laboratory studies show that animals generally don't self-administer them, although there are some interesting exceptions. Anabolic steroids don't cause the kinds of changes in the brain caused by other addictive drugs like cocaine and heroin. However, it is clear that people develop a compulsive reliance on them and willingly tolerate negative health consequences when they are using them—both of which are criteria for drug dependence. Finally, a few intriguing experiments in hamsters have shown that some animals will voluntarily take anabolic steroids. Because the effects of sex hormones in the brain can be very species-specific, we are awaiting confirmation in a wide array of species before we extend these results to humans.

Are there good health reasons for anabolic steroids to be illegal in sports? Given the real health problems caused by these drugs, this ban does make sense. In the end, the normal male body produces optimal amounts of testosterone for health and vitality, and providing suprapharmacologic amounts provides a scant benefit in terms of slightly better muscle deposition at a great health cost. The focus on success at any price, even in amateur athletics, has encouraged the use of anabolic steroids worldwide. Better education about the consequences should make people wary of using or recommending them.

12

STIMULANTS

Drug Class: Stimulants. All of the drugs mentioned in this chapter are legally considered Schedule I or II drugs (classified by the Drug Enforcement Administration as having a high potential for abuse and no accepted medical uses). Drugs that are used to treat ADHD (amphetamine, methamphetamine, methylphenidate) have a valid medical use and are Schedule II. Others are Schedule I. Purchasers must show identification to purchase stimulant precursors like pseudoephedrine.

Individual Drugs: cocaine, amphetamine (Adderall, Dexedrine), methamphetamine, methylphenidate (Ritalin), cathinone, methcathinone, 4-methylmethcathinone (mephedrone), 3,4-Methylenedioxypyrovalerone (MDPV), 3,4-methylenedioxymethcathinone (methylone)

Common Terms: coke, blow, candy, crack, jack, jimmy, rock, nose candy, whitecoat (cocaine); crank, bennies, uppers (amphetamine); meth, crystal, crystal meth, ice (methamphetamine); Ritalin (methylphenidate); cat, khat, crank, goob (methcathinone); Ivory Wave, Bliss, Bubbles, Meow Meow, Explosion, Vanilla Sky (bath salts)

The Buzz: Stimulants are aptly named: these drugs cause a sense of energy, alertness, talkativeness, and well-being that users find pleasurable. At the same time, users experience signs of sympathetic nervous system stimulation, including increased heart rate and blood pressure and dilation of the bronchioles (breathing tubes) in the lungs. These drugs also cause a stimulation of purposeful movement that is the reason for their description as psychomotor stimulants. When injected or smoked, these drugs cause an intense feeling of euphoria. With prolonged and high-dose use, the locomotor activity often becomes focused in repetitive movements like drawing repeating patterns.

Overdose and Other Bad Effects: There are three kinds of dangers with the stimulants. First and most important, at high doses (these are doses a person could take accidentally), death can result. High-dose cocaine use can lead to seizures, sudden cardiac death, stroke, or failure of breathing. Lethal doses of amphetamine sometimes cause seizures but more often can cause lethal cardiac effects and/or hyperthermia (fever). As with opiates, any of these drugs can cause death with a single dose, and this is particularly easy with cocaine. The second kind of danger is psychiatric. With repeated use of high doses of stimulants over days to weeks, a psychotic state of hostility and paranoia can emerge that cannot be distinguished from paranoid schizophrenia. With some of the new, particularly effective "bath salts," a toxic delirium with psychotic-like behavior can occur as a result of a single very high dose. Finally, profound addiction can develop to any stimulant.

Dangerous Combinations with Other Drugs: Stimulants can be dangerous when taken with over-the-counter cold remedies that contain decongestants, because the effects of the two can combine to raise blood pressure to a dangerous level. Also, stimulants can be dangerous in combination with the antidepressants known as monoamine oxidase inhibitors, because they will enhance the effects of the stimulants. Cocaine is dangerous with anything that would affect heart rhythm, such as medication taken for certain heart diseases, because these drugs would act in an additive way with the effects of cocaine on the heart. Cocaine is also dangerous in combination with anything that makes people more sensitive to seizures, such as the prescription medication buspirone (BuSpar) or extremely high levels of xanthines, like caffeine or theophylline.

CHAPTER CONTENTS

THE HISTORY OF STIMULANT USE

The yuppies of the eighties certainly did not invent cocaine use. Cocaine has been used for centuries by the natives of South America. Amphetamine, on the other hand, was the product of the pharmaceutical industry—the result of successful attempts to improve upon ephedrine as a drug for treating asthma.

THE STORY OF COCAINE

Cocaine appears in the leaves of several species of plants, including the shrubby plant *Erythroxylum coca*, that grow in the Andes Mountains in South America. Coca use as early as the sixth century is documented in archeological relics from South America, but it probably started much earlier. The natives of South America chewed coca leaves for their alerting effects and their ability to increase endurance, particularly at the high altitudes in which many of these peoples lived. This practice continues to the present day. When the Spaniards conquered the Incas in the sixteenth century, they attempted to ban the use until they realized that the Indians working in the silver mines would work harder if given their daily allotment of coca.

With the importation of coca to Europe and the purification of cocaine from the leaves by the German scientist Albert Niemann in 1860, a new era began. The Corsican chemist Angelo Mariani was partly responsible for popularizing the use of cocaine by inventing Vin Mariani in 1869. Vin Mariani was a "medicinal" wine made by steeping coca leaves in wine, and it became the rage of Europe. Soon thereafter, the American pharmaceutical industry took note, and Parke-Davis started manufacturing a cocaine-containing tonic. The success of this tonic spawned a host of imitators, including Georgia pharmacist John Pemberton's Coca-Cola, a tonic containing a (still) secret formula that included cocaine. Another pharmacist, Asa Candler, realized the financial potential of this concoction and purchased the rights to the formula. The rest is history, as his Coca-Cola Company became a fixture in the American landscape and now the world.

Sigmund Freud, known to most as the father of psychoanalysis, was also one of the major forces in the popularization of cocaine in Europe. Freud studied cocaine using the well-accepted practice of the time—self-experimentation. He took the drug and recorded his experiences. His initial reports were overwhelmingly positive: he enjoyed the sense of euphoria and energy and found little in the way of toxic effects. His enthusiasm caused him to encourage his friend Ernst von Fleischl-Marxow to try cocaine in an attempt to free himself from morphine addiction. This turned out to be a misguided idea, as his friend quickly substituted morphine dependence with cocaine dependence. His pattern of use escalated to intravenous injections of larger and larger doses until he developed psychotic symptoms, one of the first recorded cases of stimulant psychosis.

Freud was also responsible for noting the ability of cocaine to produce local anesthesia (numbing), and his mention of this quality to a friend, ophthalmologist Carl Koller, led to the widespread use of cocaine in certain types of eye, ear, and nose operations that persists to the present day.

Why isn't there still cocaine in Coca-Cola? The tale is familiar in today's environment of public activism about product safety. During the early 1900s, unregulated sales of "tonics" containing potent ingredients such as opium and cocaine boomed. Some of these formulations contained so much cocaine (hundreds of milligrams per milliliter instead of the 0.5 milligrams per milliliter in the original Parke-Davis formula) that toxicities became widespread. The medical establishment finally took note. Unfortunately, a scare campaign with racist overtones also contributed to the public furor. Reports that cocaine made African Americans powerful and uncontrollable contributed to the wave of negative publicity. In 1906, the Pure Food and Drug Act required that manufacturers list the ingredients on all tonics, and in 1914, the Harrison Narcotic Act imposed severe restrictions upon the distribution of opium and cocaine products. Today, Coca-Cola contains only caffeine, and clinical cocaine use is restricted to a few surgical procedures.

THE STORY OF EPHEDRINE AND AMPHETAMINE

The story of ephedrine and amphetamine is not dissimilar. The Chinese drug mahuang was long known to help treat the breathing symptoms of asthma. Dr. K. K. Chen of the Eli Lilly Company in the 1920s identified the compound ephedrine as the active agent in mahuang, and ephedrine quickly became an important treatment for asthma. At the time it was first identified, it was a useful medicine. However, there was not an easy way to make synthetic ephedrine, so it had to be extracted from the native plant, which was in short supply. A few years later, a chemist named Gordon Alles synthesized amphetamine in an attempt to develop a synthetic form of ephedrine. Little did he realize that he had succeeded too well. Amphetamine was quickly marketed in several forms, including a volatile preparation. Nasal amphetamine inhalers gained quickly in popularity, in part because amphetamine proved to do much more than simply dilate the bronchioles—it produced a stimulation and euphoria that ephedrine lacked almost completely. Use of amphetamine for these properties spread rapidly during the 1930s. In a parallel development, Japanese scientists synthesized methamphetamine marketed as Philopon with the same enthusiasm in Japan. Soldiers of many countries, including Germany, Japan, and the United States, used amphetamine during World War II to maintain alertness during long tours of duty. After World War II, amphetamine and methamphetamine use moved even more widely into the civilian populations, and Japan experienced the first known wave of stimulant addiction. Episodes of abuse of these highly addictive stimulants have occurred ever since. In the 1960s, amphetamine use had become widespread enough that the dangerous effects of stimulants were rediscovered and given voice in the slogan "Speed kills." The "meth" epidemic in the United States and Asia today represents the most recent of three postwar waves of amphetamine abuse. Amphetamine is still popular with the military, too. Soldiers in the Gulf War used amphetamines, and recent reports have suggested that American fighter pilots in Afghanistan maintained the tradition.

Our lack of cultural memory is remarkable: we keep rediscovering the beneficial and toxic effects of psychomotor stimulants. As soon as the popularity of amphetamine waned, the cocaine abuse of the 1970s began. The widespread availability of a volatile form (crack) that could be inhaled led to a remarkable rise in addiction and toxicity, in a manner reminiscent of the Benzedrine craze of the 1930s. Then, as the dangers of crack emerged and its popularity dwindled, a new drug appeared on the horizon. "Ice," the volatile form of methamphetamine (an amphetamine derivative), spread rapidly during the mid-1990s, sparking a new wave of addiction and toxicity. Amphetamine-related emergency room admissions increased 460 percent from 1985 to 1994 in California alone, and another 67 percent from 1994 to 2001. In 2006, law enforcement personnel in the United States listed meth as the number one drug problem they face. Today, the new wave of "bath salt" abuse is leading to a rapid rise in ER admissions for these novel psychostimulants.

WHAT STIMULANTS ARE USED TODAY?

The major stimulants used in the United States today (aside from caffeine, discussed separately in its own chapter) are cocaine, amphetamine, and methamphetamine. Although the press from law enforcement might indicate otherwise, cocaine users still outnumber meth users almost five to one. Abuse of methylphenidate (Ritalin), normally prescribed to treat attention deficit disorder, is rising in student populations. Recent studies show that up to 30 percent of college students in some surveys have used a prescription stimulant either as a study aid or recreationally. The most troublesome news on the stimulant abuse front is the rapid spread of designer psychostimulants that are so potent that they are associated with a rising number of ER visits for toxic delirium and psychotic symptoms as well as overdose deaths. These are often marketed as bath salts or plant food, labeled not for human consumption.

Cocaine is used medically as a local anesthetic, but on the street, the two most common forms are the white powder that is either snorted or dissolved for injection, and crack, a solid chunk of cocaine that is heated directly in a pipe to form a vapor that is inhaled into the lungs. Both the powdered cocaine and crack are prepared from leaves of the coca plant, which are mixed with solvents and processed through several steps to remove the cocaine from the leaves and purify it as crystals. Crack is prepared from the powder by boiling it with sodium bicarbonate. Chunks of cocaine base precipitate from this solution. This simple process has a tremendous impact on the speed with which cocaine is absorbed, as we will see in the following. With the successful suppression of cocaine distribution from Colombia, Mexican distributors are playing an increasing role in its distribution in the United States, and up to 75 percent of cocaine enters the United States through the southwest borders of California, Arizona, and Texas.

The powdered form of cocaine is usually diluted with other white powders such as cornstarch, talcum powder, lactose, or mannitol, and/or with other local anesthetics, caffeine, or, sometimes, amphetamine. The purpose of the inert powders is economic: to dilute an expensive drug with cheap substances. These ingredients provide some semblance of the sensations associated with cocaine but with cheaper drugs—caffeine or amphetamine for alertness, and local anesthetics for the numbing sensation that users associate with real cocaine. However, the purity of cocaine has been declining and was on average 50 percent in 2011, the most recent year for which the DEA provides statistics.

Users usually snort powdered cocaine, which then enters the body by absorption through the mucous membranes and into the blood vessels of the nose. Sometimes it is applied to other places, including the mouth, rectum, penis, or vagina. The purpose here is the same: to promote absorption across highly vascular mucous membranes.

Amphetamine and methamphetamine appear in diverse forms: pills, powders of varying colors, or chunks that look like cocaine. While there is some diversion from medical sources, the majority is from bootleg labs. Mexican "superlabs" have provided much of the methamphetamine in the last few years since the crackdown on small, local labs in the United States. However, the number of these local labs is increasing again as manufacturers find alternative supplies of the precursor pseudoephedrine, which has been strongly regulated in the United States since the 2006 law that required customers to show identification for any purchase of cold products containing pseudoephedrine or phenylpropanolamine. Methamphetamine is sold in many forms, including loose forms like powders or "rocks," as well as in capsules or tablets of various types. Many college students buy amphetamine or methamphetamine pills intended for the treatment of attention deficit disorder. The smokable form appears as chunks called "ice," which are heated and smoked like the crack form of cocaine. Ice is becoming one of the most common forms in circulation. Methylphenidate (Ritalin) is the well-known drug prescribed to treat attention deficit disorder. It is also a psychomotor stimulant that is used for studying as well as recreation by a growing number of students. Most users obtain it in pill or tablet form from someone who has a valid prescription for its use, or from underground sources that have diverted it from clinical use.

There is an alphabet soup of amphetamine derivatives, including trimethoxyamphetamine (TMA), 2,5 dimethoxyamphetamine, 4-methamphetamine (or Serenity, Tranquility, Peace), methoxyamphetamine (STP), methylenedioxyamphetamine (MDA), and paramethoxyamphetamine (PMA), which are all chemically related to amphetamine. These are synthesized in bootleg laboratories and appear in diverse forms. Most of these drugs have effects like those that MDMA or hallucinogens produce rather than like those of amphetamine and are discussed in the "Hallucinogens" chapter.

There are also a number of synthetic stimulants with more typical stimulant effects that enjoyed temporary popularity as appetite suppressants or asthma medications until their abuse potential became recognized. Bootleg versions of many of these are available in some places (4-Methylaminorex [4-MAX, U4EU] and pemoline are two such drugs). The synthetic stimulants are sometimes called "designer drugs" because they are produced by altering the molecular structure of parent drugs so that they have a different profile of action. Some of these structural variants have been synthesized for legitimate research purposes, while others have been created by illegal producers or drug abusers to satisfy specific preferences.

Khat (also spelled "qat" or "quat") is a stimulant in a leafy plant that grows in Africa. For centuries native peoples in Africa and the Middle East have used khat in social settings to promote conversation and improve social interactions. In recent years, with the urbanization of many native populations in Africa, khat use in certain groups has extended to Europe, Great Britain, and, recently, the United States. The active ingredient in khat is cathinone, an amphetamine-like stimulant. A synthetic variant of cathinone—methcathinone—is rapidly becoming popular. It is a much more potent stimulant with amphetamine-like actions. Both cathinone and methcathinone are prepared in bootleg labs and appear on the street either as an off-white or colored powder or in capsule form. Like cocaine, the mild stimulant properties of chewing khat leaves have been replaced by the intense high of the pure chemical substance. In an interesting "back migration" of substance-abuse habits, there are increasing reports of adverse effects from excessive khat chewing, especially among urban populations in Africa.

Finally, the last few years have seen an explosion in sales of cathinone derivatives. The most common are 3,4-methylenedioxypyrovalerone (MDPV), 3,4-methylenedioxymethcathinone (methylone) and 4-methylmethcathinone (mephedrone). MDPV is the stimulant that appears most often in the United States. Mephedrone is found more in European drug samples. Methylone appears increasingly in pills sold as "Molly" or MDMA. There are many similar variants, including para-methoxymethcathinone (methedrone), 4-fluoromethcathinone (flephedrone), 3-fluoromethcathinone (3-FMC), naphyrone, butylone (bk-MBDB), and buphedrone to name the most common. The DEA has scheduled all of these molecules as Schedule I (high potential for abuse, no currently accepted medical use) under an emergency provision.

HOW STIMULANTS MOVE THROUGH THE BODY

COCAINE

The different purification methods that produce powdered cocaine and crack have a huge impact on how they are delivered to the body. Because cocaine constricts the very blood vessels that are absorbing it, snorting is a relatively slow way to deliver cocaine to the bloodstream. Blood cocaine levels rise relatively gradually and don't reach a peak until about thirty minutes after snorting. Cocaine in its "crack" form, in contrast, forms a vapor that users inhale. This delivers cocaine as quickly to the circulation as injecting the drug intravenously. Maximum levels occur within a minute or two, and blood levels of cocaine at this time are much higher than ever observed after snorting comparable doses. Users often prefer the fast and intense rush that results from smoking crack. However, this rapid delivery of more drug also means a greater risk of addiction or overdose.

Liver and blood enzymes degrade about half of a cocaine dose in about an hour. This means that a user is usually ready for another dose in about forty minutes or less. The rapid rise in blood levels, followed by a rapid fall—a rush followed by a crash—often leaves the user wanting to reexperience the original high. This rush-and-crash phenomenon can lead the cocaine user to keep taking additional doses until blood levels accumulate to toxic levels. This "run" often continues until the user either runs out of drug or has a seizure or some other sign of toxicity.

Ingesting cocaine is a much less effective route of delivery. The process is slower, and the liver degrades much of the drug before it ever reaches the circulation. For this reason, the average blood levels of cocaine in people chewing leaves is very low compared to the amounts present in the blood after smoking crack or snorting powder. Similarly, single doses of the original patent formulas, like Vin Mariani, with fairly low levels of cocaine (six milligrams per ounce) probably resulted in relatively low blood levels of the drug with a single dose.

AMPHETAMINE AND METHAMPHETAMINE

Amphetamine and methamphetamine, like cocaine, enter the bloodstream very quickly when users smoke or inject them. This leads to a rapid high and to a greater likelihood of toxicity. Unlike cocaine, amphetamine and methamphetamine are also effective if they are ingested as pills, because they are destroyed more slowly in the liver and enter the circulation effectively. Amphetamine and methamphetamine are degraded more slowly than cocaine, and so effects last at least two to four hours. This leads to less of the rush-and-crash pattern of injecting the drug. However, heavy users still tend to use in binges over several days followed by a period of exhaustion that they call "tweak and crash."

EPHEDRINE AND EPHEDRINE SUBSTITUTES

Ephedrine is almost always ingested as either a pill or tea, and it enters the circulation easily. Ephedrine reaches its peak effect in about an hour and lasts for three to six hours. However, many supplement manufacturers have replaced ephedrine with somewhat similar molecules, including dimethylamylamine, beta-phenylethylamine, and synephrine (bitter orange). These are supplied mainly as pills that users ingest to improve athletic performance. Most of these molecules are well absorbed, but only betaphenylethylamine enters the brain well.

METHYLPHENIDATE

Methylphenidate exists typically in pill form. It is well absorbed from the intestine. The drug effects last two to four hours in a simple pill, although there are many different extended-release preparations. Addicts have been known to crush the pills and inject them. This practice is extremely dangerous because the other components in the pill can lodge in tiny blood vessels in the lung and eye and cause serious damage. Students have tried to crush the pill and snort it in the hopes that a high would result. However, absorption from this form is slow enough and the dose of most pills low enough that the buzz, if any, is not particularly different from taking a pill. Methylphenidate enters the brain but more slowly than cocaine and amphetamines, which may be one reason that compulsive abuse of methylphenidate is fairly rare.

CATHINONES

Khat in its native form is ingested as a tea or chewed as leaves of the native plant. However, users today typically snort or inject purified cathinone. Similarly, users snort bath salts (MDPV), and both MDPV and methylone appear often in tablet form. These pills often contain a variety of compounds, sometimes with other drugs thrown in. The distribution of these drugs in the human body has not been extensively studied, but all enter the brain quickly. The high lasts for several hours, longer for some like MDPV.

WHAT STIMULANTS DO TO THE BRAIN

Amphetamines and cocaine are best known for their ability to increase attention, cause alertness, and eliminate fatigue. Amphetamines are popular in the United States to increase attention and delay sleep and as medical treatments for attention deficit disorder and narcolepsy (a disease in which the patient falls asleep repeatedly during the day). Even Freud commented that the most probable use of cocaine would be for these properties: "The main use of coca will undoubtedly remain that which Indians have made of it for centuries: it is of value in all cases where the primary aim is to increase the physical capacity of the body for a given short period of time and to hold strength in reserve to meet further demands. . . . Coca is a far more potent and far less harmful stimulant than alcohol, and its widespread utilization is hindered at present only by its high cost."* People who have taken stimulants are often talkative and full of energy, movement, and confidence to the point of being restless and grandiose in thinking that they can accomplish anything.

If stimulants simply increased energy and alertness, they indeed would be the miracle medicine that Freud proposed. However, these drugs also cause an unmistakable euphoria and sense of well-being that is the basis of addiction. People who inject or smoke cocaine describe a rush of intense physical pleasure that they often compare to orgasm. When these drugs are taken in a form that is absorbed more slowly (snorting or taking a pill), this feeling is much less intense and may simply be recognized as a feeling of well-being.

Stimulants also cause an increase of movement, which is the reason for their name. Stimulant users are in constant motion—talking, moving, exploring, and generally fidgeting. At higher stimulant doses, this motion becomes a more focused, repetitive action. People who have taken high doses of amphetamine will doodle in repetitive patterns or engage in repetitive tasks or even pick at their skin repeatedly. Laboratory animals do the same thing. At low doses, amphetamine-treated animals move incessantly about the cage, as if they are constantly searching the environment. After a high dose, animals will sniff back and forth in one spot in the cage, or engage in a repetitive grooming or chewing.

At very high doses, or after prolonged use, stimulants can cause a psychotic-like state that resembles paranoid schizophrenia except that the symptoms usually resolve quickly when the user is hospitalized. These symptoms often occur when a user is at the end of a "run" of some days and blood levels are very high. However, people with excited delirium with psychotic behaviors are also showing up in emergency rooms from

---

* Freud's comments are from *Über Cocaine*, quoted by S. H. Snyder in *Drugs and the Brain* (New York: W. H. Freeman and Co., 1995).

the new bath salt preparations. One reason may be that these drugs are often supplied as a powder, and as relatively new drugs on the scene, users are inexperienced and tend to overdose. While the conventional wisdom states that these symptoms go away when the user stops drugs, there is some suspicion that this can take a very long time in a chronic stimulant user (months to years).

People sometimes use cocaine in combination with heroin or other opiates. In this case, the effect on the brain and behavior is somewhat like the addition of the two. The dreaminess of opiates is added to and cuts the edginess and arousal caused by cocaine. This combination can be particularly dangerous: often people who are injecting cocaine slow down their intake of the drug when the jitteriness gets too great, but in the presence of heroin, these feelings are not so obvious, increasing the risk of an overdose (of either cocaine or heroin). This is the combination of drugs that comedians Chris Farley and John Belushi and rap performer Chris Kelly were taking when they died.

Psychostimulants decrease appetite through actions in the brain. Amphetamine was the first diet pill and was popular for this use in the 1950s and 1960s. Its dependence-producing effects became a real problem in its use as diet aids, and psychomotor stimulants are not used for this purpose today; nonaddicting alternatives have been developed. All stimulants do this, and weight loss is a consequence of high-dose chronic use.

WHAT STIMULANTS DO TO THE REST OF THE BODY

The aphorism "Speed kills" is well deserved. It reflects the understanding that the sixties drug subculture had of the effects that cocaine and amphetamine derivatives have on body functions. Cocaine and amphetamines mimic the effects of the sympathetic nervous system: they initiate all the bodily responses of the fight-or-flight syndrome. They increase blood pressure and heart rate, constrict (narrow) blood vessels, dilate the bronchioles (breathing tubes), increase blood sugar, and generally prepare the body for emergency. These effects can be beneficial. The effects on the lungs can actually improve the symptoms of asthma. Furthermore, fat is broken down to help mobilize energy, and this effect in combination with the suppression of appetite and excessive physical activity may contribute to the weight loss these drugs can cause. However, the effects on the heart can be so excessive that they may result in a disordered heartbeat or, eventually, failure of the cardiovascular system. Most of the aforementioned stimulants have these effects, and overdose deaths from cocaine, amphetamine, and bath salts typically result from their cardiovascular effects.

Most of the stimulants also increase body temperature, which presents a real problem when amphetamines are used in situations involving exercise. At the same time, amphetamines and cocaine seem to increase the capacity for muscular work. Whether this represents a real improvement in muscle function, a better delivery of sugar to fuel muscular work, or simply the perception of greater energy, these drugs have been popular with some endurance athletes, like cyclists, and with those attending all-night rave dance parties to permit dancing all night. Extreme physical exertion increases body temperature even without the amphetamine; with amphetamine added, the increase in body temperature can become fatal.

EFFECTS ON THE FETUS

Effects on "crack babies"—babies born to women who abuse crack or other psychomotor stimulants during pregnancy—have probably stimulated more public scrutiny and more public outcry than any other consequence of drug addiction in the United States. The alarms are again being raised for meth babies. Are the minds and bodies of these infants destroyed by their prenatal exposure to the drug? The answer is very hard to know, partly because almost no person abuses only one drug. The pregnant women who abuse cocaine almost invariably smoke cigarettes and abuse alcohol as well. Furthermore, they tend to have poor access to health care and as a result often do not receive adequate prenatal care. It is very difficult to distinguish the role of cocaine itself in any problems the infants experience.

Nevertheless, exposure to these drugs in utero can cause serious problems. Many cocaine- or methamphetamine-exposed babies are born prematurely and with low birth weight; a few have experienced catastrophic events, like strokes, before they were born. Cocaine use is also associated with premature separation of the placenta from the uterus, a condition that can cut off the baby's blood supply and result in brain damage or death. However, if babies are carried to term, the consequences for many may not be drastic. There are small increases in the rate of birth defects, but this is not the major problem that it is for babies exposed to high levels of alcohol during pregnancy. Many stimulant-exposed infants are extremely irritable and overly sensitive to any form of sensory stimulus at birth. This condition usually improves, and the infants develop pretty normally. Many of the effects at birth (low birth weight, increased frequency of prematurity) are not unique to cocaine but also happen in babies whose mothers smoked tobacco during pregnancy. Nicotine and cocaine have something in common that explains this: both powerfully constrict blood vessels that supply blood to the fetus during pregnancy and deny the infant vital nutrients.

What is the prospect for these children as they grow up? As the first waves of cocaine-exposed children are moving through school, researchers are finding a higher incidence of learning disabilities and ADHD, much like the children of women who smoke heavily during pregnancy. However, they are not significantly different from peers who share a low socioeconomic status and chaotic home lives. Nor do we have a clear answer as to whether exposing children to drugs in utero increases the likelihood that they will abuse drugs as adults. Likewise, we don't know whether or how prenatal experience with drugs will affect later responses to drugs as these babies become adults: some studies find increased sensitivity to drugs in adulthood, and others find decreased response. Furthermore, biology is not destiny: many factors go into the development of drug use—not just brain biochemistry. In this regard, these children can be at an added disadvantage because they may well grow up in drug-using homes.

METHYLPHENIDATE AND USE OF STIMULANTS TO TREAT ATTENTION DEFICIT/HYPERACTIVITY DISORDER

Methylphenidate (Ritalin) may be the most controversial stimulant in America today. It is not the most dangerous, nor the most abused. However, scientists, parents, teachers, and counselors all have opinions about its value as a medication. Methylphenidate is the most frequently prescribed medication for treatment of attention deficit/hyperactivity disorder (ADHD) in the United States, although amphetamine and several other stimulant and nonstimulant drugs may be used. There is little disagreement, at least in the scientific community, about whether these drugs improve attention. They do so in almost every clinical study that has been conducted. Furthermore, they do so for everyone. The myth of the "paradoxical" effects of stimulants is just that—a myth. Stimulants improve attention in normal people and in people who have poor attention. College students have discovered this, and some buy methylphenidate from other students, the Internet, or sometimes even from cooperative doctors to study better. In some high-pressure academic environments, including colleges and medical schools, students view methylphenidate as a necessary tool in the competition for good grades.

Human imaging studies are providing new knowledge about how stimulants improve attention. We have learned that parts of the frontal cortex are active while we are paying attention and deciding whether to act upon information. This same area is also active when we are processing emotions. This part of the brain does our highest level of thinking; it is where we "think about thinking." Stimulant medication is active in these areas, and scientists think that maybe it corrects a deficiency in activity that exists in some people. These are just hypotheses, and the way that stimulants work to improve attention is still uncertain. However, the outcome is certain. So what is the controversy? The controversy arises from the difficulty in diagnosing ADHD. There is a difference between a healthy, active child and an impulsive, impaired, constantly active child. Because teachers or parents often make the call, lack of classroom obedience often goes to the top of the list of "diagnostic criteria." Many are concerned that we are medicating our children into submission, while health-care professionals argue persuasively that we need to treat children whose behavior is severely disordered. The role of medication in therapy is also a contentious issue. Health-care professionals insist that medication is not the sole solution and that it is best used in combination with appropriate behavioral strategies and lots of work with the family. It is unlikely that this controversy will be solved anytime soon. However, scientists are working hard to learn if there are any observable differences in the brain anatomy or function of people with ADHD and are studying possible genetic causes for ADHD. Finally, the use by students assumes that if it helps people with ADHD to be normal, it can help a normal person to be better than normal. Unfortunately, this is unlikely. Your frontal cortex likes just the right amount of stimulation—too little *or* too much causes a deterioration in its function. Furthermore, the evidence that stimulants improve learning and memory is controversial. They may keep students awake to study and help children with ADHD focus on a task (like a test) so that they can complete more answers and score better. However, the evidence that learning per se is better is contradictory.

HOW STIMULANTS WORK

What do euphoria, blood pressure, appetite, and attention have in common that causes them all to be affected by stimulants? These behaviors/bodily functions are all regulated by a related group of neurotransmitters—the biogenic amines, or monoamine, neurotransmitters. Norepinephrine, epinephrine, dopamine, and serotonin are the monoamine neurotransmitters. They are related in structure, but each is a neurotransmitter in its own right that regulates a particular set of behaviors. Psychomotor stimulants increase the amount of all of the monoamine neurotransmitters in the synapse. So, the effects of stimulants mimic what would happen if every one of the neurons that released a monoamine fired at once. It's no wonder that the effects of stimulants are so complicated.

Norepinephrine, as we mentioned earlier, is the chemical transmitter of the sympathetic nervous system. Epinephrine (or adrenaline) is the transmitter of the adrenal medulla, a special part of the sympathetic nervous system that is particularly important in fight-or-flight responses. Norepinephrine also exists in certain neurons in the brain. Norepinephrine neurons organize the behavioral part of the fight-or-flight response. They prepare the body and brain for emergency. This includes paying attention to your environment (not doing simple body maintenance things, like eating) and deciding whether the risk is so great that you should run away. So it also prepares the body for physical activity: making the heart beat faster, bringing glucose and oxygen to muscles, and widening the breathing tubes to facilitate breathing. Dopamine neurons do several different but important jobs. These neurons are responsible for reinforcement, or reward—the sense of pleasure—as we discuss in the "Addiction" chapter. In addition, these neurons control purposeful movement and influence release of some hormones. The loss of dopamine neurons in Parkinson's disease causes the gradual loss of voluntary movement that is so incapacitating. They also contribute to the improvement in attention and planning/prioritizing (executive function) that psychomotor stimulants cause. Serotonin is involved in the regulation of sleep and mood and also in controlling appetite, body temperature, and more "vegetative" functions, as they are strangely called (since when did a carrot control its body temperature?).

Imagine what happens when a person takes amphetamine: her body prepares for fight-or-flight both physically, by increasing heart rate and blood pressure, and mentally, by becoming hyperalert (via norepinephrine); she explores her environment, moves around (perhaps purpose-fully, perhaps not), and feels euphoric (courtesy of dopamine); she stops eating, raises her body temperature, and releases many of her body's hor-mones (through serotonin). Some of these actions seem to conflict with each other. For example, in preparing for physical activity, it would be better if your body were attempting to lose excess heat instead of gaining temperature. This is why the excessive use of stimulants can be so danger-ous physically.

STIMULANTS PREVENT MONOAMINE "RECAPTURE"

Stimulants work by interfering with the mechanism that monoamine neurons have for stopping neurotransmission and "recycling" their prod-ucts. Normally, monoamine neurons fire impulses and release their neu-rotransmitters, which go across the synapse and act on their receptors. Then the monoamine neurons recapture them by "pumping" them back into the neuron. This process eliminates the monoamines from the syn-apse and is the main way that these neurons "turn off" neurotransmission once it is started. Stimulants like cocaine, amphetamines, and bath salts block this pump. The result is that the norepinephrine, dopamine, and serotonin all stay in the synapse much longer once they are released. The end result is that all the effects of these neurotransmitters combined last much longer. There is a subtle but important difference between cocaine and the amphetamines: the amphetamines use this pump themselves to enter the nerve terminal and, once inside, cause a massive "dump" of neurotransmitter into the synapse. Therefore, they increase levels of neu-rotransmitters much more than cocaine does.

HOW NEUROTRANSMITTERS CONTRIBUTE TO
THE EFFECTS OF STIMULANTS

Norepinephrine	Increase in blood pressure and heart rate
	Relaxation of bronchioles
	Activation of fat breakdown
	Arousing effects
	Appetite effects

Serotonin	Increase in body temperature
	Appetite effects
Dopamine	Locomotor activation
	Euphoria: addiction
	Attention

HOW IS AMPHETAMINE DIFFERENT FROM METHYLPHENIDATE OR EPHEDRINE?

Amphetamine and methamphetamine, cocaine, ephedrine, and methylphenidate differ from each other in the range of psychomotor stimulant effects that they cause. What determines the differences in effects of the stimulant drugs? First of all, drugs that don't get into the brain affect only the peripheral nervous system. Ephedrine is a good example because it enters the brain poorly; therefore, its effects on the cardiovascular system and other "body" systems are much stronger than its effects on mood or appetite. However, amphetamine, cocaine, and methylphenidate all enter the brain, but they do not cause exactly the same effects. Cocaine and amphetamine cause all the possible actions of psychomotor stimulants; they increase attention and alertness and cause the pleasurable effects that become addicting. These drugs also mimic activation of the sympathetic nervous system, causing increased breathing, heart rate, and blood pressure because they increase levels of all the monoamines. In contrast, methylphenidate affects dopamine more than norepinephrine, so it has much smaller effects on heart rate and breathing. Understanding these underlying mechanisms has helped scientists quickly unravel the actions of the new bath salts. Some, like MDPV, inhibit dopamine and norepinephrine only and are extremely reinforcing and cause dangerous cardiovascular stimulation. Others, like mephedrone, act like amphetamine to release all monoamines. Methylone and mephedrone are much more like MDMA (see the "Ecstasy" chapter) in having large effects on dopamine and serotonin, but they also release norepinephrine. These drugs are reinforcing, cause significant sympathetic stimulation, and also elevate body temperature, as would be predicted from this profile of action. For many of the others, the research still hasn't been done, but it is likely that *all* of them will inhibit dopamine uptake to some extent; the balance of dopamine, norepinephrine, and serotonin will dictate their end results. All drugs that inhibit dopamine uptake or release dopamine will be potentially addictive. All drugs that inhibit norepinephrine uptake or release norepinephrine will stimulate the sympathetic nervous system and have potentially dangerous cardiovascular side effects. Drugs that also affect serotonin will have a touch of MDMA-like "entactogen" action and potentially have more dangerous effects on body temperature.

Drugs with large effects on all monoamines	Cocaine, amphetamine, methamphetamine, MDPV, mephedrone, methylone
Drugs with effects mainly on dopamine	Methylphenidate
Drugs with effects mainly on norepinephrine	Ephedrine

COCAINE CAN CAUSE SEIZURES

Cocaine has a unique effect all its own. Remember the initial use of cocaine by Freud's friend? He used it to cause local anesthesia—to block the transmission of pain stimuli. Physicians use cocaine for this purpose much less today because drugs that have this effect but not cocaine's addicting properties are available. However, the local anesthetic effects of cocaine may account for a toxicity that is unique to cocaine. At doses not much greater than those that cause maximal effects on mood, cocaine causes seizures. Other stimulants don't do this at all, or only do it rarely and at extremely high doses. Because other local anesthetics also can cause seizures, we think that this effect of cocaine is a result of its anesthetic action.

ADDICTION, TOLERANCE, DEPENDENCE, AND WITHDRAWAL

Cocaine addiction could be viewed as a problem created by successful science. Cocaine addiction is basically unknown in the South American cultures where the drug has been used for millennia to increase endurance and the ability to work. Chewed with an alkaline substance and delivered to the stomach and then absorbed slowly, coca leaves provide only a mild stimulant effect. The rush doesn't happen, and the drug is relatively safe.

The situation is quite different with the cocaine and amphetamine formulations available today. Part of the addictiveness of cocaine may have much to do with how it is delivered to the body. The extremely fast rise in blood levels may be the important factor. Just as cigarettes deliver nicotine to the bloodstream rapidly, smoked cocaine (crack) delivers cocaine rapidly to the brain. The recent explosion of addiction to ice, the smokable form of methamphetamine, lends credibility to this notion. Bath salts may prove to be the most lipophilic of all and enter the brain very fast even when snorted.

Animal experiments point out how uniquely compelling cocaine can be. Animals will press a lever hundreds of times to deliver a single intravenous dose of cocaine or methamphetamine (and very recent data suggests that they will press even more to receive MDPV). In contrast, most animals will not voluntarily ingest dangerous amounts of alcohol or nicotine and tend to limit their intake of heroin to a steady pattern. Recovering cocaine addicts usually say that the only thing that stops a serious addict during a binge is running out of cocaine. One user described it like this: "If I had been in a room full of cocaine, I would have kept using it until it was all gone, and I still would have wanted more."

Does this mean that everyone who uses stimulants becomes addicted? There are thousands of people, ranging from children with ADHD to truck drivers, who regularly use psychomotor stimulants but never develop a compulsive pattern of use. Good prescribing practice by the physician usually leads to safe use for clinical purposes. Taking the drug according to a schedule, instead of "as needed," helps to avoid a pattern of self-medication that can become compulsive. Similar differences have been observed in the laboratory. When monkeys have free access to cocaine, their intake increases to toxic levels, but if access is restricted to a few hours a day, their intake can remain stable for months. Another factor is the reasons for taking the drug and the environment. Usually, truck drivers and college students use stimulants only while engaged in a particular task in a particular environment (i.e., when on the road or pulling an all-nighter). When placed in a different environment, without all the typical stimuli associated with drug use, it is easier for them to abstain.

There is no question that psychomotor stimulants are addictive. As described in the "Addiction" chapter, the dopamine neurons on which they act play a primary role in addiction, and taking amphetamine or cocaine can be viewed simply as substituting drugs for natural reinforcers, such as food and sex. No other drugs in this book act so directly on reward systems or are so commonly addicting. Can some individuals use stimulants recreationally without addiction? Probably so, and yet we know that the drive to use cocaine or amphetamine is considerably stronger than that for any of the other addictive drugs.

Tolerance develops to some stimulant effects, such as the suppression of appetite, and develops more easily with continuous use than with irregular use. This is one reason why amphetamine isn't very useful as a diet pill. Tolerance also develops during a single run, so that the high becomes harder and harder to reach. This is why people keep taking more frequent injections ("chasing the high"). However, this rapidly developed tolerance also reverses rapidly, so a few days of abstaining can restore sensitivity. Some effects actually become progressively greater over time. The locomotor stimulation is one of the behavioral patterns that become more and more exaggerated. While people rarely show intense repetitive behaviors the first time they take amphetamine, it is a common behavioral effect on the longtime user. Do stimulants become more addictive over time? We really don't know the answer for sure, although the pattern of use probably plays an important role.

Is stimulant withdrawal dangerous? Although there are definite symptoms of stimulant withdrawal, it is not life-threatening. At the end of a long run, when people stop using, they crash. There is a period of exhaustion, with excessive sleep, often depressive symptoms, and a rebound in appetite that probably results from a prolonged period of inadequate food intake. During this period, the craving for the drug is very strong. One particularly difficult symptom is the inability to feel pleasure (anhedonia). This is not a big surprise if a person has been artificially and intensely stimulating his pleasure center with a drug. When the drug is removed, so is its artificial stimulus of the brain's pleasure center. There seems to be a suppression in dopamine neuron activity during the first few days after withdrawal. No one ever died from a few days without pleasure, but in the absence of any positive feelings, the temptation to use the drug to feel better becomes stronger and stronger. Anhedonia is thought to be a major reason why people start using stimulants after a period of attempted abstinence. We don't know for sure how long these symptoms last, but in very longtime users the craving for the drug can last for months.

DIET PILLS

Amphetamine was the original diet pill. This use was based on the ability of amphetamine and drugs like it to suppress appetite. Unfortunately, it was impossible to separate the appetite-suppressing qualities from the addictive potential. The search for an effective nonaddicting diet pill fueled millions of dollars' worth of pharmaceutical company research, resulting in a new understanding of the neural mechanisms regulating appetite. The appetite-inhibiting effects of amphetamine probably result from the release of norepinephrine and serotonin, and its addictive qualities from the release of dopamine. The newer medication sibutramine (Meridia) works more selectively on norepinephrine and serotonin, and so lacks the abuse potential of amphetamine. However (see the previous paragraph), the effects on norepinephrine have led to predictable cardiovascular stimulation with sibutramine, and it has been withdrawn from the market. Fortunately, the explosion of information about other mechanisms involved in the regulation of food intake have led to the development of other new drugs that don't target monoamine systems at all.

All effective drugs that suppress appetite require a prescription. However, there are many over-the-counter drugs marketed as effective that really have minimal or no effectiveness. Chromium is one favorite in health-food stores today for its supposed ability to burn fat—a claim based on modest research about its ability to increase the actions of insulin. However, these effects are slight at best, and the safety of long-term use has not been established.

Ephedrine was another favorite, for both its ability to suppress appetite and its thermogenic properties. There is a little more truth to this, but not much. If ephedrine is taken in safe amounts, it does not get into the brain and thus cannot suppress appetite. It might increase energy metabolism a little, but not without significant effects on heart rate and blood pressure. The ephedrine substitutes on the market (bitter orange, for example) do not enter the brain well either, so they share its effects on cardiovascular function but are not very effective as anorectics (see the "Herbal Drugs" chapter).

STIMULANT TOXICITIES AND OVERDOSES

Psychomotor stimulants can cause three kinds of severe health problems. First, single-dose toxicities can cause death through overdose. Second, chronic use of escalating doses leads to particular behavioral problems. Finally, there are a myriad of health problems associated with long-term use that are not specifically caused by the drug but that result from the stimulant-using lifestyle.

All of these drugs can kill at doses that people take recreationally. A single clinically appropriate dose of amphetamine, methamphetamine, cocaine, methylphenidate, or ephedrine would rarely cause death unless an individual had an underlying health problem (aneurysm, coronary artery disease, etc.). Yet people using bootleg drug sources rarely know the dose they are taking. Also, blood levels can gradually accumulate to toxic levels during the runs of repeated drug injections or inhalations at fairly closely spaced intervals, which are a common pattern of stimulant administration. It is commonplace for people to keep taking cocaine or amphetamine until they experience unpleasant side effects, but such warning signals may come too late if the drug accumulates in the body rapidly. This uncertainty is proving particularly problematic with the new bath salt drugs, which are often supplied as loose powder: the combination of inexperienced users and bulk marketing is leading to frequent dangerous overdoses. What happens as blood levels rise to toxic levels? The first effects are simply exaggerations of the typical drug response: energy and alertness become jitteriness or even paranoia and hostility, and increased movement becomes repetitive aimless activities, such as drawing closely spaced lines, taking watches apart and putting them back together, or talking constantly without listening. A mild increase in heart rate becomes palpitations or chest pains as the heart rhythm is disturbed, and the skin becomes flushed as body temperature rises. Headaches are common, often from effects on blood vessels. Nausea and vomiting can accompany these changes. These toxic levels can also result in strokes, heart attacks, or fatal elevations in body temperature. For cocaine, the pattern is a little different. Elevated body temperature is relatively rare, but seizures are commonplace—so much so that an adolescent or young adult arriving at an emergency room with a seizure without a previous history is almost always screened for cocaine use. Scientists once argued that the repeated use of cocaine led to an increased sensitivity to seizures, but this theory has not held up in continued study. Seizures can happen at any time during a cocaine-using "career"—the first, twentieth, or hundredth time. Many longtime users eventually have a seizure. Rather than some permanent change in the brain, the reason may be the escalating pattern of use that leads to higher and higher blood levels of the drug.

Like alcohol, in the words of Shakespeare, stimulants provoke and unprovoke. Stimulants, especially cocaine, can increase interest in sex, but sexual activity can become more difficult. Stimulants constrict blood vessels in the penis in a way that makes it difficult to maintain an erection and can delay ejaculation. In fact, this latter characteristic of cocaine is occasionally exploited by local application of cocaine to the head of the penis to prolong sexual activity!

There are also serious social consequences to chronic psychomotor stimulant use. The increasing hostility, paranoia, and belligerence associated with higher blood levels of stimulants result in more overt violence. Many high-dose stimulant users become increasingly convinced that people are "out to get them," while they also become more agitated and inclined toward action. In a country with liberal gun laws, this combination can be lethal and often is. The incidence of gun-related violence is substantial for stimulant users.

Different problems develop with chronic use. As use escalates into more and more frequent runs, the bizarre, repetitive movements become more extreme. They can take the form of very self-directed behaviors such as picking at imaginary insects under the skin or assembling and taking apart equipment, or more social forms such as repetitive sexual or conversational activity. The picking behavior leads people eventually to create large wounds in the skin that often become infected. When paranoid and hostile behavior takes over, a person in the midst of extreme chronic amphetamine intoxication resembles a paranoid schizophrenic patient, although the disordered thinking of schizophrenia is usually not present. After a few days of hospitalization the person often returns to normal, although sometimes the behavioral change persists.

What are the effects of long-term amphetamine use on major body functions? Part of the answer depends on how the drug is administered. Cocaine and amphetamine are powerful vasoconstrictors, and so they cut off the blood supply to the area where the drug is delivered. Snorting cocaine can cause ulcers in the lining of the nose from inadequate blood supply, while smoked cocaine or amphetamine can cause bleeding in the lungs as small blood vessels burst. Stomach ulcers or damage to the intestines can occur with long-term oral or even intranasal use. Heart problems are also fairly common. Long-term stimulant use seems to accelerate the development of atherosclerosis (development of fatty plaques that block blood vessels) and may cause direct damage to the heart muscle from lack of oxygen. Longtime stimulant use is also associated with many problems not caused directly by the drug. Because these drugs suppress appetite, stimulant users are often undernourished and experience all the ill effects of that condition. The incidence of hepatitis, HIV, and other infectious diseases is high in users who share dirty needles or engage in sex to obtain money for drugs.

Finally, research points to the possibility that chronic use of methamphetamine can cause long-term neurotoxic damage. High-dose methamphetamine causes long-lasting damage to the dopamine nerve endings of neurons. The nerves do not die, but the nerve endings are "pruned," or cut back, leaving a deficit in the density of nerve terminals and the amount of dopamine and serotonin available for use. What is the functional implication of this loss? Right after the loss, the system probably can compensate enough that no behavior problems are obvious. However, as people age and experience the normal aging-related loss of dopamine neurons, this deficit could potentially be revealed in movement or mood disorders. It is also possible that if users abstain, some recovery will occur (there is a little data to support this point of view). In addition, other abnormalities have been shown in the brains of heavy stimulant users: evidence of damage and attempted repair by the glial cells has been reported, resembling that seen with loss of blood supply, aging, or diabetes. These differences in brain structure seem to be associated with the difficulties with memory and decision making seen in heavy methamphetamine users. We don't know yet the extent to which these behavioral changes are reversible. One final question that has been raised but not answered is this: Does long-term use of ADHD medications have any of these effects? The answer is no for most of the worst effects because these result from very high doses. However, we don't know if the brain adjusts to the long-term use—likely it does in some ways (changes in receptor sensitivity, etc.). Research in this area is ongoing. One good bit of news is that most studies show that kids with ADHD who get effective treatment (behavioral or drug) are less likely to become addicted to drugs.

Part
II

PART

II

13

BRAIN BASICS

NOTHING CHANGES THE way we feel or the way we perceive the world unless it interacts with our central nervous system (CNS). Whether we take a sip of wine, snort a line of cocaine, or see an attractive person, our CNS is the place where the action occurs. To understand how any drug works, we need to understand some very basic principles governing brain function.

THE PRINCIPLES

1. The brain is not only the organ that tells us who we are, what we are doing, and what we have done, but it also controls some very basic and critical body functions, such as heart rate, blood pressure, and breathing. Drugs can strongly affect these functions.

2. The brain is an extraordinarily complex structure, with thousands of different sites for drug action on thousands of different kinds of nerve cells. This complexity can cause different people to have very different experiences with the same drug.

3. The CNS, especially in children and young adults, has a remarkable capacity to change in response to experience; this is called plasticity. We see it happen every day as learning and remembering, but the CNS, in response to a variety of influences, can undergo changes that occur without our awareness of them.

4. The ability of the CNS to undergo plasticity can be modified by chemicals, whether taken for medical benefit or for recreational purposes.

CHAPTER CONTENTS

SINGLE NERVE CELLS

It is laughable to think that anyone completely understands how the brain functions. Every time neuroscientists make a discovery that explains some property of the nervous system, that discovery opens new doors and raises new questions. For example, no one knows exactly how the CNS stores memories, but we do know a lot about how to alter the storage process.

Often the brain is compared to a computer. That analogy is overworked, but it's not such a bad one. Most people know how to use a computer, and they know that smashing the disks is a bad idea, but they do not know precisely how the circuits inside the computer do the job. However, not knowing just how the circuits work does not prevent the user from knowing where to insert the disk, how to turn on the monitor, and how to run a program. Likewise, there is a lot to know about the nervous system, and a little knowledge can help you keep yours healthy.

The first step is to appreciate what a miraculous structure the brain is. The real miracle is that such a complex structure can function so well even under some of the terribly difficult conditions that we impose on it.

It has an ingenious balance of excitatory and inhibitory influences coursing through it. It's like a sports car moving along a winding country road with just the right amount of pressure on the accelerator (excitation) and the brakes (inhibition). In the brain, the brakes are the release of inhibitory chemicals. They suppress the firing of nerve cells by opening channels in the cells' membranes, letting ions flow in a direction that causes the cells' electrical potential to move away from the point at which it would fire a signal (an action potential). Without action potentials, there is no action, so we say that that cell or network of cells is inhibited. An inhibited network cannot carry out its function, so that function is lost. The lost function might be thinking, feeling anxiety, staying awake, having reflexes to pain, adjusting the circulatory system, or breathing. An overly excited network is like a pot of boiling water, or like that sports car out of control at high speed. There is a chaos of discharges that randomly fire in many parts of the brain, leading to all sorts of feelings and movements. It is a miracle that in most of us, for most of the time, the brain maintains the delicate balance that permits a normal life.

The first step to understanding that delicate balance, and how drugs disrupt it, is to understand the building blocks of the CNS—the nerve cells, or neurons. There are many other CNS cells that support the neurons, but the neurons are where the information is stored, where feelings are sensed, and where actions are initiated.

Neurons look a little like trees. Did you ever see a big tree uprooted? There's the trunk and the top with many branches and the leaves that receive the sunlight. Then there is the root system that is equally branched, with a large taproot going off into the earth. Under the microscope, many neurons look the same way. They have a "top" receiving area called the dendrites, where connections from other neurons make contact. Then they have a "trunk" area, where the body of the nerve cell is located, containing the genetic information for that cell. Finally, out of the cell body emerges the axon of the cell (like the root of a tree), which goes off and branches to make contact with other nerve cells or muscle cells and transmit signals to them.

Like all cells, a nerve cell is held together by its cell membrane, which is a mixture of lipids (fats) and proteins. Many nonneuronal cells (e.g., blood cells, muscle cells) have cell membranes that are more or less the same all over. The cell membranes of neurons, however, are vastly different in different parts of the cell. These differences allow a cell to receive different types of signals from many other cells, integrate these signals, and then send out signals of its own. Even a single neuron is a very complicated bit of biochemical machinery, but this complexity is what allows the enormous information storage and processing capacity of the human brain to exist in such a compact form.

CONNECTIONS BETWEEN NERVE CELLS

The dendritic, or receiving, area of neurons is where axons (transmitting fibers) from other nerve cells make contact. These points of contact are called synapses. A single synapse is, in itself, a complex structure, consisting of the presynaptic and the postsynaptic regions. The presynaptic region is the termination point of the axon of the transmitting cell, and at that point the axon balloons from a very small fiber to a group of bulblike endings called the presynaptic terminals. These terminals contain chemicals—neurotransmitters—that are released into the space between the presynaptic terminal and the dendrite of the postsynaptic (receiving) cell. The neurotransmitter molecules react with special receptors that are sensitive only to that neurotransmitter on the postsynaptic cell, and, in just thousandths of a second, these receptors cause electrical and/or biochemical signals within the receiving cell.

A single neuron can have a large number of synapses on its dendrites, and it is the job of the neuron cell body to take in signals from all of those synapses and make a decision. That decision is whether to fire electrical signals itself down its transmitting fiber—its axon. The signals that are transmitted down the axon are called action potentials because they can cause action somewhere else. If they come from a nerve cell synapsing onto a muscle cell, they can cause the muscle cell to contract. If they come from a nerve cell connecting to another nerve cell, they can cause that follower nerve cell to either fire or stop firing, depending on what kind of signal it gets from the neurotransmitter molecules.

Thus, the input to a neuron is from synaptic connections from other neurons, while the output is a series of action potentials firing down its axon. The action potentials are all the same, just quick (about one-thousandth of a second) discharges of electrical activity. The information is carried at the rate by which these discharges occur. So, if a neuron fires lots of action potentials in a brief period (up to four hundred in one second), it can have a large influence on its follower cells, while slow firing would have less influence.

Some drugs may affect the generation and spread of action potentials down the axon, but that is not a common site of drug action. These drugs usually produce drastic and often toxic changes because they can completely stop a neuron from firing. One interesting toxin that does this is the chemical present in the ovaries of puffer fish, which are delicacies in Japan. This chemical, called tetrodotoxin, is so toxic that eating just part of a fish can paralyze the muscles responsible for breathing and lead to death. Japanese restaurants have chefs who are specially trained and licensed to remove the ovaries before the fish is served. This same class of toxin is also thought to be used in Haitian voodoo rituals to induce zombie-like behavior.

Most drugs act either at the presynaptic terminal, where the neurotransmitter is released, or at the postsynaptic membrane on the neurotransmitter receptor. The synapse is the primary site of action of the majority of drugs that affect human brain functions. So to understand how drugs affect our CNS, we must understand the synapse.

The presynaptic terminal is the place where neurotransmitters are synthesized, packaged, and released. When action potentials travel from the cell body of the transmitting neuron down to the terminal area, the electrical signals cause changes in the shape of protein molecules that reside in the terminal area. These molecules sense the electrical signals and, within thousandths of a second, reconfigure themselves to form pores, or channels, in the terminal membrane. Calcium ions flow into the terminal through these pores, and the calcium initiates a chain of biochemical reactions. The result of this biochemical sequence is that packets of neurotransmitter molecules break through the terminal membrane and move toward the postsynaptic area of the receiving cell.

What happens to the neurotransmitter molecules after they are released? After all, if they stayed around forever, the postsynaptic neuron, or muscle fiber, would constantly be under their influence and further signaling would be impossible. Removal of neurotransmitters is accomplished in three ways. First, the molecules just diffuse away into other areas where there are no receptors and are removed by the general circulation of fluids in the brain. Second, there can be specific chemicals that break the neurotransmitters into noneffective parts that are returned to the cells. Finally, there are specific sites on the presynaptic terminal that attach to the active neurotransmitter molecules and transport them back into the terminal for release again. These transport sites are often places where drugs act to prolong the presence of the transmitter in the postsynaptic area, therefore increasing its effect. Cocaine is an excellent example of such a drug, because it suppresses the uptake of the transmitter dopamine, which is important in the reward center of the brain.

This entire neurotransmitter-release process can be controlled by chemicals active at the presynaptic terminal. In some cases there are receptors for the transmitter being released that serve to suppress further release of the transmitter and thus limit the action at that synapse. In other cases there are receptors for different neurotransmitters that can regulate release. Any of these sites could be important places for drugs to act.

THE ROLE OF RECEPTORS

Next, consider the postsynaptic region of the cell, where the neurotransmitter receptors are located. The postsynaptic region contains the proteins bound in the lipid cell membrane that react with the neurotransmitter molecules. These proteins are, in themselves, very complex structures. They are three-dimensional molecules that have sites into which the neurotransmitter molecules can fit. In fact, this arrangement is just like a lock-and-key mechanism. The neurotransmitter molecules from the presynaptic cell are the keys and the postsynaptic receptors are the locks. When the key "enters" the lock by binding to the receptor molecule, the lock operates and the bioelectrical activity is initiated.

The lock-and-key analogy is good to a point, but it's certainly too simplistic. Unlike a lock, which usually has only one action (to throw a bolt into a door), a receptor can have numerous actions, and each one of these steps can be changed by drugs. The first two actions that occur at a receptor are electrical and biochemical. The fastest signal is the electrical process.

Once the neurotransmitter binds, the receptor molecule can change its shape and open channels (pores) into the cell on which it is located. These channels allow the flow of charged molecules (ions) into or out of the cell, and this movement of electrical charge causes an electrical signal to develop across the cell membrane.

Normally neurons have an electrical charge so that the inside of the cell is negative (about 0.1 volt) compared to the outside. This is called the resting potential, and when a neuron is at rest, it fires no action potentials. When the inside of the cell at the point of the cell body becomes considerably less negative (about 0.04 volts), then action potentials begin to fire and the cell is then transmitting to its follower cells.

The electrical action at the synapse can thus control whether a cell starts to fire action potentials. For example, if a receptor opens a channel that lets in ions that make the cell less negative, then the electrical potential of the cell moves in the direction of firing action potentials. If the receptor opens a channel that causes the cell to become more negative inside, then the cell becomes less able to fire. Clearly, then, with many synapses, the cell must add all of this electrical activity together, and the sum of it determines whether a cell fires. This addition of pro- and antifiring (excitatory and inhibitory) currents occurs in and around the cell body of the neuron, in a place where action potentials originate. Thus, all of the synaptic activity of the cell converges to the cell body, where the cell makes the decision to fire or not to fire, depending on the voltage across its cell membrane.

The two most common neurotransmitters in the CNS are the amino acids GABA (gamma-aminobutyric acid) and glutamate. These are referred to as inhibitory (GABA) and excitatory (glutamate) amino acid neurotransmitters. These neurotransmitters are responsible for much of the second-to-second processing in the CNS. If either of these is significantly blocked, the proper functioning of the CNS is dramatically disrupted. There are many subtypes of these receptors, and each of these subtypes has different characteristics. Some of the most interesting drug effects come from activating just a particular subtype of a receptor rather than the whole class of receptors.

Receptors can initiate a cascade of biochemical events within neurons. Either by letting calcium ions into cells or by activating intracellular enzymes directly, activated receptors can profoundly change the biochemical environment of a cell. These biochemical signals can alter the numbers of receptors for different transmitters, change the degree to which they recognize their transmitters, or even change the systems that regulate the genetics of the cell—literally, thousands of different processes. It is no wonder that drugs that interact with receptors can be so specific and so powerful.

It is this diversity of receptors and biochemical signaling pathways that allows humans to devise drugs that have quite specific effects. Throughout this book there are references to actions of a drug at a specific receptor, receptor regulation site, or biochemical-signaling pathway. Although we know much about the way these chemicals operate, it is important to remember the mantra of every pharmacologist: "Every drug has two effects—the one I know about and the one I don't know about."

COLLECTIONS OF NEURONS FORM SPECIALIZED
BRAIN AREAS

While neurons are the basic components of the brain, the ways in which
they are connected determine what functions will occur. An old cartoon
shows a neurosurgeon in the operating room saying, "Well, there go the
piano lessons." Like most humor, it's somewhat based on fact. The brain is
organized into specialized areas that control speech, hearing, vision, fine
movements, gross movements, learning, anger, fear, and much more.

It would be very useful to know which neurotransmitters and receptors
carry the information for all of these functions, because then we could
design specific drugs to modulate them with great precision. However, we
are far from having that information, and even if we did have it, there is
another complication—the pattern of connections between neurons.
While neurochemistry is important, the patterns in which neurons connect are equally important. The connections are quite specific, and while
we know a lot about the gross pathways connecting brain areas, we know
little about how cells are connected within small brain areas.

Behaviors, even simple ones, are possible because neuronal connections are complicated. For example, even the simplest reaction, such as
blinking when a dust particle gets in your eye, involves several nerves
connected to each other. So, when a drug alters one process, the effect it
has depends on how that process participates in the function of the network. Thus, our ignorance of nerve-cell connections accounts for some of
the uncertainty in knowing the effects of drugs.

THE CENTRAL NERVOUS SYSTEM CONTROLS
BASIC FUNCTIONS

In the following section, we will talk about some of the most exciting
parts of brain function, learning, and memory. But it is crucial to understand that the central nervous system controls some very important body
functions that sustain life. These are boring functions until they fail, and
then they get attention right away. The three most vital functions that the
CNS controls are the circulatory system (heart and blood vessels), the
respiratory system (breathing), and the reflex system (which instantly,
and without thinking, causes us to respond to a threat).

The circulatory system is maintained in a stable condition by its own built-in control system. However, the brain can easily modify this set point. For example, during periods of anger and frustration, the heart beats rapidly and blood pressure rises. The CNS also stimulates the respiratory system and causes breathing to increase. The brain has decided that the "normal" status is incorrect and that the body needs to be prepared for fight or flight. In contrast, when the mind is at peace, and perhaps meditative, the heart rate falls, blood pressure falls, and breathing is slowed.

The CNS reflex system is equally important but often forgotten. People who think about drugs and safety often mention hearts and breathing, but they don't put as much emphasis on how reflexes keep us safe. Take, for example, how we jerk our hand back from a hot surface. This is a pure reflex action that is signaled in the spinal cord. The sensing nerves in the fingers and hand send a powerful signal of distress to the spinal cord. This signal excites neurons that cause movement and, through a modestly complicated process, withdrawal of the hand. This all happens before the pain signals are even interpreted by the conscious brain.

A more important example is the reflex to clear the airway for breathing. Notice how fast and how strongly the body responds when something touches the airway in the back of the throat. This is a critical reflex to sustain life. If this reflex were suppressed by a drug, then something (such as vomit) could easily occlude the airway and it would not be cleared. The person would die of asphyxiation. The list of basic body functions that can be impaired by drugs goes on and on. This is not a particularly glamorous or fascinating area of drug effects, but it is one that everyone must understand.

PLASTICITY IN THE CNS—
LEARNING FROM EXPERIENCE

The third principle of this chapter stated that the CNS responds to experience by learning—that is, it reorganizes some of its neurochemistry and connections so that the experience is remembered. It is very important to understand that this plasticity is a broad concept. Not only does the CNS remember events that are consciously experienced, but it also changes in response to all sorts of signals, such as the constant presence of drugs.

The most familiar plasticity in the CNS is the simple remembering of experiences—faces, odors, names, classroom lectures, and lots more. The neurobiological mechanisms through which this kind of learning happens are not completely understood, but we have some clues. One important site of learning appears to be the synapse.

As discussed, synapses of nerve cells are quite complex, and there is extensive biochemical machinery in both the presynaptic and the postsynaptic areas. We think memory is built one synapse at a time: some synapses that are stimulated repeatedly change how they function (learn) and maintain that change for a long time. There is an electrical manifestation of this learning that scientists call long-term potentiation (LTP). It is a long-lasting strengthening (potentiation) of the electrical signal between two neurons that occurs when the synapse between them is stimulated.

We're not sure how this happens, but it is likely through a series of biochemical changes in how the first neuron releases its neurotransmitter and/or in how the second neuron responds to the neurotransmitter. On the presynaptic side, a synapse could be strengthened by increasing the number of presynaptic terminals, by releasing more transmitters from the same number of terminals, or by a reduction in transmitter removal. On the postsynaptic side, strengthening could occur with an increase in the number of receptors, a change in the functional properties of the receptors, a change in how well the postsynaptic site is coupled to the remainder of the neuron, or a change in the biochemistry of the postsynaptic neuron. There is scientific controversy about the true mechanisms of LTP, and the issue may not be clear for a number of years.

Almost every neuron can modify many aspects of its function to adapt to new conditions—by making more or less neurotransmitter, by changing the number of receptors on the surface of its cells, by changing the number of molecules responsible for the passage of the electrical stimulus down the axon, and so forth. If a neural circuit is being overstimulated, it can reduce the stimulation by removing some of the receptors for the neurotransmitter stimulating it. Therefore, even if the neural circuit is being sent lots of signals, they don't get through. Alternatively, if a neural circuit is receiving much less stimulation than usual, it can adapt by becoming more sensitive to each stimulus. This is how the brain stays in balance.

This type of biochemical plasticity goes on all the time and is part of normal brain function. However, these same changes can cause abnormal brain function. For example, we think that the tremendous mood changes in depression might result from changing numbers of neurotransmitter receptors following changing stimulation of specific neurons in the brain.

If neurons and synapses learn, do they also forget? The answer appears to be yes. We just described how stimulating a neural pathway in a certain way can cause it to "learn" to respond to stimulation differently. Stimulating it in another way (slowly, and for a long time) can cause a process called depotentiation, which appears to be the opposite of long-term potentiation. Why is this interesting? Depotentiation could be quite important because it may represent the synaptic equivalent of amnesia. Depotentiation can be produced by prolonged slow activity or by very strong high-frequency activity, like that which occurs in seizures. It may be a protective mechanism by which the CNS prevents a seizure or brain trauma from encoding new information into the circuits. Again, it is almost certainly under the control of cell-signaling pathways and thus could be manipulated by drugs.

This gradual change in the electrical strength of a connection seems subtle, but it makes intuitive sense that memories could form in this way. Can the brain actually change physically? We used to think that once a person was mature, the brain didn't change anymore. However, more and more research shows that actual changes in the shapes of neurons also can happen in response to earlier experiences. We know that the shape of certain neurons in the brain changes when different hormones become available. For example, at least in animals, treating them with hormones can stimulate the production of little protuberances, or "spines," on the dendrites of neurons. Other research has shown that synapses actually remodel themselves over time after different levels of activity. So, connections actually get lost or remade. For example, prolonged stress seems to actually shrink the dendrite on neurons, perhaps explaining the cognitive difficulties people encounter during prolonged stressful periods.

It has been known for a long time that this happened in lower animals. For example, as songbirds learn new songs, the structure of certain parts of their brains changes. It was once thought that the brains of mammals did not have this type of structural plasticity. However, more recent studies have shown similar changes in rats, and scientists think that they probably occur in all mammals.

The most exciting recent development in neuronal plasticity is our understanding that the brain can actually make new neurons. This process, called neurogenesis, was long thought to occur mostly during prenatal development, but now we find that it is happening in adult humans. Neurogenesis results from the conversion of neural stem cells into functional neurons. The rate of conversion seems to increase in response to injury or other pathologies and decrease in response to chronic stress. As with most neuroscience research, the data come primarily from animal experiments, usually rats, and as always, relevance to humans needs to be established.

There have been some intriguing findings regarding the effects of drugs on neurogenesis in animals. It appears that depression reduces neurogenesis and subsequent treatment with antidepressants restores it. More relevant to this book, the laboratory of Fulton Crews at the University of North Carolina has made the startling discovery that binge exposure to alcohol dramatically suppresses rat neurogenesis, particularly in the adolescent forebrain, which is a brain area in rapid development. The potential implications of this are enormous, because adolescents tend to be binge drinkers. Is this behavior impairing their brain development? What other drugs affect these processes? Does this really happen in humans? These questions should and will be answered by future research, but for now they alert us to the possibility that drug abuse could have profound effects on teenage brain development.

DO ALL PARTS OF THE BRAIN LEARN?

The processes that we just described do not happen in just one part of the brain. There are indeed specialized neural networks, especially in a part of the brain called the hippocampus, where learning occurs and memories are created. (People who have had damage to this part of the brain cannot learn new things, although they can remember things that happened before.) However, most forms of plasticity can occur all over the brain and affect all brain function.

For us to be able to function normally, all brain processes need to proceed unimpaired. All of the neurotransmitter systems need to be working. The brain needs to change with time to reflect previous experience—that is, learn—to restore balance if it is over- or understimulated.

THE DEVELOPING BRAIN

While the brains of adults change all the time, what goes on in adults is trivial compared to the phenomenal changes that occur while the brain is developing. The brain assembles itself carefully through the process of neurons growing out, and through chemical signals around them, gradually finding their way to the correct destination, where they make the connections that they then maintain. During this time of life, the physical changes in the brain are dramatic. New synaptic connections are being made at a high rate every day. The growing brain also has its own way of "forgetting." Many of the neurons growing out never reach their destination and die in the process. Others reshape their connections until they are correct. Through all of this furious growth, neurons must remain active or they can fail to make their appropriate connections. Therefore, changes in neuronal function that in an adult would simply shut down a pathway for a while, in a developing brain can have more drastic consequences.

Growing neurons are affected by processes that don't affect the neurons of adult brains. Exposure to substances that inhibit cell growth has some impact on an adult brain but a devastating impact on the developing brain. The neurotoxic element mercury provides a good example. Mercury affects the function of the adult brain and can lead to serious, but largely reversible, disruption of brain function. However, exposure of the brain of the developing fetus to mercury disrupts brain development so totally that severe mental retardation results. For example, an industrial spill of mercury into the water near a small, coastal Japanese town called Minamata contaminated the fish that were the local food source. While many adults experienced diseases that eventually resolved, many children born during this time frame had terrible disruption of normal brain development and remained mentally retarded throughout their lives.

Recently, medical imaging techniques have made it possible to study the development of the human brain at various points from birth to adulthood. Some of the most interesting studies use magnetic resonance imaging (MRI) with the machine set to reveal the white matter of the brain, the myelin insulation on the nerve cell axons. As the brain matures, the connections between cells become permanent, and then they are insulated with myelin. So, imaging for the myelin tells the scientist just how much development has occurred in a brain area. The big news is that the human brain is not fully developed until late in adolescence. And among the last parts to develop are the frontal lobe areas that give us the capability of inhibiting inappropriate behavior, handling complex tasks, and planning ahead. When we lecture about this, we often make the point that from the standpoint of the brain, adolescents are not "young adults," but rather, "big kids."

We believe it is very important to teach kids that their brains are still developing through adolescence. This means that they have the opportu-

nity to take some control of the final development of some of the most
critical areas of their brains.

There are an increasing number of studies examining the effects of
drugs on the adolescent brain from our laboratories and others. Most of
these studies have focused on the acute effects of alcohol and other drugs,
but some epidemiological studies have examined the associations
between drug use and brain pathology. We have discussed these issues in
the appropriate chapters, primarily those dealing with alcohol and
marijuana.

DRUGS AND PLASTICITY

Whatever the exact mechanisms are that underlie learning, there is strong
evidence that supports the correlation between synaptic changes, neuroplasticity, and learning. The best of this evidence comes from drug studies. Chemicals that block the development of LTP tend to block other
manifestations of neuroplasticity and, in particular, can block learning.

For example, a drug called AP-5 (D-2-amino-5-phosphonopenta-
noate) blocks a certain subtype of the excitatory neurotransmitter glutamate. This particular subtype, the NMDA (the N-methyl-D-aspartate)
receptor, has the very special property of letting calcium into the cell
only when the cell is receiving excitatory signals through other synapses.
The calcium causes LTP to occur at those synapses. Thus, the NMDA
receptor is like a memory switch. When the cell is receiving a signal and
the NMDA receptor is activated, the cell "remembers" the signal by
strengthening that synapse.

It is wonderful that we have been lucky enough to find the NMDA
receptor, because it appears to be one of the most important receptors for
learning and other forms of neuroplasticity. It may teach us much about
how memory occurs and how some drugs disrupt it. For example, in laboratory experiments, if we chemically block the NMDA receptor so that
glutamate cannot bind there, LTP does not occur, rats do not learn mazes,
and the CNS does not reorganize its neuronal connections following
injury. There is every reason to believe that learning and neuroplasticity
are also suppressed in humans.

Alcohol in rats blocks NMDA receptors, suppresses LTP, and suppresses maze learning. So, now we may know why we forget what we did
when we were drunk (see the "Alcohol" chapter for more information).

Many drugs affect the ability of the brain to learn—there is no question about it. But which drugs have which effects, and for how long? One of the best stories about the effects of drugs on learning was told to one of us by a drug company representative during an airplane trip. It seems that some of the professional staff from his company were making a quick trip overseas to a meeting, and they needed to sleep during the plane ride because their lectures were scheduled almost as soon as they were to arrive. So, this group had a few alcoholic drinks and then took one of their newly marketed sedatives (a benzodiazepine) to get to sleep. Everything went well, including the lectures, and the scientists returned home in a couple of days. The only problem was that when they returned, they remembered nothing of the meeting—not their lectures or those of anyone else. They did not know that the drug they chose, in the dose they chose, would have powerful amnesiac effects, especially when mixed with alcohol.

This story is legend in the pharmaceutical industry, and whether it is exactly true does not make any difference. It illustrates the point that even the people who develop and manufacture drugs by the highest standards may not know every effect they can have and how long these effects can last.

There are basically three ways in which drugs can affect learning: they can impair the ability of the brain to store information (amnesia), they can distort reality, or in some cases, they can stimulate the brain to increase learning.

By far the most common effect of drugs is to suppress learning. Almost all of the drugs that have sedative or anxiety-reducing properties impair the retention of information. Although we do not know exactly how this happens, there are three mechanisms that have been proposed at the synaptic level.

The first of these is increased inhibition. We know that many sedative drugs increase GABA-mediated synaptic activity, which inhibits the firing of neurons. The experimental data suggest that this increase in inhibition can reduce the effects of the type of neuronal firing that is usually necessary for LTP, and thus prevent neuroplasticity.

The second of these mechanisms is reduced excitation. Some drugs, such as alcohol, not only increase GABA function (and thus inhibition) but also suppress the glutamate-mediated excitatory channels (the NMDA receptor channels) that let calcium ions into the neurons. This reduction in calcium entry prevents the signaling mechanisms within the neurons that lead to long-term synaptic changes.

Finally, there are drugs, such as the THC in marijuana, that act through their own receptors to change cell biochemistry so that learning is impaired. From what we know of their biochemistry, they may directly regulate the signal-processing pathways within the cell that govern the strength of synaptic activity, perhaps by suppressing the signals that mediate LTP or, alternatively, by enhancing the processes underlying LTD and/or depotentiation.

Now that we know about LTD and depotentiation, it is easy to imagine that there would be reasons for the CNS to reduce activity in some pathways and thus "forget" some neuroplastic changes. Therefore, it is completely reasonable that some drugs could enhance this type of signaling, reducing the ability to learn.

On a brighter note, neurobiologists are exploring ways to use drug therapy to enhance learning. This research is particularly important for the many people who suffer from Alzheimer's disease or other brain disorders that impair learning. Most of the rest of us would also relish the ability to learn more or faster. There are some tantalizing clues that this may be possible.

One of the most interesting clues comes from an experience that almost all of us have had. It's the "Do you remember what you were doing when . . . ?" question. Every generation has at least one of these questions. For older people, it's what they were doing when they heard that JFK was assassinated. Nearly everyone recalls the fateful morning of 9/11. Think of an example: the first time you had a very important and emotional experience, either positive or negative.

Why is it that we remember some experiences so well, and not only the event but maybe what clothes we wore, what the room looked like, what we ate? Ongoing experiments shed a lot of light on this phenomenon. Dr. James McGaugh (of the University of California at Irvine) took two similar groups of people and placed them in separate but similar rooms with all sorts of cues, or decorations. The goal was to subject the groups to an emotional story and to see how well they remembered the story and the environment (the room) in which they experienced the event.

What makes this experiment interesting is that one group was given a drug (propranolol) that blocks a particular subtype of adrenaline receptor—the beta-adrenaline receptor. This receptor is the one responsible for the increase in heart rate and blood pressure that occurs under physical or emotional stress; the blocker, propranolol, is used to control blood pressure and heart problems in some patients. So, one group was completely normal, while the other group had their excitatory adrenaline activity blocked.

The experimental subjects were then told a heartbreaking story about an injured child. After a period of time the two groups were removed from their rooms and then asked to recall the story and the details of their environment in the room. Both groups remembered the story. However, only the normal (undrugged) group remembered the details of the room. The treated group remembered very little of their environment.

What does this teach us? We all know that we tend to learn what interests us, and we know that we remember emotional events. Now we know why. The adrenergic system apparently delivers signals to the brain that facilitate learning and remembering the environment associated with an emotionally powerful event. This is probably a very important characteristic for both humans and other animals to have, because it tends to help us remember events and places that were either wonderful or threatening, and thus adjust our future behavior accordingly. So, now it is clear why a smell or a face or a place might make you feel good or bad, even if you cannot immediately recall why: your brain is recalling an emotional experience.

This insight into learning is useful in several ways. First, it illustrates how important it is to be alert and interested in what we are trying to learn. When we are sleepy or depressed we are poor learners, in part because our adrenergic system is not activated. To really learn or teach something, we must include an emotional component.

In addition, this experiment suggests that there may be ways to facilitate learning through manipulating brain chemistry. Neuroscientists already know that the adrenergic system is not the only modulator of learning. However, increasing the function of any of these systems has proven difficult to achieve without producing unacceptable side effects.

At this point, no drug has yet been approved to increase learning. Until then, readers, you'll have to "trick" your brain by studying what is exciting and by getting excited about what you must study!

THE LATEST AND GREATEST(?): IMAGING THE BRAIN

It's hard to find a media story about the brain that doesn't refer to the latest technology for imaging the activity of the brain, most often using Functional Magnetic Resonance Imaging (fMRI). This is a powerful tool for imaging ongoing brain activity in humans as well as animals. As with structural MRI that yields "still" images of the brain, fMRI uses magnetic fields rather than radiation to image the tissue. So, as far as we know, there is no safety issue about long or repeated exposures (unless you have something in your body that can be magnetized).

fMRI depends on a particularly useful property of hemoglobin, the molecule in red blood cells that carries oxygen to all tissues, including those in the brain. As you may have learned in biology class, oxygen is bound to hemoglobin in the blood and is released from hemoglobin as blood perfuses tissues that need oxygen for producing energy. The magnetic properties of hemoglobin change as the hemoglobin releases oxygen to tissues. Thus, the fMRI system looks for changes in magnetic signals as tissues consume oxygen. The signal is called the blood oxygen level dependent (BOLD) signal.

When neural circuits are active, blood flow increases in those areas and oxygen is stripped from hemoglobin in the blood. Thus the BOLD signal changes to reflect that shift in the amount of hemoglobin that has oxygen bound to it. So literally, one can lie in an fMRI machine and decide to wiggle one's thumb and watch the brain activity associated with that movement. What you are really looking at is blood flow and oxygen-consumption changes in the brain areas that control that movement—not the electrical activity of the brain. The BOLD signal lags the neuronal activity for one to two seconds, and there is still controversy about what exactly triggers the increased blood flow and oxygen delivery. But it is safe to say that fMRI is measuring brain activity.

fMRI has its limits. First, there is the time issue we just mentioned, because the signal lags the neural activity for a long time compared to the firing rate of neurons. Then there is the issue of spatial resolution. The very best fMRI resolution (at this writing) is a cube that's about one millimeter on each side—and that requires a machine with a very strong and expensive magnet. That one-millimeter cube contains many neurons and synapses between them. So, using an fMRI to examine brain circuits is a bit like looking at a low-resolution TV—there is information there, but not as much as one would like. Another problem is that it is not possible to determine whether a BOLD signal in a brain area is a result of that area *transmitting* information or *receiving* information. All we can say is that the area is active. Furthermore, we don't know the result of that activity—it may be stimulating or shutting down its neighbor by activating neurons that normally slow down cells they contact.

Finally, the BOLD signals are very small compared to the background activity. This requires that the fMRI system average the images to reveal the relevant activity of an area. To further emphasize the active area, colors are used and the contrast is enhanced. Those techniques are very helpful to scientists but can produce images that are misleading to nonscientists. One of us was consulted by a major television network talk show about the effects of ecstasy as shown by brain images (not fMRI, but it doesn't matter) of individuals who had used the drug. The images had very high contrast, and it appeared that the ecstasy users had "holes" in their brains. In fact, there was just a small percentage difference in the true signals, but the images had been enhanced to emphasize those differences. Nevertheless, they talked about ecstasy producing holes in the brains of users.

fMRI has been used to monitor brain activity in a vast array of studies, ranging from epilepsy to lie detection. It has also been used to image the response of the brain to various drugs as scientists try and determine where in the brain a drug acts to produce a change in behavior. To some extent this works. For example, one can show pictures of cocaine to nonusers and compare their response to the response of cocaine addicts. The BOLD images can vary remarkably between brain areas. But it is hard to know exactly what these changes mean.

First, individual variations make it hard to draw conclusions about a particular individual's responses. Doing studies with groups of people and averaging the group results produces reliable images, but we are not yet at the point of being able to image one individual and draw firm conclusions. Second, even if a brain area is reliably activated in some circumstance, we don't know enough about the brain to know exactly what each area does. Probably most important, brain activities are executed by coordinated signaling between a variety of areas, and fMRI may not be able to tell us the direction of signal flow or what role an area is playing. Finally, variations in signal strength may obscure proper interpretations. This could easily happen if a very small collection of neurons exerted powerful effects on a much larger circuit. The BOLD signal from the small number of neurons initiating the activity might not even be visible, while the larger circuit would dominate and appear to be the source of the activity.

All of this is not to say that fMRI and other brain imaging tools should be ignored. They are truly fantastic tools to begin to understand the relationship between behaviors and brain activities. As they become more refined, they may be able to reveal individual differences that have diagnostic meaning. But our advice at this moment is to view the nonscientific media with a degree of caution and to not be seduced by pretty pictures.

WHY SHOULD ANYONE CARE ABOUT ALL OF THIS?

We hope that this chapter offers some good reasons to develop a respect for the brain and the body that supports it, as well as some insight into why drugs do what they do. This is especially important for teenagers, because as every teenager knows, they are different from adults.

What adults may not know is that the teenagers are right. For some time we have known that the very immature brain, as in babies, has a number of characteristics that are different from the adult brain. Now we are finding that the adolescent brain may be different also. It may respond differently to drugs, and it may learn differently.

A psychologist at Duke University, Dr. David Rubin, carried out a fascinating series of experiments showing just how different young people may be. The basic experiment was to take adults at various ages and ask them questions about events that occurred in every ten-year period of their lives, including a lot of trivia. Of course, recent events were remembered fairly well, but other than those, the events best recalled were those that occurred during young adulthood (from age eleven to age thirty). This means that a senior citizen recalled his life events and what was going on in the world during his adolescence even better than those events that had occurred just a few years earlier.

If our conclusions from this research are correct, then there is something very special about either our brain biochemistry or our psychological state during adolescence that enables us to store our experiences for life. Whatever the explanation, the implications are clear—the experiences, good or bad, that we have during our youth are very well stored in our "sober" memory systems and can be recalled for the rest of our lives. Thus, when teenagers say they are different, they are right, and when adults say that these are formative years, they, too, are right.

14

DRUG BASICS

UNDERSTANDING DRUGS AND their effects on our bodies begins with some very simple principles.

THE PRINCIPLES

1. A drug is any chemical put into the body that changes mental state or bodily function.

2. How a drug enters the body makes a huge difference in its effects. Ingesting a drug is usually the slowest route to the brain, and inhaling and intravenous injection are the fastest routes. If a drug is potentially lethal, then rapid administration of the drug by inhaling it or injecting it is the most dangerous way to take it and could result in death.

3. The length of time a drug affects the central nervous system varies tremendously across drugs. Some drugs are removed in only a few minutes, while others stay around for weeks. With any compound, it is crucial to know how long its effects will last—even those effects you do not notice.

4. The effects of drugs can change with time as our bodies adapt to the drug. This is called tolerance. As a result, when drug use is stopped, these changes cause bodies to work abnormally once the drug is no longer present. This is called withdrawal.

CHAPTER CONTENTS

The term *drug* means one thing to politicians trying to get elected, another thing to high school students, and yet another to physicians. **A drug is any substance that changes mental state or bodily function.** This can mean megadoses of vitamins, herbal medications from health-food stores, birth control pills, over-the-counter cold remedies, aspirin, or beer. Psychoactive drugs are those that affect the brain. People use psychoactive drugs from a number of sources including foods or beverages (like coffee), prescriptions from doctors to treat illnesses of the brain (like epilepsy), and from a variety of sources from the grocery store to the corner pusher for recreational purposes. There are thousands of compounds that fit this simple definition of drugs. Try to make a list of all the drugs you have ever taken. It will probably number at least twenty, even for those readers who "don't take drugs."

Some argue that certain foods are drugs (favorite culprits are sugar and chocolate). Likewise, some addiction-treatment programs view behaviors such as compulsive sex, shopping, playing video games, and gambling as similar to drugs. In this book, we assume that neither foods nor behaviors qualify as drugs. However, research over the last few years has provided some compelling evidence that there actually may be some overlap. Some behaviors like gambling, overeating, and sex as well as some foods (e.g., sugar) activate the same reward system that cocaine does (see the chapter on addiction). At least one study shows that the brains of overeaters show a profile of low dopamine receptors that resembles patterns seen in alcoholics, suggesting that engaging in this behavior might have changed receptors like the drug does. However, there just isn't enough information to know for certain, and these changes may just reflect normal adaptations the brain makes to excessive stimulation with natural stimuli. That doesn't mean they are drugs.

A toxin, in distinction from a drug, is a substance that causes bodily harm. Pharmacologists joke that the only difference between a drug and a toxin is how much you take. There is a grain of truth in this. Many drugs produce good effects at one dose and bad effects at a higher dose. There is another difference between drugs and toxins, however. Drug taking is usually purposeful. This is not necessarily true of toxins. We are frequently exposed without choice to toxins including pesticide residues on our food, air pollutants, and vapors we inhale when we put gasoline in our cars. This last example shows how blurred these definitions can be. One of the substances present in gasoline in trace amounts (toluene) is the active ingredient in inhalants that some people sniff to get high. Is it a toxin or a drug? It is both, and it is toxic to the body regardless of the intent of the drug user.

HOW DRUGS WORK: RECEPTORS

Drugs work by attaching to a particular molecule called a receptor. Many different molecules can be receptors for drugs. Proteins on the surface of a cell that normally respond to hormones circulating in the blood, enzymes that control the flow of energy in a cell, even structures like the microscopic tubes (microtubules) that give the cell its shape can all be receptors. They can occur anywhere in the body: brain, heart, bone, skin. A drug can affect any bodily function if it can bind to some element of the cell that influences that function.

When a drug binds to its receptor and activates it, the drug is called an agonist. This means that the drug has an effect. Some drugs attach to a receptor and do not activate it but keep other molecules from getting to the receptor—often the molecule that normally would be stimulating it. These drugs are antagonists. They act by preventing normal processes from happening. Many of the psychoactive drugs we have discussed in this book work by preventing the action of normal neurotransmitters.

The toxins used in poison darts provide a vivid example. One active compound in these poisons, curare, prevents the neurotransmitter acetyl-

choline from working on its receptor. Acetylcholine is necessary to transmit from brain to muscle the information that permits muscle contraction.
When curare blocks the action of acetylcholine, the muscles are paralyzed
and the dart's victim dies from paralysis of the muscles responsible for
breathing.

HOW WELL DRUGS WORK: DOSE RESPONSE

How well a drug works depends on how much a user takes. The larger the
dose, generally, the bigger the effect, until a maximum is reached. Usually
this maximum is reached because all the available receptors are occupied
by the drug. Taking more drug than this is pointless.

Why do we take more of some drugs than others? Advertisements on
TV are proud of bragging that just one tiny pill of brand X has the same
effect as three pills of brand Y. Some drugs bind so tightly to their receptor that it takes very little to activate all the available receptors. Such a
drug is very potent. LSD is a good example of a very potent drug—only
millionths of a gram can cause hallucinations. So, should you be happy to
take brand X instead of brand Y? It depends on how much they cost. If
brand X costs three times more and you take one-third as much, you have
gained nothing!

What difference between brand X and brand Y could matter? Some
drugs don't bind very well, but a large enough dose can activate all available receptors very well. Others bind very tightly but don't activate the
receptor very well. Efficacy means how well a drug does what it does—
how well it changes receptor function. It does matter if brand X has more
efficacy than brand Y, because then the one pill would have more effect
than three of brand Y. For example, both aspirin and a strong opiate like
morphine diminish the sensation of pain. However, no amount of aspirin
will match the pain relief from morphine, because aspirin has less efficacy
for this particular action. So, why take aspirin instead of morphine? First
of all, a morphine dose can kill you because the difference between an
effective dose and a toxic overdose is not great. Second, morphine is
addictive. For a garden-variety tension headache, the risks associated
with using morphine are not worth the potential benefit. However, for
very severe migraine headaches, sometimes the greater efficacy of opiate
drugs is necessary.

HOW DRUGS MOVE THROUGH THE BODY

GETTING IN

Drugs must get to their receptors to act. Even a skin cream like a cortisone ointment that relieves the itch of poison ivy must be able to pass through the fatty membrane that surrounds most cells to heal the cells that are irritated by poison ivy toxin.

Most drugs must go much farther than the skin to act. Drugs used to treat tumors deep inside the body must travel from where they are placed, through the bloodstream, to be delivered to distant organs. A few drugs pass through cells so well that when they are rubbed on the skin they travel through all the skin layers down to the layer of the skin where the smallest blood vessels (capillaries) are, through the capillary walls, and into the bloodstream. Nicotine is one, which is why the nicotine skin patch works. There is also a motion-sickness drug that can travel through the skin to the brain. What is unique about such drugs is their ability to pass through a cell membrane that is very fatty. However, most drugs just don't dissolve well enough in these fatty membranes to travel all that distance. Such drugs prefer water to oil, and they have a great deal of trouble passing through cells: these often only enter the body well after injection.

Applying drugs to the mucous membranes is a more effective way to get some drugs into the body, because the mucous membrane surfaces of the body (as in the nose) are much thinner, and the capillaries are much closer to the surface. For these reasons, placing drugs in the nose, mouth, or rectum provides a pretty efficient route for administering some drugs. Cocaine and amphetamine enter the bloodstream easily from these sites, which is why people snort them. In contrast, antibiotics, an example of drugs that prefer water to oil, cannot cross through cell membranes and cannot be given nasally.

The most efficient way to get a drug into the bloodstream is to put it there directly. The invention of the hypodermic syringe provided the most direct means we have of getting drugs into the body: we inject them directly into a vein. The drug then goes to the heart and is distributed throughout the entire body. After intravenous injection, peak drug levels in the bloodstream occur within a minute or two. Then levels begin to fall as the drug crosses the capillaries and enters the tissues.

There are other places that drugs can be injected. Most immunizations are done by injecting the vaccine into the muscle (intramuscular). The drug is delivered a little more slowly this way, because it must leave the muscle and enter capillaries before it is distributed to the body. Drugs can also be injected beneath the skin (subcutaneously). This "skin-popping" is a route used by many beginning heroin users who have not yet started injecting heroin intravenously.

Inhaling drugs into the lungs can deliver a drug to the circulation almost as quickly as intravenous injection. Anyone who smokes tobacco takes advantage of this characteristic to deliver nicotine to the brain. The drug simply has to dissolve through the air sacs of the lungs and into the capillaries. The surface area of the lungs is very large and fat-soluble drugs like nicotine can move quickly across a large surface. In addition, the blood supply of the lungs goes directly to the heart and then out to the other tissues. Therefore, smoking can deliver the drugs to the tissues very quickly. However, only certain drugs enter the body efficiently this way. They must be very fat-soluble, and they must form a vapor or gas when they are heated. Several drugs, including cocaine and methamphetamine, easily form vapors if they are in their uncharged form, which occurs when they are crystallized from an alkaline (basic) solution. In this case, the nitrogen that is present in each molecule is uncharged (it has no positive charge from a hydrogen ion). These qualities allow drugs to cross into the circulation very quickly. Drug users call this method of delivery "freebasing." Cigarette manufacturers create the same effect by making tobacco leaves alkaline (basic).

The most common way that people get drugs into their system is by swallowing them. Drugs that enter this way must pass through the walls of the stomach or intestine and then enter the capillaries. A large part of any drug that is swallowed never gets to the rest of the body because it is removed by the liver and destroyed. The liver is placed cleverly to do this job. All the blood vessels that take nutrients from the intestine to the body must go through the liver first, where toxic substances can be removed. This protects the body from toxic substances in food. Swallowing may be the easiest way to deliver drugs, but it is the slowest way to deliver a drug to the body. That is why your headache is not gone five minutes after you take an ibuprofen tablet.

To recapitulate, the way people take a drug (the route of administration) and the amount they take determine the drug's effects. Injecting drugs intravenously or smoking them results in nearly instantaneous effects because the levels of drug in the blood rise very rapidly. This speed accounts for the lure of injecting heroin intravenously or smoking crack. The drug effect occurs much more rapidly than if the drug was snorted. Injecting a drug intravenously or smoking it also offers the greatest risk of overdose. Drugs like heroin can be lethal because they take effect so quickly after intravenous injection that the drug user can reach fatal drug levels before it would be possible to get help. The same dose of drug taken orally will never exert as great an effect—some of it will be lost to metabolism because the process of absorption is gradual.

WHERE THEY GO

Once drugs are in the circulation, getting into most tissues is no challenge. There are big holes in most capillaries, and drugs are free to go into most tissues. The brain is an important exception because it has an especially tight defense—the blood-brain barrier—that prevents the movement of many drugs into it. All of the drugs we discuss in this book are psychoactive, in part because they easily pass through this blood-brain barrier.

Although there are myths that drugs "hide" in specific places in the body (such as Ecstasy or LSD hiding in the spinal cord for months), they don't really. Because most psychoactive drugs are fat-soluble enough to enter the brain, they also accumulate in body fat. THC (the active component in marijuana) and PCP (phencyclidine, or angel dust) are particularly prone to accumulate in fat. As the drug eventually leaves the fat, it enters the bloodstream again and can enter the brain but usually at levels so low it produces negligible effects.

There is a legal consequence to this storage in fat. Drugs like THC are so well stored in fat that they remain detectable in urine for weeks after the last time the drug was used. It is common in drug-treatment programs for people who have been testing "clean" to show drugs in their urine suddenly if they have been losing weight during their rehabilitation. The drug is simply driven out of the fat as the fat deposits shrink.

GETTING OUT

Most drugs do not leave the body the way they came in. Although a few drugs, like the inhalants, enter and leave through the lungs, most leave through the kidneys and the intestine. Many are changed in the liver to a form that is easily excreted in the urine. This process of metabolism and excretion in the urine determines how long the drug effect lasts. It is very difficult to change this rate, so once a dose of drug is ingested, there is no hurrying the recovery. In extreme cases, there are emergency room procedures that can accelerate the removal of some drugs by the kidneys, but otherwise we must wait.

Some drugs, like cocaine, leave the brain and bloodstream quickly. The combination of quick onset of action and rapid removal can lead to cycles of taking the drug repeatedly. Drug levels shoot up, then plummet, taking the user to an intense high followed by a "crash," which motivates him to take another dose of the drug. Some cocaine users get into "runs" of repeated doses and end up using grams of cocaine in a single sitting. This pattern often leads to overdosing—the user takes another dose as the drug effect wanes but before the earlier dose has been completely eliminated. Drug levels in the brain gradually accumulate to dangerous levels.

Marijuana presents the opposite problem. THC, the active compound, is extremely fat-soluble (and thus accumulates in body fat), and its breakdown products are also active compounds. So, as the body tries to remove it, the metabolic products continue to have psychological effects. These two characteristics of marijuana mean that users can be under its influence for many hours or even days after it is smoked.

THE EFFECTS OF DRUGS CHANGE OVER TIME

When people recall the first time they drank alcohol, most remember that they got drunker than they would now if they drank the same amount. This isn't all just fading memory. Many drugs cause much smaller reactions in the body when someone uses the same drug regularly. This change is called tolerance. Usually the lesser reaction is due to previous experience with that drug or a similar drug, but even intense stress might change the reactions to some drugs.

Think about all the drugs we take that keep working even with many doses: our morning cup of coffee, an occasional aspirin for a headache (imagine how much aspirin we all take over a lifetime!), an antacid to calm the stomach after a spicy meal. Why do these drugs keep working? The reason is that we usually take them only for a short time, or intermittently. The more frequently we take the drug, and the higher the dose, the more likely it is that tolerance will develop. So, with just one aspirin once a week or even once a day, the body has plenty of time between doses to return to normal.

Caffeine continues to provide that pleasant arousing effect that people associate with their morning cup of coffee or tea for years. However, bodies do adapt to the daily cup of coffee (see the "Caffeine" chapter), so that people who are regular coffee drinkers have smaller effects from (show tolerance to) caffeine compared to someone who never ingests it. So, tolerance builds up, but the normal daily dose is not enough to cause the effect to go away entirely.

Tolerance to some drugs can be dramatic. For example, heroin addicts rapidly build up tolerance to opiate drugs. Longtime heroin addicts will take doses that would have killed them the first time they used the drug. This tolerance can last as long as several weeks or months. Tolerance lasts this long because addicts typically take many doses a day, every day, sometimes for years, and some of the body's changes are very long-lasting.

What about antibiotics? Everyone probably remembers being exhorted to be sure to take every one of the two weeks' worth of pills, and tried (and perhaps failed) to be careful to take a dose every six to eight hours. Although no one bacterium adapts to the drug, the population as a whole often does adapt. Bacteria replicate between one and many times a day, so new generations are constantly appearing. When an individual bacterium appears that happens to be resistant to the drug, this individual and its offspring survive, and the infection becomes resistant. With the rising use of antibiotics (antibiotics in beef, antibiotics for many childhood diseases, etc.), more and more humans are carrying resistant populations of bacteria in their body that are difficult to treat with currently available antibiotics. This is drug tolerance playing out at the population level rather than the individual level, and it is becoming more of a problem worldwide.

Some drugs actually become more effective over time. Cocaine is an example. Some of its effects become greater with each passing dose. There could be a beneficial side to this effect: drugs that gradually become more active could be delivered only occasionally and still be effective. This certainly would be cheaper! Some researchers have proposed that antidepressant drugs fit into this category, and that daily treatment may not be necessary.

Fortunately, many of the drugs we rely on to treat disease are given in doses that do not cause the development of tolerance, so they can continue working over a long period of time. This is especially important for drugs that are used to treat diseases like high blood pressure, which are lifelong conditions that require therapy for years.

HOW THE BODY'S RESPONSES TO DRUGS CHANGE

How do tolerance and sensitization happen? Bodies tend to adapt to the continuous presence of drugs, so bodily functions remain normal despite the presence of drugs. We will describe the three most important ways that this happens.

The first adaptation to long-term drug use happens in the liver, which inactivates drugs with certain enzymes that change the drugs into forms that the kidneys can excrete. The enzymes that inactivate drugs are not very specific. If they were, hundreds upon hundreds of them would be needed—one for each drug. Instead, humans have between twenty and thirty, which are responsible for metabolizing all drugs.

The activity of these enzymes changes with experience. When the liver encounters frequent doses of a drug that one of the enzymes must inactivate, its cellular machinery "tools up" to deal with the excess drug by making extra enzyme to get rid of the drug. As a result, the drug gets eliminated more quickly. This process causes tolerance in a simple way: less of the drug gets to the tissue where the receptors are. Smokers, who inhale many different substances each time they smoke cigarettes, typically metabolize many drugs much more quickly than nonsmokers because the constant presence of the substances in smoke results in increases in many drug-metabolizing enzymes. This can present problems when treating diseases in smokers. In the same way, the livers of heavy alcohol drinkers metabolize many drugs more quickly.

Nasal decongestants provide a great example of the second major tolerance process. The over-the-counter medications that people use to treat stuffy noses accomplish their effect by attaching to receptors on the blood vessels in the nose. These receptors are activated by the drug and cause the blood vessels to constrict. This decreases the volume of blood in the nose and helps to reduce the inflammation and swelling. This works well for a while. However, the cells that have these receptors figure out that they are being overstimulated by them. To reestablish balance, they simply remove some of the receptors from the surface of the cells. The result is that the nasal decongestant stops working! The warnings on the bottle about not using the drug for more than a few days are based on the reality that the drug will stop working anyway. This kind of change is a very common source of tolerance. The brain adapts in much the same way: overstimulation of receptors causes neurons simply to remove receptors and bring the level of stimulation back down to normal. Likewise, if the drug prevents receptors from working, the cell simply makes more.

Pavlov's dogs salivating when they heard a bell ringing to signal the arrival of dinner provides an example of the last tolerance mechanism. Our brains "learn" to expect the drug, and act accordingly. Sometimes this means activating processes that tend to oppose the effects of drugs. If people take drugs in a familiar environment (as do many people who take addictive drugs), they learn to associate the typical environment of drug taking with the experience of the drug. For example, a heroin addict might usually buy from the same dealer and take the drug to a "shooting gallery" to inject it. Soon, this environment becomes associated with the drug experience. When the heroin addict enters the shooting gallery, he or she will start breathing faster to offset the slowing that will happen once heroin is injected. This process is powerful. Often, when people overdose after taking a dose of drug that they normally tolerate, it is because they took it in an unfamiliar place.

Unfortunately, this type of expectation can also work the opposite way. When heroin addicts have been in recovery and then return to their homes, many times simply being on the street where they used to take the drug will reawaken those same sensations and reawaken drug craving. This becomes a very strong urge and is the reason why many treatment programs urge addicts to change their lifestyle in a dramatic way and avoid people and places that they associate with drug use.

WHAT HAPPENS WHEN WE STOP TAKING DRUGS?

When the drug is no longer present, all of these marvelous adaptations are counterproductive. Let's go back to the nose of the earlier example. Imagine that someone has been taking decongestants for two weeks. She probably is taking more and more to overcome the tolerance that is developing to the drug. What happens when she stops? The blood vessels of the nose don't have their normal number of receptors anymore. They are staying unstuffy only because the decongestant has been stimulating the few that are left like crazy. Once the drug is gone, the few receptors left are not enough to do the job, and there is a huge rebound in nasal congestion. So, the cure has become the disease.

This process is called withdrawal, and it is really the flip side of tolerance. She is not addicted to nose drops, but simply tolerant: her nose is dependent on the drug. This is one of the commonest misconceptions about withdrawal and addiction (more about this in the "Addiction" chapter). A person can be dependent and go through withdrawal even from drugs that are not addicting, like nose drops.

All joking aside, the consequences of withdrawal can be life-threatening. For example, alcohol is a sedative drug that slows the firing of neurons. Imagine a neuron prevented from firing every day by alcohol. A logical response would be for it to do whatever it could to fire more often. Now imagine many cells in the brain affected in this way. They adapt by increasing receptors that stimulate neural firing and decreasing receptors that inhibit firing. Now imagine an alcoholic who enters treatment and stops drinking abruptly. All these neurons are very excitable and result in tremendous overexcitation of the nervous system. This overexcitation can actually lead to seizures and death. Fortunately, there are medications that can be given to detoxifying alcoholics to keep these withdrawal symptoms at bay while the brain returns to normal.

Understanding how drugs work is not simply a matter of which drug does what, although that is the first thing to know. Everyone needs to understand how safe it is to take a drug in a particular way, how fast it gets in, how long it hangs around, and how it gets out; and we all need to understand the consequences of prolonged use of, and withdrawal from, anything we take.

How quickly does any tissue, including the brain, return to normal when a person stops using a drug? The answer depends on how much drug the person took, how long she took it, and the extent and kind of changes that occurred. Some changes reverse very quickly. The nose drop user will have a normal nose in a few days if she stops using nose drops. Even some of the receptor changes in chronic alcoholics reverse so quickly that the worst of the withdrawal symptoms are over in a matter of days. However, other changes take longer to reverse. The longest changes may be the responses that rely on learning mechanisms—like Pavlov's dogs. These do eventually reverse—if you expect something to happen often enough and it never happens, very gradually your brain changes its response. But this can take weeks or even years. This type of change is one of the changes that develop in addiction that make recovery such a long-term process.

15

ADDICTION

THE PRINCIPLES

1. Addiction is the repetitive, compulsive use of a substance despite negative consequences to the user.

2. Addictive drugs initially activate circuits in the brain that respond to normal pleasures, like food and sex. Every brain has these circuits, so every human could potentially become addicted to a drug.

3. Drug taking persists for many reasons, including changes in the brain, the desire to experience pleasure from the drug, and the desire to avoid the discomfort of withdrawal.

4. Many different factors in the life of an individual, such as family history, personality, mental health, social and physical environment, and life experience, play a role in the development of addiction.

CHAPTER CONTENTS

WHAT IS ADDICTION?

Addiction (or psychological dependence, as some people call it) is the repetitive, compulsive use of a substance by a person despite negative consequences to his life and/or health. Use of cocaine or heroin is illegal and unhealthy, but not everyone who uses those substances is addicted to them. Likewise, addiction differs from physical dependence: simply undergoing changes when substance use is stopped (like the headache that many coffee users experience when they miss their morning cup of coffee) is a sign of physical dependence, but it is not necessarily a sign of addiction. Both psychological dependence and physical dependence coexist in people who are strongly addicted to some drugs.

This definition of addiction obviously applies to the compulsive, repetitive use of alcohol, nicotine, and opiate drugs like heroin, as well as cocaine and other stimulants. But what about activities like overeating, gambling, and sex? Some people engage in these activities to the point that there are negative consequences for themselves (and their families). Some people gamble away everything they have, or engage in promiscuous sex to the extent that they risk infection with HIV or other sexually transmitted diseases. These behaviors resemble drug-seeking behaviors in an addicted person, and more and more research shows that the same neural circuits may be involved.

HOW ADDICTION STARTS: THE NEURAL CIRCUITS OF PLEASURE

What would lead someone to abandon his job, his family, and his life or to ignore the most basic, life-sustaining impulses to eat and reproduce? There must be something fundamentally different about "addicts" that leads them into such an extremely dysfunctional lifestyle. Addiction has been attributed to personal characteristics, including a lack of "morals," having different brain chemistry, experiencing mental illness or extreme trauma, or hanging out with the wrong friends. While all of these factors influence addiction, something more primal is at work. The neural mechanisms by which addictive drugs act are present in every brain. Addiction is so powerful because it mobilizes basic brain functions that are designed to guarantee the survival of the species. Because these mechanisms exist in every brain, potentially any human being could become a drug addict. The reason lies in a complicated neural circuit through which we appreciate the things that feel good. The job of this neural circuit, presumably, is to cause us to enjoy activities or substances that are life-sustaining. If it is successful, then it is more likely that we will engage in the activity again.

How does this "pleasure circuit" work? Let's use food as an example. If a person has a really great pastry at a bakery, he will go to this bakery again because the food tasted good. The good-tasting food is a reinforcer because it increases the likelihood that the person will engage in the same behavior (going to the bakery). Animals, including humans, will work to obtain access to food, water, sex, and the opportunity to explore an environment (perhaps to find food, water, or sex). These are the "natural reinforcers"—events or substances in the world that motivate behavior.

In a laboratory, animals can learn to press a lever to obtain a food pellet. This is the laboratory equivalent of the bakery scenario. There is a critical neural circuit in the brain that makes this happen. If this circuit is damaged, even animals that are extremely hungry will not press the bar. We think that this neural circuit is the pathway that causes the animal or person to experience the reinforcers as pleasurable. It is sometimes called the reward pathway. When this pathway is destroyed, an animal loses interest in food, in sex, and in exploring its environment. It is still capable of doing all these things; it is just not motivated. On the other hand, an animal will work very hard (pressing a bar or whatever) to turn on a gentle electrical current that stimulates this pathway. It acts like it enjoys having the pathway stimulated electrically. This is called self-stimulation.

DRUGS AND THE PLEASURE CIRCUIT

It won't surprise anyone that addictive drugs are reinforcers. Here the experimental evidence is overwhelming. Most experimental animals (pigeons, rats, monkeys) will press a lever to get an injection of cocaine, methamphetamine, heroin, nicotine, and alcohol. They will not press a lever for LSD, antihistamines, or many other drugs. Furthermore, even fruit flies and zebra fish will hang out in an environment in which they have previously received a reinforcer—another test of the potential addictiveness of a substance. This list of drugs for which experimental animals will work matches exactly the list of drugs that are viewed as clearly addictive in humans.

We know that the same pathway mediates the pleasurable effects of addictive drugs. There are two particularly convincing arguments. First, if this pathway is damaged in an animal, the animal will not work for drugs. Second, animals with an electrode placed in the reward pathway find smaller currents more "enjoyable" if the animal has received an injection of cocaine or heroin, for example. The same system is activated in the brains of addicts. When cocaine addicts looked at pictures of cocaine or handled crack pipes while the activity of their brains was monitored, they reported a craving for cocaine, and at the same time, their brains showed activation in the reward pathway of the brain.

Addictive drugs (stimulants, opiates, alcohol, cannabinoids, and nicotine) can actually substitute for food or sex. This explains why rapid injection of cocaine or heroin produces a "rush" of pure pleasure that most users compare to the pleasure of orgasm. This isn't just true for certain people who lack willpower or who are engaged in a deviant lifestyle. It is true for everyone who has a brain. It automatically becomes easier to understand why addiction is such a common problem across cultures.

Although the news media have certainly overdone the "what is the most addictive drug?" contest, it is also clear that animals will work much harder to get some drugs than others. For example, rats will press a bar up to two to three hundred times for one injection of cocaine and perhaps even more for the bath salt MDPV. However, some drugs, like alcohol and nicotine, might be administered more if they didn't have unpleasant effects on the body. Humans seem to be particularly good at ignoring unpleasant side effects to obtain reinforcement from drugs. If you judged the most addictive drug by the largest number of people who have trouble stopping their use of it, then nicotine would be the clear leader.

THE SPECIAL ROLE OF DOPAMINE

The neurotransmitter dopamine seems to play an important role in the normal process of reinforcement and in the actions of most addictive drugs. One group of dopamine neurons runs directly through the reward circuit we just described. If the dopamine neurons in this circuit are destroyed, then animals will not work for food, sex, water, or addictive drugs. Furthermore, both natural reinforcers and most addictive drugs increase the release of dopamine from these neurons. Our favorite experiment was conducted by a scientist in Canada who measured the release of dopamine in the brain of a male rat before and after providing it with a female partner. Not surprisingly, access to a sexually receptive partner caused a large rise in dopamine levels in this part of the brain.

If this same experiment is done with drugs instead of natural reinforcers, the results are the same. Cocaine, morphine, nicotine, cannabinoids, or alcohol will cause large increases in dopamine in the same area of the brain in which sex causes a rise. Most neuroscientists think that addictive drugs affect neurons that connect, one way or another, with this critical dopamine circuit to stimulate its activity.

Anyone who has ever enjoyed a muffin knows that dopamine going up when something pleasant happens is not the whole story of addiction. It is not even the whole story of how dopamine is involved. To explain that, we are going back to the bakery for a second visit. The first time you went to the bakery, dopamine went up when you had an unexpected treat—a tasty muffin. The second (or the third, or fifth) time, you started to anticipate the muffin when you saw the bakery sign. We know from experiments in monkeys that dopamine starts going up in anticipation of a reward rather than when the reward arrives. Scientists now think that one important role dopamine plays is this *anticipation* for a known reward. This agrees with our common sense that muffin eating is not food addiction. The first step toward addiction may be when you expect the muffin and begin to organize your walk to work to make sure it happens. Dopamine probably contributes to that decision-making process. However, it is still not addiction. You could change your route if you needed to.

Furthermore, dopamine neurons are not "the end of the line" for detecting pleasure, but they clearly connect with other neurons. We are just beginning to understand how these other areas of the brain play a role.

THE DARK SIDE: PAIN, NOT PLEASURE

Enjoying the rush of pleasure from a drug is only part of addiction. For addicts, there is an opposing force, a yang for the yin. Once the body adapts to the drug and physical dependence develops, a daily cycle of drug taking, pleasure, gradual waning of drug effect, and the onset of withdrawal symptoms emerges. Withdrawal symptoms are different for each drug, and minimal for some (much of this is covered in detail in the chapters on individual drugs). For example, the waning of opiate effects causes an ill feeling similar to the onset of the flu. The drug user has chills and sweats, a runny nose, diarrhea, and a generally achy feeling. An alcoholic will feel restless and anxious. However, there is a common underlying feeling for withdrawal from all addictive drugs: a feeling that is the reverse of the good feeling that the drug once gave that can be accompanied by a strong craving to take more of the drug. Avoiding the unpleasant feelings of withdrawal and satisfying the desire for more drug can eventually become even stronger motives for drug taking than simply feeling good.

CUCUMBERS AND PICKLES: CHANGES IN THE BRAIN

So what changes between the fifth time that you get your muffin and the time that you waited at the bakery door until opening time each day, neglecting your job or forgetting to take your children to school? You do this even if the muffin tastes lousy. It is this sort of compulsive, repetitive involvement in drug taking despite negative consequences that most experts view as addiction.

Use of addictive drugs can be viewed in a similar way. Many people drink alcohol occasionally, or even sometimes use cocaine at parties. However, for some people, the first social experiences with drugs gradually evolve into more continual use. Alcohol use provides an example. While 50 percent of the adult population of the United States drink alcohol occasionally, of these about 10 percent drink heavily and about 5 percent engage in addictive patterns of drinking.

Clearly, something happens in addicts that makes the need to consume drugs so great that they will go to extreme lengths to obtain the drug. What changes in the brain explain this? We have heard recovered addicts compare the change in their behavior and lives to the change from a cucumber to a pickle. Once a cucumber is turned into a pickle, it cannot be turned back. Is this a real analogy? If so, then the Alcoholics Anonymous approach of lifetime abstinence from drugs becomes a convincing solution to alcoholism.

Most scientists think that changes gradually occur in the reward circuit of the brain as it adapts to the continuous presence of the drug. However, we don't completely understand exactly which changes are the most important for addiction. The simplest change is easy to understand: with daily stimulation by addictive drugs, the reward system comes to "expect" this artificial stimulus. When people stop using drugs abruptly, the reward system is shut down—it has adapted to the daily "expectation" of drugs to maintain its function. We know of one biochemical change in the brains of all addicts that may explain this result. The brains of alcoholics, methamphetamine addicts, heroin addicts, and even compulsive eaters show a common biochemistry—they have low levels of one of the receptors that normally receive dopamine. This makes sense—in response to a constant barrage of dopamine, the cell that receives it is just trying to shut down. Recovering heroin addicts often report that every time they inject heroin, they are trying to recapture the feeling of their early experience with the drug, which gave a pleasure that they never quite reached again. People who are in a stimulant "binge," taking hits every few hours, can have the same experience. They respond by "chasing the high," taking the drug every hour or so to recapture the first rush. Only when they stop taking the drug for a while does their initial sensitivity return.

Some recovering cocaine addicts say that they do not feel pleasure in anything for a while after they stop using cocaine. Imagine how difficult it must be to stop using a drug that gives incredible pleasure, when even things that are usually enjoyable give no pleasure during withdrawal. This inability to feel pleasure may be one of the powerful reasons why people have great difficulty giving up cocaine. If there is a substance at an addict's fingertips that can make him feel better immediately, clearly the impulse to take it can become overwhelming.

Some of the changes in the brain of a person who uses addictive drugs repeatedly are just a result of normal learning in the brain. Let's go back to our bakery one more time. As our imaginary muffin addict approaches the store each day, he remembers the route and looks forward to the smell of newly baked muffins wafting down the street. Pretty soon, the smell of the bakery alone can cause an intense longing for the pastries before he gets there. What happens when our muffin addict decides that the daily search for muffins is taking too long, or when the bakery raises prices so much that he won't pay? If he goes "cold turkey" and quits muffins altogether, he had better find another way to go to work, because he will find that the route to the bakery, the smell of the muffins, and many of the experiences associated with going to the bakery will cause an intense longing for a muffin. This type of longing has ruined many a diet, and this type of learning plays an important role in addiction as well. Simply showing a former cocaine user a photograph of a crack pipe will trigger a strong craving for the drug, and recent studies of brain activity show that areas of the brain involved in memory are activated while he looks at these pictures.

There is another kind of "learning" that happens in the brains of addicts that makes it hard for them to stop using drugs. This is the part of the brain that plans for the future. Under normal circumstances, if an animal or person finds a reinforcer, her brain remembers where and how it happened and plans to check back the next time she needs food or sex. This ability to plan for the future is perhaps the most sophisticated thing our brain does. However, in a crack user, what this part of the brain focuses on is finding crack—the repeated stimulation with this one reinforcer can also "hijack" these planning centers in the same way. So it isn't simply the pleasure the drugs cause that motivates drug use but our ability to remember and plan for future pleasure. This may be one of the most long-lasting changes that happen in the brain.

New research shows that there is a final step in addiction: when taking the drug becomes as automatic as tying your shoes. Scientists have shown that another part of the dopamine system that is important for the transition of this learning to something automatic gradually changes, too, but more slowly. Eventually, hitting the bar to get an injection of drug becomes a habit. This behavior has become an automatic and controlling part of your behavior.

IS THERE A DEFICIENT BRAIN CHEMISTRY IN ADDICTS?

If everyone with a brain can become an addict, why are there (relatively) so few addicts? Could there be a unique group of people whose pleasure circuits are abnormal in some way so that these drugs feel particularly good? Or could there be a group of people whose pleasure circuits don't work very well, so that they are inclined to drink alcohol, smoke, or take cocaine to feel normal? There are probably people in each of these categories. In studying these questions in human addicts, there is a real "chicken and egg" problem. If brain function is abnormal, it is impossible to know whether the abnormality was caused by years of substance abuse or was present before. This is one challenge about the aforementioned dopamine receptor finding. Some scientists have tried to solve this problem by studying the children of alcoholics. There are certain EEG (brain wave) changes that have been noted in some alcoholics and in their sons. However, we don't really understand the significance of this EEG anomaly yet. The only way to be sure is to study these children until they become adults to see if this difference predicted alcoholism. Such studies are underway, but they take a long time. We can do these experiments in animals, and we have found that even with free access to cocaine, only a certain percentage of animals (about a fifth) progress to the stage of compulsive use.

Are these differences due to a deficient gene that could simply be repaired? The mapping of the human genome has really speeded up the search for genes related to addiction as well as other diseases. Many candidates have been identified. Some are specific to specific addictions. A variant of one gene for the receptor through which ethanol acts is associated with alcoholism, and a variant for a receptor that narcotics act upon is associated with narcotic addiction. Others, like the dopamine D2 receptor, are related to all addictions. Others have been surprises. One of the best genetic "predictors" of nicotine dependence is a gene that controls the breakdown of nicotine in the liver—not anything related to brain function at all. Finally, there are genes that seem to protect people from addictions. Two genes involved in alcohol degradation fit into this category (see the chapter on alcohol). So, as many scientists predicted, drug addiction is a complicated disorder that can involve many genes. Can we fix the affected genes? Not yet. Do we want to? Because most of these genes affect normal brain activities, we are not even vaguely close to knowing if changing them would treat addiction without causing other troubles. And even if we could, the ethical questions raised by such manipulations are huge.

Finally, it is important to realize that biology is not destiny. People are more than bags of genes that produce behavior. They are influenced by their environment and can control their behavior voluntarily. Simply possessing a particular gene that has been found in the brains of some alcoholics does not mean that an individual must become an alcoholic. If he or she abstains from alcohol, for one thing, there will never be a problem.

Maybe these slightly abnormal genes provide some benefit to the person that we don't fully understand. On the other hand, people with no genetic predisposition may experience such traumatic life circumstances (being sexually abused during childhood, for example) that they develop compulsive use of alcohol or other substances in an attempt to self-medicate their psychological trauma. The bottom line is that everyone with a brain can become an addict. Given the diversity of human brains, it is likely that some people will find the experience more compelling than others, but we have not really defined exactly what brain chemistry leads to this vulnerability yet.

PERSONALITY AND DRUG ADDICTION

How many people reading this book have worried about the possibility that they or a loved one may have an "addictive personality"? Although this concept is a favorite of some drug-abuse treatment professionals, psychology classes, and self-help books, there seems to be little agreement about what an addictive personality is. Furthermore, the personality type prone to substance abuse changes with the times. In years gone by, the obsessive-compulsive personality was described as prone to drug abuse. Today, there is concern that risk-taking and impulsive people are more likely to develop substance-use problems. Many of these theories probably have a grain of truth to them. For example, if a person is uninhibited about trying new experiences, including those that are risky, he may be more likely to take drugs the first time. So, the risk of addiction in these people might rise from the greater likelihood that they will experiment with drugs. As with genetic arguments, it is important to remember that such traits do not condemn a person to drug addiction. Many risk takers channel their energies into daring activities like bungee jumping.

LIFE EXPERIENCE AND DRUG ADDICTION

Life experience can certainly contribute to addiction as well as protect potential addicts. The life histories of people who have entered drug-treatment facilities show that certain characteristics appear more frequently in substance users than in people without substance-use problems.

Substance abusers are more likely to have grown up in a family with a substance-using parent. Alcoholism can be passed on by the experience of living with an alcoholic parent (although almost as often this experience will motivate a life of abstinence). Do people growing up in an alcoholic household simply learn to respond to stress with alcohol? Possibly. Children of alcoholics also are more likely to experience physical and emotional abuse at the hands of their parents, and a past history of physical and emotional abuse is another characteristic of many substance abusers. This is particularly true among women. In studies of hospitalized alcoholics, 50 to 60 percent typically report having experienced childhood abuse.

Why should bad early experience lead to adult substance use? One group of theories suggests a psychological origin for the substance use. However, a biological theory was developed from experimental work done on monkeys. Scientists at the National Institutes of Health and elsewhere have shown that when infant monkeys are neglected or abused by their mothers, they have a number of behavioral problems as they grow up. As adults, they tend to get into fights, and if given the chance to drink alcohol, they drink to excess. This is not just a genetic tendency, because infants from perfectly normal mothers will show these tendencies if they are raised by neglectful mothers. None of this is surprising. What is surprising is that these behavioral problems are accompanied by changes in the brain. The alcohol-drinking monkeys show lower levels of the neurotransmitter serotonin in their brains. This study indicates that this early life experience may produce long-lasting changes in the brain that contribute to these behaviors.

We know that associating with drug-using peers increases the chances that a person will choose to try drugs. Also, early use of cigarettes, alcohol, or marijuana is associated with later use of other drugs. This association has led to the popular "gateway theory" of drug addiction. This theory is based on evidence that most people who use illegal addictive drugs first used drugs like alcohol, tobacco, or marijuana. These drugs are viewed as a gateway to the use of more dangerous drugs. However, the vast majority of people using cigarettes, alcohol, and marijuana never use "harder" drugs. Although the statistics are correct, this situation reminds us of our favorite statistics teacher, who is fond of saying that statistics don't prove how things happen. It is possible that people who are risk takers, or mentally ill, or living in chaotic families, or hanging out with deviant friends are more likely to experiment with many deviant behaviors, including drug use. The drug use could just as likely be a symptom as a disease.

MENTAL ILLNESS AND DRUG ADDICTION

Depression and some other mental illnesses also occur more frequently in substance users. Did the drugs cause the problem, or did the problem cause the drug use? Once someone's life has become complicated by substance addiction, the turmoil that has been created can certainly contribute to the development of depression. This fact makes it very difficult to understand the complicated relationship between mental illness and drug addiction. However, some recovering addicts will describe an opposite cycle: that their anxious or depressed mood led them to drink or to use other substances to deal with feelings of inadequacy or despair. Then, as time passed and substance use became more frequent, the substance use became the dominant problem. This "self-medication" process probably contributes to addiction in many people.

THE BOTTOM LINE ON ADDICTION

The bottom line on addiction is that anyone with a brain can get addicted to drugs. However, most people don't, and there are a lot of reasons. First and foremost, if a person does not experiment with addictive drugs, then she won't get addicted. Second, if a person is mentally healthy, has a stable family and work life (including supportive and non-drug-using peers), and has no family history of substance abuse, she lacks some important risk factors and is less vulnerable. However, she still has a brain, and she is not immune to addiction. During the cocaine craze of the 1970s and '80s, plenty of constructive, highly educated, well-employed professionals became addicted to cocaine despite positive factors in their lives.

Finally, there may be some people for whom the pleasurable experience of these drugs is exceptionally high, and the drive to use the drugs is thus more compelling than for others. If these people do not try drugs, this underlying quality will not present a problem. However, if they have access to them, and if they do choose to use them, they are at significant risk. It is no accident that the rate of drug addiction among professionals in the United States is highest among medical personnel, who have easy access to such drugs.

16
LEGAL ISSUES

IT IS SAID that your life can change forever in a matter of seconds. When a person mixes alcohol or other drugs and the legal system, the combination can easily become life-changing. For a variety of reasons, the law-making bodies of most countries, especially the United States, have decided to suppress illegal drug use by making drug laws harsh and certain. All who deal with drugs in an illegal manner are thus at risk for penalties that can disrupt their own lives and those of their families.

The use of almost all the drugs discussed in this book could involve violations of the law, depending on the circumstances. Many of these drugs are illegal in all circumstances—manufacturing, distribution, and possession. Others are legal when prescribed, but not for recreational use. Still others, such as alcohol, can be legal for adults, but their use is prohibited for underage individuals and for activities such as driving a car or operating a boat.

This chapter is written to inform readers about very basic laws and principles that come into play around drug issues. It is not intended to give advice about dealing with the law-enforcement community or the judicial system. If you feel that you need that advice, find a good lawyer and ask her all of your questions before you become legally involved.

THE PRINCIPLES

1. While laws exist regarding the rights of a law officer to search some-one's car or home, this very complicated issue is often decided in the courts in individual cases. Generally you have the greatest "expecta-tion of privacy" in your home. There is less expectation of privacy in a car, and the least when you are out in public.

2. If a law-enforcement officer suspects you of a crime and really wants to search you or your car, you will be searched, whether or not you give permission. If you give your permission, the search will almost certainly be considered legal. If you refuse permission, the search may or may not be legal, but it may happen anyway. The debate over whether the search was permitted and legal will begin in the court system. The easiest way to avoid trouble is to avoid situations in which a random and unexpected search will yield anything illegal.

3. A person who is innocent of any crime but is with someone arrested for possessing drugs may become involved with the legal system until her innocence is proven. By that time, she may have incurred large financial burdens (e.g., an expensive lawyer), terrified her family, and spent some time under arrest.

4. The penalties for drug-related activities can be horrendous, especially in the United States federal judicial system, and particularly for selling drugs. Many casual drug users do not realize that simple possession of a modest amount of a drug can automatically be considered "intent to distribute," whether or not they actually plan to sell the drug.

5. You do not have to be on government property to be in violation of federal law. The federal drug laws apply everywhere in the United States and US territories at all times.

6. State and federal laws can be extremely strict about the use of guns in the commission of crimes. The possession of a gun—even just having one in the vicinity of a drug-law violation—can add many years onto the sentence for the original crime.

7. Many people believe that they are "safe" from serious legal consequences because they know the local officials, or because they believe the penal-ties are not serious. They are wrong. First, if a local official were to inter-fere with a prosecution, she could be prosecuted for obstruction of justice

or public corruption. Second, an arrest by a state or local officer can easily be referred to federal prosecutors not subject to local political influence. Third, in many states and in the federal system there is no parole. Even worse, in some cases "minimum mandatory" sentencing laws give the judges practically no leeway for reduced sentences.

8. Your rights as a US citizen do not apply in foreign countries, and the legal consequences of drug-law violations in some places can literally mean death.

CHAPTER CONTENTS

DRUG LAWS

The drugs in this book are subjected to a variety of laws. Tobacco and alcohol are legal to possess and use in the United States, as long as you are at least eighteen years old (for tobacco) or twenty-one years old (for alcohol). The same pertains for many of the over-the-counter cold medications that can be used as precursors of methamphetamine and for dextromethorphan—if you show identification and are at least eighteen years old, you can possess amounts for personal use. Most herbal drugs we discuss (except ephedrine) can legally be purchased and possessed by anyone.

Most of the other drugs are covered by the Controlled Substances Act. According to this federal law, some substances cannot be purchased or possessed by anyone, while others can be used if they have a prescription from a doctor. There are different "schedules" that are based on the danger of abuse, and the medical use. These are described in what follows. These drugs can be purchased and possessed only with an appropriate license from the Drug Enforcement Administration (DEA) or a prescription from a physician.

- **Schedule I:** Drugs in this class have no currently accepted medical use in the United States, a lack of accepted safety for use under medical supervision, and a high potential for abuse. They cannot be purchased or possessed by anyone. Some of the drugs in this category are all forms of marijuana (natural and synthetic), heroin, all serotonin-related hallucinogens (LSD, psilocybin, and all their derivatives), MDMA and all its congeners, and all cathinone derivatives (bath salts). These can be possessed only for research purposes with an appropriate license.
- **Schedule II:** Substances in this schedule have appropriate medical use but a high potential for abuse that may lead to severe psychological or physical dependence. This includes many opiates, such as methadone, morphine, opium, oxycodone, fentanyl, meperidine, and codeine; some sedatives like pentobarbital; and stimulants that are used clinically, including amphetamine, methamphetamine, and methylphenidate.
- **Schedule III:** Substances in this schedule have a potential for abuse less than substances in Schedules I or II, and abuse may lead to moderate or low physical dependence or high psychological dependence. Drugs in this class include combination products containing some opiates like hydrocodone with acetaminophen; buprenorphine formulated with naloxone (Suboxone), which is used to treat opiate addiction; the anesthetic ketamine; and testosterone.
- **Schedule IV:** Substances in this schedule have a low potential for abuse relative to substances in Schedule III. Drugs in this category include many benzodiazepine sedatives, including diazepam (Valium), alprazolam (Xanax), and triazolam (Halcion).
- **Schedule V:** Substances in this schedule have a low potential for abuse relative to substances listed in Schedule IV and consist primarily of preparations containing limited quantities of certain narcotics.

This list is *not* comprehensive, but it provides enough examples. The penalties that result from purchasing or possessing them vary by the schedule and by how much you have in your possession, so you should consider this only as an introductory guideline. You need to understand that if you purchase or possess anything in these schedules without a doctor's prescription, you are breaking the law. In addition, state laws may differ from federal laws. For example, marijuana is scheduled much lower by most states, but many states have broadly liberalized availability for medical purposes (although it is not completely legal in any state).

We have a word of caution about the scheduling of drugs. While this list describes the various schedules for drugs, placement at a given level in the list does not necessarily represent the degree of safety of the drug. For example, marijuana is a Schedule I drug, but it is almost impossible to die from it acutely. On the other hand, benzodiazepines are Schedule IV drugs, and with regular use over a period of time, an individual can become very tolerant to them. At that point, stopping their use can be almost impossible without medical help. If you take one of these drugs, get good information about it and don't depend on the level of scheduling to keep you safe.

Not all psychoactive drugs are controlled substances and, therefore, are on these schedules, but they do require a prescription. In most situations, you are breaking the law if you possess these drugs without a prescription and particularly if you give or sell them to another person.

GETTING SEARCHED

There's this joke about a very large canary: Where does an eight-hundred-pound canary sit? Anywhere he wants to! Likewise, a law-enforcement officer will search just about anywhere if he really wants to do it. Eventually the courts could decide whether the search was legal, but if an officer has reason to believe that a crime is being committed, he may well initiate the search process and let the lawyers settle the issue later.

Laws in the United States on the subject of a search are extremely complicated, in part because the legal rights of individuals have been defined over the years by many different court cases. However, there are a few general principles that govern when someone can legally be detained and searched.

First is the "expectation of privacy." The expression "A man's home is his castle" applies here. To search a residence usually requires more stringent legal prerequisites than searching elsewhere. Often a search warrant signed by a judge is required, unless there is evidence of a major and immediate threat to public safety.

Next is the automobile. This is the place where most individuals confront the law. An officer will see a traffic violation in progress, stop the vehicle, and then come to suspect that illegal drug activity is being carried out. If an officer reasonably believes that a crime is being committed, then he probably has the right to detain the occupants of the car until a legally proper investigation can be carried out. Remember, this officer can stop and hold someone if he believes that a crime is being committed, even if he is wrong!

A court official gave us an extreme example: Say a murder has been committed in the course of a bank robbery and the killer is driving away in a 2007 blue four-door sedan. In the heat of the moment, an incompetent 911 operator becomes confused and broadcasts that the killer is leaving the scene in a 2003 red pickup truck. An officer down the road sees a 2003 red pickup truck and stops it, removes the occupants, and searches the truck for weapons. He finds illegal substances. Was the search legal? Probably, because the officer had reason to suspect that the occupants were criminals. He was wrong, but with good reason, and the occupants may well be convicted for whatever offense they committed.

There are equally odd outcomes in which convictions are not possible because the officer was found to have no reason to search a vehicle. That is why most officers ask permission to search a car before doing so. That permission usually makes the search legal and any evidence is thus legally obtained. If permission is not given, then the officer may choose to detain the individuals further and call for a drug dog or other assistance to examine the vehicle. This issue then gets very complicated.

The practical side of all this is that a law officer has quite a lot of power to detain and arrest, because the lawmakers have decided it is in the public good to be able to temporarily detain potential criminals and, to some extent, to ask questions later. Even if an officer is eventually found in court to be wrong, the suspected individuals would have suffered loss of time and perhaps arrest, legal bills, and considerable life discomfort.

Finally, there is the situation when a person is out in public and walking about. This is the least "private" act, and so there is the least expectation of privacy. In this case a law officer has much more leeway in searching a person for the protection of the officer herself and for that of the general public. For example, imagine that an officer sees a person walking down the street in and out of traffic, in an erratic manner. She has the right to stop and talk to that person to ensure that he and the driving public are safe. If in the process of that stop the officer suspects that the individual may be carrying a weapon, she could search him by doing a pat down. If in the course of that search the officer feels something she recognizes to be an illicit drug, the officer can seize the drug. Can the person be convicted of a drug-law violation? It is very likely that he can because the search was legal.

The same rules might apply at a concert. Let's say that two students are obviously intoxicated and fighting. An officer moves to stop the fight, the students resist, they are appropriately searched for weapons, and illicit substances are discovered. If the officer chooses to charge them, there is a good probability that the charges will stick.

Do law-enforcement officers have a pathological agenda to harass drivers and students at a concert, looking for drugs everywhere? Rarely. Most law officers see their work as a job, not a mission. Think of all the traffic laws that are broken every day and how seldom stops occur. Think of how seldom someone who is innocent of any law violation is stopped in a car or interdicted at a concert. By and large, the legal community just does its job.

ILLEGAL ACTS

The drug laws are complicated, and the states differ from each other and from the federal system. So, there is no easy way to explain them in detail. However, there are a few very powerful and relatively unknown aspects of the law that should be explained to everyone.

First is the difference between a felony and a misdemeanor. A misdemeanor is a minor crime that might result in a fine, public service, or a short prison sentence—typically less than one year (in the federal system)—and usually is associated with traffic violations, minor theft, or sometimes possession of a very small amount of an illegal drug. A felony (murder, armed robbery, sale of drugs) usually carries a sentence in excess of one year and is considered such a serious crime that convicted individuals lose many rights that ordinary citizens enjoy. This includes the right to hold many kinds of highly paid jobs. A felony conviction is truly a life-changing event. Understanding this is important for drug users because possession of some amounts of some drugs can be considered a misdemeanor, while larger amounts are always felonies.

The law always sets the level of punishment based on the amount of a drug that one possesses or distributes, and in this case size counts a lot.

For example, there is a current public controversy because the federal laws are terribly tough for possession of even a few grams of crack cocaine, but one would have to possess much more powdered cocaine to receive the same punishment. Anyone who contemplates drug usage should understand the severity of the penalties that various levels of drug possession invoke. (As we write this, the US Department of Justice has decided to modify the way US attorneys may charge cocaine/crack dealers. Now they can make the charge without stating the amount of drug, so that the penalties are more consistent between crack and powdered cocaine. The problem is that this is an executive decision and can be reversed in any case and at any time. The actual law regulating possession and distribution of these drugs has not been changed.)

Most people know that conviction for selling drugs (distribution) results in stiffer penalties than for possession. What they don't know is that simply possessing certain amounts of a drug can be considered an "intent to distribute" and thus may subject a person to the much stiffer distribution penalties. Moreover, money may not have to change hands for distribution to take place from a legal perspective. Simply handing a package of a drug from one person to another can be considered distribution.

Another obscure criminal area is conspiracy. In drug cases, there are many convictions for conspiracy to commit a crime because very often a drug deal involves much more than the simple transfer of money and drugs. The conspiracy laws are broad and powerful, and even people peripheral to the planning of a crime, who may not have participated in the crime itself, are often charged under these laws, sometimes in the hope that they will cooperate with the court officials to convict others. Anyone hanging around individuals involved in drug possession and distribution should be aware of the risk of being charged with conspiracy for seemingly innocent acts, such as lending a boyfriend a car, cashing a check, or allowing a friend who is a dealer to use a telephone if it can be proven that in doing any of these seemingly innocent acts you knew why the person wanted you to do them. From the standpoint of law enforcement, drug dealing is considered a business (although it is illegal), and just as in a legal business, different people play different roles and have different levels of importance. In general, being around drug dealing is legally very risky.

Finally, there is the issue of the confiscation of property. Most of us have heard about auctions where the property of drug dealers is sold. This happens because of forfeiture laws that allow property used in drug dealing to be confiscated and sold by the government. The particularly devastating aspect of this is that the property of a more or less innocent individual might be confiscated because it was being used in violation of drug laws. Imagine, for example, a student distributing cocaine from his father's home and car. Suppose the father knew something about this and told the student to stop it. If the prosecutor could prove that the father knew something and allowed it to continue, it is possible that both the home and the car could be confiscated as part of the criminal prosecution.

What about marijuana? It's now legal, right? Some states have "legalized" marijuana possession for medicinal purposes; others have made the possession of small amounts for recreational use either legal or punishable as a misdemeanor. But the US federal law makes it a crime in all fifty states. In general, federal law overrules state law, so you might well be in a state in which possession is legal but prosecuted under federal law. As we are writing this new edition, President Obama has asked the Department of Justice to refrain from enforcing the marijuana laws in certain circumstances for states that permit its possession. But that is an executive decision that can be reversed at any time. Moreover, the specific conditions under which the federal law might be enforced may not be crystal clear. So, be aware that no matter what a state law says, federal law still has this drug illegal everywhere in the United States.

GETTING CAUGHT

Most people believe that they will not get caught. Teenagers, in particular, have the feeling that they are "beyond the law." But it does happen. It happens to grandmothers, teenagers, lawyers, doctors, and the most ordinary people on the face of the earth.

Many drug arrests come from the most random events imaginable. In Virginia, an officer stopped a car for having something hanging off the rearview mirror. He became suspicious, legally searched the car, and found major quantities of cocaine. Another drug transporter thought he had the perfect scheme and filled fruit juice cans with cocaine, then resealed them. It is a regular practice for tourists to bring back food from vacation in the Caribbean, and he expected to walk right through customs. What he did not realize was that customs officials knew there was no reason to bring canned fruit juice from the Caribbean, where it is expensive, to the United States, where it is cheap. He was arrested and convicted for transporting millions of dollars' worth of cocaine.

Even grandmothers are not immune to arrest. A pair of DEA agents working a bus station in North Carolina noticed an elderly woman behaving oddly. When they approached her, she moved away and they became suspicious. They conducted a legal search and found a large quantity of cocaine in her luggage.

A college student came back to her dorm room to find the place crawling with campus and city police. While she had absolutely no role in any illegal activity, a friend of her roommate had come to town from another college with a shipment of drugs. Another student, obeying the honor code, had called the campus police. Fortunately, the innocent student was not arrested because the roommate cleared her, but it was a very close call.

The law-enforcement community is actually quite sophisticated in its drug-enforcement efforts. DEA agents work all over the world trying to prevent the transport of drugs into the United States. They have agents working major and minor airports, and even bus stations. The highway patrols of most states have drug interdiction units looking for suspicious vehicles. This is not a trivial effort, and it results in so many convictions that both the state and federal prison populations have grown dramatically.

Yet everyone realizes that most countries are overrun with drugs. It is usually easy to buy the most common illegal drugs in many areas of cities and on college campuses. So why is the legal interdiction effort perceived as failing? It is not exactly failing, but rather it is being overwhelmed. Many, many people are caught in the legal system, but there is always someone else to replace each person caught. Routine usage of cocaine, crack, or heroin can be a very expensive habit, and the only way that most people can maintain such expensive behavior is to turn to dealing. As we say elsewhere in this book, cocaine and opiates can be extremely reinforcing, and they are also expensive in the quantities that habitual users consume. The combination of dependence and expense often leads users to become dealers until they are stopped by medical intervention, arrest, or death.

What does this have to do with the average reader of this book? Anyone who can read this book no doubt has the ability to do honest and legal work and have a successful life. Such a reader might feel that she is above being caught, or just not in the "wrong" circle of friends. This naïveté might be the most dangerous attitude of all, because, like most jobs, illegal drug dealing depends on knowledge, skills, and having a network of people. Most casual dealers do not have the knowledge or, fortunately, are not willing to do what is necessary to involve themselves fully in the drug culture. Thus, they approach the whole issue as amateurs, and like many amateurs in anything, they fail miserably. Only in this case, the stakes are much higher. They can get caught, lose a lot of money, become victims of criminal violence, or become heavily dependent on the substance they are dealing.

As we all know, some people think they have few opportunities and only a short time to live. They will deal drugs no matter what anyone says. In their lives they see jail time as just the cost of doing business. However, a district attorney who has prosecuted thousands of drug cases had just one bit of advice: people with families, an opportunity for education, and a supportive network of friends have so much to lose from being on the wrong side of the legal system that they should never become involved with it. A felony conviction can strip a person of so many opportunities in this society and can cost families so much in pain, suffering, and financial loss that no amount of money or drug experience is worth the risk.

GETTING CONVICTED: THE PENALTY BOX

The penalty laws of most states and countries are built on a series of legislative acts that happened over a long period of time, and thus, they are complicated and not easily summarized. Possession of modest amounts of marijuana can result in a slap on the wrist in some places and serious jail time in others. The same is true for other drugs, although they are usually taken more seriously, even in very small amounts. Often the prosecuting attorney has some leeway about the level of crime with which to charge an individual. The problem is that it is difficult to be sure of (1) the latest changes in the law, (2) the attitude that the prosecutor is taking toward drug crimes, and (3) whether that individual will be charged under state or federal statutes. Thus, conviction for the possession of a small, recreational amount of heroin or cocaine could result in either a modest sentence or a huge fine and a long prison term, depending on the exact circumstances and the mood of the legal officials overseeing the case.

It is important to recall that in some states and in the federal system there is structured, or guideline, sentencing. That means that once an individual is convicted of some drug crimes, the sentence is regulated by law and might not be alterable by the judge, no matter what the circumstances. Coupled with the fact that there is no parole in the federal system (and increasingly in the state systems), a conviction can mean long prison time, even if the prosecutor and judge wish it were otherwise.

Here's an example of how things can go terribly wrong as a consequence of alcohol, a prescription drug, and harsh laws. One of us (WW) testifies as an expert in legal cases, and a recent one illustrates how the law, the prosecutor, and the courts can interact to ruin the life of an individual. A man was at a party with his neighbors outside of his home. He consumed a modest amount of alcohol throughout the evening, but at some point he decided to go to bed and took his nightly medicine, which included the sleeping pill zolpidem (generic for Ambien). Before going to bed, he came back to the party but soon appeared intoxicated. He then prepared for bed and went to sleep. Shortly thereafter, he awoke and came out of the house without his shoes, false teeth, or hearing aid, clearly having just awakened. But he had a gun, which he had retrieved from his bedside where he kept it. He fired twice as he yelled an obscenity to the individuals at the party. No one was hurt. The police were called, and he was arrested.

The man was charged with aggravated assault, and everyone thought he was intoxicated with alcohol. In the law of most states, that is considered "voluntary intoxication" and thus is *not* a defense against any charges. His defense team argued that he was not intoxicated with alcohol, but with his prescribed zolpidem, which is known to produce odd behaviors such as sleep driving, sleep sex, sleep shopping, sleep eating, and so forth. If it were the zolpidem, that would be "involuntary intoxication," and that *is* a defense against such charges.

The jury heard the case and decided that he was intoxicated by alcohol and was therefore guilty. Now, here is where the disaster occurred. In that state, commission of many crimes (such as aggravated assault) with a gun is a *mandatory* ten-year sentence. If the gun is fired, the mandatory sentence is twenty years. In this case the prosecutor chose to charge the man for each of the six people present at the party, and the law requires that the mandatory sentences apply to each charge and be served consecutively. This means the man (who has not been sentenced at this writing) must, by law, be sentenced to 120 years in prison. The judge has no discretion in this case.

This is a terrible example of the interaction of intoxication, harsh laws, vigorous prosecution, and finally, the presence of a gun where a sleepy, intoxicated person could access it and fire it. This man had no history of behavior like this and was a decorated soldier. It is very likely that the zolpidem produced the bizarre behavior, but the prosecutor and jury did not see it that way.

The lesson from this is that if a person chooses to intoxicate himself and then commits a crime, that intoxication is usually not a defense against any crime he committed, no matter how impaired he was at the time of the crime.

WHERE DO WE GO FROM HERE?

There is an ongoing debate in the United States about the legalization or decriminalization of drugs by society. Several states have either passed laws or are considering laws that allow the use of marijuana for medical and possibly recreational purposes, but these laws are still controversial, and there is the additional problem that these state laws can be in conflict with federal laws. As a result, no one knows what the outcome will be even though it appears that federal officials are beginning to limit some prosecutions.

A number of prominent Americans—including the conservative Republican senator Rand Paul—have concluded that the War on Drugs is leading to injustices. As this is being written, Senator Paul and Democratic senator Patrick Leahy want to change the law and have introduced the Justice Safety Valve Act, which will allow judges more discretion in sentencing.

On the other side, many people believe that any effort to reduce the pressure on drug users and dealers will result in a flood of illegal substances that, in their worst nightmares, will become readily available to children. Unfortunately, drugs are already readily available to anyone, including children, from all economic levels. So that nightmare is here right now.

To reduce demand, we need to increase education. As we have said elsewhere in this book, effective drug education is not just a matter of exhortations to refuse all drugs, because many individuals believe that the drugs they use are harmless. It is a matter of teaching the basic science that can help us appreciate what complex and delicate organisms our brains are, how body chemistry may vary from person to person, and how little we know about the many ways, both positive and negative, short-term and long-term, that the powerful chemicals we call "drugs" can affect us. Good education is expensive, but with it we will be healthier, and as a society, we will save the enormous costs of lost wages, law enforcement, and prisons that drugs have brought us.

FURTHER READING

DOING YOUR OWN RESEARCH

If reading this book has raised your level of interest and you want more specific information, or you want the straight story about a new development, there is no substitute for doing your own research.

Reading both scholarly review articles and original research papers is much easier than most people believe. In fact, one of the first steps in writing this book was gathering such research. Much of the library work for the first edition was done by two college students, neither of whom had any previous experience using a medical library. Should you decide to investigate for yourself, here are some suggestions about where to begin.

Public libraries are not likely to have the sorts of journals and books you will need. Because there is such a vast amount of medical literature published, most universities with a medical school have a separate library just to house all this information. Find a medical library at a nearby medical school. If for some reason you cannot get to a medical school, check to see if there is a college or university biology department nearby and use the library they use.

Next, go to the library and make friends with the reference librarian, because you will need his or her help until you are familiar with the library and the search mechanisms. The most efficient way of searching the literature is to use MEDLINE or PubMed, databases of the National Library of Medicine, a US government institution that allows you to search almost all the published medical literature on any subject you can think of related to health. You can search by author, title, subject, keyword, institution, and many other descriptors.

In most cases you will find far more information than you need. A good place to start is with reviews. Reviews are documents that consolidate and summarize the research and literature available in a given area, and they are usually written in less technical language. Reading several recent reviews about the topic you are researching will help you form a base of knowledge about the subject. Practice using MEDLINE by starting out with simple concepts; for example, search for marijuana articles. There are hundreds of them, and many of the titles will be so technical that they might seem indecipherable. So tell the computer to select marijuana review articles. This will reduce the number markedly.

If you have read *Buzzed*, then you know that one of the active ingredients in marijuana is THC. Try searching for THC and you will get more articles. Refine your search by asking for reviews of THC and you will get articles different from those you did when you searched for marijuana in general. Play with the database and have fun. Search for all kinds of combinations of keywords, like THC and learning, or THC and adolescent. You will soon have an idea of the enormous amount of information there is about just this chemical. Understand, though, that no one study tells the whole story.

As a final note, we caution you not to accept everything you read as directly applicable to the human condition. Often scientists employ very high levels of a chemical to test for toxic effects in animals, and sometimes the chemical levels they use in/on animals are hundreds or thousands of times higher than a human would ever use, taking into account the weight of the human compared to the animal. Consequently, some of the toxic effects seen in animals may not apply to humans. On the other hand, animal experiments cannot reveal many subtle effects of chemicals, particularly psychological ones, and thus animal studies almost certainly miss some important effects that humans will experience. So, as you read a scientific paper, remember that it is just a small part of the literature about a drug, and while the data may be true, it is important to understand that data in the context of everything else known about the drug.

GENERAL REFERENCES

Brunton, L., B. Chabner, and B. Knollman, eds. *Goodman and Gilman's The Pharmacological Basis of Therapeutics.* 12th ed. New York: McGraw-Hill, 2010.

Drug and Alcohol Dependence, 1–2 June 1998: Entire issue devoted to review articles about drugs of abuse. Topics include addiction, reward, relapse, genetics and addiction, imaging the addicted brain, prenatal effects of drugs of abuse, opioids, stimulants, alcohol, nicotine, cannabis, hallucinogens, caffeine, and inhalants.

Erickson, C. K., and J. Brick. *Drugs, the Brain, and Behavior.* 2nd ed. London: Routledge, 2013.

Hart, C., and C. Ksir. *Drugs, Society, and Human Behavior.* 15th ed. St. Louis: McGraw-Hill, 2012.

Iversen, Leslie L., Susan D. Iversen, Floyd E. Bloom, and Robert H. Roth. *Introduction to Neuropsychopharmacology.* New York: Oxford University Press, 2008.

Karch, S. B., and O. Drummer. *The Pathology of Drug Abuse.* 5th ed. Boca Raton, FL: CRC Press, 2013.

Koob, G., and M. Le Moal. *The Neurobiology of Addiction.* London: Elsevier Press, 2006.

Musto, D. F. "Opium, cocaine and marijuana in American history." *Scientific American* 265 (1991): 40–47.

Schivelbusch, W. *Tastes of Paradise.* Trans. D. Jacobson. New York: Vintage Books, 1993.

Sowell, E., P. Thompson, C. Holmes, T. Jernigan, and A. Toga. "In-vivo evidence for post-adolescent brain maturation in frontal and striatal regions." *Nature Neuroscience* 2 (1999): 859–861.

Weinberg, B. A., and B. K. Bealer. *The World of Caffeine.* New York: Routledge Press, 2002.

White, A., and H. S. Swartzwelder. *What Are They Thinking?! The Straight Facts about the Risk-Taking, Social-Networking, Still-Developing Teen Brain.* New York: W. W. Norton, 2013.

ALCOHOL

Acheson, S., R. Stein, and H. S. Swartzwelder. "Impairment of semantic and figural memory by acute ethanol: Age-dependent effects." *Alcoholism: Clinical and Experimental Research* 22, no. 7 (1998): 1437–1442.

Barron, S., A. White, H. S. Swartzwelder, R. L. Bell, Z. A. Rodd, C. J. Slawecki, C. L. Ehlers, E. D. Levin, A. H. Rezvani, and L. P. Spear. "Adolescent vulnerabilities to chronic alcohol or nicotine exposure: Findings from rodent models." *Alcoholism: Clinical & Experimental Research* 29, no. 9 (2005): 1720–1725.

Brown, S., M. McGue, J. Maggs, J. Schulenberg, R. Hingson, H. S. Swartzwelder,, C. Martin, et al. "Underage alcohol use: Summary of developmental processes and mechanisms, ages 16–20." *Alcohol Research and Health* 32 (2009): 41–52.

Diamond, I., and A. S. Gordon. "Cellular and molecular neuroscience of alcoholism." *Physiological Reviews* 77 (1997): 1–20.

Herz, A. "Endogenous opioid systems and alcohol addiction [review]." *Psychopharmacology* 129 (1997): 99–111.

Hobbs, W., T. Rall, and T. Verdoorn. "Hypnotics and Sedatives; Ethanol." This is chapter 17 in *Goodman and Gilman's The Pharmacological Basis of Therapeutics*, listed in the general references.

Koperafrye, K., S. Dehaene, and A. P. Streissguth. "Impairments of number processing induced by prenatal alcohol exposure." *Neuropsychologia* 34 (1996): 117–1196.

Monnot, M., S. Nixon, W. Lovallo, and E. Ross. "Altered emotional perception in alcoholics: Deficits in affective prosody comprehension." *Alcoholism: Clinical and Experimental Research* 25 (2001): 362–369.

Musto, D. F. "Alcohol in American history." *Scientific American* 274 (1996): 78–83.

The National Clearinghouse for Alcohol and Drug Information (www.health.org/index.htm) is a national resource sponsored by the US government. For users of the Internet, it has the advantage of providing searchable databases (www.health.org/dbases.htm) that allow the user to search for references to research papers on any topic related to alcohol actions or use.

NIAAA-funded consortium for research on the enduring effects of alcohol exposure during adolescence, http://nadiaconsortium.org/.

Streissguth, A., P. Sampson, H. Olson, F. Bookstein, H. Barr, M. Scott, J. Feldman, and A. Mirsky. "Maternal drinking during pregnancy: Attention and short-term memory in 14-year-old offspring—a longitudinal prospective study." *Alcoholism: Clinical and Experimental Research* 18 (1994): 202–218.

US Dept. of Health and Human Services. *Tenth Special Report to the U.S. Congress on Alcohol and Health: Highlights from Current Research*. Alexandria, VA: EEI, September 2000.

White, A. M., and H. S. Swartzwelder. "Age-related effects of alcohol on memory and memory-related brain function in adolescents and adults." *Recent Developments in Alcoholism* 17 (2005): 161–176.

CAFFEINE

Cauli, O., and M. Morelli. "Caffeine and the dopaminergic system." *Behavioural Pharmacology* 16, no. 2 (2005): 63–77.

Edwards, B. *America's Favorite Drug: Coffee and Your Health*. Berkeley, CA: Odonian Press, 1992.

Evans, S., and R. Griffiths. "Caffeine withdrawal: A parametric analysis of caffeine dosing conditions." *Journal of Pharmacology and Experimental Therapeutics* 289 (1999): 285–294.

Jurich, N. *Espresso: From Bean to Cup*. Seattle: Missing Link Press, 1991.

Lamarine, R. J. "Selected health and behavioral effects related to the use of caffeine." *Community Health* 19 (1994): 449–466.

Lane, J., and R. Williams. "Cardiovascular effects of caffeine and stress in regular coffee drinkers." *Psychophysiology* 24 (1987): 157–164.

Lane, J. D., C. F. Pieper, B. G. Phillips-Bute, J. E. Bryant, and C. M. Kuhn. "Caffeine affects cardiovascular and neuroendocrine activation at work and at home." *Psychosomatic Medicine* 64 (2002): 595–603.

McLellan, T., and H. Lieberman. "Do energy drinks contain active components other than caffeine?" *Nutrition Reviews* 70 (2012): 730–744.

Satel, S. "Is caffeine addictive?—A review of the literature." *American Journal of Drug & Alcohol Abuse* 32, no. 4 (2006): 493–502.

Shapiro, R. E. "Caffeine and headaches." *Neurological Sciences* 28, suppl. 2 (2007): S179–183.

Thompson, W. G. "Coffee: Brew or bane?" *American Journal of the Medical Sciences* 308 (1994): 49–57.

Weinberg, B. A., and B. K. Bealer. *The World of Caffeine: The Science and Culture of the World's Most Popular Drug*. New York: Routledge Press, 2001.

ECSTASY

Clemens, K. J., I. S. McGregor, G. E. Hunt, and J. L. Cornish. "MDMA, methamphetamine and their combination: Possible lessons for party drug users from recent preclinical research." *Drug & Alcohol Review* 26, no. 1 (2007): 9–15.

Kalechstein, A. D., R. De La Garza II, J. J. Mahoney III, W. E. Fantegrossi, and T. F. Newton. "MDMA use and neurocognition: A meta-analytic review." *Psychopharmacology* 189, no. 4 (2007): 531–537.

Morgan, M. J. "Ecstasy (MDMA): A review of its possible persistent psychological effects." *Psychopharmacology* 152 (2000): 230–248.

Parrott, A. C. "MDMA, serotonergic neurotoxicity, and the diverse functional deficits of recreational 'Ecstasy' users." *Neuroscience & Biobehavioral Reviews* 37, no. 8 (2013): 1466–1484.

Reneman, L., J. Boik, B. Schmand, W. van den Brink, and B. Gunning. "Memory disturbances in 'Ecstasy' users are correlated with an altered brain serotonin neurotransmission." *Psychopharmacology* 148 (2001): 322–324.

Ricaurte, G. A., A. L. Martello, J. L. Katz, and M. B. Martello. "Lasting effects of (±) 3,4-methylenedioxymethamphetamine (MDMA) on central serotonergic neurons in nonhuman primates: Neurochemical observations." *Pharmacology and Experimental Therapeutics* 261 (1992): 616–622.

Rosenson, J., C. Smollin, K. A. Sporer, P. Blanc, and K. R. Olson. "Patterns of ecstasy-associated hyponatremia in California." *Annals of Emergency Medicine* 49, no. 2 (2007): 164–171.

Rudnick, G., and S. C. Wall. The molecular mechanism of "ecstasy" [3,4-methylenedioxymethamphetamine (MDMA)]: Serotonin transporters are targets for MDMA-induced serotonin release." *Proceedings of the National Academy of Sciences* 89 (1992): 1817–1821.

GHB

Galloway, G. P., S. L. Frederick, F. E. Staggers Jr., S. Gonzales, and D. E. Smith. "Gamma-hydroxybutyrate: An emerging drug of abuse that causes physical dependence." *Addiction* 92, no. 1 (1997): 89–96.

Maitre, Michel. "The gamma-hydroxybutyrate signalling system in brain: Organization and functional implications." *Progress in Neurobiology* 51 (1997): 337–361.

Mason, P. E., and W. P. Kerns. "Gamma hydroxybutyric acid (GHB) intoxication." *Academic Emergency Medicine* 9, no. 7 (2002) 730–739.

Nicholson, K. L., and R. L. Balster. "GHB: A new and novel drug of abuse." *Drug and Alcohol Dependence* 63 (2001): 1–22.

Van Amsterdam, J. C., T. M. Brunt, M. T. B. McMaster, and R. J. M. Miesink. "Possible long-term effects of gamma hydroxybutyric acid (GHB) due to neurotoxicity and overdose." *Neuroscience & Biobehavioral Reviews* 36, no. 4 (2012): 1217–1227.

HALLUCINOGENS

Abraham, H. D., A. M. Aldridge, and P. Gogai. "The psychopharmacology of hallucinogens." *Neuropsychopharmacology* 14 (1996): 285–298.

Cunningham, C. W., R. B. Rothman, and T. E. W. Risinzano. "Neuropharmacology of the naturally occurring kappa-opioid hallucinogen salvinorin A." *Pharmacological Reviews* 63, no. 2 (2011): 316–347.

Griffiths, R. R., M. W. Johnson, McCann U, Jesse R. "Psilocybin occasioned mystical-type experiences: Immediate and persisting dose-related effects." *Psychopharmacology* (Berl) 218, no. 4 (2011): 649–665.

Halberstadt, A. L., and M. A. Geyer. "Multiple receptors contribute to the behavioral effects of indoleamine hallucinogens." *Neuropharmacology* 61, no. 3 (2011): 364–381.

Holmstedt, B., and N. Kline, eds. "Ethnopharmacologic search for psychoactive drugs." Public Health Service Publication no. 1645 (1967).

Jacobs, B. L. "How hallucinogenic drugs work." *American Scientist* 75 (1987): 386–392.

Marek, G. J., and G. K. Aghajanian. "Indoleamine and the phenethylamine hallucinogens: Mechanisms of psychotomimetic action." *Drug and Alcohol Dependence* 51 (1998): 189–198.

Schultes, R. E. *The Botany and Chemistry of Hallucinogens*. New York: Thomas Press, 1980.

Schultes, R. E., and A. Hoffman. *Plants of the Gods*. Rochester, VT: Healing Arts Press, 1992.

Vollenweider, F. X. "Recent advances and concepts in the search for biological correlates of hallucinogen-induced altered states of consciousness." *Heffler Review of Psychedelic Research* 1 (1998): 21–32.

Zawilska, J. B., and J. Wojcieszak. "Salvia divinorum: From Mazatec medicinal and hallucinogenic plant to emerging recreational drug." *Human Psychopharmacology* 8, no. 5 (2013): 403–412.

INHALANTS

Balster, R. L. "Neural basis of inhalant abuse." *Drug and Alcohol Dependence* 51, no. 1–2 (1998): 207–214.

Bowen, S. E., J. Daniel, and R. L. Balster. "Deaths associated with inhalant abuse in Virginia from 1987 to 1996." *Drug and Alcohol Dependence* 53, no. 3 (1999): 239–245.

Brouette, T., and R. Anton. "Clinical review of inhalants." *American Journal on Addictions* 10, no. 1 (2001): 79–94.

Cruz, S. L. "The latest evidence in the neuroscience of solvent misuse: An article written for service providers." *Substance Use and Misuse* 46, no. S1 (2011): 62–67.

Dinwiddie, S. H. "Abuse of inhalants: A review." *Addiction* 89 (1994): 925–939.

Meadows, R., and A. Verghese. "Medical complications of glue sniffing." *Southern Medical Journal* 89 (1996): 455–462.

Nitrites and volatile anesthetic gases are well described in *Goodman and Gilman's The Pharmacological Basis of Therapeutics*, listed in the general references. This book contains numerous references to the research literature.

Sharp, C. W., F. Beauvais, and R. Spence, eds. National Institute on Drug Abuse Research Monograph 129 (1992). This can be obtained from the National Institute on Drug Abuse at 6001 Executive Boulevard, Room 5213, Bethesda, MD 20892-9561; www.nida.nih.gov.

Soderberg, L. S. "Immunomodulation by nitrite inhalants may predispose abusers to AIDS and Kaposi's sarcoma." *Journal of Neuroimmunology* 83, no. 1–2 (1998): 157–161.

MARIJUANA

Abood, M., and B. Martin. "Neurobiology of marijuana abuse." *Trends in Pharmacological Sciences* 13 (1992): 201–206.

Adams, I. B., and B. R. Martin. "Cannabis: Pharmacology and toxicology in animals and humans." *Addiction* 91 (1996): 1585–1614.

Aryana, A., and M. A. Williams. "Marijuana as a trigger of cardiovascular events: Speculation or scientific certainty?" *International Journal of Cardiology* 118, no. 2 (2007): 141–144.

Castle D. J. "Cannabis and psychosis: What causes what?" *F1000 Medicine Reports.* 5 (2013): 1, http://f1000.com/prime/reports/m/5/1.

Cha, Y. M., A. M. White, C. M. Kuhn, W. A. Wilson, and H. S. Swartzwelder. "Differential effects of delta9-THC on learning in adolescent and adult rats." *Pharmacology, Biochemistry, and Behavior* 83 (2006): 448–455.

Chang, L., and E. P. Chronicle. "Functional imaging studies in cannabis users." *Neuroscientist* 13, no. 5 (2007): 422–432.

Clarke, R. C. *Marijuana Botany.* Berkeley, CA: And/Or Press, 1981.

Cota, D., M. H. Tschop, T. L. Horvath, and A. S. Levine. "Cannabinoids, opioids and eating behavior: The molecular face of hedonism?" *Brain Research Reviews* 51, no. 1 (2006): 85–107.

Devane, W. "New dawn of cannabinoid pharmacology." *Trends in Pharmacological Sciences* 15 (1994): 40–41.

Ehrenreich, H., T. Rinn, H. J. Kunert, M. R. Moeller, W. Poser, L. Schilling, G. Gigerenzer, and M. R. Hoehe. "Specific attentional dysfunction in adults following early start of cannabis use." *Psychopharmacology* 142 (1999): 295–301.

Grinspoon, L., and J. Bakalar. "Marijuana as medicine." *Journal of the American Medical Association* 273 (1995): 1875–1876. See also the replies to this article in volume 274 (1995): 1837–1838.

Haney, M., A. W. Ward, S. D. Comer, R. W. Foltin, and M. W. Fischman. "Abstinence symptoms following smoked marijuana in humans." *Psychopharmacology* 141 (1999): 395–404.

Hollister, L. "Health aspects of cannabis." *Pharmacological Reviews* 38 (1986): 1–20.

Justinova, Z., S. R. Goldberg, S. J. Heishman, and G. Tanda. "Self-administration of cannabinoids by experimental animals and human marijuana smokers." *Pharmacology, Biochemistry & Behavior* 81, no. 2 (2005): 285–299.

Lichtman, A. H., and B. R. Martin. "Delta 9-tetrahydrocannabinol impairs spatial memory through a cannabinoid receptor mechanism." *Psychopharmacology* 126 (1996): 125–131.

Malchow, B., A. Hasan, P. Fusar-Poli, A. Schmitt, P. Falkai, and T. Wobrock. "Cannabis abuse and brain morphology in schizophrenia: A review of the available evidence." *European Archives of Psychiatry and Clinical Neuroscience* 263 (2012): 3–13.

Maldonado, R., and F. Rodriguez de Fonseca. "Cannabinoid addiction: Behavioral models and neural correlates." *Journal of Neuroscience* 22, no. 9 (2002): 3326–3331.

Meier, M. H., A. Caspi, A. Ambler, H. Harrington, R. Houts, R. S. E. Keefe, K. MacDonald, A. Ward, R. Poulton, and T. E. Moffitt. "Persistent cannabis users show neuropsychological decline from childhood to midlife." *Proceedings of the National Academy of Sciences* 109 (2012): E2657–E2664.

Neurobiology of Disease 5, no. 6 (1998): 379–553. Series of excellent review articles about the basic biology of cannabinoid receptors and their actions.

Pollan, M. "How pot has grown." *New York Times Magazine*, February 19, 1995.

Schramm-Sapyta. N. L., Y. M. Cha, S. Chaudhry, W. A. Wilson, H. S. Swartzwelder, and C. M. Kuhn. "Differential anxiogenic, aversive, and locomotor effects of THC in adolescent and adult rats." *Psychopharmacology* 191, no. 4 (2007): 867–877.

NICOTINE

Audrain-McGovern, J., D. Rodriguez, and J. D. Kassel. "Adolescent smoking and depression: Evidence for self-medication and peer smoking mediation." *Addiction* 104 (2009): 1743–1756.

Julien, R. M. *A Primer of Drug Action*. New York: W. H. Freeman, 1995.

Naqvi, N. H., D. Rudrauf, H. Damasio, and A. Bechara. "Damage to the insula disrupts addiction to cigarette smoking." *Science* 315, no. 5811 (2007): 531–534.

Picciotoo, M. R., B. J. Caldarone, S. L. King, and V. Zacharious. "Nicotinic receptors in the brain: Links between molecular biology and behavior." *Neuropsychopharmacology* 22 (2000): 451–465.

Porchet, H. "Pharmacokinetics and pharmacodynamics of nicotine: Implications for tobacco addiction apprehension." In *Drugs of Abuse and Neurobiology*, R. R. Watson, ed. Boca Raton, FL: CRC Press, 1992.

OPIATES

Compton, W. M., and N. D. Volkow. "Major increases in opioid analgesic abuse in the United States: Concerns and strategies." *Drug & Alcohol Dependence* 81, no. 2 (2006): 103–107.

De Vries, T. J., and T. S. Shippenberg. "Neural systems underlying opiate addiction." *Journal of Neuroscience* 22, no. 9 (2002): 3321–3325.

Di Chiara, G., and R. A. North. "Neurobiology of opiate abuse." *Trends in Pharmacological Sciences* 13 (1992): 185–193.

Hammer, R. P. *The Neurobiology of Opiates*. Boca Raton, FL: CRC Press, 1993.

SEDATIVES

All legal sedatives are well described in *Goodman and Gilman's The Pharmacological Basis of Therapeutics*, listed in the general references. This book contains numerous references to the research literature.

STEROIDS

Angell, P., N. Chester, D. Green, J. Somauroo, G. Whyte, and K. George. (2012). "Anabolic steroids and cardiovascular risk." *Sports Medicine* 42, no. 2 (2012): 119–134.

Kazlauskas, R. "Designer steroids." *Handbook of Experimental Pharmacology* 195 (2010): 155–185.

Kuhn, C. M. "Anabolic steroids." *Recent Progress in Hormone Research*, 57 (2002): 411–434.

Wilson, J. D. "Androgen abuse by athletes." *Endocrine Reviews* 9 (1988): 181–191.

Yesalis, C. E., ed. *Anabolic Steroids in Sport and Exercise*. 2nd ed. Champaign, IL: Human Kinetics Pub., 2000.

Yesalis, C. E., and V. S. Cowart. *The Steroids Game*. Champaign, IL: Human Kinetics Pub., 1998.

STIMULANTS

Afonso, L., T. Mohammed, and D. Thatai. "Crack whips the heart: A review of the cardiovascular toxicity of cocaine." *American Journal of Cardiology* 100, no. 6 (2007): 1040–1043.

Baumann, M. H., J. S. Partilla, K. R. Lehner, E. B. Thorndike, A. F. Hoffman, M. Holy, R. B. Rothman, et al. "Powerful cocaine-like actions of 3,4-Methylenedioxypyrovalerone (MDPV), a principal constituent of psychoactive 'bath salts' products." *Neuropsychopharmacology* 38, no. 4 (2013): 552–562.

Baumann, M. H., J. S. Partilla, and K. R. Lehner. "Psychoactive 'bath salts': Not so soothing." *European Journal of Pharmacology* 698, nos. 1–3 (2013): 1–5.

Chang, L., D. Alicata, T. Ernst, and N. Volkow. "Structural and metabolic brain changes in the striatum associated with methamphetamine abuse." *Addiction* 102, suppl. 1 (2007): 16–32.

Everitt, B. J., and M. E. Wolf. "Psychomotor stimulant addiction: A neural systems perspective." *Journal of Neuroscience* 22, no. 9 (2002): 3312–3320.

Hammer, R. P., ed. *The Neurobiology of Cocaine*. Boca Raton, FL: CRC Press, 1995.

Hatsukami, D. K., and M. W. Fischman. "Crack cocaine and cocaine hydrochloride—Are the differences myth or reality?" *Journal of the American Medical Association* 276 (1996): 1580–1588.

Joseph, H., ed. "The neurobiology of cocaine addiction: From bench to bedside." *Journal of Addictive Diseases* 15 (1999).

Karch, S. B. *A Brief History of Cocaine*. Boca Raton, FL: CRC Press, 1998.

Kuhar, M. J., and N. S. Pilotte. "Neurochemical changes in cocaine withdrawal." *Trends in Pharmacological Science* 17 (1996): 260–264.

Lakoski, J. M., M. P. Galloway, and F. J. White, eds. *Cocaine: Pharmacology, Physiology, and Clinical Strategies*. Boca Raton, FL: CRC Press, 1992.

Lehner, K. R., and M. H. Baumann. "Psychoactive 'bath salts': Compounds, mechanisms, and toxicities." *Neuropsychopharmacology* 38, no. 1 (2013): 243–244.

Smith, M. E., and M. J. Farah. "Are prescription stimulants 'smart pills'? The epidemiology and cognitive neuroscience of prescription stimulant use by normal healthy individuals." *Psychological Bulletin* 137, no. 5 (2011): 717–741.

Van Dyke, C., and R. Byck. "Cocaine." *Scientific American* 246, no. 3 (1982): 128–141.

Williams, R. G., K. M. Kavanagh, and K. K. Teo. "Pathophysiology and treatment of cocaine toxicity: Implications for the heart and cardiovascular system." *Canadian Journal of Cardiology* 12 (1996): 1295–1301.

Zimmerman, J. L. "Cocaine intoxication." *Critical Care Clinics* 28, no. 4 (2012): 517–526.

ADDICTION

Berke, J. D., and S. E. Hyman. "Addiction, dopamine and the molecular mechanisms of memory." *Neuron* 25 (2000): 515–532.

Dalley, J. W., T. D. Fryer, L. Brichard, E. S. Robinson, D. E. Theobald, K. Laane, Y. Pena, et al. "Nucleus accumbens D2/3 receptors predict trait impulsivity and cocaine reinforcement." *Science* 315, no. 5816 (2007): 1267–1270.

Di Chiara, G., and A. Imperato. "Drugs abused by humans preferentially increase synaptic dopamine concentrations in the mesolimbic system of freely moving rats." *Proceedings of the National Academy of Science* 85 (1988): 5274–5278.

George, O., M. Le Moal, and G. F. Koob. "Allostasis and addiction: Role of the dopamine and corticotropin-releasing factor systems." *Physiology and Behavior* 106, no. 1 (2012): 58–64.

Goldstein, A. *Addiction: From Biology to Drug Policy.* New York: W. H. Freeman, 1994.

Kiyatkin, E. A. "Functional significance of mesolimbic dopamine." *Neuroscience & Biobehavioral Reviews* 19 (1995): 573–598.

Koob, G. F., and N. D. Volkow. "Neurocircuitry of addiction." *Neuropsychopharmacology* 35, no. 1 (2010): 217–238.

Parvaz, M. A., N. Alia-Klein, P. A. Woicik, N. D. Volkow, and R. Z. Goldstein. "Neuroimaging for drug addiction and related behaviors." *Reviews in the Neurosciences* 22, no. 6 (2011): 609–624.

Pierce, R. C., and V. Kumaresan. "The mesolimbic dopamine system: The final common pathway for the reinforcing effect of drugs of abuse?" *Neuroscience & Biobehavioral Reviews* 30, no. 2 (2006): 215–238.

Robinson, T. E., and M. K. C. Berridge. "The neural basis of drug craving: An incentive-sensitization theory of addiction." *Brain Research Reviews* 18 (1993): 247–291.

Ron, D., and R. Jurd. "The 'ups and downs' of signaling cascades in addiction." *Science's STKE* [electronic resource]: *Signal Transduction Knowledge Environment,* 2005(309).

Samaha, A. N., and T. E. Robinson. "Why does the rapid delivery of drugs to the brain promote addiction?" *Trends in Pharmacological Sciences* 26, no. 2 (2005): 82–87.

Volkow, N. D., G. J. Wang, J. S. Fowler, D. Tomasi, F. Telang, and R. Baler. "Addiction: Decreased reward sensitivity and increased expectation sensitivity conspire to overwhelm the brain's control circuit." *Bioessays* 32, no. 9 (2010): 748–755.

Wickens, J. R., J. C. Horvitz, R. M. Costa, and S. Killcross. "Dopaminergic mechanisms in actions and habits." *Journal of Neuroscience* 27, no. 31 (2007): 8181–8183.

LEGAL ISSUES

We do not recommend that anyone act on any legal information obtained from any source without first speaking with a legal expert. The laws of each state and the federal system are different from one another and extremely complicated. What may be legal in one place may be a felony in another.

For general reading on search, seizure, and privacy, we recommend McWhirter, Darien A. *Search, Seizure and Privacy.* Exploring the Constitution Series, edited by Darien A. McWhirter. Phoenix, AZ: Oryx Press, 1994.

For information on US government laws, drug scheduling, and penalties, we recommend the DEA website: www.dea.gov.

BUZZED WEBSITE

Check www.dukebrainworks.com for more information from the authors.

INDEX

CYNTHIA KUHN is a professor of pharmacology at Duke University Medical Center and heads the Pharmacological Sciences Training Program at Duke. She is married with two children.

SCOTT SWARTZWELDER is a professor of psychology and neuroscience at Duke University and a clinical professor of psychiatry and behavioral sciences at Duke University Medical Center. He is also a senior research career scientist with the U.S. Department of Veterans Affairs. He is married with three children.

WILKIE WILSON is a professor of prevention science at the Duke University Social Science Research Institute and the Center for Child and Family Policy. He is married with two daughters.

LEIGH HEATHER WILSON is a graduate of Meredith College with a degree in Spanish language and literature. She is pursuing a career in educational consulting.

JEREMY FOSTER is a graduate of the University of North Carolina, Chapel Hill, with a degree in journalism and mass communication. He is currently working as a specialist in international development.